Overleaf: Stonehenge

WORLD ARCHITECTURE

AN ILLUSTRATED HISTORY

INTRODUCTION BY H.R. HITCHCOCK □ SETON LLOYD DAVID TALBOT RICE

NORBERT LYNTON ANDREW BOYD ANDREW CARDEN PHILIP RAWSON JOHN JACOBUS

GENERAL EDITOR: TREWIN COPPLESTONE

CHARTWELL BOOKS INC.

The illustrations on the half title page, from l. to r.

Statue of Rameses II: Paul Popper. Wu Men, Peking: Colin Penn. Jingoji Temple, Kyoto: Wim Swaan. Royal Mosque, Isfahan: John Donat. Votive Stupa, Kanheri Cave: R. Lakshmi. Stained glass window, Fairford Church, near Gloucester: Kersting. Staircase in Dijon: Eric de Maré. Caracas: Camera Press.

The publishers wish to extend their thanks to the following for permission to reproduce and redraw illustrations:

The Athlone Press, University of London: *A History of Architecture on the Comparative Method*, Banister Fletcher. Cambridge University Press: *Handbook of Greek and Roman Architecture*, D. S. Robertson. Hirmer Verlag, Munich: *Egypt*, Max Hirmer. Penguin Books Ltd (Pelican History of Art): *The Art and Architecture of Japan*, Robert Treat Paine and Alexander Soper. Princeton University Press: *Evolution of Buddhist Architecture in Japan*, Alexander Soper. Thames and Hudson Ltd: *The Art of the Ancient Near East*, Seton Lloyd. The Estate of the late Andrew Boyd. Andrew Carden, A.R.I.B.A.
Drawings by Peter Pratt and Martin Weaver, architectural draughtsmen.

PUBLISHED BY

CHARTWELL BOOKS INC.,

A DIVISION OF BOOK SALES INC.,

110 ENTERPRISE AVENUE

SEACAUCUS

NEW JERSEY 07094

© THE HAMLYN PUBLISHING GROUP LIMITED 1963

FIRST EDITION 1963

TENTH IMPRESSION 1977

LIBRARY OF CONGRESS CATALOG CARD NO. 76–11617

ISBN 0–89009–061–0

Depósito legal: TO-282-1977

Printed in Spain
by Artes Graficas - Toledo S.A.
Polígono Industrial Toledo

CONTENTS

Reproduced by Gracious Permission of H. M. The Queen: 763
A.C.L., Brussels: 642
Aerofilms Ltd: 43, 88, 161, 521, 523, 665, 841
Airviews (M/CR) Ltd: 517, 828, 846
Alinari: 139, 157, 166, 192, 195, 463, 465, 471, 480, 482, 528, 567, 607, 608, 660, 662, 686, 690, 693, 694, 695, 701, 702, 704, 705, 707, 709, 719, 721, 723, 726, 727, 730, 735, 737, 738, 739, 741, 742, 745, 746, 748, 788, 790, 792, 794, 801, 805, 810, 812, p. 233
Anderson-Alinari: 469, 663, 718, 799
Wayne Andrews: 904, 942, 952, 954, 956, 957, 958, 964, 966, 984, 985, 986, 1008, 1013, 1024
Annan-Glasgow: 970
Architects' Journal: 1014, 1021
Austrian State Tourist Department, London, 939
Barnaby's Picture Library: 97, 199, 204, 843, p. 130, XIX, XXI
Bauhaus-Archiv: 995
Bildarchiv Foto Marburg: 52, 59, 64, 71, 114, 168, 171, 172, 174, 178, 191, 206, 410, 417, 467, 474, 476, 488, 489, 493, 495, 497, 501, 504, 507, 520, 527, 529, 531, 533, 535, 536, 537, 539, 556, 566, 571, 572, 573, 576, 579, 581, 583, 587, 592, 594, 596, 597, 611, 613, 614, 630, 631, 632, 635, 646, 654, 655, 656, 657, 666, 678, 687, 692, 729, 754, 772, 773, 781, 795, 796, 798, 803, 817, 818, 819, 824, 825, 830, 848, 850, 852, 853, 855, 860, 861, 862, 863, 864, 867, 868, 874, 877, 901, 926, 928, 929, 930, 931, 936, 972, 974, 975, 976, 998, p. 297
G. Douglas Bolton: 677, 775
Boston Museum of Science: 42
Boudot-Lamotte: 399, 405, 420, 449, 462, 478, 522, 554, 621, 628, 644, 749, 757, 770, 808, 884, 888, 1011
British-China Friendship Association: 236, 241, 242, 243, 258, 259, 266, 273, 275, 280, 282, 283, 285, 287, 289, 290, 292
British Museum: 230, 231, 234, p. 81
Miss Bromley: 288
Buffalo and Erie Historical Society: 983
Camera Press: 210, 215, 216, 217, 218, 219, 220, 269, 286, 894, 895, 896, 897, 899, 922, 944
Casa de Portugal: 755
J. Allan Cash: 93, 120, 121, 126, 205, 207, 374, 453, 456, 640, 722, 1012, p. 111, XV; p. 339, XLIX
Chevojon – S.P.A.D.E.M.: 920
Chicago Architectural Photo Company: 959, 960, 962, 963, 979, 981, 982
Chicago Historical Society: 961
Colour Library International: p. 288, XLII
Combier: 518, 560
Bernard Cox: 574
Eric de Maré: p. 269, XXXIX
Department of Archaeology, Government of India: 339
Department of Archaeology, Pakistan: 338
Department of Public Works, Amsterdam: 774, 950
Director General of Antiquities, Iraq: 17, 22, 23
Director of Archaeology, Mysore: 378
R. E. Dixon: p. 164, XXVI: p. 181, XXVIII
John Donat: 27, 28, 29, 33, 408, 437, 1026
Ronald Doyle: 155, 200
John Ebstel: 1023
Egypt Exploration Society: 63
Finnish Travel Information Centre, London: p. 340, LIII
Olga Ford: 181, 182, 183, 187, 434
Claude François-Portal: 563, 589
Fox Photos: 935
French Government Tourist Office, London: 651, 652, 1005
Gabinetto Fotografico Nazionale: 158, 175, 177, 179, 460, 481, 484, 697, 698, 699, 700, 712, 714, 716, 724, 732, 733, 734, 736, 791, 804, 807, 809

De Burgh Galwey: 208, 212, 670, 915, 918
Leonard and Marjorie Gayton: 832, 844, 879
General Department of Information and Broadcasting, Teheran: 407
German Archaeological Institute, Athens: 135
German Tourist Information Bureau, London: 866
Giraudon: 232, 562, 569, 580, 626, 826
Peter Goodliffe: 685
Greek State Tourist Office, London: 69, 95, 131
Solomon R. Guggenheim Museum, New York: 944, 1020
Musée Guimet, Paris: 361
Studio Haig, Amman: 404, 477
Paul Hamlyn Ltd: 160, 696, 720, 744, 811, 870
Hedrich-Blessing: 999
Heikki-Havas: 1018
Lucien Hervé: 1000
Michael Holford: 878, p. 163, XXII; p. 236, XXXVIII
E. O. Hoppé: 185, 524, 683, 857, 865, 941
Hsinhua News Agency: 222, 235, 238, 239, 244, 246, 248, 249, 250, 251, 260, 261, 268, 271, 272, 277, 282, 291
Hunting Surveys: 32
Independent Features: 342, 358, 381
Indian Government Tourist Office, London: 386, 387
Irish Tourist Office, London: 887
Alan Irvine: 1002, p. 322, XLVI, XLVII, XLVIII; p. 339, LI; p. 340, LII, LIV, LV, LVI
Ise Shrine: 297
Italian Institute, London: 717
Italian State Tourist Department, London: 119
Japan National Tourist Association, London 299, 303, 305, 308, 311
A. F. Kersting: 41, 67, 68, 406, 424, 468, 494, 516, 519, 525, 538, 540, 541, 542, 593, 598, 599, 600, 601, 609, 616, 617, 618, 620, 622, 659, 661, 664, 667, 669, 671, 672, 673, 674, 679, 681, 684, 691, 706, 777, 783, 785, 786, 787, 815, 827, 831, 834, 840, 845, 847, 858, 859, 875, 880, 883, 889, 891, 905, 910, 912, 916, 917, 919, 933, 947, frontispiece; p. 24, II, III; p. 75, VI; p. 76, IX, X; p. 164, XXIII; p. 181, XXVII; p. 182, XXX; p. 199, XXXII; p. 200, XXXIII; p. 217, XXXIV; p. 218, XXXV; p. 235, XXXVI; p. 236, XXXVII; p. 288, XLIII; p. 321, XLIV
Keystone Press Agency: 816, 822, 1019
R. Lakshmi: 340, 348, 349, 354, 355, 368, 383, 392, p. 129, XVIII; p. 130, XX
E. Lessing - Magnum: p. 287, XLI
Lichtbildwerkstatte 'Alpenland': 782, 968, 969
Mansell Collection: 76, 78, 79, 80, 91, 92, 94, 101, 103, 104, 106, 107, 526, 647
A. Martin: 851, 924
Maryland Historical Society: 906
Mas: 971
Photo Maywald: 430
Terence Mead: 762, 882
Federico Arborio Mella: 615
Albert Morance, Paris: 1003, 1004
Mondadori: p. 58, V
Mustograph Agency: 221, 543, 885
National Buildings Record, London: 595, 602, 604, 605, 606, 675, 680, 764, 842, 908, 911, 923, 938, 946, 948
William Rockhill Nelson Gallery of Art, Kansas City: 233
Nelson's Atlas of the Classical World: 214
Netherlands Embassy, London: 835, 836, 837, 838, 849, 854, 990, 991, 992, 996, 997
David Nettheim: p. 164, XXV; p. 339, L
Newport (Rhode Island) Historical Society: 955

New York Historical Society: 965
Nordisk Pressefoto: 907
Öffentliche Kunstsammlung, Basle: 643
Oriental Institute, University of Chicago: 20, 30
Orion Press, Tokyo: 293, 296, 301, 306, 313, 318, 332
Colin Penn: 256, 257, 264, 267, 276, 278, 279
Antonello Perissinotto: 19, 473, 496, 499
Photo Researchers: 423
Pictorial Press: p. 321, XLV
Picturepoint: 57, 85, 98, 105, 108, 110, 115, 116, 117, 118, 432, 458, 490, 515, 676, 768, 839, 913, 914, 934, 945, 973, 1006
Pix Photos: 932
Paul Popper: 49, 366, 371, 373, 376, 382, 390, 401, 403, 438, 439, 457, 778, 892, 893, p. 23, I; p. 57, IV
Josephine Powell: 70, 72, 74, p. 182, XXXI
Press and Information Bureau, Government of India: 356, 372, 377, 380, 388, 389, 451, 452, 455, 1007
Radio Times Hulton Picture Library: 156, 394, 398, 411
Rapho: 552, 1015
Philip Rawson: 341, 344, 345, 346, 347, 350, 351, 352, 353, 360, 362, 363, 364, 365, 367, 391, 393
Marc Riboud – Magnum: p. 93, XI; p. 94, XII, XIII, XIV
Rijksdienst Monumentenzorg: 771
Roger-Viollet: 82, 419, 422, 431, 433, 435, 440, 442, 559, 568, 582, 584, 585, 610, 612, 634, 641, 645, 649, 650, 653, 751, 752, 753, 760, 766, 820, 821, 829, 886, 898, 925, 927, 937, 1010, p. 147
Jean Roubier: 532, 534, 547, 548, 549, 550, 551, 553, 555, 557, 558, 561, 564, 565, 577, 578, 586, 591, 629, 636, 638, 639, 731, 740, 759, 765, 767, 769, 780, 902, p. 167
Royal Commission on Historical Monuments (England): 761
Royal Institute of British Architects: 237
Sakamoto Photo Research Laboratory, Tokyo: 294, 295, 298, 304, 310, 312, 314, 315, 317, 322, 326, 335, 336, p. 109
Scala: 502
Toni Schneiders – Photo Researchers: p. 270, XL
Julius Shulman: 1022
Society for Cultural Relations with the U.S.S.R.: 506, 509
Staatliche Museen, Berlin: 16, 31
Vic Stacey: 1009
Stad Antwerpen Dienst voor Toerisme: 658, 949
Stato Maggiore Aeronautica Militare: 153, 196, 871
Dr Franz Stoedetner: 856, 903, 977, 978, 987, 988, 989
Ezra Stoller Associates: 1025
Wim Swaan: 84, 211, 300, 302, 316, 333, 334, 337, 357, 359, 369, 379, 385, 395, 396, 397, 443, 454, 459, p. 127
Wim Swaan – Camera Press: p. 112, XVI, XVII; p. 164, XXIV
Tass Agency: 510, 511, 512, 513, 514
John Topham: 603, 967
Trans-World Airlines, by Ezra Stoller: 1016, 1017
Turkish Ministry of Information and Broadcasting: 441, 485, 486, 505
United Arab Republic Tourist and Information Centre, London: 38, 48, 50, 55, 56, 65, 412, 413, 415, 418
United States Department of Defense, Washington: 940
View Point Projects: 146, 147, 197, 198, p. 75, VII, VIII
E. Wilford: 448, 498, 500, 503
Hed Wimmer: 209
Professor Rudolf Wittkower: 800
Yan: 152, 193, 194, 425, 426, 427, 428, 588, 590, 750, 756, 758, 872

BY HENRY-RUSSELL HITCHCOCK

Buildings that survive from the past are fossils of civilization. For certain early cultures that left no written records, or whose records have not been deciphered, monumental remains are the principal sources of information. Even of so-called 'high' periods—Periclean Greece, say, or Hadrianic Rome—such edifices as the Parthenon and the Pantheon are, for many people, the most impressive manifestations. Nearer to our own time the architecture of the nineteenth century provides evidences of achievement and of failure hardly to be found in political chronicles. Some writers even attempt, rather prematurely, to judge our own twentieth–century civilization, in part at least, by its man–made setting. They contrast favourably or unfavourably our vast industrial and business structures with the cathedrals and palaces of the past, or they try to read the degree of success or failure of various 'Welfare States' in the quality of their housing and their schools. That will be quite legitimate for future historians, but it is likely to be tendentious and arbitrarily opinioned if attempted too soon.

Architectural history is always a part, sometimes even the most important part, of history in general. It can be interesting intellectually even in periods whose products appeal little or not at all to mid–twentieth–century taste. Yet to consider architectural history merely as a part of general history is to miss a great deal of its potential interest. Despite the social, technical, and functional aspects of building—those that link architecture most closely to other aspects of history—architecture exists in the realm of art, more specifically of the visual arts. The artistic value of individual buildings or, indeed, of whole cities and regions at certain periods may have been low or even, so to put it, negative—doubtless more buildings are and always have been, if not ugly rather than beautiful, at least of negligible visual interest—yet we turn to the history of architecture not merely to become informed but in the expectation of visual pleasure. We even distort statistically the history of building by habitually throwing emphasis on those aspects of the production of the past that have the most positive visual qualities, paying far more attention to the temples than to the houses of the Greeks, and studying the churches of the Victorians with greater assiduity than their equally characteristic factories. This is no serious error if we are fully aware of what we are doing. Indeed, one may admit that for certain portions of architectural history, such as the story of castles and fortifications of cities in the Middle Ages and succeeding periods, or the development of low-cost state-aided housing in the nineteenth and twentieth centuries, a predominantly non-visual approach has its value.

There are significant aspects of architectural history that can be treated conceptually, using chiefly words; or, in matters of construction, with simple diagrams (since all buildings considered as physical objects are within the realm of solid geometry). But considered as an art, architecture is a visual matter, and it is through pictures—today chiefly photographs—that it must be apprehended. In the actual presence of a building other senses are affected, but even within a great man-created space the response of the other senses is mostly dependent on what the eye sees rather than direct.

front., 19
27, 69-83
892-9
84, 191-2

901-40,
946-69

997, p.339
p. 200
p. 217
831, 861
1010,
1014-15,
1021

84, 115
933

516-25

1014-15

475

The height of a tower may perhaps be realised by climbing it, but that of an interior is usually experienced merely by our sub-conscious interpretation of what the eye reports.

Ideally all buildings should be visited; but there is certainly no human being who has seen all the buildings which such a world history of architecture as this must, even minimally, include. Furthermore, in the very presence of a building there is also information worth having which the eye alone cannot provide. Fully to comprehend, say, a great medieval cathedral (or, for that matter, an extensive modern housing estate), one needs the schematic evidence provided by plans on paper and probably by cross-sections as well. To understand any but the simplest and most naked types of building construction further schematic diagrams are needed, perhaps even more than are plans and general sections. Moreover, to the average visitor certain aspects of buildings are in practice inaccessible—the frieze of the Parthenon, for example, even those portions of it still in situ on the Acropolis, or the stained-glass windows high up in the clerestories of Chartres or Bourges. Thus, in fact, although certain major architectural qualities of mass and, above all, of space are truly apprehensible only before or within the building, the history of architecture that can be presented in illustrated lectures or books is by no means merely—as is usually the case with painting or sculpture—a feeble echo of reality. On the contrary, by the skilful selection and juxtaposition of images—general views, inside and out, views of inaccessible areas, details of all sorts in photographs, combined with various diagrammatic drawings, especially of plans and sections—the reality of a building can be rounded out so effectively that it is necessary, or at least very desirable, to have such derivative images at hand for consultation even when visiting the actual building, or at any rate some clear memory of them.

The very idea of a history of any subject assumes a sequence of discrete events (in the case of architecture, of individual buildings) that are rarely to be found in close proximity. The Chicago skyscraper story, for example, cannot be studied in that city alone, since two of the architect Sullivan's major works are elsewhere, in St Louis and in Buffalo. To follow the sequence of development of Greek temples or French cathedrals requires at least as extensive travelling to see all the principal originals. In the pages of a book, such sequences can be clearly ordered, and all sorts of comparisons can be readily made that would take days or weeks if they could be made only by seeing first one and then another of the buildings themselves.

If the sequences that the idea of history implies be not too long and the contexts not too disparate, most students come to feel that these sequences have real meanings that are of considerable intrinsic interest, however debatable the particular formulations of those meanings by one historian or another may seem. The simple one-line evolution from the primitive hut to the mature Greek temple, which appealed so much to certain eighteenth-century theorists, is today hardly an acceptable pattern for any of the principal historical sequences in architecture. Yet one cannot deny that if five or ten buildings, products of the same culture and not too far apart in date, are lined up chronologically—whether they be medieval parish churches, Georgian coun-

627, 633, 668, 682

140-144

p. 58

649

960-963

115-119, 628-647

101

try houses or modern skyscrapers—some 'plot' or 'form' will almost always appear to be discernible in the development. Thus the historical study of architecture has a dimension of temporal depth necessarily lacking in the appreciation, so much more sensuously direct, of individual buildings, even the very greatest or most complex.

892-899

For obvious reasons, the various sequences—the historical chapters, one might call them—that have succeeded one another in various countries of the Western world from antiquity to the present have been more thoroughly analysed than the sequences in the Asiatic or pre-Columbian cultures that are remote from us in every way and concerning which parallel political and social-historical documentation is either lacking or relatively inaccessible. Moreover, there are phenomena of architectural history in the Western world, not necessarily lacking in other cultures but less readily apprehensible to all but specialists, that provide certain continuities: on the one hand, the renaissances and revivals that are almost as evident in late antiquity as in the fifteenth-to-sixteenth or the eighteenth-to-nineteenth centuries; on the other hand, and not unrelated, the history of architectural theories as articulated in books and realised, partially but rarely completely, in executed work.

697, 704,
1000-1007

The history of architectural theory is largely an intellectual matter that can be of great interest for its own sake quite apart from the effect of theory on production. But it certainly should not be ignored in considering the buildings erected by such theorists as Alberti, Pugin or Le Corbusier, not to speak of the many architects who accepted and followed with greater or less devotion the highly articulate leadership of such men. There are, indeed, students of architecture, more critically than visually minded, who today and in earlier periods judge, and have always judged, architecture not by its fruits but by its programmes; and even do so when those programmes (as for most periods before the fifteenth century) are, in fact, largely what has been deduced by later observers from what was actually produced. But direct study of the monuments should, and in most cases does, lead to scepticism concerning the importance of theory. Rather we come to realise that buildings, in so far as they are works of art, are most likely to be, whether their names be known to us or not, creations of individuals who would today be called architects; and, in so far as they are also works of craftsmanship, the products of technical traditions that are the result of total social situations and the specific availability or non-availability of certain materials. This is as true of the concrete or structural-steel craftsmanship of modern technics as of the stone craftsmanship of earlier France or the brick craftsmanship of Holland.

1011, 920

This dual background for the production of architecture permits of two separate approaches. On the one hand, there is the 'great man' approach that presents architectural history as a series of illustrated biographies, from Brunelleschi's in the fifteenth century to Frank Lloyd Wright's or Le Corbusier's in the twentieth. This treatment is obviously ill-suited to the architectural history of earlier periods and remoter cultures. In contrast there is the approach which sees architecture in any time or place as the ineluctable result of the technical status of the building industry as it then

686-690,
979-983, 1008
1000-1007,
1010-1012

and there was. There is, moreover, a real dichotomy here: some great architects have, in fact, built rather badly, because they didn't master or know how to command the best craftsmanship of their day. Much of the finest stone-work, brickwork and, *a fortiori*, steel or concrete-work, on the other hand, can be found in buildings that hardly rise high in the scale of works of art because the creative control of a designer of talent—whether builder, architect or engineer—was not utilised.

In most countries there is to be found a vernacular, especially in country villages and isolated farmhouses, that owes little or nothing to conscious design. The peasant dwellings of Friesland, the hamlets of the Cotswolds, the small towns of New England, the pueblos of the American south-west often show an instinctive command of particular materials—respectively, brick and tile, limestone rubble, painted wood, adobe—that the trained architect, by his very sophistication, is unable to equal. Nor, at this level, can one ignore the charms of weathering—effects that the architect leans on at his peril but which, in moss and lichen, in softened corners and sensuously mixed textures, are the result not of man's intentions but of nature's mellowing.

The difficulty of a world history of architecture is that in covering so much territory it is hardly possible to present, with equal thoroughness for all periods, the individual works of great geniuses—named or unknown—and also the general run of building of a period or place which more often than not determines the total architectural character of a city or a region. Masterpieces—and so far as possible they *must* be included—are never, by definition, typical. Indeed, there are important periods, such as the Age of Justinian, that exist for us only in a handful of major monuments and of whose general production we have little idea. On the other hand, some of the most successful macrocosmic entities, not merely medieval or Renaissance towns such as San Gimignano and Santiago de Compostela, but later cities like Bath and Nancy—whose architects are, in fact, known—were not the product of genius, or even of exceptionally high individual talent, but of political, social and material circumstances (the availability of fine, easily handled building materials, for example) not, to the same degree at least, to be found in the contexts within which certain of the most intense individual creators—Guarini, say, in seventeenth-century Italy, or Gaudí in nineteenth- and twentieth-century Spain—were forced to work. Cerebral architects, indeed, seem often to be rather scornful, or at least very aberrant, in their response to materials. Intrinsically difficult materials, of the sorts ordinarily rejected as ugly, can fascinate architects like the Victorian Butterfield or the twentieth-century Le Corbusier, not to speak of the architects just mentioned.

485-488
p. 181

812-815
971-975

933
p. 340

There have often been what might be called 'immanent' architectures, possibilities of carrying further and realising more completely the formal aspirations of original geniuses who were under-employed, or even of periods that were abruptly terminated by extra-architectural events. Here lies the fascination of certain unrealised projects, hints of great buildings that never came to material fulfilment, suggestions for further development of style-phases that never quite matured, yet occasionally in another day and another coun-

900-903

try could inspire later designers more effectively than what had already been executed and was thereby limited in potentiality. A general history of architecture cannot, therefore, ignore altogether certain architects who built very little or nothing, such as François Blondel in seventeenth-century France or Sant'Elia in twentieth-century Italy, nor 756 such an exotic and peripheral movement as the Manoeline in Portugal.

Theorists writing about architecture generally stress that it is a practical art providing shelter and serving various human needs. Actually, the further we penetrate into the past the more such a highly proper modern attitude requires 43 drastic modification. The pyramids of Egypt provided shelter only for the dead, and much of the greatest architecture has intentionally served the needs of gods rather than men. But, of course, sheltering the dead was a more important matter to the Egyptians than sheltering the living, which in their climate was relatively simple; and in serving their gods men have been serving also their own religious needs, which they have often put well ahead of more practical and everyday ones. So excellent are our own factories, on 997 the other hand, that the builders of the Parthenon or of 84 Chartres might well accuse us of giving better thought to 636-641 sheltering machines than men, much less gods; and the concept of shelter is hardly adequate to explain the motivation for enormous palaces such as those of the ancient 828, 846 East or seventeenth- and eighteenth-century Europe.

Shelter seems, indeed, to have been a minor consideration in many of the early cultures; and the sort of space creation in which they often excelled consisted in the enclosure of 16, 49, 50, 196 courts, in the modelling of terrain by vast terraces and, in general, in effects more closely related to the landscape or garden arts of the Western world than to what might be called the 'will to hollow form' of the Roman Pan- 192, 919 theon, the Victorian Coal Exchange or the Guggenheim Museum.

The art of architecture is concerned with the manipulation at relatively large scale of three-dimensional elements. But the three dimensions may apply to a solid, as with the pyramids or Greek temples—which latter had, of course, modest interiors; to hollow interior spaces, ranging in size and complexity all the way from a modest domestic room to a vast cathedral; or to the spaces around and between buildings, more usually considered as urbanism or as gardening rather than architecture, but not separable theoretically from the formal organisation of the elements of individual free-standing structures.

Moreover, every building has a physical context. Sometimes, the designer may have ignored that context out of scorn for surrounding structures and on the assumption that they would be replaced by a setting more to his own taste. More often, it is posterity that has destroyed a once appropriate context and substituted one hardly imaginable 160 to the original designer. That is the case with archaeological 841 sites and also in modern cities. Wren's churches in London or Upjohn's in New York have long been all but lost

among the tall business buildings of the nineteenth and twentieth centuries. Yet for some buildings the context is all-important: one may well feel at Vaux-le-Vicomte or at 827-828 Versailles that the garden-designer Le Nôtre's contribution was greater than the architect Le Vau's. For other situations the context may be inconsequential, the perfection of the individual structure as a creation of interior space so notable, as at St Sofia, that the exterior and the setting can be 485-488 ignored. In this connection, the contrast with the Istanbul mosques, built by Sinan a thousand years later, is very 448-450 striking, since their exteriors and their settings are, in fact, of some real consequence, while their interiors follow closely the Justinianic model.

In introducing a general history of architecture, it is hardly possible to call attention to all the different ways in which buildings can profitably be seen and studied. Properly, the authors of the texts for the different sections each stress those aspects of architecture most relevant to the periods or regions with which they are concerned. Ideally, not an introduction but a conclusion might hope to summarise and wind up the story. But the history of architecture, unless it be arbitrarily terminated at 1800 or at 1900, is open-ended. That present, concerning which Mr Jacobus has written, will already be past by the time this book appears. It is an inevitable temptation of historians to turn to propaganda or to prophecy; to assume that because there certainly are lessons to be learned from the past of architecture they can, at the least, suggest how those lessons should or will in the future be applied. But this is an illusion. The first lesson to be learnt from the history of architecture is that at any moment the next stages of development are uncertain. Who would have expected the late northern Gothic to accept—admittedly very gradually—the 751 Renaissance of Italy; why should the reaction against the 753-754, 761-763 Rococo have led to a Classical Revival; why didn't the in- p. 270, 866, 889-891, creasing use of new materials in the nineteenth century lead 900-903, 917-929 at once to a wholly new architecture? Since such questions have so far proved to be more or less unanswerable, so today we can have little idea of what is likely to come next. The very character of the study of the history of architecture today, so different from what it was even in the relatively recent past, will affect the future. There were those among the last generation who saw the study of architectural history as a danger, leading inevitably (as it certainly had in certain earlier periods) to imitation. Actually it seems, in the mid-twentieth century, to have no such effect, but rather to inspire a yearning to rival in originality the great ages that are past. We should read history not to lose ourselves in the past but to set high goals for our own achievement. Nor need we be discouraged. Already our own century has produced many buildings not unworthy to stand with those of the past, and three or four architects active since 1900—Wright, certainly, Le 1008, 1007, 999 Corbusier, Mies van der Rohe, perhaps one or two others—need not fear comparison with the greatest names that have come down to us.

ANCIENT AND CLASSICAL

1 Khirokitia in Cyprus
Neolithic village of circular houses.
The circular, domed structure,
whether of brick or snow blocks,
is one of the primary
structural forms that persist until
the present day.

2 Arpachiyah in Iraq
Tholos-type house.
Tholoi were beehive houses entered
through an outer rectangular
apartment. From earliest times,
man felt the need for
indirect entry to his living space.

**3 Plan of temple at Tepe
Gawra**
Al'Ubaid period.
Centuries immediately before
3000 B.C. More substantial
brick building now followed the
reed-and-mud form.

4 Farmhouse at Hassuna, Iraq
Adobe buildings such as
these soon gave way to
more substantial structures
of mud-brick.

5 Plan of Hacilar II. c. 5000 B.C.
Small walled
settlement in south-west Anatolia,
approximately contemporary
with Hassuna.
Reconstruction of building in
level II, perhaps a shrine.

6 Hacilar in Turkey
Reconstruction of a house in the
Hacilar II enclosure.

7 Plan of Hacilar VI
More formally planned house in
a late neolithic settlement at
Hacilar.

1

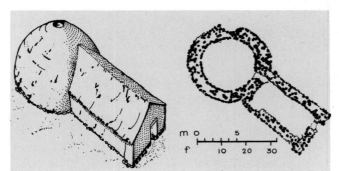

2

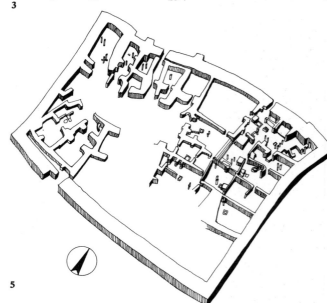

3

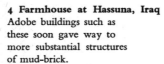

4

5

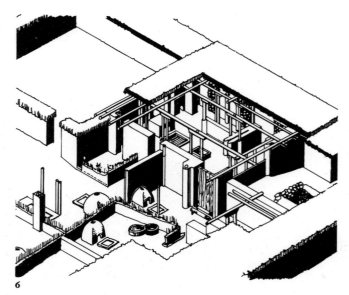

6

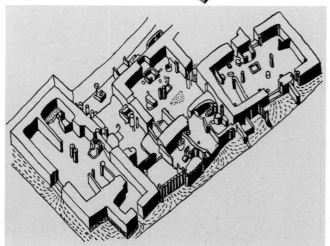

7

PREHISTORIC AND MESOPOTAMIAN

In its first evolutionary stages, the pattern of man's existence was tribal and nomadic. Gathering vegetable food or hunting animals and moving from place to place in search of them, caves or natural shelters provided him with a home, which for the time being satisfied his primitive needs. Rather less than 10,000 years ago, he discovered the possibilities of agriculture, and from then onwards new factors were introduced into his life, which restricted his movements and resulted ultimately in the permanent settlements of a farming community. Under these circumstances individual homes acquired a new significance: the space in which certain domestic functions regularly took place needed to be enclosed and protected, and the craft of building was devised for this purpose. The primary functions to be considered were eating and sleeping, both of which, as modern analogies show, can be performed with equal facility in a compartment of almost any shape. When, therefore, stone was available and could be piled up to make a wall, a rectangular hut with an opening in one side might suggest itself, whereas the plasticity of clay might lend itself to the construction of a circular building. Timber beams would point to a flat roof and their absence to some sort of corbelling. The form and appearance of the earliest buildings were in this way dictated, literally, by material considerations. But except in the most rigid, dictionary sense, this was not yet architecture.

Today we find ourselves able and anxious to distinguish the special qualities which elevate mere buildings to the status of architecture, and their immediate definition here may have certain advantages. The most elementary requirement of architecture is that a builder or designer shall have consciously contrived the form and appearance of a building in such a way as to provoke predictable reactions in those who see or use it—reactions, that is, either of personal satisfaction or aesthetic pleasure. We think that in doing this there are at least four principles which need deliberate consideration. Two of these, the structural and functional principles, speak for themselves. The soundness of a building's structure must be evident and even impressive. It must also be designed for a specific purpose and must adequately express that purpose inside and out. The spatial principle, which comes next, is a more abstract consideration. We have already mentioned the elementary intention of a building, which is to enclose space: in the interior of a building the designer is accordingly concerned with the shaping and disposal of spatial elements in an articulate manner. The building's external appearance introduces the fourth or formal principle, and in applying this he will find himself subject to limitations imposed by all the others—structural, functional and spatial. Architectural design consists entirely in the observation of these cardinal principles. With superficial ornament we are not yet concerned.

In the primitive buildings which we were discussing, with the possible exception of the structural principle none of these matters was yet understood. The rectangular hut could serve equally well as a house or a stable; grain-stores were circular dwellings on a smaller scale. As for spatial

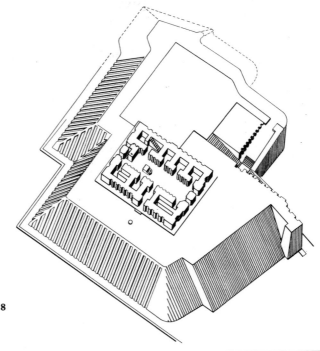

8

8 The White Temple, Uruk
Early third millennium B.C.
This edifice stood on a platform forty feet high. Entrances at either end suggest the elaboration of worshipping ritual between god, priest and congregation.

9

9 Plan of temple VII at Eridu.
c. 3000 B.C. A late building in the Al'Ubaid series at Eridu. Already standing on its own platform, the central shrine or cella is now flanked by subsidiary chambers and the façade ornamented with buttresses.

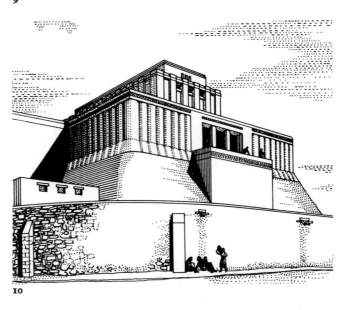

10

10 Temple I at Eridu
Early third millennium B.C.
Reconstructed.
The temple platform has now reached an advanced stage of evolution. In part faced with stone, it terminates in a mosaic of gypsum cones sheathed in polished copper.

11

11 Section through a tomb at Ur
End of third millennium B.C.
An early and skilful use of untrimmed stone blocks for the construction of corbelled vaults.

12, 13 Eshnunna
Plan and elevation of the Gimilsin
temple and the Palace of the
Rulers.
Tell Asmar, the ancient Eshnunna,
was a provincial city compared
with Ur. The square building on
the right is a temple for the
worship of Gimilsin, deified king
of Ur. The temple, planned around
a single axis, is typical Babylonian.

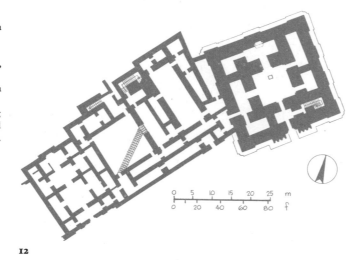

12

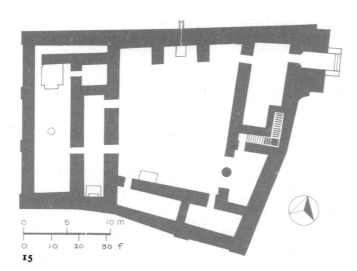

13

14, 15 Khafaje
Plans of Sin temples II and VIII.
Third millennium B.C.
The more open plan at Uruk
has been modified in the case of
these temples to suit shrines
situated among houses.
The irregular plot of land has
been walled to serve as a forecourt,
and entrance to the shrine is
from one side only.

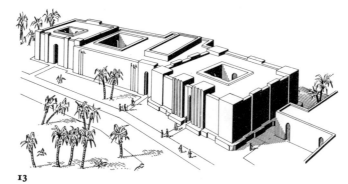

14

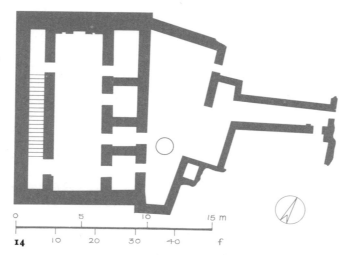

15

proportion or exterior form, any effect obtained from these
was still unpremeditated. Yet this age of architectural inno-
cence was to be short-lived.

It was in the Near East that village communities made
their earliest appearance, and it is among them that archaeologists have detected the first germ of an impulse towards
architectural design. During the neolithic period, contrasts
in the conventional shapes of buildings were perhaps already
dictated by tradition. In Turkey, for instance, on the fringes
of the Anatolian plateau, there were houses substantially built of mud-brick on stone foundations, still consisting of a single rectangular compartment. But they had
a doorway in the centre of one side and the position of
the domestic hearth directly opposite is emphasised by a
formal niche in the wall behind it. At Khirokitia in the is-   1
land of Cyprus, houses were circular with a beehive-shaped
vault of mud-brick; and a raised wooden sleeping-platform
created, perhaps for the first time, an upper floor. A little
later in Crete and northern Iraq, there were again similar
beehive buildings called *tholoi*, but they were entered   2
through an outer, rectangular compartment, which does not
explain itself unless they were partly buried in the side of
a hill and required a *dromos* approach like the much later
beehive tombs at Mycenae. At Jericho in Jordan, meanwhile, a circular stone tower, twenty-seven feet in diameter,
seems to point to the fortification of a contemporary settlement. And here, another significant find was a building
evidently devoted to some cult; square, with a portico
screened by wooden posts and two doorways leading one
through a tiny vestibule, all consciously arranged on a single axis. Here already the functional principle at least was
being considered.

Yet it was more than 2,000 years before the seed of this
abstract idea seems effectively to have germinated. Then,
in the proto- and pre-Sumerian settlements of southern
Mesopotamia, amid a crescendo of creative invention, real
architecture suddenly materialised as a setting for the complex functions of newly developed civilization. The earliest
dwellings here were of reeds and mud. Simply rectangular
in plan but of an elaborate and ingenious construction, they
must exactly have resembled the great *mudhifs* still built
by the Marsh-Arabs today; upright bundles of reeds with
their heads bent together to form a vault, and a filling
between them of mud-plastered wicker-work. By Sumerian times these had long been abandoned in favour of
more substantial brick buildings, but memory of their external appearance conditioned Sumerian design for many
centuries to come, and the complicated pattern of their
entrance façades survived both as a form of ornament and
as the pictographic symbol of a temple. For already, in
the middle of the third millennium B. C., temples and
shrines were the buildings upon which the new-found fac-
ulty of architectural expression was mainly concentrated.
At Eridu, one of the oldest religious foundations in the   10
world, a shrine which had started as no more than a small
hut with doorway facing an offering-table and altar, had
become a well-proportioned building with long central
sanctuary, side chambers and a façade elaborately fretted
with vertical buttresses and recesses, to perpetuate the
marsh-building tradition. Far from those marshes at Tepe

16

16 The Great Sanctuary of Marduk at Babylon. c. 550 B.C.
The ziggurat ('Tower of Babel') carrying the high temple stands in an open precinct, E-temen-anki, surrounded by priests' quarters and storerooms. The lower temple, E-sagil, is seen in the foreground.

17

18

17 Ziggurat at Ur. c. 2125-2025 B.C.
The remains of this great ziggurat give a clear outline of its original form and scale.

18 Ziggurat at Ur
Reconstructed.
An elaborate architectural setting for an elevated shrine. The ramped, stepped and buttressed form developed out of the temple platform of earlier times.

19

20

19 Choga Zambil ziggurat
Thirteenth century B.C.
A remarkably preserved five-tiered Elamite ziggurat near Susa with a labyrinth of internal chambers and stairways.

20 Khorsabad. Wall painting from a minor palace in the citadel. 722-705 B.C.
The painted bands, depicting bulls and winged genii, are bright blue, red and white, their colours somewhat subdued by the limited light which entered only through the arched doorways.

21 Ischali. Temple complex
Early second millennium B.C.
An important shrine dedicated
to Ishtar, and two subsidiary
sanctuaries, are incorporated
into a magnificently monumental
lay-out, in which terracing is
cleverly exploited.

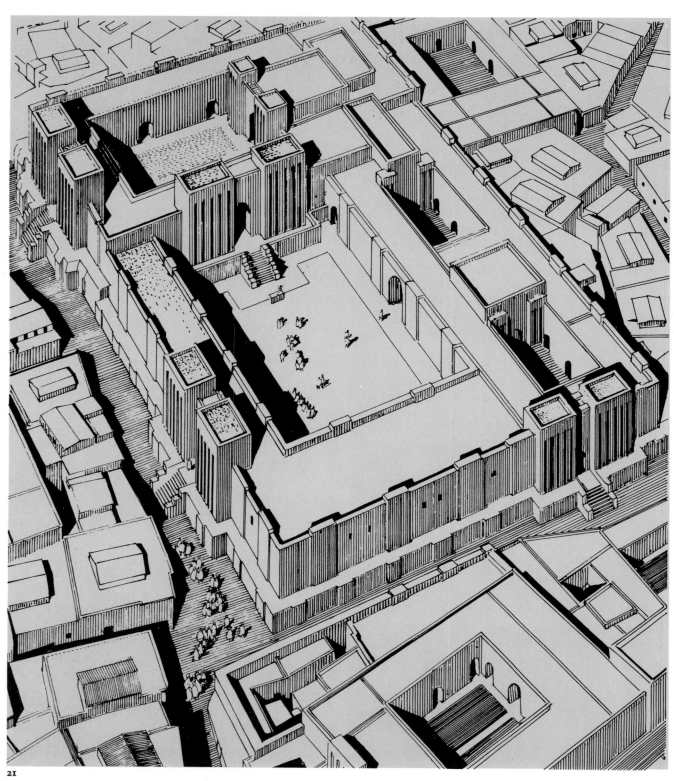

21

**22, 23 Khafaje. Sumerian temple
oval**
Third millennium B.C.
The main shrine stood on a
platform in the centre of
an oval precinct or temenos, with
a portico entrance.
A priest's residence was
included in an outer oval.

22

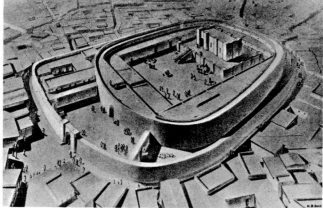

23

3 Gawra in the north, a group of three temples on an acropolis faithfully imitated the same design.

And now at last in these buildings one sees proper attention being paid to the cardinal principles of design which we have earlier enumerated. The loss of their upper parts and our consequent ignorance of their roofing principle deprives us of certainty about their structural qualities. But their functions are properly articulated, so that the part played by almost every element in the plan can still be identified, and the allocation of space is perfectly intelligible. Even more significant is the attempt to give formal expression to a newly conceived abstraction. The building stands upon a podium or raised platform, which is clearly intended to emphasise the exalted purpose to which it is dedicated. Nor can one fail to notice how the low walls flanking the steps by which the platform is approached initiate an architectural device which was never afterwards forgotten. The Sumerian architect is already beginning to understand his job, and in the great period of universal discovery which follows, he is able to make his own striking contribution, designing now with confidence and creative ability.

16, 17   The idea of sublimating a religious ritual by elevating the shrine in which it took place, was one which persisted through Sumerian times and culminated in the high *ziggurat*
18, 19   towers of Babylon and Assyria. In the prehistoric temple at 'Uqair, the platform is already ten to fifteen feet high and made to look higher by vertical panels in the brickwork. The temple itself has the same structural and functional characteristics as its prototype at Eridu, but a new element has appeared in the form of superficial ornament. The whitened mud-plaster of the interior wall-faces is covered with painted decoration. The fact that this is already competently adapted to architectural requirements, with bands of geometric ornament supporting or enclosing formalised figures of men and animals, need not surprise us. Pottery had already been decorated in this way for many centuries, and the designs of mythical figures had more recently been perfected in small-scale relief carving. Both here and in the
8   so-called White Temple at Uruk, another form of wall-ornament took the form of terra cotta mosaic cones, inserted contingently in the plaster to form a band or pattern. The White Temple itself, now standing on a pyramidal platform forty feet high, had entries at either end of the sanctuary, as though to suggest an actual confrontation between the worshipper and his god. In other respects it differed little from that at 'Uqair, but an adjoining building, the Pillar Temple, had free-standing columns eight feet thick and half-columns against the sidewalls, all completely covered with mosaic. The coloured ends of the cones (many thousands in number) were arranged in a varying diaper pattern and must have created a decorative effect of extreme brilliance.

At Eridu, the only Sumerian site where any stone seems to have been available, even more elaborate façade ornament was used in the latest prehistoric temple. Here, the ruins of earlier temples to which we have referred, were enclosed in a stone-faced retaining-wall, and above this rose the serried bastions of the platform, ornamented in this case with bands of huge gypsum cones, their ends sheathed in polished copper. Fallen from the temple itself were found smaller cones chipped out of coloured stone and little rectangular cement bricks, perforated for the attachment of other architectural ornaments.

In these prehistoric temples the primary characteristics of Mesopotamian architecture were already present. The Sumerian dynastic period (first half of the third millennium B. C.) showed few innovations save for the elaboration of planning and formal arrangement. The main sanctuary was now incorporated in a complex of subsidiary chambers and courtyards, sometimes enclosing smaller shrines dedicated to minor deities. In an interesting setting at Khafaje   14, 15 on the south bank of the Diyala River, the main shrine stood on its platform in the centre of an oval-shaped precinct or *temenos*, protected by double enclosure-walls and   22, 23 entered through a formal portico. An exactly similar temple at Al'Ubaid, near Ur, showed evidence of having been embellished with costly and elaborate architectural ornament, remnants of which were found stacked against the base of the platform after its destruction; copper bulls' heads, bands of inlay ornament with religious scenes carved in white limestone on a dark ground, columns inlaid with coloured stone and an enormous copper lintel with mythical figures in high relief.

It becomes clear that these elevated temples, towards the end of the third millennium, were dedicated to a distinctive purpose. They provided a setting for the sacramental ritual around which the Sumerian fertility cult centred. The shrines themselves, all of which have now vanished, are known from external evidence to have been simple affairs, probably consisting of a single compartment. But the platform on which they stood had been heightened and elaborated beyond all recognition. These 'staged-towers', with their monumental stairways and superimposed porticoes, now became the most conspicuous features of Sumerian temple-cities. They were constructed of solid mud-brick, with layers of matting set in bitumen between courses and heavy cables of plaited reeds to reinforce them. Parts of the facing and the treads of the stairs were of kiln-baked bricks, and their successive 'stages' were painted in different colours. They stood usually in a fortified *temenos* or sacred enclosure and were surrounded at ground level by more ordinary temples dedicated to individual deities of the Sumerian pantheon. These were for the most part conventionally planned, with entrance, vestibules, central court and sanctuary all arranged on a single axis which terminated in the niche where the cult-statue stood. Good examples of how such temples were grouped can be seen in the great *temenos*   16 at Ur or in the sacred enclosure at Ashur, which had three separate *ziggurats*. A huge provincial temple at Ischali shows   21 how the elements of such a complex can be combined in a single building. The gateways leading from one to the other are flanked by projecting towers; a common architectural feature from this period onwards.

In discussing Mesopotamian architecture, it is religious buildings which monopolise one's attention. Far less care was lavished on secular construction, as may be judged, for instance, from the negligent design of an administrative building attached to a fine temple at Tell Asmar. Its only conventional feature is a rectangular throne-room or *divan*, approached on its short axis from a square open courtyard.

24 Plan of the city of Khorsabad
End of eighth century B.C.
A temporary capital of the Assyrian empire, built by Sargon II on an open site but abandoned after his death in 704 B.C. Only the major and minor citadels were excavated.

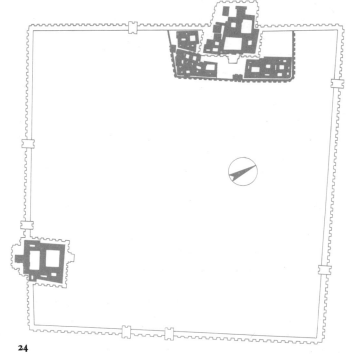

24

25 Khorsabad
Reconstruction of part of the main citadel.
The Assyrian passion for symmetry is most apparent in Khorsabad despite the frequent failure to achieve perfect right angles. This was due to empiric planning and an inadequate knowledge of surveying.

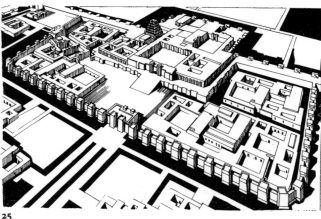

25

26 Khorsabad. Plan of the palace of Sargon. 722-705 B.C.
Dominating the citadel of the city, Sargon's palace comprised an impressive complex of reception suites and temples arranged around successive courtyards and covering an area of twenty-three acres.

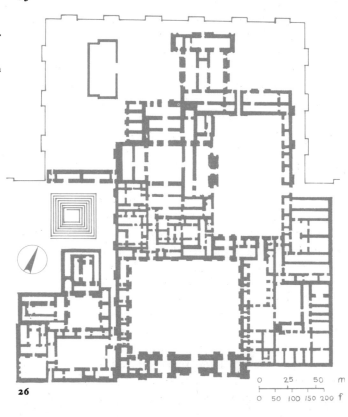

26

0   25   50   m
0   50 100 150 200 f

Private houses too were of the 'introverted' type, their rooms having no outward exposure, obtaining their light from a central court. With the flat façades of its fortifications relieved by alternative buttresses and recesses and punctuated by towered gateways, the general appearance of a typical Mesopotamian city is relatively easy to imagine. Flat roofs and the limitations of mud-brick construction restricted the possibilities of formal design, and, though little is actually known of parapet treatment or terminal ornament, the picture conceived is that of flattened prismatic elements rising tier above tier over an accumulation of earlier ruins, to where a group of religious buildings gain prominence from the vertical treatment of their façades, but are overshadowed by the rectilinear bulk of a *ziggurat*. Only these latter gave expression to the aspirations of a plain-dwelling people; for, like beacons in an otherwise featureless landscape, each tower must have been remotely visible to its neighbour.

The geological environment of the upper Tigris valley gave a slightly distinctive character to buildings erected by the Assyrians during the eighth and seventh centuries B. C. Soft gypsum limestone was easily quarried in the hills north of Nineveh and lent itself to architectural sculpture, which now became a conspicuous feature of public buildings. As might be expected from the exalted attributes of Assyrian royalty, more attention was paid to palaces than to sacred buildings, and it was the interior of these which received the major share of ornament. Five centuries earlier, the Kassite kings of Babylon had used moulded brick or painted frescoes to form an ornamental dado around the walls of their banquet-halls. For these the Assyrians substituted upright slabs of stone (orthostats), their faces sculptured in low relief with historical and other scenes, forming a continuous frieze, sometimes as much as nine feet high. Above this, in throne-rooms and other important chambers, the plastered walls would again be decorated with frescoes in the Kassite manner and the ceiling similarly ornamented. Sculpture-in-the-round was rarely used, but to embellish the main doorways and entrances, a new form of portal-sculpture was devised, once more following a five-hundred-year-old precedent established this time by the Hittites. It consisted of pairs of symbolical beasts such as winged bulls or lions; 'double-aspect' sculptures, often provided with five legs in order to perfect their appearance either from the front or from the side. These would stand somewhat higher than the sculptured orthostats of the interior, and above them the bricks of a semi-circular arch would be enriched with coloured glaze. Coloured designs in glazed brick would also form panels at the base of the projecting towers flanking the entry on either side.

The semi-circular arch with radiating *voussoirs*, to which brick construction was easily adapted, had been favoured by Mesopotamian architects since prehistoric times. From its use by the Assyrians over deeply recessed openings, one might infer an understanding of barrel-vaulting. And indeed, Assyrian buildings have often been reconstructed with vaulted chambers and even domes. But conclusions of this sort depend on evidence provided by the rare representations of architecture in Assyrian relief-carvings, and it is probably safer to infer that a plentiful supply of timber from neigh-

II   III

bouring forests (also depicted), made flat roofs more practical. Certainly free-standing columns were of timber, though their bases and capitals were sometimes carved from stone. It is again the reliefs which provide the only evidence regarding the external appearance of buildings. They show crenellated battlements and also occasional rectangular windows.

At Khorsabad, which has provided the most complete plan of an Assyrian royal city, it is the king's palace which is now elevated on an artificial platform, raised level with the parapet of the city wall, while the temples are no more than subsidiary features of the plan. The palace is connected by a wide ramp with a complex of low-level public buildings, having its own towered fortification and sculptured gateways. The whole lay-out is a small masterpiece of monumental planning, with the massing and relative heights of the buildings carefully considered. It may well have inspired the central composition of Nebuchadnezzar's Babylon 200 years later.

Apart from ornament and facings, Assyrian buildings were still constructed of solid mud-brick. Their immensely thick walls, like the grandiose subjects of the reliefs which adorn them, gave to the architecture of the period an almost Victorian complacency. But when certain engineering works became necessary their architects were compelled to build in stone; and then, in structures such as bridges and aqueducts, their qualities of thoroughness and structural solidity became more obvious assets.

In the sixth century B.C., after the fall of Nineveh, the focus of historical events shifted southwards again to Babylonia, and during the cultural renaissance which followed, some principles of Assyrian architecture were adapted to the old Sumerian tradition. Under Nebuchadnezzar there was a great revival of building activity, and everywhere ancient temples were reconstructed on a pretentious scale. Above all, on the lower Euphrates the city of Babylon itself was enormously enlarged and replanned. The inner city was now magnificently laid out with broad streets intersecting at right angles, some parallel to the river quay, others terminating in huge bronze gates in the city wall or smaller ones leading to landing-stages on the river bank. The 'Champs Elysées' of this composition was the so-called Procession Street, along which the images of the gods were carried to the New Year's Festival. Where it passed through the inner wall, the famous Ishtar Gate made an 'Arc de Triomphe', and it skirted the imperial palace with its Hanging Gardens before reaching the great temple of Bel, Etemenanki, whose *ziggurat* had now also been rebuilt on an ambitious scale.

In Babylonia there was no stone for sculptured reliefs, so it was the outer façades of these buildings that were enriched. They were covered to their full height with glazed bricks in brilliant colours, while heraldic animals or patterns of foliage, modelled in low relief beneath the glaze, contributed a texture of delicate shadows. Against the monotonous geometry of otherwise undecorated clay buildings and the monochrome of an alluvial landscape, the glittering wall-faces of this precinct must have acquired an exaggerated brilliance, like the gilded domes and ceramic façades of mosques in a modern Islamic city.

24
25
26

31

27

27 Persepolis. 518–465 B.C.
These Persian buildings of the Achaemenid dynasty derive something from the architecture of Assyria and more from that of her northern neighbour Urartu. They are distinguished from the former by the plentiful use of columns.

28

28 Persepolis. Double dragon, upper part of capital
Resting directly on the shaft of the column, these double images were also made in the shapes of men, bulls or bulls with men's heads.

29

29 Persepolis. Relief sculpture, hall of Darius and Xerxes
The Achaemenid relief carvings have the hard precision of metalsmiths' work. They differ from those of Assyria in that they decorate the outside façades of buildings only.

30

30 Tell Tayanat. Column base
Eighth century B.C.
Wooden columns were a feature of Syrian architecture at this period. The carved ornament has no equivalent in Assyria.

31 Ishtar Gate. 605-565 B.C.
Reconstructed.
Standing at a point where the
Procession Street entered the
inner city of Babylon, this
great portal had façades decorated
with heraldic animals
modelled in relief and
covered with brightly coloured
glazes.

31

32 Persepolis
Aerial view.
The palaces and audience halls
of the Achaemenid kings cover
this wide terrace in a lay-out
which may recall the grouping
of pavilions in the centre of
a nomadic encampment.

33 Persepolis
Architectural and sculptural
remains. Persepolis abounded in
architectural sculpture. All the
stairways, and most of the terraces,
were lined with reliefs.
The columns, beautifully fluted,
have a character of their own.

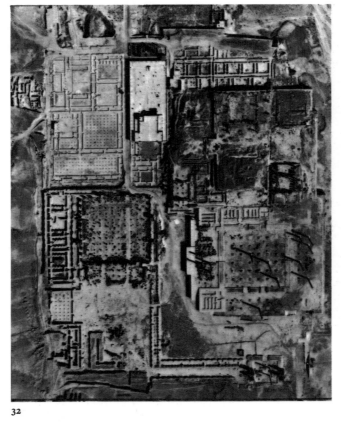

32

33

34 Boghazköy
Plan of Temple I. Fourteenth-
thirteenth centuries B.C.
The most impressive huge stone
temples built by the Hittites
were to be found at Boghazköy.

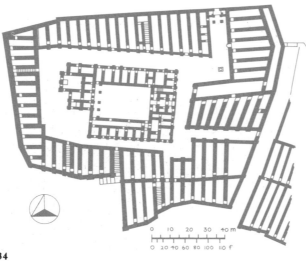

**35 Boghazköy. Inner and outer
side of King's Gate. c. 1360 B.C.**
The elliptical opening,
flanked by great towers, had
corbelled arches standing
on monolithic stone jambs.

34

35

During this same period in the sixth century B.C., some aspects of Assyrian architecture were reflected in the cities of south-western Iran, from which a dynasty of Achaemenian kings ruled a large part of the Near East. At Persepolis, which they made their capital, the great rock-hewn terrace on which their palaces stood makes a significant comparison with those of Assyria and Babylon. For here, as immediately becomes apparent, one is dealing with a totally different tradition of building. The interest in monumental planning, the cellular composition and interrelation of buildings of which we have seen so much evidence in Mesopotamia, appears to have been non-existent among Persian architects. The grouping and character of the individual palaces at Persepolis were still reminiscent of a nomadic tradition in which a cluster of gaudy tent-pavilions formed the nucleus of a tribal assembly. Strikingly proportioned in themselves and lavishly decorated, the various throne-rooms and banquet-halls are disposed almost at random on their elevated emplacement, and the magnificently ornamented stairway which forms the main approach seems unconnected with any one of them.

The most striking quality of these Persian architectural remains lies in the field of plastic ornament. For this also an origin must be sought in regional tradition, and it is immediately apparent in the aptitude for fine drawing and modelling, particularly of plant and animal motifs, which has always distinguished Iranian art. Persian architects emulated the Assyrians in decorating their buildings with sculptured reliefs, but preferred the Babylonian principle of applying this ornament only to the exterior façades. The carving of the reliefs is as formalised as the Assyrian, but more meticulously detailed, so that at times it resembles goldsmith's work in its hard precision. The human figures are stereotyped and sometimes monotonous, as though carved with waning interest; but interest and aptitude alike revived when animal motifs were handled, and decorative shapes like the magnificent double-bull capitals in the Hall-of-a-Hundred-Columns made a welcome challenge to the Persian sculptor's ingenuity.

Another peripheral development from Assyrian architectural tradition appeared during the eighth and seventh centuries B.C. in the vassal states of northern Syria and Taurus, inhabited by remnants of the imperial Hittites. The Hittites indeed had a tradition of their own, inherited from the mid-second millennium when they ruled eastern Anatolia from their heavily fortified capital at Hattusas (Boghazköy). Their buildings were of timber-framed mud-brick on a sub-structure of irregularly jointed stone; impressive in structural strength when their purpose was military and occasionally of striking design, as in the case of an all-stone temple at Boghazköy. But the sculpture with which they were adorned is derivative in style, of indifferent workmanship and of little more than archaeological interest.

EGYPTIAN

The beginnings of architecture in Egypt date from the centuries before 3000 B.C., which we have called the prehistoric period. Their style may have been influenced by contemporary brick buildings in Mesopotamia, though one can imagine only the most tenuous physical link between countries at that time so separated. Certainly the brick superstructures of early *mastaba* tombs are otherwise difficult to explain. The complicated designs of their niched façades faithfully reproduce those of early Mesopotamian brick buildings in which elements of reed-construction are seen to have been retained; and in Egypt these have no known antecedents to suggest the coincidence of a parallel development. But although they contributed the embryo of an idea which led eventually to the design of pyramids, architecturally these buildings are no more than a 'false start'. Early in the third millennium, stone became the conventional material for monumental building, and soon a new code of architectural formulae created an inflexible stylistic tradition. Indeed, it would be true to say that of all national styles of architecture, that invented by the Egyptians was the most homogeneous and long-lasting. The twenty dynasties of Egyptian kings who ruled during the third and second millennia B.C., are historically divided into sub-phases known as the Old, Middle and New Kingdoms; but the style of building which they perfected outlasted all these and even survived the Persian conquest in the sixth century. Temples erected still later by the Ptolemaic rulers after the death of Alexander can easily be mistaken for more authentically dynastic buildings.

The character of Egyptian architecture was directly and profoundly influenced by geological and climatic conditions in the Nile valley. The sense of confinement between parallel barriers of desert, flattened earth and canopy of sky, gave to the world of the ancient Egyptian a sort of rectilinear stability, which must have seemed as permanent and inevitable as the unchanging climate and predictable rhythm of the Nile flood. It is no great feat of imagination to see this reflected in the prismatic forms and spatial arrangements of his buildings, or producing a formative impulse in the design of tomb-chambers, which were of special significance owing to his preoccupation with personal survival.

A more tangible aspect of Egyptian environment was the presence in the Nile valley of much building stone. In the desert escarpment, approximately from modern Cairo to Luxor, there is an abundant supply of limestone. Sandstone is found in the extreme south and elsewhere granite, alabaster, basalt and porphyry. Palm-trunks were the only form of timber available, and at an early stage these were discarded as roofing material for any but the least pretentious buildings. But the limestone slabs which took their place and which continued to be used almost until the end of the Middle Kingdom, could span no more than eight or nine feet; so long, narrow chambers could only be avoided by multiplying the number of free-standing supports, and a form of architecture resulted which is sometimes described as 'columnar and trabeate'. Climatic conditions also had their effect. Perpetual sunshine and cloudless winter skies made it less important to admit light than to exclude heat. If one adds to these the architect's impulse to express human aspirations on a worthy scale, the primary ingredients of Egyptian architectural design are mostly accounted for.

All these stone buildings, then, are dedicated to religious

**36 Zoser complex, Sakkara.
2778 B.C.**
The group, uncovered in recent
years, comprises a funerary
temple, chapels and residential
quarters for the king's use in a
vast rectangular enclosure.

37 Zoser's Hall of Pillars
Entrance hall reconstructed.
The architecture of Zoser's
scheme is delicate and precise in
detail and finish.

38 Zoser complex
Wall detail.
Early Egyptian architecture
has a lightness
and elegance never repeated in
later work. The ribbed walls
obviously derive from brick
technology, now carried out
in stone for the first time.

**39 Tomb of Queen Merneith,
Sakkara**
Reconstructed.
First dynasty tomb attributed
to Merneith. Façade treatment is
notably similar to that
in temples of protoliterate
Mesopotamia.

**40, 41 Step pyramid of Zoser,
Sakkara**
The first known pyramid.
The stepping seems to have been
for structural rather than
ritual purposes. The courses
slope inwards for stability, a
derivation from the mastaba.

36

37

38

39

40

41

or monumental purposes; and with few exceptions it is they whose ruins have survived above ground or been considered worthy of excavation. This has resulted today in a slightly unbalanced conception of what an Egyptian city in fact looked like. And had there been no exceptions to the rule, such as the palaces of El Amarnah or the astonishing Middle Kingdom fortress at Buhen in Nubia, one might have been tempted to forget that all the private dwellings and the overwhelming majority of other secular buildings were constructed of mud-brick with palm-trunk roofs and limited by these materials to comparatively simple architectural forms.

Surprisingly enough, the first, and in some ways the most attractive style of Egyptian architecture in stone appeared, already fully perfected, in the third dynasty of the Old Kingdom. This is illustrated by the pyramid complex of King Zoser; a group of buildings only revealed by clearances in comparatively recent years. The interior walls consist of ashlar masonry in even courses, and engaged columns are used, sometimes on short wing-walls, to lessen the span of the limestone beams above. Some are decorated with delicate reeding, others with flutes (to which disproportionate attention has been paid owing to their anticipation of the Doric order). Ornamental elements are charmingly adapted from vegetable forms; ceilings often imitate palm-trunks and capitals papyrus motifs, some with pendant leaves. The limestone was quarried in small manageable blocks, but the refinement of its facing is deceptive, since little care was taken over jointing that was not superficially apparent.

The complex of buildings laid out around Zoser's tomb at Sakkara is the first major example of monumental design and planning. The name of Zoser's architect, Imhotep, is known, and it is hardly surprising to find that he was afterwards deified. The group comprises an elaborate funerary temple as well as palaces and chapels for the king's use during the Jubilee Festival, all contained within a vast rectangular enclosure. The step pyramid in the centre was the first erection of its sort, and itself creates the most conspicuous link with subsequent architectural forms. The *mastaba* tombs of that time were rectangular platforms with sloping sides, built over the tomb shaft to enclose a ritual chamber and other appointments. One would assume that the stepped form of the pyramid was arrived at by superimposing diminishing versions of the original platform; but if this idea was ever in mind, it is not reflected in the physical anatomy of the pyramid. For, though the central core is of *mastaba* shape, it is attenuated to the full height of the structure and to it are added concentric accretions of masonry, increasingly truncated, with their stone-courses sloping inwards to ensure stability. This device was retained as a basis of pyramid construction long after the steps had been eliminated and the whole structure had acquired the simplicity of an unequivocal geometric form. It is well illustrated by a section cut through the fifth dynasty pyramid at Abusir.

Pyramids and other funerary monuments also best illustrate the characteristic style of the Old Kingdom, which became prevalent in the fourth dynasty. Imhotep's elegant designs were now a thing of the past. Their freedom and

36

37

40, 41

42 The building of the pyramids
Model in Boston Museum of Science.
It is necessary to remember that with two crops grown per year, the greater part of the male population was available for public works projects for nine months of the year.

42

43

43 Gizeh. The pyramids. c. 2723–2563 B.C.
The pyramid is really a giant cairn, a heap of stones over a grave.
Its primary aims are practical ones – permanence and concealment.

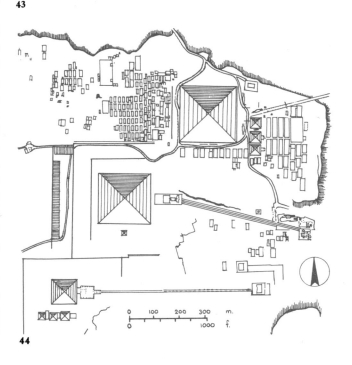

44

44 Gizeh. Plan of the pyramids
The plan of the pyramid group is in a way more impressive than the pyramids themselves, showing as it does the austerity of form and geometric exactitude with which such a scheme was conceived.

43, 44

45 Gizeh. Section of the pyramid of Cheops
There are three internal chambers in the largest pyramid, the result of changes made during construction. The king's chamber, containing the granite sarcophagus, was used instead of the so-called queen's chamber.

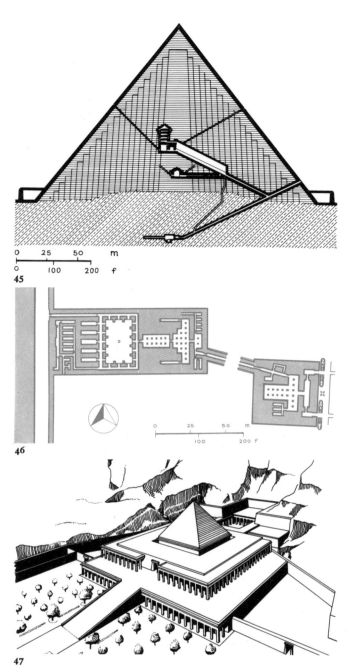

```
0    25   50        m
0        100   200  f
```
45

46 Gizeh. Chefren funerary temple group
This includes the Sphinx. The funerary temple on the pyramid's terrace was connected by a long causeway to the landing stage temple on the Nile below.

```
0      25    50     m
         100    200 f
```
46

47 Deir-el-bahari, Thebes. Temple of Mentuhotep. 2065 B.C.
Here the pyramid has been reduced to a symbolic tombstone. The great pyramids had already been found not to be thief-proof, and the king was buried elsewhere.

47

48 Deir-el-bahari. Detail of Queen Hatshepsut's temple
On the highest terrace of this elaborate building stands a series of arches, richly decorated and incised.

48

individuality were replaced by the ponderous formalism of an authoritarian convention. Granite from Assouan was now often substituted for limestone and quarried in blocks of cyclopean proportions. Ornament was abandoned in favour of monolithic simplicity. With jointing perfected and improving standards of structural integrity, the superficial virtuosity of Zoser's masonry was rapidly forgotten.

The most famous group of pyramids is that at Gizeh, containing the tombs of Cheops, Chefren and Mycerinos. The Cheops pyramid is 755 feet square by 481 feet high, and geometrically it makes an angle of forty-five degrees at the intersection of the sides. The dual aims behind pyramid design were practical ones — permanence and concealment; and the severity with which these functions were expressed precluded the use of ornament even in the internal chambers. Structural perfection must also have been a central objective, yet the weight-relieving devices over these chambers suggest a lack of confidence in its attainment. All else was subjected to the sheer scale of the central conception; and this may have been given extra emphasis by the low horizontality of the subsidiary buildings which completed each of the three complexes. Architecturally these are perhaps more interesting than the pyramids themselves. In the case, for instance, of the Chefren group (which is best preserved and includes the colossal sculpture now known as the Sphinx), one sees how the funerary temple on the pyramid terrace is connected by a long causeway to a smaller 'valley temple' on the river bank below. The chambers themselves in these buildings account for so small a proportion of their cubic content that the plan resembles that of a rock-cut tomb; but they are faced entirely with red granite and the roof is supported by granite monoliths. In both temples there was also a formal arrangement of colossal statues, mostly of green diorite, which must have provided a contrasting colour in the dim light diffused by vertical shafts in the walls. Simple reliefs had already been carved to enrich the walls of Zoser's Festival chambers at Sakkara; but this was the first use of free-standing figures and it initiated the close association between architect and sculptor which persisted throughout the subsequent history of religious building in Egypt.

One of the few major buildings to survive from the Middle Kingdom is the funerary temple of Mentuhotep at Deir-el-bahari. Dramatically situated at the foot of the Theban cliffs, it is composed of low colonnaded terraces with a small stone pyramid in the centre. The efficacy of a pyramid as protection for a tomb had now proved an illusion and the king was buried elsewhere; but plain square piers still formed the colonnade, and the interior was sparingly decorated with painted ornament. The terraces of a much larger funerary building, laid out beside it during the brilliant eighteenth dynasty of the New Kingdom, makes an interesting counterpoint. Erected by Queen Hatshepsut, this temple also was adapted in form to the unusual requirements of the site, but its terrace walls in the shade of the colonnades were richly adorned with sculptured reliefs, and the two buildings together make an architectural ensemble of such memorable beauty that its reflection is sometimes still recognisable today in the achievement of modern lay-outs.

45
46
47
48-50

49 Deir-el-bahari
Aerial view.
Here can be seen the graceful
juxtaposition of the temples
of Mentuhotep (left) and Queen
Hatshepsut (right), the first
built 500 years before the larger,
which echoes it in form.

49

**50 Deir-el-bahari. Temple
of Queen Hatshepsut.
1520 B.C.**
The queen was buried in a corridor
tomb deep in the mountains behind
this mortuary temple dedicated to
Amon. An avenue of sphinxes
connects the temple with the valley.

50

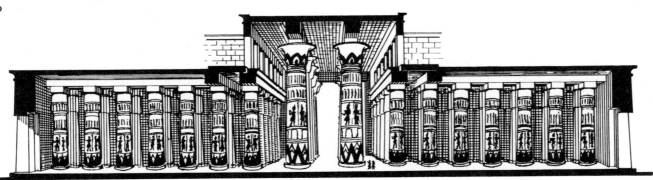

**51 Karnak. Temple of Amon.
1530–323 B.C. Section of
Hypostyle Hall**
This impressive hall, part of the
Great Temple of Amon,
is a symmetrical forest of columns,
134 in sixteen rows.
The increased height of the
central colonnades make clerestory
lighting possible.

51

**52 Karnak. Temple of Amon.
1530–323 B.C.**
Oblique rays of sunshine
penetrating through stone
grilles were the only
form of lighting.

52

**53 Karnak. Plan of the temple
of Amon**
The plan is strongly axial and
formal. The processional form
shows that this was
the dominating liturgical feature.

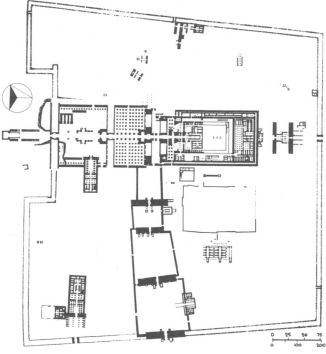

53

**54 Karnak. Section of temple
of Khons. 1198 B.C.**
This smaller temple at Karnak is a
fine example of the cult temple
consisting of pylons, hypostyle hall,
sanctuary with the sacred
boat of Khons and surrounding
chapels.

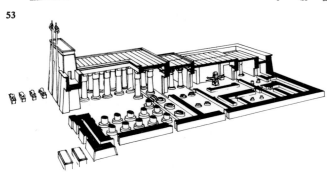

54

The city of Thebes, New Kingdom capital of Egypt,
stood in open country on the right bank of the Nile, where
Luxor stands today. Facing it across the river were funerary buildings like those we have already described, and
thousands of rock-cut tombs transformed the hills behind
into a vast necropolis. In the city itself, each Pharaoh in
turn contributed either a temple of his own or an annex
to some existing group of buildings such as we must now
describe. But first, the function of Egyptian temples needs
to be understood. They were not intended to provide a
setting for public worship and prayer, like the congregational establishments of Christendom or Islam. Liturgy
and ritual were performed by a hierarchy of priests, and
none but they was admitted to the temple precinct. The
esoteric purpose and abstract intention of the buildings
within can be understood perfectly from a single glance
at their planning. Their component elements are ranged   53, 54
out along a single and much protracted central axis; a
fulcrum on which developments in breadth and formal
dualities may be balanced. The meaning is unmistakable.
Each element marks a prescribed stage in the ritual approach to some ultimate mystery, and it is in a cult-chamber
associated with this mystery that the axis usually terminates.
For the benefit of the outside world, the significance of
this arrangement is indicated by an extension of the approach beyond the limits of the building, sometimes
between avenues of sculpture. But the layman's exclusion
from participation in the actual ritual is emphasised by the
uncompromising symbolism of a 'Sublime Porte' at the
entrance to the sanctuary.

To create portals of this sort, gigantic stone pylons were
used in pairs, and these sometimes attained so great a
size that they may be thought of as successors to the
pyramids of an earlier age. Their sloping faces were
sometimes covered with reliefs and chased vertically to
support ornamental masts, perhaps carrying banners.
Within the precinct, successive pairs of such pylons might
occasionally be used to create a secondary approach to
the sanctuary. This device is well illustrated in the great
temple of Amon at Karnak, which, in addition, embodies   53
almost all other conventions usual in such buildings.
Entered through pylons, and open to the sky, an outer
colonnaded courtyard gave access, once more between
pylons, to the great Hypostyle Hall, which occupied the   51
full breadth of the building. Architecturally this was its
most striking feature and, like the crossing and transepts
of a cathedral it was calculated to produce a temporary
climax in one's emotional reactions. In the three central
aisles, columns of colossal height made possible a system
of clerestory lighting through stone grilled windows. They   52, 66
themselves were thus illuminated by oblique rays of
sunshine, while smaller pillars on either side seemed to recede
into almost total darkness. From the Hypostyle Hall one
progressed between further pairs of pylons into an inner
courtyard surrounded by a labyrinth of minor halls and
cult-chambers, all enclosed in a double outer wall. There
were many variations on this system of planning, but
the main architectural conventions and the function
which they expressed remained unchanged.

The New Kingdom builders had discovered sandstone

quarries at Silsilah, near Thebes, and this material made wider spans possible for lintels and roofing slabs. But the appearance of temple interiors was still conditioned by the need for innumerable columns. Almost always their shapes echoed vegetable forms. Shafts, swelling at the base to resemble a bunch of lotus stalks, stood upon circular stone bases, their bud-shaped capitals creating a silhouette very common at the time. Another was produced by a simple tapered shaft, crowned by the inverted-bell form of an open papyrus flower. In the Hypostyle Hall at Karnak, the huge central columns took this latter form, while the capitals of the lower order on either side imitated the shape of a closed flower. Other more cumbersome architectural features were introduced from time to time, such as the so-called 'Hathor-headed' capitals which incorporated human features and the rudiments of a shrine; or the 'Osiris-pillars', found mainly in mortuary temples, which could be considered forerunners of the Greek 'caryatids'. Then there were obelisks, as a setting for which special courts were sometimes provided, and occasional free-standing sculptures. But everywhere a special distinction was given to the interiors of these buildings by the ubiquitous ripple of relief carving and hieroglyphic inscriptions. Even the shafts of columns were sometimes covered with such ornaments, which could consist of incised intaglio carving or true relief. In a building like the temple of Sethos I at Abydos, both techniques were employed side by side and there as elsewhere a very general use was made of colour.

It is only when we turn to the external façades of these temples that all character appears to be lacking. Egyptian architects confined themselves to a single cornice moulding of an extremely simple form, apart from which all ornament was restricted to the entrance gateways and the pylons on either side of them. In the realm of structural security too we find one curious idiosyncrasy. Little attention was paid to foundations. Eleven of the largest columns at Karnak, which fell flat in 1899, were found to have been supported on friable little blocks of stone placed loosely together in holes beneath their bases. This fact becomes more surprising when we consider the volume and variety of experience in dealing with stone, which Egyptians had accumulated throughout the centuries. One example of their technological virtuosity may be seen in the rock-hewn temples of Nubia, of which that designed by Rameses II at Abu Simbel is the most spectacular. Here, a fantastic and apparently pointless *tour de force* is achieved by carving 'in negative', out of the solid rock, a full-scale and conventionally designed temple of the sort we have been describing above, and decorating its entrance with four seated statues, sixty-five feet high, themselves also carved out of the cliff-face.

In Egypt, as we have said earlier, there is a natural tendency to concentrate one's attention on stone buildings and to forget how ludicrously incomplete a picture is thus created. To correct this impression, one needs only to glance for instance at the completed plans of the Ramesseum or the Medinet Habu temple at Thebes, in which the mud-brick dependencies of the main stone buildings have been added. The central structure then appears almost submerged in a warren of storage-chambers and priests' quarters.

55

55 Karnak. Papyrus capitals in the Temple of Ptah
Several variations on the same theme are seen in this group.

56

56 Medinet Habu. Columns in the Temple of Rameses III. 1198 B.C.
Lotus-bud capitals of an early complicated form, which is seen simplified in figure 52.

57

57 Deir-el-bahari. Sculptural detail from the temple of Queen Hatshepsut. c. 1520 B.C.
The colonnades against the terraced walls were richly adorned with relief sculptures.

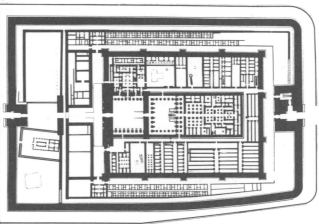

58

58 Medinet Habu. Plan of the temple of Rameses III
The stone temple was almost submerged in a warren of storage chambers and priests' quarters in mud-brick.

**59 Luxor. Temple
of Amon-Mut-Khons.
1408-1300 B.C.**
Here we see increase
of span followed by an even
greater increase of columnar size.

**60 El Amarnah. Central quarter
of the city. 1366-1351 B.C.**
Akhenaten's short-lived capital
at El Amarnah had elegant
mud-brick palaces and mansions
with wood-pillared rooms,
formal gardens, and ornamented
pavilions.

**61 El Amarnah. Plan
of north palace**
Inhabited for only eighteen years,
the palace of Akhenaten
was built with precious material
and richly decorated.

**62 El Amarnah. Mansion
of Vizier Nakht**
The better houses of the town
may have had as many as
four storeys, and were set in their
own grounds, with groves,
gardens and pools.

**63 El Amarnah. Restored
model of Egyptian mansion**
This clay model of an Egyptian
dwelling of c. 1400 shows
the buildings of crude brick,
with door and window openings
dressed in stone. The central
hall was raised high enough to
permit clerestory light on
at least one side. Bright colours
were used for internal decoration.

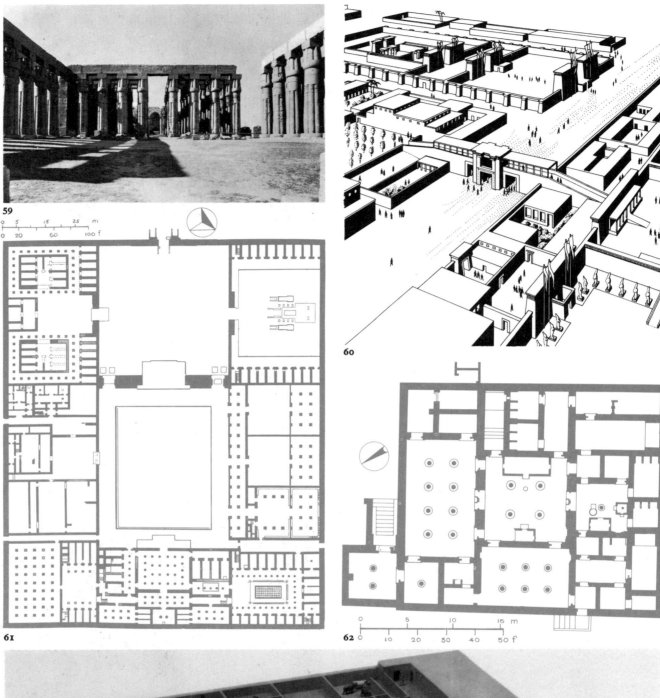

Again, elaborate reconstructions are available both of palaces and of minor domestic buildings in brick, such as those excavated at Akhenaten's short-lived capital at El Amarnah. To decorate these some of the most beautiful frescoes in the history of Egyptian painting were used, and the severity of religious convention was relieved by picturesque contrivances such as balconies and bridges between buildings. Even the private houses had thoughtfully designed interiors lit by clerestory grilles, which illuminated the attractively painted ceilings, and showed a formal architectural treatment of the sort which occasionally required a dummy window or door to complete its symmetry. The gardens too, with their cloistered pools and pavilions, provide a clue to the secular predilections of the ancient Egyptian, of which purely religious monuments would leave one in ignorance. In the realm of military architecture, there are striking fortifications for instance at Uronati, as well as the great fortress to which we have already referred near the Nubian frontier at Buhen. And if the more prosaic planning of proletarian dwellings is sought for, it can be found in the purposefully planned housing of labourers at Amarnah and Kahun.

CRETAN AND AEGEAN

Moving westward across the great land-bridge which connects Asia and Europe, we come to the coast-lands of the Aegean Sea and the tiny but formidable, ancient stronghold of Troy, which symbolises both geographically and historically the transition from one world to another. The period to which it brings us is the so-called Bronze Age, in which the shadowy antecedents of classical architecture must be sought. The region where we find them is a corner of the eastern Mediterranean, including not only Greece but the shores of Asia Minor, which in early times the Greeks also made their own. Here, small mountain ranges, thrust out like fingers from the Asiatic coast, reappear first as a pattern of Aegean islands and afterwards find counterparts in the promontories of the Greek mainland. To the south its limits are softly outlined by the island of Crete. Its land- and sea-scapes are of remarkable beauty, and one sees how the form of architecture perfected in this setting by the Greeks twenty-five centuries ago was not only inspired by but perfectly adapted to it.

In discussing Aegean architecture then, Troy can significantly be chosen as a point of departure. Basic traditions and practices which give character to the lives of a particular people are considered as together composing what is loosely termed a 'material culture'; and during the complex migrations which took place in these parts late in the third millennium B.C., Troy and other stations on the Aegean coast seem to have been the channel through which one such 'culture' was transmitted from the hinterland of Asia Minor to the islands, including Crete, and eventually to the Greek mainland. At this stage in its history, the 'city' (which covered no more than five acres of ground) was architecturally conspicuous for two reasons. Already, a thousand years before the Hittites were heard of, it had fortress-walls whose lower parts were soundly built of stone in rectangular blocks. Secondly, inside the fortress, was a

60, 61
62, 63

64 65

Negative intaglio carving was often used on temple exteriors in strong light.

65 Thebes. Detail of capital in the Ramesseum, funerary temple of Rameses II. 1301 B.C.
Heavy beams obtain a bearing on the square abacus.

66 Karnak. Temple of Amon. Reconstruction of clerestory, Hypostyle Hall. 1312-1301 B.C.
The roof of stone slabs is supported by 134 columns in 16 rows. The columns of the central nave, 69 feet high, rise above the side aisles, allowing stone grilles to be inserted, through which clerestory light is admitted.

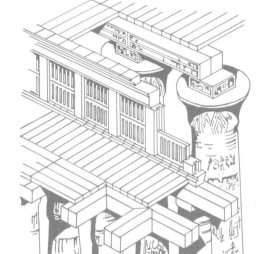

66

67

After the Alexandrian conquest, a certain reduction in labour sources led to a smaller building in which economy and elegance combine.

68 Edfu. Birthhouse of the Horus temple. 140-124 B.C.
The Graeco-Roman temple of which this forms a part is one of the best preserved examples of the period.

68

69 Mycenae. The Lion Gate. c. 1250 B.C.
Part of the massive walls circuiting the palace, the Lion Gate is its landmark. Above the sixteen-foot lintel is the triangular opening containing the sculpture of rampant lions; between them is recorded the shape of the downward-tapering Aegean column.

69

70 Mycenae. Dromos, 'Treasury of Atreus'. c. 1325 B.C.
The beehive tomb is entered through a rectangular dromos. Like the Lion Gate, the doorway has a flat lintel and corbelled relieving arch.

70

71 Mycenae. North gate
Roughly squared stones were used, not in regular courses. Their enormous size gave rise to the name Cyclopean for this type of masonry.

71

palace, or more likely a Hall of Assembly, composed of a single rectangular chamber twenty-five feet wide, with a circular hearth in the middle and side walls extended to form an open porch at one end. These and other details (such as clay benches for sitting or sleeping and timber facings on the ends of the wing-walls) exactly reproduced the so-called Greek *megaron*, which Homer described a thousand years later. This equation gains more than academic interest when one is reminded that the *megaron*, surrounded by a screen of columns, provided the classical shape of a Greek temple. For this reason and in spite of geographical evidence offered by the Trojan examples, most art historians have contrived a purely Greek origin for the form; whereas it is in fact part of our Anatolian 'culture', transmitted through Troy, first to such islands as Lemnos, where it shaped the first Bronze Age house, and later to Greece itself. Excavators at Beycesultan, seventy miles east of the Aegean coast, found a recognisable *megaron* built before the Bronze Age started. A little later, as far east as Kultepe in central Anatolia, another was found already to have adopted the form—square, with a huge circular hearth and four columns—which it took in the Mycenaean palaces a thousand years afterwards.

Here then was the first basic conception of the form which a dwelling-house should take—a form completely unknown in the Near East—spreading from the Asiatic mainland to Greece and the islands and making so conventional an image in the Aegean mind that for classical Greece it became a religious symbol. With it, in the sphere of practical building construction, came an architectural tradition every bit as important. Timber was now used in the composition of walls as well as of roofs. In the countries south and west of the Black Sea, a single method of building became practically universal. Walls rested on a substructure of undressed stone, strengthened with timber, above which came a timber framework, with vertical posts tied in to the roof and panels between filled with crude or kiln-baked brick. Above all, this device afforded the structural elasticity so necessary in a region continually subject to earthquakes. It was one which only deforestation could render impractical, and despite the latter has survived to the present day. Its weakness lay in danger from fire, as may be seen in the tangle of charred beams and vitrified brick from which some fine half-timber buildings of the Bronze Age have been reconstructed. But from Crete and Greece to the inland cities of Anatolia and Syria, it dictated the main principles of design in small and great buildings alike; and among these were the Bronze Age palaces of the Aegean.

If architectural developments in this part of the world also are to be taken in chronological order, we must start at its southernmost limit in Crete, where a precociously advanced civilization came to maturity in the early centuries of the second millennium B.C. Partly owing to its geographical situation, the Bronze Age culture of this island was sharply differentiated from that which developed elsewhere in the Aegean. Whereas on its northern side Crete encloses the sea-ways between Greece and Asia Minor, to the south it looks towards Egypt and the Levant, and from the earliest times Cretans were good sailors. Unlike

72

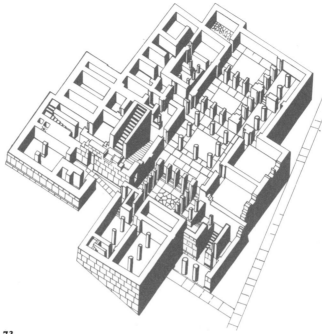

73

72 Mycenae. Tholos tomb. Treasury of Atreus. c. 1325 B.C.
A very advanced form of beehive-domed chamber, closely resembling those in Egypt in the twelfth dynasty and bearing witness to close contact therewith. Similar corbelled structures are found in Crete.

73 Cnossos. The 'Little Palace'
Stairways, colonnades and open light-wells are typical of the island palaces; the columns were of the downward-tapering type and made of wood. The walls were generally plastered and covered with bright frescoes.

74

74 Cnossos. The palace of Minos. c. 1800–1600 B.C.
Here also there were columns of wood, narrower at the foot than at the top (as in furniture legs), returning flights of stairs, bathrooms and plumbing and folding, all innovations in East Mediterranean architecture.

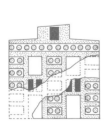

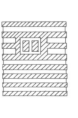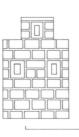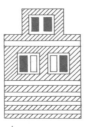

75

76

75 Restored models of Minoan houses
These buildings, with square-cut window openings, are decorated in a way which shows their part timber construction.

76 Cnossos. The grand stairway, palace of Minos
This stairway is built around a light-shaft whose walls are supported on tapered columns.

77 Mycenae. Plan of the palace
The Mycenaean palaces are typically groups of suites of rooms arranged round a main hall with a porch – the megaron form. Sometimes several of these complexes are grouped round an inner courtyard.

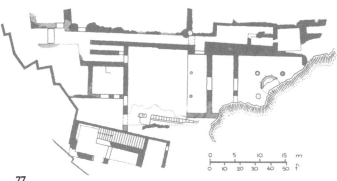

77

78 Cnossos frescoes
These are true frescoes on plaster. This example gives a lively representation of performers in the Minoan bull-ring.

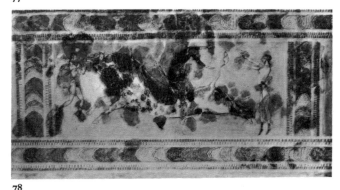

78

79 Cnossos. Royal chamber
The royal chambers had plastered walls painted in fresco above and lined with a dado of thin marble slabs below. Here the brilliance of colour was given full strength by the natural lighting which came from the colonnaded light-wells.

79

80 Cnossos. Queen's megaron
Although the use of these quarters for the queen has been disputed, the fact is that they did contain, as well as the sprightly dolphin frescoes, some of the most advanced sanitary arrangements, including a W.C. with flushing device.

80

their northern neighbours therefore, their most instructive contacts were with the peoples of the Near East. This is apparent in their architecture, where Egyptian or Syrian forms or techniques are curiously combined with more northerly traditions. An increasing use of squared masonry, gypsum orthostats, formal staircases and columns, sometimes fluted or reeded, were Eastern features which they adopted, and the true frescoes used to ornament their walls compare favourably with the Egyptians' tempera painting. All these refinements were superimposed on structural principles which were basically Aegean. But formal elements elsewhere associated with these, such as the *megaron* hall, seem not to have reached the island, and planning was a disorderly affair, casually adapted to regional requirements and predilections. The Cretan temperament, which was sensitive, ingenious and light-hearted, manifested itself in the romantic and somewhat disorderly character of Minoan architecture; in its agglomerative compositions and distaste for symmetry.

During these centuries, Crete developed an urban civilization as complicated and advanced as those of the Near East itself; but in strange contrast to the latter, it produced no major religious buildings. The animistic beliefs of these people centred round mysteries of the sort which could be performed in natural settings, such as mountain caves or secret cult-chambers. Its public ceremonials, such as the famous bull-leaping spectacles, could take place in the courtyards and theatrical arenas of royal palaces, which also served as the seat of government. These buildings were the great monuments of the age, on which Cretan architects lavished so much skill and ingenuity. Remains of them have been found at three main centres: Cnossos, Phaestos and Mallia. In the form which we know from their ruins, they date from the three centuries following 1700 B.C., and though their character owes much to periodical accretions and reconstruction after earthquakes, their general appointments are in each case broadly similar.

The Palace of Minos at Cnossos, which was finally destroyed by fire in about 1400 B.C., is the one which provides most material for study. Alone it covers almost five acres of ground and, like the others, its buildings are grouped around a central court with a double-square proportion, a feature for which there is an earlier precedent in Anatolia. It consists of innumerable rooms, generally rather small, and ranges of long storage-chambers, accessible through inner courts, yards and corridors. In the west wing at ground level store rooms and ritual chambers, including a throne-room, support an upper suite of reception rooms (*piano nobile*), and this is approached by monumental stairways from the main entrance and from the courtyard. Placed lower down the hill on the east side, in order to give these a clear view over the valley, are the residential apartments of the royal family, again on two storeys connected by stairs. These apartments are perhaps the earliest example we have of living quarters both elegantly and ingeniously planned to suit the climate. Main chambers and annexed loggias are separated only by ranges of doors, which fold back into the stone piers between them, so that the whole suite can be thrown open for summer air and space on ceremonial occasions, or closed for intimacy

78

81–83

73, 74
76, 79
80

and winter warmth. Interior wall-faces are dignified with dadoes of stone slabs, and the plaster above enriched with frescoes, whose brilliant and naturalistic designs are occasionally and rather unexpectedly varied by a reproduction in paint of the half-timber structure beneath. Columns are of painted wood, usually tapering downwards (a device more often associated in our own minds with furniture), and their capitals are composed of square and cushion-shaped elements which foreshadow the abacus and echinus forms of classical times. In the outer façades of these buildings (as in those of minor dwellings of which small models have survived), square or rectangular windows are conspicuous and other forms of ornament once more emphasise the structural pattern.

Tombs in Crete, like those in Egypt, make little contribution to the repertory of architectural practices. But circular *tholos* burials with rectangular antechambers, like much earlier examples which we have noticed in Mesopotamia, anticipate imminent developments on the Greek mainland

None of the Cretan palaces or the towns surrounding them showed any traces of military defences, nor is there much evidence to suggest that the Minoans were a warlike race. Nevertheless, they were undoubtedly a maritime people with far-reaching trade connections. Whether by peaceful association or by actual conquest, during the fifteenth century B.C. their culture dominated almost the whole Aegean area. Mycenae, due west of Athens in the Peloponnese, was already at this time the seat of an important mainland principality, and the contents of the famous 'shaft-grave' burials discovered there by Schliemann in 1876, though architecturally irrelevant, reveal the richness of Minoan art in the provincial centres of the period. But at a date usually estimated at about 1400 B.C., some great migratory upheaval seems to have transformed the ethnic composition of the Aegean peoples and to have ended the hegemony of the Cretan nation. When a clear picture once more emerges, it shows the Minoan palaces in ruins and the island, in common with the whole Aegean area, dominated by a people whose written language is now tentatively identified as Greek. Related by speech and heredity, they are not so much a nation as a federation of maritime principalities and their regional seats of government are in cities such as Mycenae, Tiryns and Pylos on the Greek mainland. Their kings or princes, afterwards to become the heroes of Homeric legend and classical myth, built themselves palaces which bore little resemblance to the Minoan labyrinths of the preceding age.

Mycenaean palace plans are well illustrated for instance by that discovered at Pylos. The central unit is a *megaron*, of which the hall has become a squarish compartment with a central hearth, twelve feet in diameter, and four columns, probably to allow clerestory lighting or outlets for smoke. It is separated by an inner vestibule from the usual columned porch. In a similar building at Tiryns the subsidiary chambers on either side include a smaller *megaron*, and in both examples the central unit is as it were partially insulated from these by a surrounding corridor. It faces a courtyard, colonnaded at Tiryns, and entered by a gateway with columned porches inside and out.

77

83

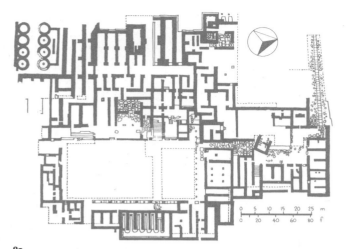

81 Mallia. Plan of the palace
Middle of second millennium B.C. The palaces at Mallia, Hagia Triada and Phaestos were complexes of rooms arranged round a series of inner courtyards, a form already familiar elsewhere in the Near East.

81

82 Phaestos. Part of the palace of Radamanthus
Middle of second millennium B.C. Minoan towns and palaces show that these people were able to deal systematically with town-planning problems. There was an ordered system of sewers and freshwater canals. Warehouses were built for food storage.

82

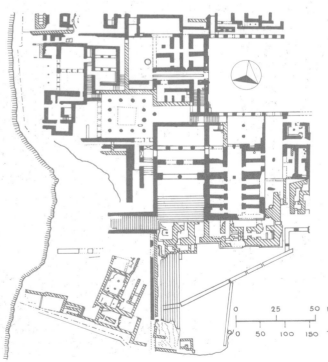

83 Phaestos. Plan of main portion of palace
Destroyed by earthquake. The main feature of Hellenic houses of 1,000 years later, the peristyle court, is here anticipated.

**84 The Parthenon, Athens.
447-432 B.C.**
This best-known of all Greek
temples, the apogee of Hellenic
architecture, is still a pitched-roof
building surrounded by
a colonnaded verandah which
originally sheltered brick walls
from sun and rain.

84

**85 Treasury of the Athenians,
Delphi. c. 500-485 B.C.**
The first Doric building
to be built entirely out of marble.
Like most treasuries
it looked like a miniature temple
with only two columns
and a very short cella.

85

Every one of these features has a precedent a thousand years earlier in Anatolia, and the only resemblance to Cretan palaces lies in the familiar half-timber construction and the frescoes which ornament the plaster-faces. Later in the fourteenth century B.C. these palaces seem to have been converted into military strongholds by the addition of powerful fortress-walls, often built of huge rough stones, which the Greeks of later days termed 'Cyclopean'. Nevertheless, before the end of the thirteenth century B.C. they were all destroyed by fire and never rebuilt.

One opening in the outer fortification at Mycenae is known as the 'Lion Gate'. Two huge blocks of stone form the door-jambs and another the lintel, which is relieved of the weight above it by a system of corbelling. The triangular opening thus left is filled by a sculptured slab, on which two rampant lions support a cult pillar of the sort often represented on Cretan seals. A more pretentious architectural treatment distinguishes the *tholos* tombs in which the princes of this age were buried. Of these the so-called 'Treasury of Atreus' is the most striking example. It is a beehive-shaped affair with a round interior, forty-four feet in diameter and forty feet high, partly submerged in the side of a hill, with a low circular retaining wall supporting the earth above. The corbelled vault was built of carefully dressed and jointed masonry, ornamented here and there with bronze rosettes. The tomb itself is approached by a rectangular *dromos*, and the doorway between the two makes a striking architectural composition, flanked by elaborately carved half-columns in green stone. Above the lintel once more there is a weight-relieving triangular opening; but this was afterwards masked by a panel of spiral and other ornament in stones of various colours, framed on either side by downward-tapering pilasters.

Little more is known of Mycenaean architecture. These few surviving remains suggest Minoan stylistic influence on basically Anatolian forms and the occasional introduction of Egyptian motifs. Its parental relationship to that of classical Greece is by no means conspicuous.

GREEK AND HELLENISTIC

With the end of the Bronze Age in sight, we are approaching one of the greatest turning-points in architectural history. In about 1100 B.C., world events of which we have little understanding brought Mycenaean civilization to an abrupt end, and for the moment there was nothing to replace it. Historically there ensued a curious interlude of retrogression; a period of four centuries during which the Aegean peoples relapsed into a state of poverty and impotence almost comparable to that from which they had emerged during the third millennium B.C.

It is towards the end of the eighth century B.C. that the first symptoms are to be seen of a new and distinctive civilization materialising from this period of gestation. Mycenaean citadels, in an age when temples were practically unknown, had usually been crowned by the palace of a ruling prince. Now there were no princes, and the most prominent building housed the statue of a god. Furthermore, since Greek religion now combined the worship of ancient heroes with that of personified natural phenomena,

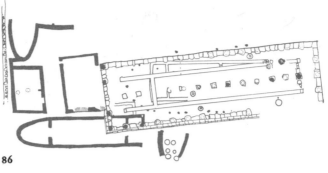

86

86 Plan of the temple of Apollo, Thermum. Before 600 B.C.
At first the temples were built of mud-brick with timber framing. The columns were of wood, and the sculptural decoration was painted terra cotta. The whole stood on a stone platform.

87

87 Plan of temple, Selinus. 600 B.C.
The megaron plan is here not yet standardised.

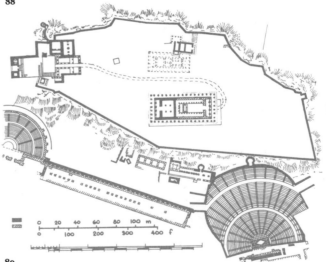

88

88 The Acropolis, Athens
The Acropolis was originally a Stone Age site, owing its origin to the presence of fresh-water springs on a high plateau. It later became a fortress-citadel and shows traces of every phase of Greek architecture before its final state just prior to the fall of Athens.

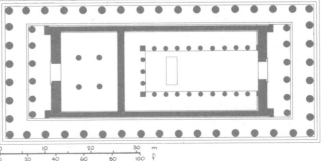

89

89 Plan of the Acropolis, Athens
The plan was dictated by the traditional siting of holy places, rather than as a dramatic processional way. Indeed, the Parthenon had the rear end towards the gate house, and a procession had to go round it in order to enter.

90

90 Plan of the Parthenon, Athens
In this final development of the Greek temple plan, the megaron form is partly concealed by a surrounding colonnade or peristyle. Behind the sanctuary, with its statue, is a second chamber used as a treasury.

91 The Erechtheion, Athens.
421–405 B.C.
An irregular plan adapted to
sacred landmarks. Projecting
porticoes are added to a main
building which is a classical
example of the Ionic order.

91

92 The Erechtheion, Athens.
Caryatid porch
Here sculptured figures, never
again so effectively employed,
replace the columns.

92

93 The Propylaea, Athens.
437–432 B.C.
Both Doric and Ionic orders
were used together in
the gate house to the Acropolis.
Here also were elegant
mullioned windows and hipped
roofs.
The Peloponnesian war prevented
the completion of the buildings
as originally planned.

93

94 The Propylaea
North wing, behind monument
of Agrippa.
The stepped approach to the
marble constructed Propylaea from
the Beulé gate led the eye
continually upward and then
directly through the
centre of the building
to the Acropolis beyond.

94

a temple might be dedicated to the very individual
whose palace had previously occupied the same site. In
Aegean tradition as we have seen, the central and indispensable element in any sort of dwelling-house was the 'hall-
and-porch' structure known as a *megaron*, and it is in no
way surprising that this basic form should now have been
chosen for the dwelling-place of a deity. The subject to
which we find ourselves thus abruptly introduced is that
of the Greek temple.

When the earliest temples appeared in the seventh century B. C., the structural practices of the Bronze Age had
not yet been discarded. Walls were still of timber-framed
mud-brick on a stone substructure, and roofs were generally flat. The temple in its simplest form, as may be seen
from the reconstruction of a Cretan example, had no more
than the elementary features of a *megaron*; a rectangular   86, 87
chamber (*cella*) with some sort of altar replacing the domestic hearth and a central doorway, approached through
an open portico. Only the square pillar which, in conjunction with pilasters in the wing walls, supported a beam
over the entrance, can already be seen to anticipate the
columns *in antis* of later times. The spatial principle of a
new type of building having thus been determined by the
adoption of an ancestral precedent, its external form was
next drastically transformed by the addition of a verandah
or colonnade all round the main structure. Whether this
was done for purely aesthetic reasons or for some practical purpose, such as the protection of mud-brick from the
weather, will probably never be known. But the device
in itself served at once to supply a primary characteristic
of the Greek temple.

The proportions of the *cella* now began to be greatly
elongated. The altar was removed to the end furthest from
the entrance and, when a row of columns was tentatively
added down the middle, it needed to be placed a little
on one side in order to be seen. Sometimes also a false
porch was provided at the back of the *cella*; and this feature, which appealed to the Greek sense of symmetry, became a fairly usual convention. An alternative, at this early stage, was an apsidal end to the building; a device which
presented no problem in roofing as long as thatch was the
material used. At the end of the seventh century however,
thatch gave way to roofing-tiles of baked clay; and from
then onwards rectangular buildings with pitched roofs
were standardised. A gable-end appeared above the porch,
and the retention beneath it of a horizontal lintel over the
entrance formed a triangular feature afterwards known as
a pediment. Almost all the standard elements of a temple
were now present, but a long process of modification and
refinement was still required.

One innovation which gave a new stimulus to design
was the use of dressed stone to replace the brick-and-tim-
ber construction of earlier times. When this happened, no
change was at first made in the broad system of structure
and ornament, each traditional feature being conscien-
tiously reproduced in the new material. In the earliest stone
temples dating from the beginning of the sixth century
B.C., every detail of the timber-framed prototype was
imitated in stone, down to the wooden pegs which held
the beams together. Soon however increasing familiarity

with the new material brought a better understanding of its possibilities and limitations. Its tensile weakness, for instance, made a reduction in beam-spans desirable, whereas the squat proportions at first assigned to columns proved an unnecessary precaution. Once such principles were understood and architects became capable of thinking in terms of the material which they were using, new aesthetic notions could be applied to the refinement of design. Meanwhile, the component features of a building, both structural and ornamental, were standardised and a canon created governing their position and shape. It was thus that the so-called 'orders' in Greek architecture came to exist.

As the end of the sixth century approached, the Doric order came to be accepted throughout the Greek mainland and the western colonies as a basic formula for architectural composition. Yet many improvements in shape and proportion were made possible by the Greek architect's increasing sensibility and confidence. As early as 525 B.C., marble came into general use to replace stone in the structure of buildings, and it was soon found that even roofing-tiles could be made of the same material. At first Parian and other island marbles were preferred, but from about 480 B.C. onwards, the Pentelic quarries near Athens became the most popular source. Fine polished surfaces could now be obtained and a new definition in the carving of ornamental detail.

Elsewhere in the Aegean, other interesting developments were taking place. The Ionic order, whose genesis in the islands and cities of Asia Minor occurred a little later than the Doric, seems to have been less hampered from the start by memories of half-timber construction and retained in its composition less evidence of 'petrified carpentry'. Technical improvements in masonry also now led to a new interest in proportion, and columns became more than ever attenuated. Where new subtlety was introduced into the design of carved ornament, major features still retained their conventional formality; and this persisted until the invention of the Corinthian capital whose freely carved foliage carried naturalism to an opposite extreme. A third order, differentiated in few other respects from the Ionic, was thus conceived.

The purpose of a Greek temple, as we have said, was usually to house a cult-statue or emblem; but more rarely it could contain an oracle. The statue was invariably placed facing towards the rising sun through the main doorway; and the great altar, at which both sacrifices and offerings were made, stood outside the building on the east side, usually connected to it by a stone causeway. (The Parthenon has none, since, when it was built, an earlier building was still in use for the purpose.) A second purpose of the building then was to protect an accumulation of valuable offerings. The sanctuary itself in which the statue stood occupied the greater part of the *cella*, but there was also sometimes a rear hall (*opisthodomos*) connected either with it or with the back porch, and this may have served as a treasury. The enclosure of the porches themselves of Doric temples with metal grilles between the columns perhaps served the same purpose. In at least one Hellenistic example of those which survive, the treasury is a vaulted chamber beneath the sanctuary.

95 Temple of Niké Apteros, Athens
Fifth century B.C.
A small gem of classical design. Its miniature size was adapted to the bastion on which it stands.

95

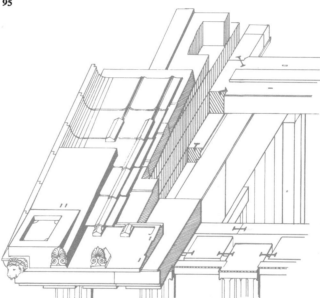

96 The Parthenon roof construction
Early Greek builders effectively converted timber forms into stone. At first they underestimated the strength of the stone and built unnecessarily heavily; later they not only built lightly but gave even greater lightness by optical illusion.

96

97 Temple of Olympian Zeus, Athens. Begun 174 B.C.
An example of the Corinthian order, which became increasingly popular in the Hellenistic period. This building was not completed by the Greeks. Subsequently in A.D. 132 Hadrian finished and dedicated it.

97

98 Temple of Aphaia, Aegina
Early fifth century B.C.
This Doric temple is the third to
this obscure goddess on the same
site. No metopes have been
found, but these may have
been of wood.

98

**99 Plan of the temple
of Aphaia,
Aegina**
Early fifth century B.C.

**100 Plan of the Theseion,
Athens**
Mid-fifth century B.C.
Built immediately before
the Parthenon.

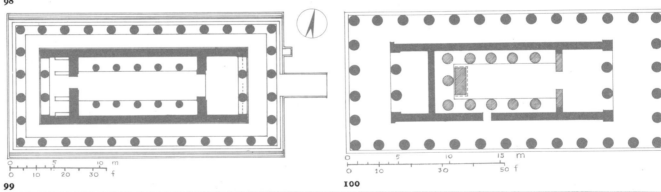

99   100

101 The Theseion, Athens
Mid-fifth century B.C.
An edifice built almost entirely
of marble in peripteral hexastyle.
Its well-preserved state is due
to its having been converted
into a church by Byzantine Greeks,
who built an apse at the east end.

101

In the plan of a temple the next important feature was the arrangement of columns to form the porticoes and the colonnade or peristyle surrounding the whole building. This, in conjunction with components of the design, gave rise to a whole vocabulary of Graecisms, which need tabulating if they are to be understood or remembered. The plan of the Parthenon for instance is ultimately derived from that of a normal *megaron* with two columns *in antis*, (i.e. between the wing walls) at either end. This number has been increased to four (distyle *in antis*). Next the wing walls have been truncated, leaving the porch-ends supported by rows of six free-standing columns (amphi-prostyle hexastyle): and finally the whole arrangement has been enclosed in a single peristyle with eight columns at each end (peripteral octostyle). But there are many other variations. Sometimes the peristyle in such a building is duplicated (dipteral decastyle): sometimes the inner peristyle is then eliminated, and at others there is more than one row of columns inside the antae of the main porch. Occasionally there are engaged columns against the outside walls and there are rare examples of circular temples.

Usually a temple stood in a *temenos* or sacred enclosure, often on top of a high rock or *acropolis*, as at Athens. Other buildings were as a rule disposed in a studied relationship to it. The position for instance of the *propylaion*, through which the *temenos* was entered, assured a diagonal approach to it, which was considered the ideal viewpoint. That of subsidiary temples might be dictated by less practical considerations. The classical Doric practice was to build upon a solid stone platform, of which the upper four courses appeared above ground and were set back to form steps all round the building. Smaller steps interposed between them, or even a flat ramp, facilitated the approach to the eastern porch (*pronaos*). The floor of the *cella* also was raised a little above that of the peristyle, directly upon which the columns rested without intervening bases. Inside the colonnade, the stone walls of the *cella* started at pavement level with tall upright slabs, recalling the orthostats of earlier times. It ended in a sculptured frieze, and above this stone cross-beams supported coffered ceiling-slabs. The masonry between the capitals and the verge of the tiled roof (entablature), corresponding in a timber building to the lintel-beams, joist-ends and eaves, formed a pattern exactly prescribed by the canon of Doric design and proportion. Its construction in stone can be far more easily understood from a perspective reconstruction than from a verbal description. The same, however, does not apply to the interior of the *cella*; for considerably less is known about it and conflicting theories offer a variety of possible restorations.

In the sanctuary or *naos* there were lateral colonnades, serving to reduce the span of the roofing beams: in the Parthenon and some later temples they were united by a third range of columns across the end of the chamber. These were on a much smaller scale than those outside and, in order to obtain the required height, a second range of even smaller pillars, sometimes conforming to the Ionic or even Corinthian order, was superimposed upon them. Probably the 'nave' and 'aisles' thus created were then covered by timber ceilings; but the reconstruction of these

90

84

88, 89

93, 94

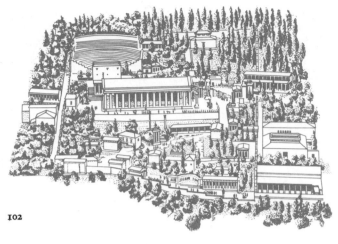

102

102 The temenos, Delphi. 700 B.C. onwards
Set apart from the city on high ground, the temenos or sacred precinct, usually walled, contained the main sacred buildings. Here the temple of Apollo occupies the main, central position; the theatre is behind it, to the left; the treasuries in the foreground.

103

103 Temple of Apollo, Corinth. c. 540 B.C.
Only seven monolithic columns remain of the original thirty-eight. The capitals were carved separately, surfaced with a stucco made of marble dust.
The inner building had two cellas back to back, containing two rows of smaller columns.

104

104 The Acropolis, Athens
Architectural remains.
By the middle of the fifth century Greek masonry had achieved a finesse hitherto unparalleled even in Egypt.
No mortar was used, and blocks were fitted together with extraordinary precision.

105 The marble tholos, Delphi. c. 390 B.C.
Doric and Corinthian columns were used in two circles of the rotunda. The architect, Theodorus of Phocaea, who here adapted temple architecture to a circular structure, established a pattern for the tholos.

105

106 The Erechtheion, Athens. 421-405 B.C.
The Ionic columns in the north porch.
The eyes of the volutes were gilt and those of the guilloche ornament filled with glass beads of four colours.

107 Choragic Monument of Lysicrates, Athens. c. 334 B.C.
This is the first building in which the Corinthian order was used externally and exclusively. The columns, although appearing to be pilasters, are in fact free-standing, the curved wall being infilled panels.

106

107

depends on diverse theories regarding the main structure
of the pitched roof, which has in every case vanished. All
one can safely say about this is that the Greeks never seem
to have mastered the use of triangular tie-beam trusses.

In the mid-fifth century, however, Greek masonry attained a finesse hitherto unparalleled even in Egypt. No
mortar was used, and the blocks were fitted together with
extraordinary precision. By making their bedding-surfaces
slightly concave, it was found possible to obtain what builders call a hair-joint on the face of the wall. Each block
was joined to its neighbours by a metal dowel, more often of iron than of bronze, and these were fixed in position with molten lead. Exposed faces were left rough and
then dressed *in situ*. This method was also applied in the
case of columns, whose circular faces temporarily remained undressed when placed in position, except for narrow bands of completed fluting at top and bottom. Metal
dowels connecting the drums together were encased in
wood to prevent them splitting the stone. The several patterns of carved enrichment were standardised like everything else, and each was used exclusively for a particular
moulding or ornament. As for the figure sculpture with
which the building was adorned, one can here do hardly
more than mention the positions which it occupied. As
we have seen, the summit of the *cella* façades made a suitable position for a continuous frieze of relief sculpture,
subtly lit by reflected sunshine from the marble pavement
below. Figures in deeper relief could be empanelled in the
square spaces (metopes) between the imitation beam-ends
(triglyphs) in the main entablature. The pediments have
space for more ambitious groups of sculpture, which now,
after much experiment, were admirably composed to fit
their triangular shape. But generally speaking, the important status of sculpture in the whole composition of the
building can hardly be over-emphasised. It would be true
to say that the architect's primary motive in designing a
temple was not only to house a particular statue but to
provide a setting for other sculptured groups. And it is
less surprising to find the sculptor Pheidias apparently 'su-
pervising' the work of the Parthenon architects, when one
remembers that the intrinsic value of the chryselephantine
cult-image alone far exceeded the cost of the building.

Before leaving the subject of masonry, one must mention the 'refinements' applied by Greek architects to the
cardinal forms of a temple building. Sometimes this involved the actual positioning of architectural features; the
adjustment, for instance, of inter-columniation, by which
corner pillars were placed more closely together. But most
important of all were the ingenious calculations whereby
the main lines of the building, including even the surface
of the stylobate, were imperceptibly distorted to counter-
act the effects of perspective and foreshortening. Like the
geometrically calculated curve in the tapering silhouette
of a Doric column, these too must have been arrived at
by a long process of trial and error.

Finally there is the subject of colouring by pigmentation,
which must so drastically have conditioned the actual appearance of such buildings. It is a subject which can be
seen to have proved distasteful to some modern critics,
who have found archaeologists' tentative reconstructions

96

98

108

**108 Temple of Poseidon,
Sunium. 444-440 B.C.**
The columns are an attenuated
Doric, similar in proportion
to those of the Theseion at Athens.
By the building are the remains
of a frieze which seems to show
the battle of the Centaurs and
Lapiths and the story
of Theseus.

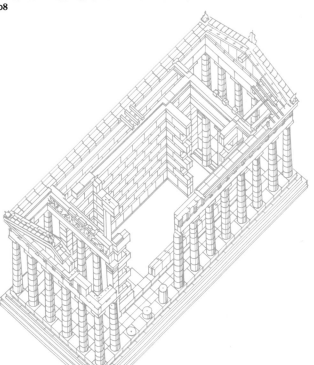

109

**109 Temple of Poseidon,
Sunium**
Restored.
The Doric order was perfected
shortly after the middle of
the fifth century, and at Sunium,
the perfect proportion
between side and end columns
was used (thirteen to six).
There were two temples
at Sunium, the first having been
destroyed around 490 B.C.

110

**110 Temple of Aphaia,
Aegina**
Detail of Doric capitals,
also showing the superimposed
colonnades, c. 490 B.C.

111-113 The three orders
The Doric and Ionic were
contemporaneous; the Corinthian
was a later modification of the
Ionic. The Doric was the simplest,
the Corinthian the most ornate.
At first the Doric and
Ionic orders were used separately,
but latterly architects combined
them. Ionic sculptured friezes
were used over Doric columns,
and slender Ionic columns
were used in the
interior of Doric buildings.
111 Ionic column from temple
on the Ilissus, Athens
112 Doric capital
from the Theseion, Athens
113 Corinthian capital
from the Choragic Monument
of Lysicrates, Athens

111

112

113

114 Doric capital
Temple of Aphaia, Aegina.
Here, in this almost perfect
example of the early Greek temple,
the highly refined Doric
order was used throughout.

114

difficult to accept. Architectural taste in our own time is
rarely sympathetic to the colouring of stone with paint;
and few can reconcile themselves easily to the undoubted
fact that, in a Doric temple, all ornamental features and
some others were brightly painted in traditional colours,
mostly red and blue.

Details of the Greek orders have been a subject of comparative study ever since the time of the Roman emperor
Augustus, to whom the architect Vitruvius dedicated a critical work on the subject. Ideal proportions for the component parts of the design are calculated in multiples of a
unit called a 'module', equal to half the lower diameter
of the column. For students they can be presented in dia-
grammatical form and are easily memorised. In the Doric
order perhaps the most striking and distinctive feature is
the capital, which is clearly a stone-carver's invention and
has no timber origin. The gradual refinement of the curved
member (echinus) beneath the severely squat impost (abacus) can well be seen by comparing early examples like
those in the beautifully preserved temple of Poseidon at
Paestum, with the perfected version seen in the Parthenon. Other classical examples of the Doric order at its best
are the temples of Aphaia at Aegina, of Poseidon at Sunium and the Theseion at Athens.

The home of the Ionic order was in the islands and
Asiatic coastal cities of the Aegean, and it too was evolved
during the first half of the fifth century B.C. Once more,
its most striking and distinctive feature was the form of
capital used. Conscientious and sometimes ingenious attempts have been made to identify the origin of this form
with, for instance, Egyptian papyrus designs or archaic terminal ornaments in the islands of Cyprus and Lesbos. But
in truth, we simply do not know what first induced Aegean designers to superimpose upon a Doric echinus-form
something in the shape of an open scroll with its ends curved
into graceful volutes. Certainly it provided an opportunity for additional ornament, and another was supplied
by the same designer's addition of moulded bases to his
columns. Indeed, in archaic times, much attention seems
to have been paid to these lower parts of the building,
which presented themselves to the human eye at close
quarters. In the oldest temple of Artemis, whose remains
were found beneath twenty feet of alluvial clay at Ephesus,
each column stood on a cylindrical plinth ornamented with
sculptured figures. The Ionic builder also made the steps
leading up to the stylobate of more humanly manageable
proportions. His columns, which unlike their Doric counterparts, came accurately into line with the *cella* walls, had
small flat fillets between the flutes. In the entablature, the
alternating triglyphs and metopes so characteristic of the
Doric order were replaced by a continuous frieze, usually
sculptured; and the architrave beneath was often divided
into three receding fascia-planes.

An ornate but extremely fine example of the Ionic
order is to be seen, once more on the Acropolis at Athens,
in the temple known as the Erechtheion. This is an unusual building, asymmetrical in plan, because it is intended
to accommodate various immovable relics, such as a sacred
olive-tree and a well. It is in its eastern portico that classical specimens of the Ionic capital are found; and one

112, 11

117
98
99, 110
108, 10
100, 10

111, 12

91, 100

115

116

117

118

119

**115-119 Doric temples
in southern Italy and Sicily**
Some of the finest early Doric
temples are to be found
in southern Italy and Sicily.
At Paestum, three well-preserved
temples display the Doric order
at its most typical,
although the trachelion
(the necking) of the columns of
the 'Basilica' (116) shows traces
of Ionic influence.
The other two – the temple of
Poseidon (117) and that
of Demeter (115, 118) – and the
temple at Segesta in Sicily
(119), even earlier than
the Paestum examples, have the
monolithic quality which
has come to be associated with this
temple type. The capitals are
heavy and wide-spreading, the
columns have pronounced entasis.

120, 121 Examples of Ionic and Corinthian capitals
North porch
of the Erechtheion (left);
Temple of Olympian Zeus,
Athens (right).
Bases of columns
From the Erechtheion (left);
Temple of Zeus, Athens (right).

120   121

122 Plan of the agora, Athens
The market-place of Athens,
roughly square in shape, stood
below the Acropolis and
contained various public buildings,
a temple to Ares and several
stoas. That of Attalus which
has been reconstructed (see 126)
is shown at the top of
the plan. Before it,
traversing the agora, was
the Street of the Panathenaia.

122

123 Stoa of Attalus, Athens
Plan and section
Built by Attalus II
of Pergamon around 150 B.C.
It filled the east side of the agora,
was two-storeyed and had
shops behind it. The walls
and columns were of marble.
The height of its roof was such
that it provided shade from
the high summer sun, but the low
winter sun shone straight into
the open side.

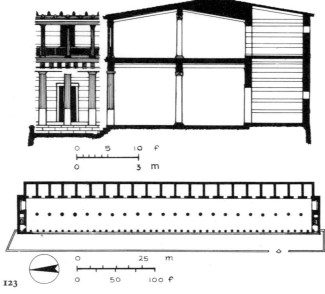

123

sees here how those over the corner pillars are provided with one diagonal volute so that their appearance in both façades may be identical. In another porch, sculptured human figures are substituted for columns; one of these famous caryatids was brought to the British Museum by Lord Elgin and has since been replaced by a terra cotta model. Structural sculptures of this sort were a device not unknown to the Greeks. In the Doric temple of Zeus at Agrigentum, built in 480 B.C., and distinguished also by a solid outer wall to which columns were attached, human figures supported the roof of the *cella*.

The use of diagonal volutes beneath a curved abacus was also adopted in the design of the Corinthian capital. Perhaps the most ornate of all Greek ornamental devices, this was also the first to be enriched with a pattern carved to imitate foliage. How far in fact the sculptured acanthus differed from the living plant, one may judge from seeing the two side by side among the ruins of Greek cities. But there can be no doubt that it makes a versatile form of ornament and, as the Greeks later discovered when the drill came into more general use, it is easy to carve. The Corinthian capital, in any case, was used sparingly in classical times. One of the best-known occurrences is again in an unconventional building at Athens. This was the so-called Choragic Monument of Lysicrates, a circular erection with six columns and an Ionic entablature around a central structure of ashlar. Fragments have also survived of a most elaborately carved scroll ornament which adorned the roof. Another Athenian monument, the Tower of the Winds, had small Corinthian columns without volutes.

The direct simplicity with which the formal elements present in temple architecture were adapted to the requirements of other buildings is well illustrated in the Propylaea, through which one entered the Athens Acropolis. Porticoes with Doric and Ionic orders of varying heights were combined in a composition fitting the asymmetrical approach to the summit. One wing was extended to enclose a picture-gallery (*pinakotheke*) and balanced on the opposite side with intuitive dexterity by a bastion supporting the tiny Ionic temple of Wingless Victory (Niké Apteros). Most cities boasted an acropolis like this one at Athens, on which their principal religious shrines were set. But, as a focal point of communal life, the citadel was rivalled in importance by the *agora*, another indispensable amenity of every Greek city. It is difficult in any other language to find a term which would express the multiple functions fulfilled by the *agora*. In addition to being a market, it served as a place for litigation, political meetings, entertainments and minor religious functions. Throughout the course of its history, as the Greek political system changed from monarchy to aristocracy and finally adopted the principles of democracy, public interest concentrated itself on the *agora* as the centre of government. But it was government of a kind which seemed to require no specific form of accommodation. In classical times a platform (*bema*) for a speaker, with space around it, or even an elevated rock like the Areiopagus, seemed quite adequate for the purpose, and formally designed council-chambers did not appear until Hellenistic times.

For the rest, one very simple type of building seemed to

121

107

93, 94

95

122

124, 1

124 Restored view of the agora at Assos
The agora was the general city meeting place for all purposes – political, business, legal, religious and entertainment – and the focal point of government.

124

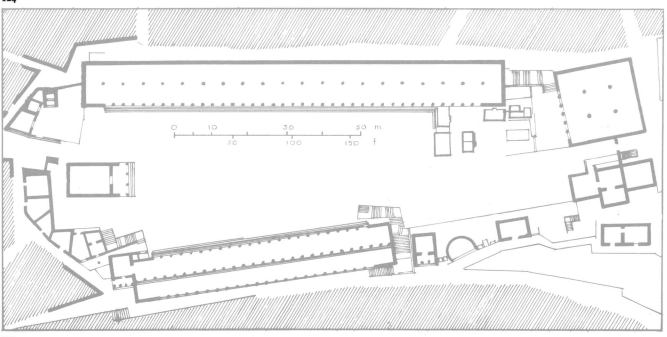

125 Plan of the agora, Assos
Here the stoa was built on a slight slope descending from the agora. Behind it was a market which ran through to the front. Facing it across the agora was a two-storeyed building, the upper part of which contained public baths; behind it was a street leading to the theatre.

125

126 The reconstructed stoa of Attalus, Athens
Recently built by the American School of Classical Studies at Athens, this admirable reconstruction is to house the finds of American excavations in the Athenian agora.

126

127 Plan of Priene
Third century B.C. The town wall follows the natural contour of a rocky outcrop. The streets are laid out on a rectangular grid.

128 Plan of the agora, Priene
This is an especially fine agora, with an extremely regular plan.

129 Plan of houses, Priene
Probably late fourth or third century.
A series of rooms around a central courtyard, built of stone. The outer walls were blank; windows looked inwards, very much as in houses in Asia Minor today.

130 Priene. The ekklesiasterion
This council house could hold all citizens entitled to vote. The tiers of seats rising on three sides for debate resemble those in a modern senate or parliament house.

131 Theatre at Delphi
Third century B.C.
Here the banked seats arranged round the stadium-theatre were built out against masonry retaining walls where the hillside fell away. The remains of the temple of Apollo are directly in front of the theatre.

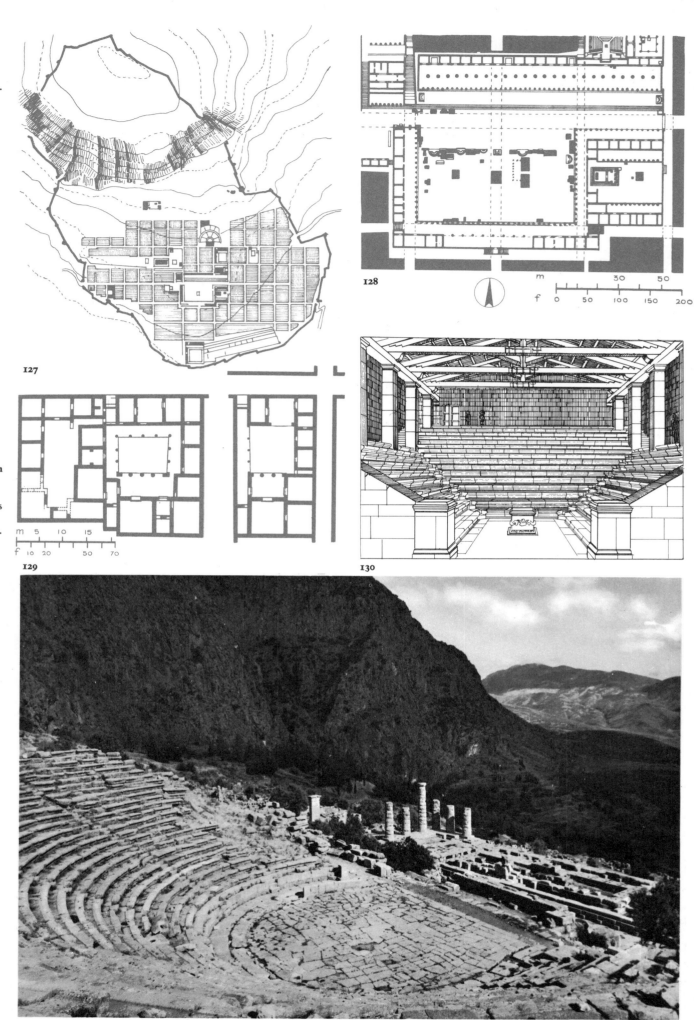

127

128

129

130

131

meet all the requirements of those whom business or pleasure brought to the *agora*. This was the elongated porch or *stoa*. Several such buildings usually grouped themselves around the central space, arranged in such a way as to catch the sun in winter and to afford shade in hot weather. At Athens the most famous of all was the so-called Painted Porch, beloved of the philosopher Socrates; but this has not survived and today we have to be content with a Hellenistic example, the Stoa of Attalus, which has been skilfully reconstructed by archaeologists. It shows the conventional use of a Doric and Ionic order respectively for external and internal colonnades, beneath a double-pitched roof and a row of small chambers behind.

When other types of buildings appeared in the *agora*, they seem in plan to be distributed almost haphazardly. But the contours of the site often show the reverse to have been the case. Better than at Athens, this can be seen in cities such as Delphi or Olympia where, owing to their religious associations, the attributes of acropolis and *agora* are combined. At Delphi, for instance, additional features include numerous monuments, sanctuaries, treasuries and even a stadium, all arranged to obtain the maximum pictorial effect from the steep proclivities and elevated position of the natural terrace on which the famous oracle was located.

But it is in Hellenistic times, and geographically perhaps in the Ionian cities of Asia Minor more than elsewhere, that one sees civic architecture and the planning of Greek cities around their religious monuments logically considered and accomplished with real ingenuity. On the Asiatic coast in the centuries immediately preceding the birth of Christ, little remained of the original classical cities. For their earliest settlements the colonists of archaic times had usually chosen sites on small islands or little promontories projecting into the great estuaries; and it was to the neighbouring shores that the growing cities spread. Frequently however, it was the action of the rivers themselves which brought about their downfall. Year by year, as their burden of silt was deposited, the level of alluvium rose until either the water-line receded, rendering their harbours useless, or the tide of grey mud rose over the quays and flowed into the streets. In a score of cases, by the end of the fourth century B.C., it proved necessary to find a new site for the city on higher ground. When this happened, only the architects and planners were pleased by the prospect of wholesale reconstruction. To them we owe some of the finest examples of Greek architecture in the developed style characteristic of its Hellenistic aftermath.

One very small city, beside the one-time estuary of the Meander River, has a history exactly following the pattern we have described. The site chosen for Priene in Hellenistic times was a natural terrace some hundreds of feet above the original harbour town, with cliffs behind rising to a high rock which could serve as an acropolis. With all the most characteristic features of a Greek city present in miniature, it perfectly illustrates the contemporary conception of civic architecture and planning. The whole city area is surrounded by a fortress wall, which straggles up on either side to encompass rather loosely the summit of the acropolis rock. Inside, we see for the first time the

Margin references: 3, 126 · 102 · 105 · 134 · 127

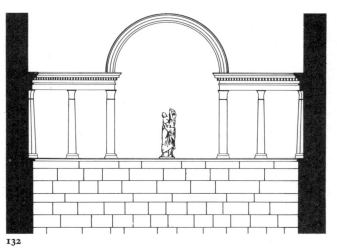

132 Lower gymnasium, Priene
During the Hellenistic period, the gymnasium became a very formal structure with open courts for athletics, pools for bathing, dressing rooms and rooms in which to rest and meet.
There were seating arrangements for spectators, store rooms and lecture halls. These gymnasia foreshadowed the Roman thermae.

132

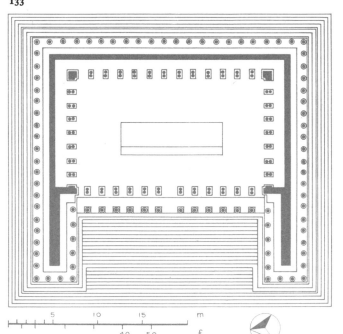

133

133 Plan of theatre, Epidaurus. c. 350 B.C.
The Greeks took advantage of a natural hillside site, terracing and excavating where necessary. The theatre had four parts: a segmental arrangement of tiered seats, a circular orchestra, and proscenium in front of the skene, below which the actors dressed and waited.

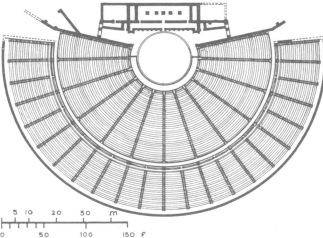

134

134 Plan of Altar of Zeus, Pergamon. c. 180-150 B.C.
Opposite a temple there usually stood a broad altar, often with steps for the officiating priest, to which worshippers brought offerings and at which sacrifices were made.
The Pergamene altar had a long frieze portraying the battle of the gods and giants, in a form highly realistic, theatrical and emotional.

135

135 The town of Naxos
Late sixth century.
Known for its wines, Naxos was a centre of Bacchic worship, and its sculptors were famous in early Greek art. There are still unfinished statues to be seen in its quarries. The remains of a Dionysian temple are on an island not far from the town.

128

130

129

136 Mausoleum, Halicarnassus. 353 B.C.
This giant memorial to the ruler of Caria, Mausolus, all restorations of which are conjectural, gave us the word mausoleum.

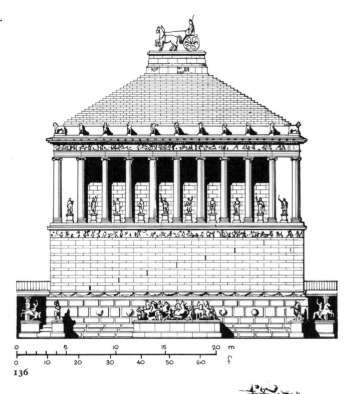

136

137 Detail of restoration of entrance to the agora, Priene
The gateway to the agora, built around 150 B.C., is an early example of a Greek ornamental arch; it spans an opening of about twenty feet.

138 Plan of stadium at Delphi
The stadium was almost 600 feet long and was 90 feet wide in the centre. A shallow tier of seats ran along one side and around the semi-circle, with the judges' seats half-way along.

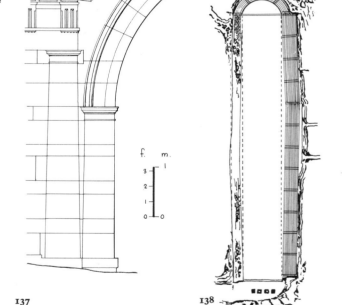

137

138

139 Stadium at Delphi
Competitions in running, spear-throwing, discus-throwing and the long jump were held here.

139

'Hippodamian' system of planning, with roads intersecting at right angles to form a regular grid. A convenient area in the centre, tangential to the broadest streets in either direction, is reserved for the *agora*, which is enclosed by colonnaded *stoas* at two different levels. Temples and other public buildings are effectively placed elsewhere; and they include the most perfectly proportioned miniature theatre, gymnasium and stadium, as well as a skilfully designed council-house (*ekklesiasterion*) which would probably accommodate the whole adult male population of the little community. It had rising tiers of stone seats on three sides, with an altar in the middle and a timber roof spanning thirty-two feet without intermediate support.

As for the private dwelling-houses at Priene, some of the larger examples show a surprisingly archaic arrangement of planning. As elsewhere, the rooms are grouped around a central court, from which light is obtained; but the main reception unit is an old-fashioned *megaron*, with a porch and two columns *in antis*, which can easily be restored to resemble the end façade of a miniature temple. It is by no means impossible that this tradition survived all through the classical centuries. Our uncertainty in the matter is perhaps mainly due to the fact that, as the Greeks themselves boasted, people in those times 'gave all to the state and lived in houses of mud'. Certainly on the acropolis at Larisa, there are remains of houses much older than those at Priene, whose planning seems to comprise a cluster of *megaron* forms. But at Priene itself, particularly in the later period of its history, the peristyle type of house became as popular as it had long continued to be in the rest of the Hellenistic world. In it, the *megaron* porch is extended to form a widely spaced colonnade all round the central court, and the rooms around are loosely arranged according to individual requirements.

On the acropolis rock at Priene few remains of buildings have survived; and as an example of a citadel where the reverse is the case, and for the sake of other strange contrasts, we must turn to the great city of Pergamon, a hundred miles to the north. Pergamon differs from Priene in very many respects. It stands in an inland valley of Mysia, some miles from its own small harbour town of Elaea. It was built for the most part after 200 B.C. and its claim to represent one of the most spectacular achievements of the Greek imagination rests mainly on the siting of its so-called Upper City, in which most of its temples and other important buildings are concentrated. This is an isolated rock over a thousand feet high, and at its summit they are disposed on a series of terraces and rocky platforms to form a remarkable composition. A lower city with temples of its own, is spread over the southern slope and outwards from the base of the rock; but the citadel is more than a mere acropolis. It has an *agora* of its own, as well as a vast theatre, whose spectacular setting is perhaps unrivalled anywhere else in Greece. On the west side of the summit, its auditorium is fitted into a hollow between two shoulders of rock, so that the 20,000 spectators could look beyond the stage over a wide landscape towards the distant sea. The stage prolonged itself into a formal terrace, beneath whose parapet the cliff-face fell almost vertically to the valley beneath. Its complement of temples was increased in numbers when its last Attalid ruler bequeathed the Pergamene state to the Romans. Its most impressive monument however was purely Hellenistic; the great Altar of Zeus, which early in the present century came to be partially restored in the Berlin Museum. The altar itself, with its perpetual column of smoke, stood on an enormous stone plinth, which also supported a double colonnade of Ionic columns enclosing it on three sides, and was approached by a stairway sixty feet wide. The plinth and the colonnade were ornamented with two friezes of sculpture portraying one of those scenes of furious action which characterise the Pergamene school of Hellenistic art.

Some other buildings which we have named as characteristic features of a Greek city deserve more detailed reference. The first of these is the theatre. The earliest purpose of the Greek theatre was to be a setting for periodical festivals in honour of Dionysus, at which dancing and miming took place and hymns were sung by a fairly numerous chorus. Like all other buildings with a primarily religious intention therefore, much attention was paid during the late fourth century B.C. to the improvement of its design. Unfortunately, evidence on which to base any exact reconstruction of the classical theatre is by no means plentiful. This applies in particular to the Athenian theatre, whose parental relationship to all subsequent designs confers special interest on such of its remains as have survived later rebuildings. It started as a circular earthen floor, placed in such a way that the spectators could take advantage of the sloping rock on the southern flank of the acropolis. And this circle, subsequently known as the 'orchestra', with its central altar soon became an indispensable theatrical convention. In the mid-fourth century, regulations were devised to which the performance of Greek drama had to conform; and these necessitated the addition of a long *skene* or changing-room, placed tangentially to the orchestra. Its façade, which faced the audience, could be used for painted scenery, and a raised wooden stage was constructed in front of it. The *skene* had three central doorways (entrance through each of which implied a particular provenance from which the actor made his appearance), and lateral ramps leading to the orchestra entrances. At Athens a stone auditorium early replaced the natural amphitheatre and was made to surround about three-fifths of the orchestra. It sloped at an angle of about twenty-five degrees. Radiating gangways and two horizontal terraces or girdles gave access to the tiers of seats. The whole arrangement is perhaps best seen in the comparatively well-preserved theatre at Epidaurus, whose remains also give an idea of the beautiful setting contrived for such buildings in classical times. The actual magnitude to which Hellenistic models attained, is well illustrated by the theatre at Miletus, where a small section of the auditorium now supports the ruins of a fairly large medieval castle.

Few other types of building need to be dwelt on here. The stadium, for instance, was no more than a simplified version of the theatre, elongated to an appropriate shape. Tombs were curiously designed, especially in Caria and Lycia, but fall outside the category of architectural composition. One funerary monument whose fame was assured

134

131

133

, 139

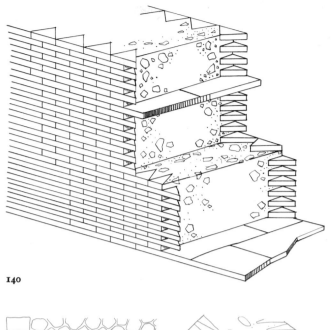

140

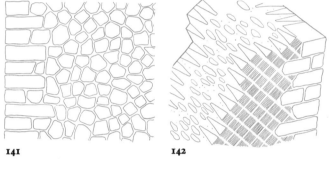

141   142

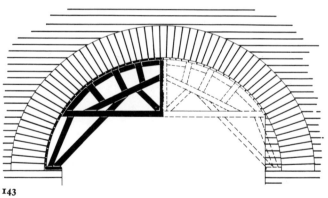

143

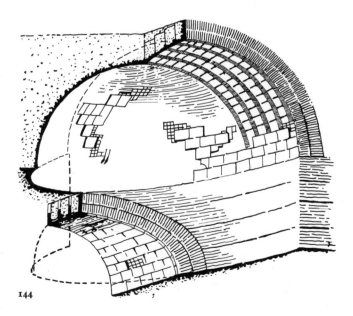

144

140-142 Roman concrete
Roman cement was extremely hard and durable.
The aggregate was sand and volcanic gravel. Courses of bonded flat bricks served as ties and as shuttering during erection. Roman concrete was never left exposed, for practical as well as for aesthetic reasons.

143 Roman arches
The Roman stone arch was a true arch. Ledges were sometimes left at the springing to carry the temporary wooden centring, and afterwards built up, making the arch segmental.

144 Roman vaults and domes
The Roman method of using brick ribs with light concrete between made vaulting possible on a very impressive scale.

145 Vault in the Minerva Medica, Rome. c. A.D. 260
Decagonal in plan, this garden building is topped by a dome on pendentives, a form which the later Byzantines adopted extensively. This dome has box ribs embedded in it, tied in with horizontal tile courses. Remarkable strides have here been made in the understanding of structural principles.

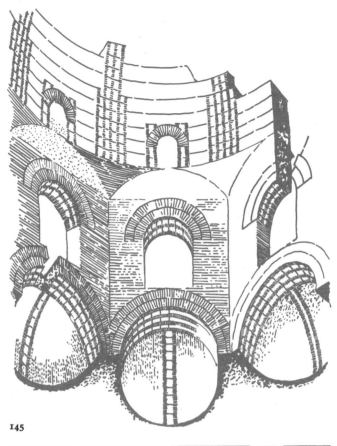

145

146, 147 Vaulting of the Thermae of Diocletian. A.D. 302
It is worth remembering that the giant buildings of the time of Caracalla and Diocletian were built during the decline of the empire. Emperors were following one another in quick succession, and these enormous buildings were erected at incredible speed.

146

147

by its inclusion in the Seven Wonders of the World was the Mausoleum, dedicated to a Persian Satrap who had brought prosperity to the Greek city of Halicarnassus; but its form is known only from contemporary descriptions, copied by Latin writers, and surviving fragments in the British Museum.

136

ROMAN

During the archaic and classical periods of Greek history, the numerous colonies founded in southern Italy and Sicily made those lands an integral part of the Greek world (*Magna Graecia*). Northern and central Italy however, continued to be occupied by tribes of miscellaneous extraction, of whom the most notably civilized were the Etruscans. These people, whose origin was said by Herodotus to have been in Asia Minor, extended their influence from Etruria northwards to the Alps and, at one time, southwards as far as Naples. Their art in some respects rivalled that of classical Greece: the influence of their architecture is discernible in that of the Romans, whose history may be said to have begun when the city of Rome became emancipated from the Etruscan kings in about 500 B.C. A hundred years later all the Etruscan cities became subject to a rapidly expanding Roman Republic.

Some of the individual qualities and characteristics of Roman architecture began to be apparent in Rome itself during the Republican period. But in the conquered territories so many of the cities had been Greek, that for the time being little needed to be or could be done to enhance the dignity or utility of public buildings. In Greece itself and Asia Minor, Hellenic or Hellenistic temples could be enriched or rebuilt to please the communities which they served; but as these for the most part retained their autonomy under the direction of Roman magistrates, Greek taste and conventions continued to prevail among them throughout the centuries directly preceding the Christian era. In cities like Ephesus and Miletus therefore, it is difficult to fix an exact date at which Hellenistic architecture was finally superseded. In some of the remoter provinces, certainly it outlasted the Republic. Elsewhere it was not until the Empire had reached its greatest extent, with its generals everywhere founding new cities and rebuilding old ones, that new practical requirements demanded a new architecture, and characteristically Roman forms came to predominate. Of Rome itself Augustus said that he found it a city of bricks and left it a city of marble. But it was the emperors who followed him during the three centuries after the birth of Christ—Nero, Vespasian, Trajan, Hadrian, Septimius Severus, Caracalla and Diocletian—who were the great patrons of architecture and supplied a new kind of world with the civic equipment which it demanded.

The pre-Roman way of life and its adaptation to changing conditions during the first century B.C. is well illustrated by the residences of ordinary citizens in the two small Italian towns, commercial Pompeii and residential Herculaneum, buried by the eruption of A.D. 79. Here, in houses which are no different from those of Priene, except that the atrium has been roofed in, Romans lived elegantly against a decor which was still entirely Greek.

IV *Palace of Minos, Cnossos*

Elsewhere in Italy however, far-reaching changes had by now begun to take place. In circumstances where even wheat could be imported from conquered territories, interest in agriculture had diminished and the attractions of town life greatly increased. With huge concentrations of a hitherto rural people in the larger cities, new principles of mass accommodation had to be devised. Rome itself had now reached the size and complexity of a modern European capital, and the communal needs of its huge population were multiple and urgent. Domestically they could partly be met by accommodation in tenement buildings; public activities were a different matter. The Romans were above all a well-disciplined people. Obedience to authority came naturally to them, and parental training had promoted in them a capacity for law-making and the orderly conduct of their public affairs. But these required an appropriate setting. Not only had legislature and litigation to be considered, but commerce and the complex functions of political and social life. Athletics and public entertainment were hardly less important and their demands increased the need for new forms of accommodation and spatial organisation. The manner in which the architects and planners of Imperial Rome satisfied all these requirements and the character of the buildings which they devised are all the more remarkable for the fact that a host of new problems were solved by the use of completely new materials and structural contrivances.

One practice which distinguished Roman architecture from a very early stage was the use of the semi-circular arch with radiating *voussoirs*. In Hellenistic architecture this device appears on rare occasions but can be recognised as no more than a self-conscious *tour de force*. It was used more purposefully by the Etruscans and adopted from them by the Romans as a basic principle in their new system of construction in brick and concrete. Their discovery of concrete also was a momentous event, since, once its potentialities came to be properly understood, it determined the primary characteristics of their buildings. The principle of arcuation led logically to the construction of barrel vaults and, where these intersected, groined or quadripartite features had to be devised. From here it was only a short step to the contrivance of a semi-circular dome. The disappearance in this way of horizontal beams and lintels eliminated also the numerous small uprights necessary to support them and concentrated the weight of the building on fewer but more massive piers. In this way wide, unencumbered floor-spaces became a practical possibility, and interior design acquired a new interest. The principal and most characteristic achievement of Roman builders was their discovery that the organisation of internal space could be as important as that of external architectural forms. Their experiments from the beginning were bold and rational. Once the technical adaptation of new materials was achieved, buildings on a magnificent scale became possible.

By contrast to all this, Roman ornament and superficial decoration fell a good deal below Greek standards of refinement. This is partly explained by the fact that their central purpose was to give scale to the major forms of the buildings. The Greek orders, whose rectilinear motifs could

143

140

4-147

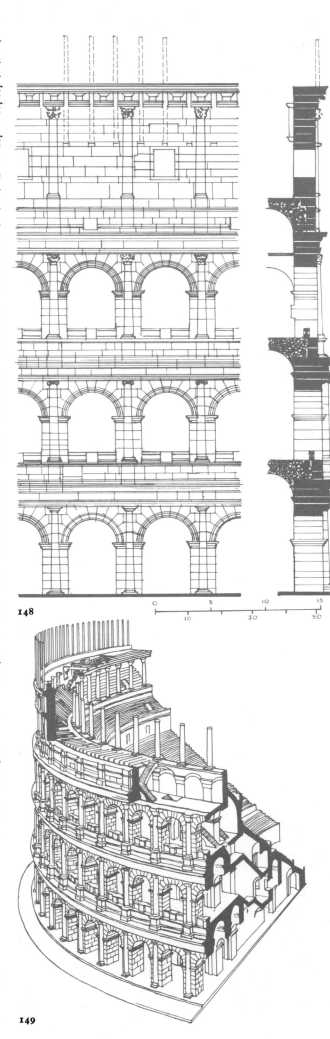

148

149

148 Columnar façade of the Colosseum, Rome. A.D. 72-80
The Romans rarely used columns structurally save in porticoes and porches. They tended to apply the orders as ornament to a façade. On the Colosseum, the orders are used one above the other, the heavy Doric at the bottom and the decorative foliated orders at the top. The Romans invented two more orders for use in this way – the pseudo-archaic 'Tuscan' and the combined Ionic and Corinthian Composite.

149 Section, Colosseum, Rome
The Greek theatre was removed from its hillside and built in the centre of a town, the tiers of seats carried on a series of arches whose arcades provided galleried access to the tiers. Amphitheatres such as this were used for gladiatorial combats and other popular entertainments.

**150, 151 Celsian library,
Ephesus. A.D. 115**
Front elevation and plan.
The best-preserved Roman library.
The building is partly
submerged in sloping ground so
that the emphasis falls on the
main façade. Inside are niches for
bookcases, a colonnade
for an upper gallery and an apse
for statue of Athena. Beneath the
apse a vaulted chamber contains
sculptured sarcophagus of Tiberius
Celsus, to whose memory the
library is dedicated.

150

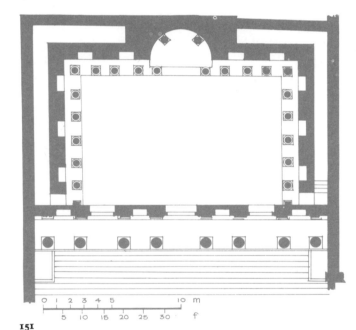

151

152 The Forum Romanum
On the left is the temple of
Castor and Pollux, 7 B.C.-A.D. 6.

152

not easily be adapted to the Roman system of arcuation, were now used almost exclusively for decorative purposes and provided a conventional pattern for the treatment of façades. Into these also, the ubiquitous arch now intruded itself between attached columns deprived of their practical function. Only in the realm of temples and other religious buildings did the rigidly conservative tradition of classical beliefs inhibit structural changes: and one new type of building, the basilica, appeared, conforming to the temple pattern in which its design may have originated.

But it was the use of concrete which provided the key to the development of Roman architecture. Its mixing required no more than an adequate supply of unskilled labour, while its main ingredients, lime and sand, were plentifully available. If dressed stone were also used in a building, the masons' chippings made an excellent aggregate. 'Shuttering' was rendered unnecessary by the use of prefabricated brick facings. The tiles preferred for the purpose were no more than two inches in thickness but two feet square and split diagonally down the centre, so that their inward-facing corners provided a 'key' for the concrete. 'Through courses' were inserted at intervals to give greater strength. Stone was also used for facing, in panels framed with brick; a mosaic of pyramidal stone pegs, whose square heads were set diagonally in the wall-face to create a 'reticulate' pattern. For decorative purposes also, there was a wide choice of granites and marbles, which could be supplemented by bronze.

By the mid-first century A.D., the Romans had mastered the use of *pozzolana*, a reddish volcanic sand, perfectly adapted to making a hard, light concrete for vaults and domes. Great ingenuity was now displayed in the construction of these with a minimum of temporary wooden centring. Barrel vaults, for instance, could be composed of successive brick arches, the spaces between them divided by linking-tiles into concrete-filled 'boxes'. A similar construction was used to form 'ribs' composing the skeleton of a quadripartite vault, the curved surface between being faced with flat tiles, keyed into the concrete. The hardsetting quality of the *pozzolana* consolidated such vaults into homogeneous structural units, devoid of any lateral thrust which might require abutment. Domes also, constructed in this way, acquired the independent solidity of an inverted porcelain saucer. The use of concrete gave to the Roman architect a new kind of freedom in planning, since curves could now be used and niches or alcoves added, to which vaults or semi-domes were easily adapted. Only the construction of pendentives—the spherical triangles whereby the base of a dome is adapted to a square compartment—seems to have presented a problem in solid geometry which he was unable to master.

In spite of all these innovations, the craft of building in stone was by no means neglected, though confined now for the most part to certain traditional classes of monument. The volcanic stones *tufa* and *peperino* had been popular in the early days of the Republic; but the latter in particular proved too coarse to be serviceable for facings and needed to be covered with stucco. Later the *travertino*, which is seen everywhere in Rome today, came into general use. Ashlar masonry was laid in mortar or jointed with metal

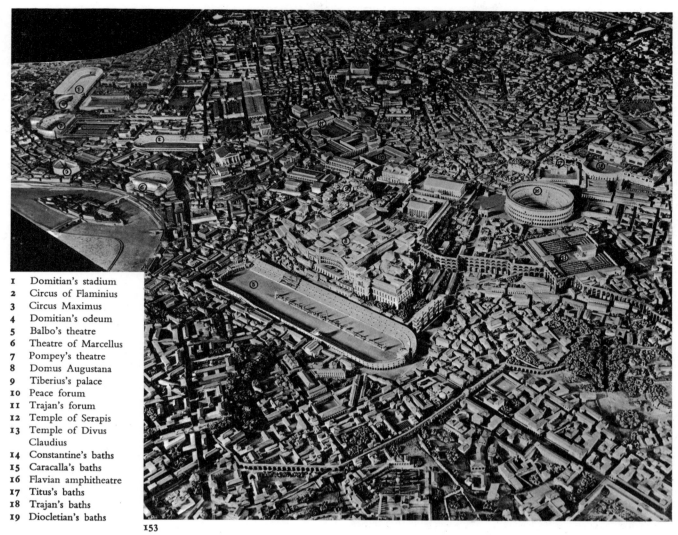

153

1   Domitian's stadium
2   Circus of Flaminius
3   Circus Maximus
4   Domitian's odeum
5   Balbo's theatre
6   Theatre of Marcellus
7   Pompey's theatre
8   Domus Augustana
9   Tiberius's palace
10 Peace forum
11 Trajan's forum
12 Temple of Serapis
13 Temple of Divus
    Claudius
14 Constantine's baths
15 Caracalla's baths
16 Flavian amphitheatre
17 Titus's baths
18 Trajan's baths
19 Diocletian's baths

153 Imperial Rome
Restored model.
An example of controlled axial planning on a scale larger than any in Egypt. The main thoroughfare was the sacred processional way.

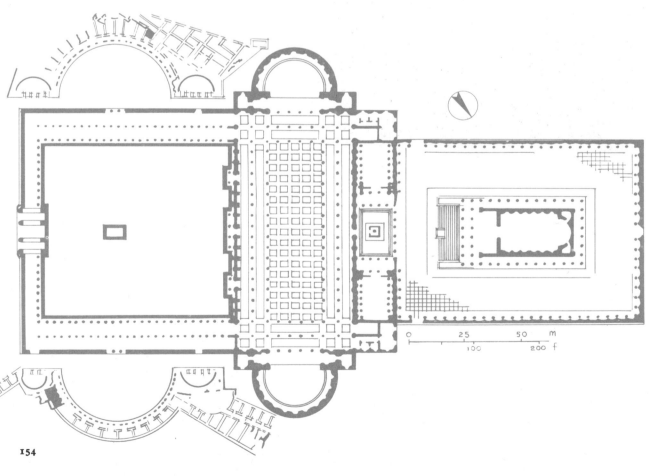

154

154 Plan of the Forum of Trajan, Rome
The forum was entered through a triumphal arch.
At the far end stood the great basilica and the law court.
In a small colonnaded court stood Trajan's column.

155 Trajan's Column, Rome. A.D. 113
The column stood next to the basilica in Trajan's forum in an open court with galleries from which the sculpture on the column could be viewed. Made entirely of marble, it stands approximately 115 feet high. At ground level is the entrance to Trajan's tomb.

156, 157 Trajan's Column
Details of sculpture. Carved in a spiral, the bas-reliefs portray scenes from Trajan's war with the Dacians. There are something like 2,500 human figures.

156

155   157

158 The Colosseum, Rome
An elliptical amphitheatre, it was begun by Vespasian in A.D. 70, and completed by Domitian in A.D. 82.

158

159 Plan of the Colosseum
In plan the Colosseum is an awe-inspiring ellipse, measuring 620 by 513 feet. There were eighty external openings on each storey, those on ground level giving entrance to the tiers of seats. The arena in which the spectacles were staged was actually surrounded by a fifteen-foot wall, containing an area of 180 by 287 feet.

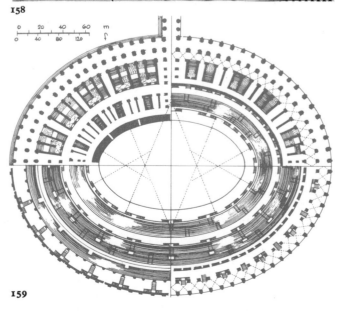

159

dowels in the Greek manner; but an innovation was the 'drafted margin' which leaves all but the outer border of the block-face rough and in basement courses gives an impression of solidity.

We must now see how these structural devices, as well as the spatial and formal contrivances which they made possible, could be applied variously to old and new types of building. Where the Greeks, as we have said, required only an *agora* and a couple of *stoa*-porticoes to accommodate the functions of their public life, the needs of the Roman people were far more sophisticated. Yet they too, in the early days of their city's life, started with no more than an open precinct—the old Forum Romanum—around which their principal monuments were built, and which served also as a meeting-place, market, social and political rendezvous. Through its centre, the sacred processional way (Via Sacra) led past the House of the Vestals and skirted a variety of other religious shrines before ascending the Capitoline Hill. To this forum, in the course of time, significant additions were made: triumphal arches, pillars of victory, a basilica, senate-house and colonnades of shops. And when, in the Imperial age, it became inconveniently congested, successive emperors extended it by appending their own forums, each one on an increasingly ambitious scale. When space was required for these lay-outs, slum clearances were at first undertaken, but later it became necessary to cut into the rocky hill on the north side. In the end the whole complex of buildings and forums covered more than a hundred acres of ground.

We are thus confronted with the first example in architectural history of axial planning on a colossal scale; and it already shows a complete mastery of the principles involved. Unlike the Greek acropolis or *agora* in which a variety of individual buildings were asymmetrically disposed with an artifice that was semi-intuitive, the Roman forum was geometrically planned as a coherent composition, in which component units were functionally related by 'movement' implicit in the general arrangement. In this respect the Forum of Trajan was perhaps the most characteristic and also the most finely conceived. One entered through a triumphal arch into an immense court, 280 feet square, flanked by double colonnades to right and left. It was enclosed on the far side by the façade of a colossal basilica, oriented at right angles to one's approach and occupying the full breadth of the site. Next, on the main axis came a small colonnaded square, dominated by Trajan's famous sculptured column; and on either side were two comparatively small libraries. Still on the central axis, one then passed into a second pillared courtyard and was confronted by the temple dedicated by Hadrian to Trajan after his death. This was approached by a wide stairway ascending between wing-walls to the podium and octastyle portico. Shops and markets, again protected from the weather by screens of columns, spread out in wide hemicycles beyond the outer walls, symmetrically subordinated to the main building.

The Romans retained the three Greek orders (with a slight attenuation in the proportion of the Doric column and subordination of its curved echinus), but they added a 'composite' variation, combining elements of the Ionic and

153
160

154

155-1

162-1

160

160 The Forum Romanum
The oldest and largest of
the forums, its expansion required
the removal at various times
in its history of minor functions to
other parts of the city, until
only state buildings, temples,
basilicas and public monuments
were left. The theatrical displays
which once took place here
were housed in the theatres and
circuses, and the shops were moved
elsewhere. Even so, lack of
space necessitated the building
of new forums by emperors who
wished to commemorate
their glories.

161

161 Cyrene, Libya
Aerial view.
Cyrene was the capital
of the ancient Cyrenaica, and one
of the greatest of the Greek
colonies. At its height it is said to
have had over 100,000
inhabitants. The city passed to
Rome in 96 B.C., and continued
to flourish, Hadrian being
responsible for much rebuilding.

162–165 The Roman orders
The Roman column was often
decorative and not, as was
the Greek, invariably structural.
This led to a weakening
of form; in the main,
the capitals were over-
refined, the shafts longer, more
slender and frequently unfluted.
162 Doric
from the Theatre of Marcellus,
Rome.
163 Ionic
from the Theatre of Marcellus,
Rome.
164 Composite
from the Arch of Titus, Rome.
In their search for new and
richer forms, the Romans combined
the Ionic and Corinthian orders.
165 Corinthian
from the Pantheon, Rome.

**166 Temple of Fortuna Virilis,
Rome**
First century B.C.
A small Ionic building, referred
to as pseudo-peripteral because
of the engaged columns at the side
and back. The corner capitals
have a third volute, diagonal
so as to give the capital a
face on two sides.

**167 Plan of the Maison Carrée,
Nîmes**
Beginning of the first century A.D.
Like the Fortuna Virilis temple, the
Maison Carrée is on a podium
and is pseudo-peripteral.
The columns are Corinthian.

168 The Maison Carrée, Nîmes
A provincial example.
This temple was placed at
the end of an open court which was
surrounded by a subsidiary
colonnade, and faced an
outer entrance.

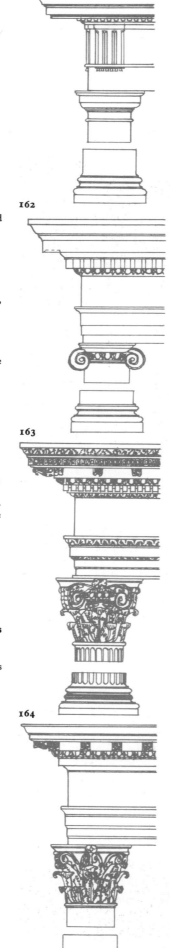

162

163

164

165

166

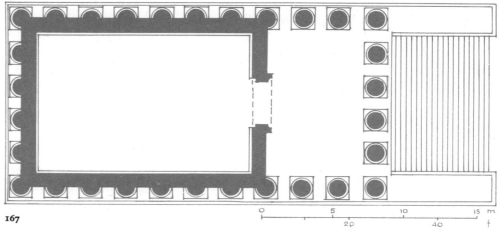

167

168

162 Corinthian. The 'Tuscan' order, which Renaissance writers professed to recognise in Roman buildings, was hardly distinguished from the Doric, except by its unfluted column-shaft. Yet, if we are to judge from reconstructions made on the authority of Vitruvius, the Etruscan temple had a character of its own. In the first place, it was of all-timber construction, and its upper parts were heavily encrusted with terra cotta ornament. It had no peristyle. The *cella*, in deference to its frequent dedication to a triad of deities, had three separate compartments, each with its own doorway; and in front of these was a low, open portico, two columns deep, approached by a stairway between wing-walls. Both eaves and pediment had an unusually wide overhang, equal in fact to one-quarter the height of the column.

166 One temple plan, that of Fortuna Virilis at Rome, may be taken to illustrate the adaptation of some of these features to Roman requirements. Though the triple sanctuary has now been discarded, the building once more stands on a podium, approached only from the front by a flight of steps between wing-walls. The rear and side walls of the Etruscan *cella* had presented blank faces; but these have now been screened with half-columns, continuing the line of the portico colonnade to make the edifice 'pseudo-peripteral'. But there is still no doubt that it is intended to be seen from directly in front. Its rear end could in fact be set against an enclosure-wall or screened by subsidiary colonnades without impairing the design, while its frontal approach was exactly suited to the termination of an axial vista in any characteristically Roman lay-out. From now onwards this 'hermit-crab' disposition became a feature of Roman temples. Quite often, as may be seen in examples 57, 168 as far removed from Rome as the so-called Maison Carrée at Nîmes, they were placed at the end of an open court, itself surrounded by a subsidiary colonnade, and faced towards an outer entrance which again emphasised the axial approach. An exception to this arrangement was the great 9, 170 Temple of Venus and Rome, in which twin *cellas* were placed back-to-back. As a concession to the new fashion in architectural forms, each ended in a semi-circular niche covered by a semi-dome.

Another type of building which retained something of the classical tradition both in design and construction, has already been mentioned. This is the basilica—a truly indispensable feature of Roman city planning, which combined the communal functions of a social and political meeting-place with those of a law-court. It has often been said that it resembled a Greek temple turned inside-out: but internally its colonnades enclosed a central nave, which rising above the side-aisles, made clerestory lighting possible. Both were covered by pitched timber roofs in the Greek manner; and those over the aisles of the larger examples were required to span openings up to eighty feet wide. Although the timber fabric of all such roofs has long ago perished, one is compelled to conclude that Roman architects were by now familiar with the principle of trussed tie-beam construction. As may be seen in a section through the Basilica Ulpia in the Forum of Trajan, the aisles were built in two storeys, corresponding to superimposed orders in the nave, and were themselves duplicated by central colonnades. In this case also, the rectangular severity of the

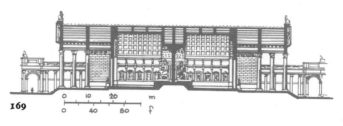
169

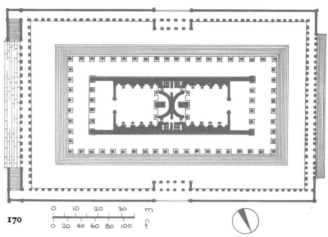
170

169, 170 Temple of Venus and Rome, Rome.
A.D. 123-135
Section and plan.
In this temple built for Hadrian two cellas were placed back to back. This building was surrounded by a superb colonnaded portico some 545 feet long by 330 feet wide.

171

171 Temple of Portunus, Rome.
c. 31 B.C.
This circular temple in the Forum Boarium stands on eight marble steps; the design of the twenty Corinthian capitals suggests that they may have been the work of Greek carvers.

172

172 Basilica of Maxentius, Rome. A.D. 310-313
Also known as the Basilica of Constantine, it adjoined the Forum Romanum. The enormous groin vault topped the central nave at a height of 120 feet.

173 Basilica of Maxentius, Rome. A.D. 310-313
The basilica was a law court where all civil litigation was heard; also agreements and contracts were made there before a magistrate.

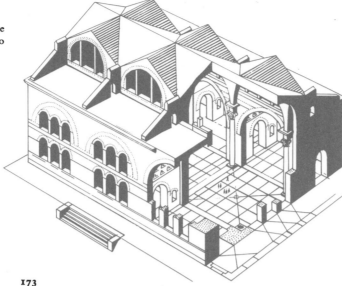

173

174 Basilica of Maxentius
The basilicas stood ready for Christian adaptation. Features such as the semi-circular apse, the vestibule and the atrium were found in some Early Christian churches.

174

building was relieved by the curve of huge projecting hemicycles at either end.

In their simpler form, such buildings have a special interest in that they seem to have been adopted as a prototype for a quite different class of edifice in later times. In conventional examples, the semi-circular apse appears at one end of the building only and has in its centre a seat or throne for a presiding official. At the reverse end there is an arcaded vestibule ('narthex') facing onto an open forecourt ('atrium'). All these features reappear in some of the earliest Christian churches.

A third feature which appears in the Forum of Trajan, and of which there are more famous examples in the old Forum Romanum, is the triumphal arch. These monuments illustrate how the conventional pattern of a classical order can be used as a superficial framework of ornament around an essentially Roman form: the deeply soffited archway. One sees also, for instance in the Arch of Titus, the addition of other characteristically Roman decoration in the form of incised lettering and terminal statuary. But the culminating result of a compromise between the rectilinear forms of Greek architecture on the one hand and the predominantly circular lines of Roman construction on the other is best seen in the Colosseum—that huge amphitheatre, built near the entrance to the old Forum by the Flavian emperors in the mid-first century A.D. In its travertine façade, the four Roman orders are superimposed in conventional succession. But the columns are half-columns with no purpose other than decoration, and the openings between them are crowned with semi-circular arches. This arch-and-column motif, repeated indefinitely around an interminable oval façade, has a soporific effect which blunts all perception of the purpose for which the orders were originally contrived.

The amphitheatre was an elliptical affair with an arena in the middle. The overall dimensions of the Colosseum were 620 by 513 feet. The internal arrangement of its seating and many staircases was a masterpiece of ingenuity, and so well considered that the building could have been cleared of spectators in a few minutes. The stairways and corridors, including those under the arena, which provided accommodation for gladiators and wild beasts, were for the most part built of stone with concrete vaulting. Mouldings and stucco panelling were their only ornament. The vernacular style of the building was in fact in keeping with the colossal vulgarity of the spectacles presented there. Only its sheer size impresses one.

These great stadiums, of which there were impressive examples even in Britain, belong to a category of Roman buildings contrived for the entertainment of the well-disciplined Roman masses. Circuses, like the great Circus Maximus at Rome, which according to Pliny could hold half-a-million spectators, differ only in the 'hair-pin' shape of the *dromos* around which the seating is arranged. The elliptical shape of the Colosseum on the other hand might have been arrived at by placing two Roman theatres back to back. For these differed slightly from their Greek predecessors in that the auditorium was now an exact semi-circle, the old 'orchestra' being occupied by seats for special dignitaries. The structure of the building also tended to

175

176

177

**175 Arch of Titus, Rome.
A.D. 81**
Built to commemorate the capture
and sack of Jerusalem.
The engaged columns are of the
Composite order. The reliefs
were the high-water mark of
Roman narrative art. These
impressive monuments were
erected in many areas
conquered by the Romans.

**176 Monumental archway at
Palmyra**
First century A.D.
Erected at the intersection of four
main streets, this
impressive arch at Palmyra
was the focal point of
the splendid colonnaded streets.

**177 Arch of Septimius Severus,
Rome. A.D. 203**
This commemorates the Parthian
wars and is dedicated to the
emperor and his two sons,
Caracalla and Geta. Detached
Composite columns are seen in
front of the three arched openings.

**178 Baths of Caracalla, Rome.
A.D. 211-217**
From a print of 1832.
Bathing was therapeutic, and
the baths were centres for every
kind of entertainment,
including shops, libraries, theatres
and halls for boxing and
wrestling matches.

178

**179 Plan of the baths of Titus,
Rome. A.D. 80**
The baths were built on part of the
site of Nero's 'Golden
House'. Here the famous
Laocoon sculpture was discovered.

180

180 Baths of Caracalla

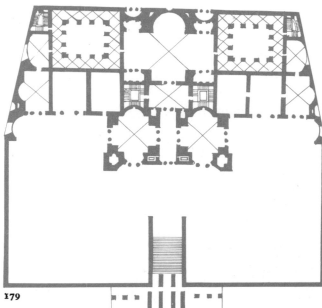

**181 Baths of Trajan.
The library**

179

181

depend less frequently on the support of a natural amphitheatre and could be completely free-standing. Also, the *skene* wall which formed a background to the stage could be given an elaborate architectural treatment by a very free use of the classical orders, sometimes combined with statuary. There is a magnificent example at Aspendos in Pamphylia, which has been cleverly reconstructed. It shows over the stage a sloping wood canopy, which must have served the dual purpose of protecting the actors from the weather and improving the acoustics.

178-181 In contrast to these popular amenities, the *thermae*, or bathing establishments, were provided for the leisure of a more sophisticated and privileged social stratum. They are also of greater architectural interest, because the scale on which they could be conceived and the elaboration of which they were capable appealed to the aesthetic imagination and gave full scope to the structural virtuosity of contemporary architects. Looking at drawings of a building such as the Thermae of Caracalla, one sees how, for the first time in history, the plan alone is a design in itself, an essay in the symmetrical arrangement of fancifully contrasted shapes. The thermal establishments were communal centres catering for a luxurious form of leisure. That of Caracalla comprised a sumptuous main building surrounded by an elaborate enclosure with gardens and an open-air gymnasium. Among the amenities of the baths themselves were a vaulted central hall with clerestory lighting (*tepidarium*), a circular domed hot-room (*calidarium*), and a swimming-pool (*frigidarium*), perhaps open to the sky.

Extravagant planning with elaborately curved and polygonal shapes was carried a stage further in the palaces of the Roman emperors. One Latin writer's description (Suetonius: *De Vita Caesarum*) of the 'Golden House' which Nero built after the great fire of A.D. 65 on the site later occupied by the Colosseum, reads like a fantasy of the Arabian Nights. But more is known about them from excavations on the Palatine Hill and also from the considerable remains of Diocletian's palace at Spalato (Split). There can be no doubt that they strained the trabeated forms of Greek architecture to breaking point: and one sees there how the orders were now regarded simply as a convenient repertoire of loosely variable patterns. A classical entablature could suddenly curve upwards into an arch beneath the angle of a pediment or an arcade of arches spring directly from a row of attached columns (a foretaste of Romanesque design). But in a sense, none of these developments could be said to be new, for their temerity had long been outclassed, as we shall presently see, by the 'baroque' fantasies of Pompeian ornament.

We must turn to another world-famous masterpiece of Roman architecture, a religious building which could not, for obvious reasons, be included in the category of traditional temples. This is the great domed 'rotunda' known 187-189 as the Pantheon, one of the best preserved but also in a 191, 192 sense the most enigmatic of all Roman monuments. In the first place, we do not know for certain which parts of it were built by whom and when. Most authorities are satisfied on archaeological grounds that both rotunda and dome were built by Emperor Hadrian between. A.D. 120 and 124, though his name appears nowhere in an inscription.

182

182 Circus Maximus, Rome
Restored model.
Scarcely anything remains of this oldest of Roman circuses, which was enlarged by Julius Caesar and embellished by subsequent emperors.
The circus was a track for chariot races. Gladiatorial combats were originally held here, but in the first century B.C. were moved to the amphitheatre.

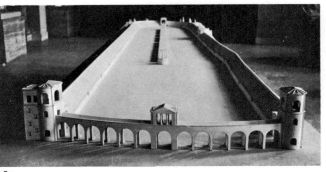

183

183 Circus of Maxentius, Rome A.D. 311
Restored model. Built on the Via Appia. The spina, or central wall, seen here, was oblique in order to adjust the distance for various starting positions.

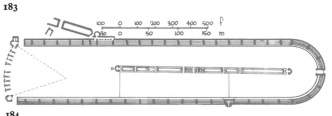

184

184 Plan of the Circus of Maxentius

185

185 Amphitheatre at Verona. A.D. 290
A characteristic Roman arena, with most of the stone seats remarkably well preserved. Little is left of the upper part of the external wall.

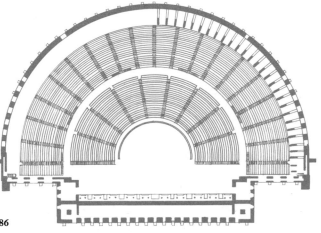

186

186 Plan of theatre at Aspendos
The auditorium was restricted to a semi-circle rather than the two-thirds circle of the Greek theatre. In this theatre a wood canopy over the stage protected the actors from the weather and improved the acoustics.

187 The Pantheon, Rome. A.D. 120-124
This shows the gabled portico in contrast with the domed building behind.

187

188, 189 Plan and section of the Pantheon, Rome
Both vault and walls are of concrete, bonded with brick and stone clad internally. The vault is lightened and strengthened by coffering.

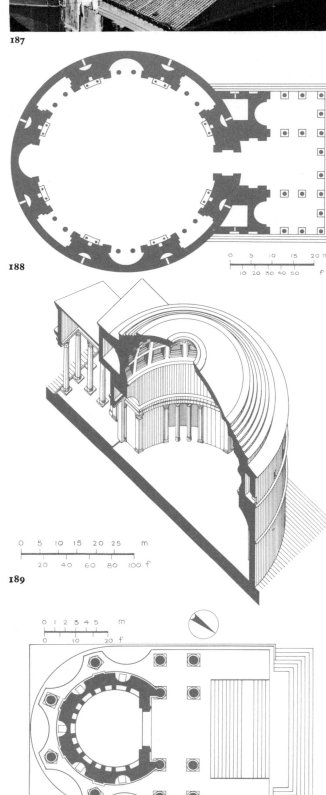

188

189

190 Plan of temple of Venus, Baalbek. A.D. 273
This highly interesting building has concave
curves running counter to its circular plan, a theme later fully exploited by the
architects of the Baroque period.

190

But there is also the columned portico, which stands upon the foundations of an earlier building, and between the two there is a rectangular projection which is structurally unconnected with either. Inscriptions show the earliest building to have been the work of Agrippa in the time of Augustus (27 B.C. to A.D. 14) and the portico in its present form to be that of Severus and Caracalla. Also, little is known about the dedication of the building, beyond that which is suggested by its name. Finally, it has never been possible to ascertain exactly how the great concrete dome was constructed, since there are, for instance, no outward signs of an internal system of brick arch supports. One must content oneself with accepting it as ultimate proof of the Roman engineer's capacity for imparting to his domed structures sufficient independent rigidity to eliminate all lateral thrust. Though it was originally covered with gilded bronze plates, its actual weight must have been slightly reduced by the deep coffering with which its soffit was ornamented.

Like the dome, the rotunda also is of concrete, faced with brick. It was originally embellished on the outside with slabs of Pentelic marble and inside with coloured marble and porphyry. Its thickness of twenty feet leaves room for deep recesses at ground level, and the weight of the wall above is deflected from these by means of relieving arches in the fabric above. Pairs of columns screening these recesses, and the pilasters that match them, support a continuous entablature. The modest size of the order gives scale to the rotunda itself, whose inner diameter and height alike measure 142 feet. In the portico, the Corinthian columns are unfluted monoliths of granite and marble. The huge bronze doors were plated with gold, and there was originally a segmental vault of bronze plates beneath the timber roof.

It is hard to speak objectively of the Pantheon as an architectural design. One is impressed above all by the geometrical simplicity and colossal scale of the interior: also by the remarkable effect of lighting obtained from a single opening, twenty-seven feet wide, in the crown of the hemispherical dome. For thirteen centuries Christian worshippers have venerated its antiquity while repressing the memory of its pagan origin. Visitors from all over the world have accepted its testimony to the wealth and accomplishments of Imperial Rome.

When we speak of technological accomplishments, we are reminded that Roman competence in practical engineering produced spontaneous architectural forms which commend themselves to the modern mind seeking 'functional expression'. This is well illustrated by bridges and aqueducts. There is for instance the Mulvian bridge at Rome, whose arches of tufa and travertine spanned openings sixty feet wide. There is Trajan's bridge over the Danube with its timber piers 170 feet apart; and Augustus's aqueduct at Segovia with 128 arches ninety feet high. This was built of uncemented white granite, and the Pont-du-Gard at Nîmes was similarly constructed of dry-jointed masonry. Here and elsewhere one also sees traces of the devices used to support temporary wooden centring for the great arches of Roman times. Ledges in the pier-face and slightly projecting *voussoirs* intended for this purpose are still visible.

187

193, 1

191

191 The Pantheon, Rome
Engraving by Giovanni Battista
Piranesi (1720–78).
His large prints of classical and
post-classical buildings are
characterised by their dramatic and
romantic grandeur as well as
their unparalleled accuracy. They
did much to encourage a wider
interest in classical archaeology in
the eighteenth century.

**192 Interior of the Pantheon,
Rome**
The vault and much of the interior
remains of the original structure
although a considerable restoration
has occurred at various
times. The granite and porphyry
pavement was restored in the
nineteenth century. The circular
wall was at first faced with pilasters.
The entrance forms one of eight
arched recesses, the other seven
probably being used for
statues of gods.

192

193, 194 The Pont-du-Gard, Nîmes. c. A.D. 14
Roman engineering works often reached the sublime simplicity and nobility which the architecture lacks. The magnificent Pont-du-Gard was part of an astonishingly well-constructed aqueduct, twenty-five miles long, which brought water to Nîmes from Uzès. It is over 800 feet long and 155 feet high. It was built without mortar.

193

194

**195 Hadrian's Villa, Tivoli.
A.D. 124**
Restored model.
This was a series of pavilions
and gardens covering over seven
square miles; it was more
like a city than a residence.
Hadrian was a great patron
of the arts and commissioned
copies of Greek sculpture.

195

196 Hadrian's Villa, Tivoli
Aerial view.
In addition to the emperor's own
house, this complex contained
colonnades, courts, terraces,
baths and theatres, as well as
many trees and gardens.

196

Roman houses

The apartments were built round an atrium or courtyard which was more of an open-air room than a central 'garden'. The house looked inward as in the East. A roofed colonnade round the atrium served as a catchment for rainwater and provided shelter from the summer sun and winter winds. Houses of well-to-do owners were richly painted, and had mosaic and tile floors, under which was hot-air central heating. In towns Romans lived in blocks of flats, the wealthy often occupying the main floor with slums above.

197 Street of shops in the region of Trajan's Forum, Rome

198 Street of the Balconies, Ostia Antica

197   198

199 Basilica at Pompeii
As the building for the administration of the law, the basilica occupied, as in all Roman towns, a focal point in town-plans.

200 House of the Faun, Pompeii
First century A.D.

199   200

201 Basilica at Pompeii
Plan.

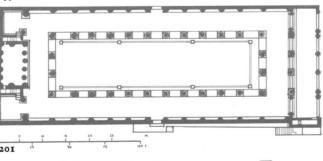 

202 House of the Faun, Pompeii
Plan.

201   202

203 House of the Faun, Pompeii
Elevation.

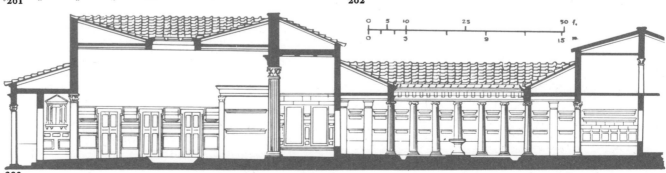

203

VI Roman theatre, Aspendos VII Forum, Pompeii VIII House of the Vetii, Pompeii

VI VII VIII

Another common Roman practice directed to this end was to set back the actual springing of an arch a few inches behind the inner face of the pier, leaving a ledge for the centring to bear upon. When the wooden structure was removed, the space between soffit and reveal was filled, giving the arch itself a slightly flattened segmental shape.

As to private dwellings, in Rome, as we have said, tenement buildings could accommodate a large part of the population. Concrete made multiple storeys possible, and living conditions must at times have been extremely squalid. At this social level however, the male section of the community who, to our way of thinking, received more than their share of consideration, now spent much of their lives in the open air or in artificially heated public buildings. Quite a different aspect of domestic life in a Roman town is revealed by the Pompeian residences to which we have already referred. They were luxurious even by modern standards. Standing in narrow stone-paved streets, these houses presented blank façades to the outside world. They obtained their light from a peristyle—the wholly Greek colonnaded court, around which the private part of the house was arranged—and from a second partially covered court, corresponding to the Greek atrium. This was protected from the weather by a lean-to roof, supported by columns and draining into a central pool, which also served as an ornamental feature (*impluvium*). The main part of the house had pitched timber roofs covered with tiles and occasionally an upper storey. Heating was by brazier, but water was distributed by 'rising mains' and drawn from taps. Like the Greek houses at Priene, floors were at first decorated with delicate mosaics—a border of floral or geometric design around a central picture (*emblema*)—and later these gave way to more freely distributed patterns. Walls and vaulted ceilings made a setting for painted frescoes in the distinctively Pompeian manner.

These famous wall-paintings, which art historians have classed in four successive 'periods', embody some of the most sensitive and elegant forms of Roman ornament. The earliest date from the second century B.C., and were executed directly on the plaster in fresco, tempera, oil or colours mixed with melted wax. Public rooms in Pompeian houses of the time had panelled doors with fanlights and formal architraves around them; and it was between these that the decoration was applied, first in forms that imitated marble veneers and panelling. In Empire times motifs became immensely more complicated. The simulation of architecture became prevalent and whole wall-faces were covered with an elaborate framework of improbably attenuated classical shapes, sometimes presented in an elementary form of perspective. Never had such liberties been taken with the classical orders. The content of the enclosed panels was even more remarkable; for in addition to *emblemata* consisting of figured pictures, open-air scenes were sometimes depicted as though through a window.

Towns like Pompeii of course had their own public buildings, secular and religious, arranged around a forum, as well as theatres, baths, etc. The forum itself was placed in the south-west corner, at the intersection of two important streets. And this seems also to have been the common practice in newly built Roman cities, which were laid out like

204

205

206

204 **Temple and statue of Apollo, Pompeii**
The greater part of the west side of the forum is occupied by two buildings, a basilica, which is the largest edifice in Pompeii, and the temple of Apollo, which presents its side to the forum. An imposing building, it is surrounded by a portico of columns, outside which is a wall bounding the sacred enclosure.

205 **Mosaic fountain at Pompeii**
A characteristic feature of Roman towns was the many fountains in streets and squares, welcome reliefs from the hot, dry climate. In Pompeii, the typical fountain was lined with mosaic, the water coming from lions' or gorgons' heads.

206 **Villa of the Mysteries, Pompeii**
The villa owes its name to the frescoes on its walls which illustrate the Dionysiac rites. The dwelling is on the outskirts of the city near one of the gates, and was clearly the out-of-town house of a wealthy citizen.

207 Temple of Bacchus, Baalbek
Second century A.D.
A Roman army branch was responsible for architecture in the colonies.

207

208 Temple of Bacchus, Baalbek
Detail of columns. The inner walls of the temple have engaged columns of the Corinthian order with fluted shafts. Between the columns are two rows of niches, the upper with a pediment and the lower arched.

209 El Djem. c. A.D. 240
Ancient name Thysdrus, in Tripolitania. The unfinished amphitheatre is modelled on the Colosseum.

210 Baalbek. Temple of Jupiter

208

a military camp with central gates in the four sides of a square enclosure. Judging from impressive town-plans like that of Timgad (Thamugadi) in North Africa, the streets were arranged in a regular grid, something on the lines of the Hippodamian system of Hellenistic times. Those adopted by the Romans from their Greek or Etruscan predecessors, remodelled and fortified in their own more practical idiom, were undoubtedly the more attractive to the eye.

One leaves the subject of Roman architecture with an uneasy feeling that the emotions which it arouses do less than justice to its greatness. Certainly this was one of those periods in which building, as a form of self-expression, reached a crescendo of portentous eloquence. But history had seen others, particularly in the countries of the Near East: and there were more to come. As the Roman epoch ends, one is left with a foretaste, not of the European aftermath with its leitmotif of 'regret and remembered glory' but of later centuries under another empire: of Victoriana and the Neo-classicism of the Industrial Revolution. It is with relief that one turns eastward to watch the rise of a more exotic culture on the Bosphorus.

In looking back on the whole of these earliest variations on the theme of architectural invention, if one might be permitted a moment of selective nostalgia, the subject would hardly be in doubt. Most easily in one's mind, vignette pictures arise of Greek cities like Priene; and one remembers the self-contained perfection of its miniature public buildings; the tiny theatre and small dignified council-chamber. And because such architecture was an indispensable complement to Greek life, one is reminded finally of a quotation which Plommer has taken from the Greek writer Phocylides. He says, 'A small city on a hill, well governed, is better than stupid Nineveh.'

214

209

210

211

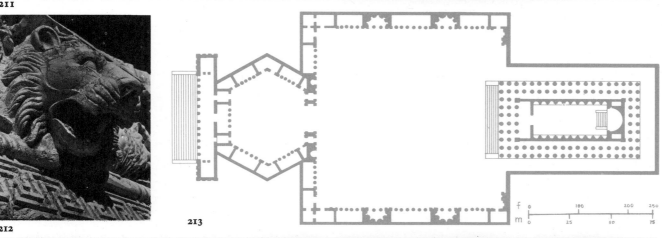

212   213

214

211 Baalbek. Temples of Jupiter and Bacchus
The magnificent temple group at Baalbek comprised the temple of Jupiter (the columns of which are seen on the right) and that of Bacchus (left foreground).
The Jupiter temple suffered depredation by Arabs and Turks, and before them, in the fourth century, by Theodosius the Great.

212 Baalbek
Sculptural detail.

213 Plan of the great sanctuary, Baalbek
The temple of Jupiter stood within the main sanctuary which was surrounded by a high wall.
The temple of Bacchus, not seen on the plan, was outside the sanctuary but was near the Jupiter temple.

214 Timgad
Second and third centuries A.D. Aerial view.
Roman colonial towns were based on the military camp.
Rectangular or square, they were entered by four gates, one in each wall. The streets were laid out on a rectangular grid.
The main axis was a processional way, and along it was placed the forum, the basilica and various temples.

Primitive and nomadic
In providing shelter for himself
from available materials under
primitive conditions,
man laid the foundations
upon which architecture grew.
The circular hut, prototype
of the tholos, the Pantheon and
the Dome of the Rock,
is found made of reeds in the
tropics (215) and blocks of snow
in the Arctic (216).
The mud-brick hut with
a thatched roof (217), sometimes
with wide, overhanging eaves
supported by tree-trunk
columns to keep heavy rain clear
of the walls and to provide
open shelter from the sun, is the
prototype of all verandahed
buildings, headed by the Parthenon.
In much of south-eastern Asia,
the sea and the rivers are
the only means of communication.
Shore- and river-dwellers build
their houses from the materials of
the jungles and raise them on
stilts against flooding (218, 219).
Often a great deal of time
and trouble is spent in elaborate
decoration of primitive dwellings,
as in the Ndebele huts (220)
and the gypsy caravans (221),
the latter an adaptation
of a dwelling to a nomadic way
of life in countries which
are generally highly developed, with
good roads.
Here the gypsy calls upon
the specialised skill of the
nineteenth-century wheelwright.

215 Swaziland, southern Africa
Small domed grass hut.
216 Arctic region
Typical igloo structure.
217 Basutoland, southern Africa
Mud-brick and thatch house.
218 Borneo. Longhouse with
tanju, or communal platform, in
front.
219 Jesselton, North Borneo
Sea-dweller's homes.
220 Pretoria, South Africa
Ndebele dwellings.
221 The Fens, Cambridgeshire
Gypsy encampment.

215

216

217

219

218

220

221

Ornamental Brick, Han Dynasty

CHINESE

**222 The Great Wall.
221-210 B.C.**
Refaced during the fifteenth and
s xteenth centuries, the wall with
its watch towers is much later
than the early buried walled cities
of central Asia, from which the
pattern may have spread both
east and west.
At this period, China may be
considered as part of the whole
Bronze Age culture which spread
all over the Eurasian continent.

222

223 Chinese beam frame system
The pine or cedar columns,
often of great length and girth,
rested on stone bases to
protect them from the damp and
were often elaborately carved.
The columns were held in both
directions by beams of diminishing
length, separated by short
vertical members. On these were
placed the roof purlins, a system
which could avoid the straight line.
Most Chinese buildings were
built in this way.

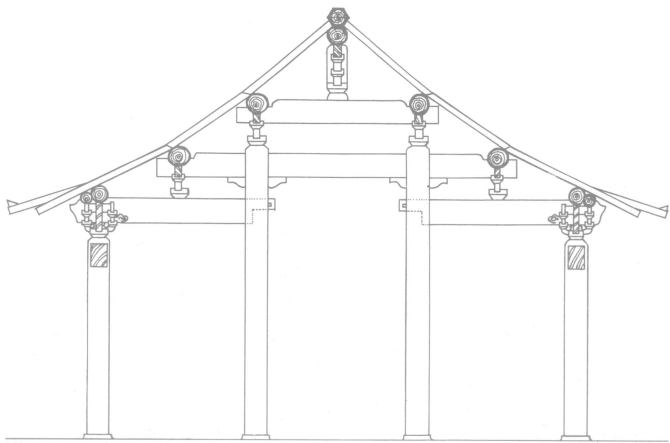

223

INTRODUCTION

Chinese civilization, growing out of its own neolithic culture on Chinese soil and independent, to an unusual extent, of contributions from outside, attained to an early pre-eminence and maintained a rather complete and self-conscious continuity from the development of Bronze Age culture in about 1500 B.C. right into the present century.

Chinese architecture, which is a typical and in some ways integral part of Chinese civilization, and early developed its own special characteristics, with an unusual degree of systematisation, continued, too, in a more or less unbroken tradition, into the twentieth century. It is this continuity, and not, of course, any real antiquity, which helps to make the unique interest of Chinese civilization.

A rather paradoxical effect of this, however, is the comparative rarity of anything old. There are fewer old buildings in China than in Europe, none of the age of the Pantheon, none of the age of St Sophia, few, indeed of the age of Salisbury Cathedral. Peking, supreme example of Chinese town-planning, physically dates only from the fifteenth century, and many of its famous buildings have been more or less completely rebuilt since. What is actually seen of the Great Wall itself, completed about 210 B.C., is the Ming re-facing of the fifteenth or sixteenth centuries.

THE CHINESE BUILDING

The individual building can be thought of as divided into a number of distinct elements, elements which were indeed kept aesthetically distinct by the Chinese architects. There was the podium or base, of hard rammed earth for humbler buildings, faced with brick or stone for grander ones, varying in height and elaboration according to the 'rank' of the building. On the podium timber columns were placed on stone bases, carved in a great variety of forms. The timbers mainly used were pine and a kind of cedar. The columns were tied in both directions by beams, sometimes more than one tier of beams, let into their upper part. But the essential difference from European construction is seen in the cross-section. In the West, besides the timber arch to support the roof purlins, the rigid triangulated truss was developed. In the Chinese cross-section, the place of the arch or truss was taken by a system of beams of diminishing lengths placed vertically one over another across the plan between columns and separated from each other by struts, above which the purlins were placed.

This basic bay was capable of expansion in all directions. Across the plan in the direction of the span, the cross-section itself could be increased in width by increasing the number of beams, by adding columns, forming verandah bays or inner spaces of varying widths. Lengthways it could be extended, of course, by mere repetition. It could be extended upwards by varying the heights of different parts of the cross-section, forming lower verandahs with a higher internal room, clerestories, galleries surrounding a higher internal space; or by the addition of upper storeys.

It is a striking feature of the Chinese cross-section that, not being based on a triangle above column level, it allowed considerable freedom in the design of the roof-line. The relative positions of the purlins, which controlled this,

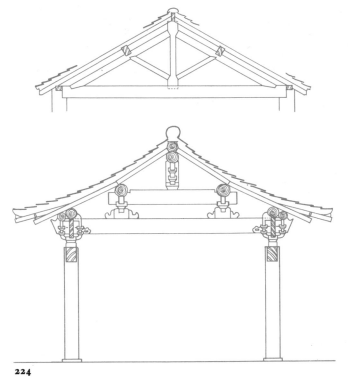

224 Western and Chinese roof construction compared
As well as the timber arch, the West developed the triangulated truss, a rigid construction which inhibits expansion, whereas the beam frame system of China, not based on the triangle above column level, is capable of considerable expansion in all directions.

224

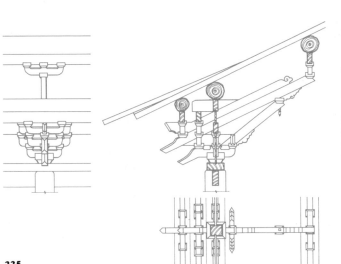

225 The high raked bracket, or 'ang tou-kung'
The brackets used to support the eaves overhang underwent many changes, especially during the T'ang and Sung periods. The high or raked bracket in the Sung dynasty became an independent, asymmetrical structure of great elegance supporting the eaves purlin as well as a purlin higher up the roof slope.

225

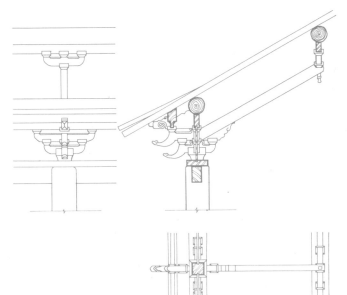

226 Variation of the high raked bracket

226

227 Bracket cluster, or 'tou-kung'
The basic device for carrying the eaves overhang was the cantilever bracket, somewhat resembling the extraordinary Chinese puzzles, pieces locking together endlessly.

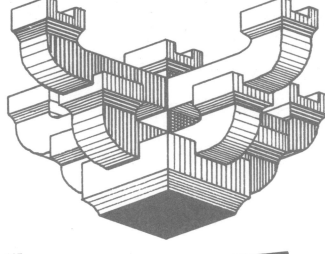

227

228 'Tou-kung' in position
The cluster was capable of many extensions in order to carry the rafters as far out as possible beyond the outermost columns.

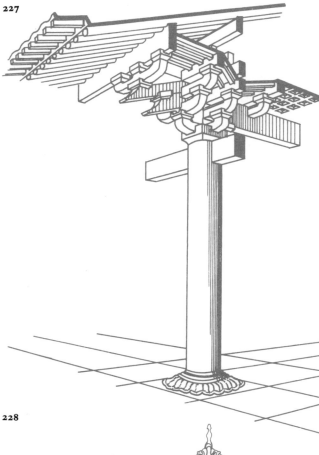

228

229 Lower Hua-yen temple at Ta-t'ung
Twelfth century.
End or flank wall.
Even external walls in Chinese houses were not load-bearing, but were screens often sloping back and disclosing the top brackets, supporting beams and roof. Thus, there were no cornices to construct.

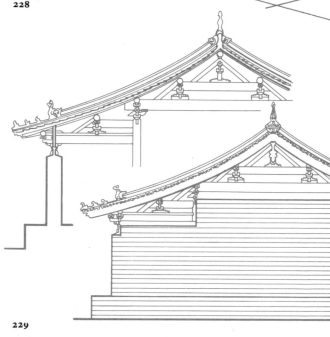

229

could be varied so as to be either in a straight line or in any required curve. Even the ridge did not have to be angular. One strut in the centre of the cross-section, resembling a queen-post, produced a straight ridge and therefore an angle. A pair of struts, one on either side of the centre line, could produce a roof which swept over in a curve without any ridge. The struts and purlins could, in fact, be placed so as to produce a roof-line wholly straight, wholly curved or any combination of the two, and all forms were used on occasions. The straight line tended to be used for humbler and more utilitarian roofs, while those of importance came to be usually one of the other types.

Another feature of the roof, which had its obvious functional connections but which was deliberately emphasised, more at some periods than at others, was the eaves overhang. A timber structure and an open plan or a verandah demand protection from the weather by means of the eaves. There were many and various applications of the cantilever used to achieve this, but the main device used to carry the rafters as far out as possible beyond the column, and also to perform many other internal cantilever supporting functions, came to be the cluster of brackets or *tou-kung*.   227, 2

Above the beams and brackets the purlins, commonly round in section, carried rafters also round in section and made of bamboo, on which boarding was fixed, covered with an insulating layer of clay, on which again were laid two layers of segmental tiles. Tiles were either natural colour (in the north, grey) or glazed in various colours: blue, purple, green or yellow.

Roof forms were of four basic types: the gabled, the hipped, the half-hipped, half-gabled, and the pyramidal.

All the roof timbers were ordinarily meant to be seen, but in important buildings an internal wooden ceiling fixed to or suspended from one of the levels of crossbeams was often provided as a decorative feature. These were basically a squared framework forming panels or coffers, which were painted. A central space in an important hall would often be ceiled in an octagonal, circular or dome-like shape, formed by means of brackets and carved woodwork.

Systems of standardisation varied from period to period but were mainly based on a range of standard rectangular timber sections appropriate to different spans and situations. Proportions of columns, *tou-kung*, etc., were by rule, and bracket arrangements with other details, though numerous, were all part of a known *repertoire*, so that the main part of a building could be erected without detailed drawings, only from description and specification of a typical bay.

There were fairly considerable differences between northern and southern practice. The timber sizes of the northern construction were more robust. The most conspicuous visual difference was the southern tendency to an exaggerated upturn to the corners of the eaves. It is the northern tradition which on the whole dominated Chinese architecture and which is mostly illustrated here.

Walls and partitions in buildings were not used structurally; they were screens. Internal partitions were commonly framed in timber and not always carried up to full height. Even thick external walls were not used to carry the loads of beams, floors or roofs; independent timber columns carried these loads and were either half-embedded   229

230

232

233

231

234

**230 Han dynasty house.
206 B.C.–A.D. 220**
Pottery model.
This is the simplest form of Han
dynasty house, a rectangular
hut-like structure, single-storeyed,
with tiled roof and walls of
rammed earth.
Most houses of this period
however were two-storeyed,
incorporating a walled courtyard;
the ground floor was used
for livestock.

231 Han dynasty tower
Pottery model.
The model clearly shows the part
corbel, part cantilever
construction at the eaves corners.

**232 Han dynasty pleasure
pavilion**
Pottery model.
This simple two-roomed pavilion,
with its sturdy construction
and sparse decoration
clearly has a rustic provenance.

**233 Han dynasty five-storey
house with small gateway**
Pottery model.
This may have been a town house.
It is a semi-fortress with
look-out towers at the gate corners.
The scale is distorted to make
a manageable tomb model.
The house was highly decorated
with a revealed timber frame.

234 Han dynasty watch tower
Pottery model.
The curved eaves line began
to make its appearance in Chinese
building during the Han dynasty.
This watch tower is interesting
in that two of the three eaves have
a marked upward curve,
the other is straight.

235 Yun Kang caves, near Ta-t'ung, Shansi
Fifth century.
These rock-cut Buddhist shrines were on a grander scale than Tun-huang. Interiors were sometimes decorated with coloured high- and low-relief carvings.

235

236, 237 Caves of the Thousand Buddhas, Tun-huang
Begun fourth century.
Tun-huang was an important point on the main trade route to India and thence to the West.
The rock-cut shrines have obvious Indian parentage.
They were begun by Buddhist pilgrims and eventually finished under state patronage.
The caves were lined with painted plaster and finished as Buddhist chapels.
Wooden porticoes originally protected the entrances. These were rebuilt and elaborated from time to time.

236

237

238 Mai-chi Shan. Cornrick Mountain, near T'ien-shui, Kansu
Sixth-eleventh centuries.
This rock stands about 500 feet high and is honeycombed with artificial caves, 194 in all.
The largest shrine was carved in imitation of a seven-bay hall with columns, beams and draperies in stone.

238

in the walls or were separate from them altogether.

The screen character of external walls was often skilfully expressed and emphasised. A striking example can be seen in the massive battered walls, pierced with deep openings, of the corner towers on the city walls in inner Peking. These external screens are simply sloped back at the top and stopped short, disclosing the timber structural work behind, sprouting into brackets and supporting the eaves and the roof. The same kind of expression can be seen in the screen-walls on the front of the Ta Hsiung Pao Hall.

It is one of the most interesting qualities of Chinese architecture, and one which has not been common in history, that the whole building is designed in colour as well as in form. The functional basis was the protection of the timber members from decay and parasites; the aesthetic aim was that the timbers played a major part in a totally polychromatic building. The actual colours varied according to time and place. Their general distribution was: enclosing walls and base walls, if plastered and not left in natural materials, one colour, often red, also white, yellow or black. Balustrades on top of such a wall or podium, with their steps and ramps, one colour, if painted at all and not left natural, e.g. white marble. Columns, one colour, often red. Beams, brackets, rafters, eaves members and ceilings, a range of vivid colours and patterns. Roof, one colour throughout, including the decorative and symbolic ornaments at the ridge and eaves.

The individual building was only part of an ensemble of buildings, and all the subtlety and grandeur of Chinese city-planning is based on a few simple principles and practices which were widely applied, whether to the plan of a little homestead, the lay-out of a temple, a palace or a whole city. These were (a) walled enclosure, (b) axiality, (c) north-south orientation and (d) the courtyard.

(a) The word for 'city' and 'wall' was the same: ch'eng. But not merely was a city walled; the principal internal parts of a city were walled. Every important ensemble of buildings and spaces was a walled enclosure in itself, and if large enough would be composed of separate walled enclosures. The palace was a labyrinth of walled enclosures. Not only a temple, a library, a tomb would be walled enclosures; a 'house' was a walled enclosure, and a great house a complex of many enclosures.

(b), (c) and (d) Within the walls or sometimes forming part of the walls, buildings, usually rectangular in plan and more usually in later centuries of one storey than of two or more, were planned around a courtyard or series of courtyards, with every important building having its long side facing south, with subsidiary, often lower, buildings on the east and west sides, and any series of important buildings standing one behind another in a north-south line, facing south on to courtyards. Even compact houses of two or more storeys will often be found on examination to be planned round a small courtyard. This south-facing orientation has its obvious functional basis, but it also appears to have been conventionalised early in the Bronze Age in connection with ancestral ceremonies and those of the worship of heaven and earth.

The roads of a city ran north-south and east-west, dividing it into a rectangular grid. The principal street was typically north-south, and the principal gate typically in the centre of the south wall. The enclosure-walls, both of the city and of its constituent parts, were the most massive elements, not only in themselves but in the buildings built on them at points of entrance and at the corners. A road encountering an enclosure did not open it up but stopped, or if it entered it passed through openings in the walls and under buildings on the wall above.

By such principles, the application of which was, of course, varied by topography, chance, growth and economics, architectural compositions of sizes varying from a single 'cell' to a whole city, of which an imperial palace would be only a part, were assembled into a unified whole, the whole and parts built up of south-facing, axial, walled enclosures.

1500–221 B.C.

The first millennium of Chinese architecture has to be passed over very rapidly indeed, if only for lack of examples. Until 221 B.C., there was one dominant type of social and economic organisation, based on bronze and then gradually changing and breaking up with the introduction of iron in about 600 B.C. This system, called by the Chinese 'slave society' and by Dr Needham* 'Bronze Age Proto-feudalism', came to be a pattern of small states ruled by princes who held them as fiefs from a king, to whom they paid tribute and owed the obligation to supply troops. The walled town grew up as the fortified home of the kings, princes and nobles, the granary for tribute grain, a centre of manufactures and of trade. Thus, Chinese society, basically agricultural, was early based on the town, from which the lord dominated a portion of the surrounding countryside. As flood-control, water conservancy and water transport developed, and as long-range trade expanded, the cities grew in importance. As cultivated land extended, they grew in number. Thus, a cellular pattern of walled towns, living off the surrounding countryside, spread over China.

The basic producers of society were slaves, working in agriculture and in urban crafts, a class formed principally from prisoners captured in the many wars, and peasants, not tied to the land, but not owning the land either. They held it in common, from their lord, subject to *corvée* and to many exactions in produce and manufactured goods.

Excavations at Anyang in Honan, the site of the Shang kings' capital, have brought to light traces of a city-wall of rammed earth and (eleventh century B.C.) foundations of large buildings, which already show some of the special characteristics of Chinese architecture—the podium or raised floor formed of successive thin layers of earth tamped with narrow staves to form a really hard permanent slab, the shaped footings of stone for the timber columns. The columns themselves had vanished, but their regular spacing in dimensions appropriate to timber construction show that the timber post and beam construction of Chinese architecture was already established. It appears likely from the remains that the light-weight panel between columns was also established. No trace of tiles was found, and the roofs were possibly of thatch.

The hegemony of the Shang kings was taken over in

* *Science and Civilisation in China*, Joseph Needham, F.R.S. Cambridge University Press. Vol. I, 1954. Vol. II, 1956, etc.

239

240

239, 240 An-chi bridge at Chou-hsien, Hopei. 605-16 Remarkable for its antiquity, its span, the flatness of its segmental arch, its spandrel arches and the beauty and economy of design. The spandrel arches relieve the abutments of dead load and provide an overflow for high water. The bridge originally had a fine fretted balustrade.

241

241 Pagoda of the Sung Yueh temple, Mt Sung, Honan. 523 The pagoda was originally a tower over a Buddhist shrine. It has its formal origin in the multi-storeyed combined house and water tower, the idea being generated by the Buddhist stupa from India and Ceylon. This example is the oldest surviving brick building in China.

242 Pagoda of the Tzu-en temple, Ch'ang-an (Sian). 704
Originally part of a monastery. The abbot who ordered its building had made a journey to India. The eaves are corbelled of brick work but modelled to imitate the more usual Chinese timber methods.

242

243 Hall of Kuan Yin. Tu Lo temple, Chi-hsien, Hopei. 984
The three storeys are galleries round a central well containing a colossal statue of Kuan Yin.

243

1027 B.C. by that of the Chou, which nominally continued until 221 B.C. Meanwhile the introduction of iron in about 600 B.C. (actually later than in Britain) had its greatest effect in the improvement of agricultural implements. A comparatively rapid expansion in cultivated lands took place with the clearing of forests and grasslands, leading eventually to a complete change in social relations.

By the time of Confucius (551-479 B.C.), the picture is that of a turmoil of states constantly at war. Confucius was one of the growing class of scholars who made themselves useful to the feudal princes as secretaries, advisers and diplomats. In a flamboyant age of lawlessness, exaggerated personal initiative and crushing exploitation, he preached order, good administration and social peace, based on benevolent autocracy, mutual obligations among different classes of society and among members of the family, and on a wide expansion of unprivileged education.

The flux of society was paralleled in the flux of ideas. This was the period of the 'hundred flowers' blooming and the 'hundred opinions' contending, from which the modern slogan was drawn, and several important schools of thought followed. Confucius was amplified by Mencius (Meng-tzu), opposed by Chuang-tzu and the Taoists, later by the Legalists, and so on. Taoism must be specially mentioned because its influence on Chinese thought and art became second only to Confucianism itself. The two modes of thought exercised, in fact, a kind of dual or complementary influence, Confucianism dominant and Taoism critical and unorthodox. While Confucianism was conservative, paternalist, rational and conformist, venerating precedent and hierarchy, perfectly adapted to become the orthodoxy of a bureaucratic empire, Taoism was anarchical, mystical, anti-rational, experimental and popular, venerating nature and teaching the contemplation of nature.

As these developments, basically deriving from the spread of iron, took place with increasing momentum, a period of still greater brilliance ensued (the 'Warring States' period, 475-221 B.C.), with advances in agriculture, technology and art. Cultivated lands were further extended, the animal-drawn plough appeared, the crossbow was perfected, iron mines sprang up everywhere. A money economy developed, ambitious irrigation schemes were launched, manufactures and trade, and with them the city, grew vastly.

THE UNIFICATION OF CHINA

The rival states reduced themselves to seven, of which one, the state of Ch'in, became the conqueror of all the other six and the unifier of China. The king of Ch'in assumed the title of Ch'in Shih Huang-ti, or First Emperor, in 221 B.C. At once many acts of unification were started, such as the creation of the Great Wall, the standardisation of coinage and measures, the simplification of the script to forms closely resembling those in use ever since, a programme of road building and the obliteration of interstate boundaries.

The Great Wall (221-210 B.C.), China's most famous   222
work of engineering, was, in fact, a joining and extension of walls already built by previous feudal states. It was none the less a colossal work carried out at extraordinary

244

245

244, 245 Pagoda of the Fo Kung temple, Ying-hsien, Shansi. 1056
Exterior and section.
Because of its date, this is an important building in Chinese architecture, one of purely Chinese timber design and construction. Octagonal in plan and 216 feet in height, it has five main storeys which are expressed and mezzanine floors which are not.
The bold eaves projections, supported on four-tier bracket systems, illustrate the flexibility of the Chinese beam frame.

246

246 Fo Kuang temple, Mt Wu T'ai, Shansi. 857
This is the earliest wooden building in China.
Thirty clay figures of Buddhist personages crowd the dais at the back of the central portion of the hall.
They are original T'ang figures, although redecorated. In this early example, the bracket ends supporting the beams are heavy corbels; later examples are developed into cantilever brackets.

247 Fo Kuang temple, Mt Wu T'ai, Shansi. 857
Section and south elevation.
Here Chinese timber technology can be clearly seen.
Basically the method is that of primitive log cabin building.
Half-lapped, jointed logs are laid in an intersecting, criss-cross pattern.
The taper is outwards and upwards.

247

248 Shen Mu hall, Chin-tzu, Shansi. 1023-31
In front of the hall (Hall of the Sacred Mother) is the square fish-pond crossed by a cruciform ramped bridge, all on a central axis to the hall, which is double-roofed with seven bays and a verandah.

248

249 Lung-hsing temple at Cheng-ting-hsien, Hopei
Eleventh century.
One of three large buildings giving a clear expression of the disposition of a Sung group. The fourth building is a largely destroyed pavilion which houses the gigantic bronze Kuan Yin.

249

speed by the only method available for great public works, a conscription of labour on a vast scale. The Great Wall runs from the Gulf of Pohai westwards to Chia–yu–kuan in Kansu, a distance of 1,684 miles. Its total length, however, which generally follows contours and includes considerable loops, is more than 2,484 miles. The original was of rammed earth construction, but successive generations of rulers constantly maintained and rebuilt it; and it was in the fifteenth and sixteenth centuries under the Ming that the last and most extensive repairs and refacing with stone and brick took place.

Now began the second great period of Chinese history, which lasted until the nineteenth century, and formally until 1911, called, by the Chinese 'feudalism' and by Dr Needham 'bureaucratic feudalism'. Slavery, for production, gradually disappeared. Land was privately owned and was saleable and rentable; it became, in fact, the main form of investment. A money economy prevailed on the whole, though rent and taxes were often paid in grain or silk. The 'free' peasant and wage-earning artisan were the basic producers (and taxpayers) of society. But since the small peasant lived near the borderline of subsistence, he could easily be forced, by natural calamities or harsh taxation, to borrow on, then sell, his land and become a tenant farmer or wage-earning labourer. Thus, there was always a tendency for the large landowners to become still larger and the peasants to be forced into greater dependence on them.

The power of the central government was, by European standards, immense and was based on a number of state institutions which were less developed in Europe until a much later age: a network of good roads and post systems for the swift passage of information, goods and armies; a system of state waterways; huge public works programmes, such as flood control, water conservancy and national defence works; state monopolies, e. g. in iron production; an army conscripted, in theory, from the whole population. Perhaps the most important instrument of the central government and the most characteristic feature of the whole system was a large, educated state bureaucracy or civil service, appointed and controlled centrally, cutting across local interests and controlling all parts of the administration, including the army. This huge 'class', from which most of the great men of letters, scientists, painters and statesmen in Chinese history were drawn, was recruited in theory by open competition from all classes, in practice mainly from those who had the means and leisure to be educated, the landowners and merchants.

Architecture, already set, went through a gradual development, which however for centuries can be seen only from funerary models, paintings and the like. The pattern of towns did not change but was merely developed further in this second period. The town ceased to be the domain of a lord but became an administrative centre, the seat of officials of the central government and the home of the many subsidiary officials, scholars and employees of the bureaucracy. Landlords of the surrounding countryside tended to live in the city, as well as vastly increased numbers of merchants, tradesmen and craftsmen of all kinds. Libraries, archives, temples, schools, warehouses, markets, inns and

250

251

250 T'ang frescoes from Tun-huang
These show various forms of architecture. Although the early development of technology in China is a byword, the Chinese built mainly in perishable material, and no really early buildings survive. Instead we have to turn to such records for examples.

251 Liao-ti T'a ('Enemy Observation Pagoda'), K'ai Yuan temple, Ting-hsien, Hopei. 1001-55
A typical brick-built pagoda of the Sung dynasty. It was built as a watch tower in an important frontier town. The pure masonry design has no timber-derived imitation brackets and details.

252 Fang Hsin-kan's house, Hsi-hsien, Anhui
Ming dynasty.
A house in a village street.
An example of walled enclosures taken to extreme.
The high walls round the house are taken to within a few feet of the windows of the buildings they enclose. The main entrance, from the south-west, was through a courtyard containing some outhouses. Inside the courtyard were two paved pools which collected rainwater from surrounding roofs and also from the courtyard paving. Verandahs ran along two sides of the yard. The main hall is in the centre of the floor plan (upper plan), and the upper storey (lower plan) contained bedrooms, but no privy.

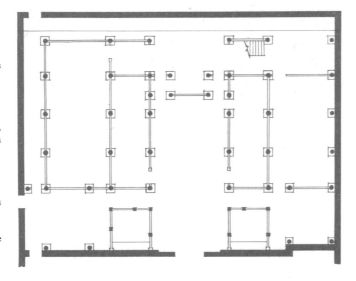

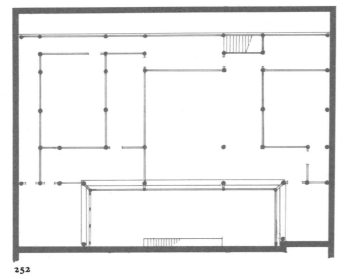

252

253 Typical courtyard house in Peking
Roof and ground plan.
These highly formal enclosures were so closely guarded that the doors themselves contained a deflectory arrangement of barrier-screens. The outer court, surrounded by the kitchen and rooms for children, guests and servants, was paved with stone slabs with a small lotus pool in the centre. The inner court, separated from the outer by a long guest hall, was the parents' domain. In one corner of the inner court was a strangely shaped stone and two peony beds.

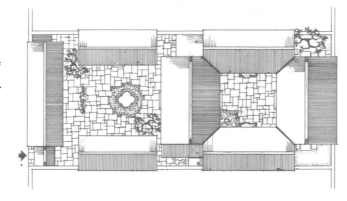

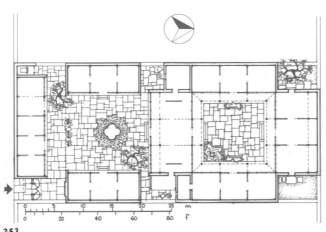

253

shops multiplied, and large numbers of towns grew into great centres of trade, luxury and culture.

THE INTRODUCTION OF BUDDHISM

About A.D. 65 an undoubted influence from abroad arrived, the introduction of Buddhism from India. On the whole Buddhism built within the secular Chinese tradition, but it did contribute one special type of building—the pagoda. In origin strictly a Buddhist building, housing the *sutras* or enshrining some sacred object, it came to be used scenically as a vertical element in the artificial landscape and not even attached to a monastery. The two 'parents' of the pagoda were, no doubt, the Buddhist *stupa* or *dagaba* from India and the Chinese many-storeyed timber-built *lou*. But it should be remembered that India, too, possessed these two distinct types, and that both contributed to the development of the tower or *shikhara* in Indian temple architecture. The pagoda of the Sung Yueh temple 241 on Mount Sung in Honan was built in A.D. 523 and is the oldest surviving building in China, a twelve-sided plan of solid brick construction. The Indian origin of the whole form is obvious.

The rock-cut Buddhist temples or shrines in China again have clear Indian origins, e.g. the Caves of the 236, : Thousand Buddhas at Tun-huang, an important station on the great east-west trade route connecting China with India, central Asia and the Western world. The cutting and dedication of these caves began in A.D. 366 and continued irregularly until the tenth century. The Yun Kang caves near Ta-t'ung in Shansi were cut in the fifth 235 century; another famous group of rock-cut shrines is on Mai-chi Shan, Cornrick Mountain, near T'ien-shui. 238

The Sui dynasty (581-618) virtually secured the unity of China once for all by radically improving the connection beween the northern and south-eastern areas. Extending previous waterways, they created the Grand Canal, linking the Yellow River, the Huai and the Yangtse. The canal was an extension of roadway, too, for over important parts of its length, roads lined with trees, whose 'shadows overlapped each other', were constructed along both banks.

This development demanded a high level of bridge-building, and the earliest surviving bridge, which cannot have been the first of its kind, is the famous segmental arch An-chi ('Safe Crossing') bridge at Chou-hsien in 239, Hopei. The date of this remarkable work was between 605 and 616, and the engineer's name Li Ch'un. It has been in continuous use ever since, or rather until 1954, when a new bridge was built nearby to save further wear on the structure.

The Sui dynasty was brought down by the unpopularity of its engineering works leading to massive peasant insurrection, out of which the great T'ang dynasty (618-907) was founded. By continuing but less drastic efforts in canal-building and transport, by skilful concessions to the peasants without too much interference with the interests of the landlords, by successful frontier wars leading to internal peace, by tolerating trade and welcoming all sorts of foreigners, the earlier T'ang rulers introduced, or rather allowed to develop, a period of extraordinary

XI *Temple of Heaven, Peking*

XII

XIII XIV

vigour and prosperity, combining receptiveness with expansion. The empire, production, trade and manufactures, cities, shipping and waterways all grew. Printing and porcelain were the most striking technological advances, but all forms of intellectual life flourished and almost all the arts developed to classic heights.

Of the capital, Ch'ang-an, largest, richest and grandest city of the world at that time, only one building remains. The general lay-out of the city has been recorded and reconstructed. This is based on plans published in the Ch'ing dynasty but appears to be accepted as substantially correct by Chinese archaeologists. Possibly the Chinese will soon be in a position to re-create the whole plan of Ch'ang-an with greater accuracy. The Chinese Institute of Archaeology have already made extensive excavations in the famous palace of the T'ang emperors, the Ta-ming Kung, the excrescence at the north-east corner of the rectangle of the city plan. The area of this enclosure was just under 823 acres—one and two-fifths miles north to south by just over a mile wide at the south side. The area of the main rectangle of the city alone, excluding the Ta-ming Kung and the parks to the east of it, was about 19,155 acres or nearly 30 square miles, and its perimeter just under 22 miles.

242 The one building which remains is the Tzu-en monastery of A.D. 704, originally built in 652 by order of the famous traveller to India, Hsuan Tsang (604-64), who was abbot of the Tzu-en. It was a brick structure of five storeys, but in 704 it was remodelled and two more storeys were added making its height about 190 feet.

Since the buildings of the Han dynasty, some of the specially familiar features of Chinese architecture had appeared: a greater emphasis on the roof, a greater eaves overhang, the curved roof-lines and the bracket cluster —and these were surely all connected.

247 There is actually a T'ang dynasty wooden hall surviving: the main hall of the Fo Kuang temple near Mount Wu T'ai in Shansi, dated by the Chinese exactly to the year 857. It was not a building of great importance in its time and not very large as Chinese halls go. Its seven bays are just under 119 feet overall on plan. Its height is 58 feet from the level of the platform to the top of the ridge-end ornament, and the depth of the plan is 66½ feet between outside faces of columns and back wall. The eaves overhang is 14 feet from the centres of columns. A thick screen-wall between columns encloses the sides and the back. The five centre bays to the front or south, which are equal, open fully with solid nail-studded doors. The two end bays are slightly smaller and correspond on plan to an ambulatory at the two sides and behind the long dais at the back of the central portion of the hall. About thirty clay figures of Buddhist personages, some very large, crowd this dais, and these, too, are original T'ang figures, though redecorated in later ages. Almost all the impressive features of this unique building are those which are specially typical of the T'ang: the low-pitched roof slope rising slightly towards the ridge, the subtly and slightly curved lines of the ridge, the hips and the eaves, the massive tile-ridge and its ornaments, the great eaves overhang supported by the main four-tier clusters of cantilever brackets,

occurring over the columns, with only one lesser cluster between columns, the bold and massive structure of beams and brackets, visible inside the hall, the simple and almost severe shallow coffering of the suspended ceilings. All these features can be compared with the more familiar Ming and Ch'ing buildings in Peking.

A short period of partition and confusion followed the T'ang from 907 to 960, which was not disruptive enough to stop new advances in printing, or to prevent the new period under the Sung (960-1274) from continuing to a still greater development of commerce and industry, to still greater heights in science, technology, philosophy and some of the arts. Advances were made in hydraulic engineering and shipbuilding. Gunpowder was invented and various military applications developed, such as the explosive grenade, the incendiary missile and the flame–thrower. Education spread, and private schools multiplied. Many famous physicians lived and worked, and a great medical encyclopedia was compiled. Moveable–type printing was invented, and there was, in fact, a mass of publishing on many subjects, including a famous manual of architecture. Paper money made its appearance. Of Sung pottery and painting it is hardly necessary to speak, since their perfection of technique and subtlety of form have long made them famous in the West. There is no doubt that T'ang and Sung China was the leading civilization in the world in these centuries, pre–eminent not only over Europe but also over India and the rest of Asia. In defence, however, Sung China had declined since T'ang times in spite of the invention of explosives, and after 1044 the Tartars in the north, while nominally paying allegiance to the Sung, actually carried on a separate government with Peking as its capital, while receiving subsidies from the Sung.

The Sung capital was first at Pien–liang (modern Kai-feng), but after a disastrous raid in 1126 and the capture of the emperor it was moved to Hangchow. Scenes of Pien–liang are shown in the superb scroll painting *By the river at the Ch'ing–ming festival*, of the eleventh century. The scroll follows the river in from the countryside, and most of the scenes are of ships, barges, small streets, shops, hotels and 'riverside cafés' in the suburbs. After showing a magnificent segmental arch timber bridge the scroll passes through a gate building and enters the city proper. We see a rather larger three–storey hotel just inside the gates; then almost immediately the scroll breaks off, the remainder being lost.

From the Sung dynasty dates the second oldest timber building, and even grander than the Fo Kuang temple, the Kuan Yin hall of the Tu Lo temple, Chi-hsien, Hopei, 243 of 984. Kuan Yin, who had become for some reason in China a feminine personage, was the Bodhisattva Avaloki-tesvara, the Lord of Compassion. The building is five bays, somewhat more than 66 feet long and 50 feet in depth, not counting the eaves overhang, which was again about 14 feet from the column centres. Its height is 73 feet, and it is of three storeys, or two and a mezzanine. These floors are galleries round the outside of the plan, leaving a well of the full height with an octagonal cupola above. This well contains a colossal clay statue of Kuan Yin, nearly 50 feet high. Again we see, on the ground floor,

254 Huang Chuo-fu's house, Anhui
Ming dynasty.
A small and simple house.
Living rooms, reception and two bedrooms were on the ground floor (upper plan). The kitchen was built on. The main room on the first floor (lower plan) was a ceremonial room for ancestral tablets and family records, rather like the Roman atrium.
The other rooms were bedrooms.
The entrance was from the one courtyard on the south-west.

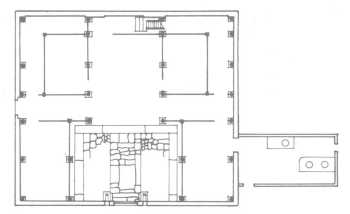

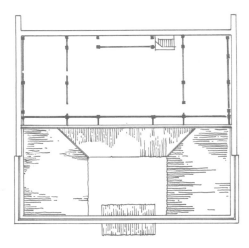

254

255 Ch'ing dynasty house in Anhui
An isolated house with the addition of two courtyards and several one-storey buildings.
The entrance, as with other buildings in this tradition, was from the south-west into a courtyard. Principal rooms and halls are found at the centre of each floor with bedrooms at the sides.

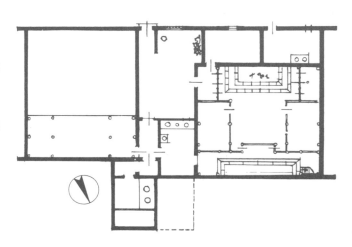

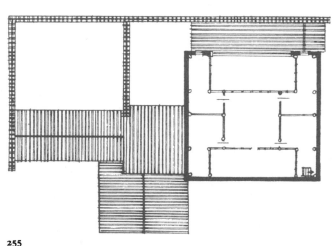

255

the great bracket clusters on the columns, five tiers in height and four steps outwards, supporting the eaves.

As individual works this and the Fo Kuang hall are surely the finest examples in the whole of remaining Chinese architecture, a tantalising remnant from an age, at least up to the end of the Sung, when buildings of this quality and finer must have been standing in their thousands, to say nothing of the larger compositions, the palaces and cities of those times made up of such buildings, all now wholly vanished. In these two examples one recognises an architectural integrity uniting the clearest expression of structure and function with the utmost subtlety of line and proportion, which the straighter, fussier, prettier buildings of later times never equalled.

Another interesting hall is the Shen Mu in Chin-tzu, near T'ai-yuan, Shansi, built between 1023 and 1031, a double-roofed, seven-bay hall with a verandah in front, which connects with a cruciform bridge over a fish-pond, 248 with steps to the front and ramps down to left and right from the sides. The bridge was extensively repaired in 1953. The steps in front lead to a little building called the Hsien Tien, built in 1168.

From the Sung dynasty also dates a very fine pagoda, that of the K'ai Yuan temple of Ting-hsien, Hopei, 251 the 'Enemy Observation Pagoda', built between 1001 and 1055. Octagonal in plan and more than 262 feet in height it had no timber floors but was wholly constructed in brick with brick vaults and corbelling and brick floors. Furthermore, the detailing is of pure masonry design, with no timber-derived decorations or imitation brackets. There were stairs, passages and a central room at each floor. Its name derives from its actual use as a military watch tower in what was a strategic point in the frontier between the Sung and the Liao territories.

The Fo Kung temple pagoda of 1056 is a building of 244, 2 purely Chinese timber-design and construction. It is octagonal on plan and 216 feet in height. The five main storeys are expressed, but there are mezzanine floors which are not expressed, except that the verandah on the ground floor adds a second tier to the base.

The Sung dynasty, too, was the time of the famous book *Ying-tsao Fa Shih*, or *Architectural Methods and Patterns*, whose first edition was published and *printed* in 1103 in Pien-liang (Kaifeng). The author was Li Ming-chung, a scholar, painter and calligraphist, who held various civil service posts, and eventually was Inspector of Works, head of the Board of Works with a deputy, assistants and a largish staff. Besides writing this book, a commission from the emperor, he himself carried out many building schemes.

Illustrations from this book are interesting because they tend to show that the colour schemes of the Sung period were more varied and subtle than those of the Ming and Ch'ing periods which are seen today, partly because of a far greater use of white. One must imagine these colours under the blue-green glazed tiled roofs of Sung palaces and not the orange-yellow tiles of later imperial roofs.

Other differences in the T'ang and Sung ensembles from those of the Ming and later, which can be glimpsed from paintings, are their generally more open and pavilion-like character, and the greater play with the massing of

256

257

256 Courtyard house, Peking
This detail of a courtyard
shows a subsidiary suite of rooms,
probably bedrooms, with, at the
right, a lower gallery to join
them to the principal living rooms.
The court is paved and set
with ornamental trees such
as crab apple, and flowers in pots
were set along the edges.
Here celebrations were held, and
in an outer courtyard, a
temporary stage might be set up
when actors were hired for
birthday parties.

257 Courtyard houses, Peking
The basic Chinese house
had buildings facing inwards
on three or four sides of a central
courtyard, the walls being blank
on their outer sides.

buildings of different heights and sizes and the greater variety and intricacy of roof shapes.

THE MONGOL INVASION

Some remarkable reforms put forward in the latter half of the eleventh century by Wang An-shih failed because of the opposition of landlords and officials, and peasant revolts broke out as usual. But the Sung were finally swept away by an external force, the Mongol empire of Genghis Khan, which had already spread over Asia and penetrated Europe to the Danube. China fell after a fifty years' struggle, but it was ruled by means of Chinese institutions and public works (e.g. the post roads and canals) which were maintained by the Mongols for military reasons (Yuan dynasty, 1279-1368).

It was now that the Polos arrived, and Marco took service under Kublai Khan (1280-95). His travels give valuable glimpses, among other things, of Kublai's Peking, laid out according to purely Chinese design, and of what was really the Sung capital city of Hangchow*, where life went on very much as before except for the highly unpopular Mongol garrisons, curfew and other aspects of military rule. Marco Polo, though innocent of artistic interests, and oblivious to much that he saw**, was an acute social observer; as a business man he was specially impressed with the wealth and luxury of the contemporary China. His account of Hangchow especially should be read.

The Mongol regime lasted only seventy-three years after Kublai's death. Secret societies of resistance and peasant rebellions sprang up in increasing numbers. The first Ming emperor was, in fact, a man of poor peasant origin, who had become a leader of the peasant armies. With the Ming dynasty (1368-1644), which came in on a tide of patriotism and national renewal, we enter the period of actual examples. In building, it was an age of enormous productivity.

By this time, of course, there were several differences in the style of individual buildings from what had gone before. The roof became higher and steeper. The ridge and eaves lines straighter and more mechanical. The columns therefore became equal in height; they also lost their slight taper and entasis. The eaves overhang was considerably reduced, and the bracket system, instead of visibly throwing out the eaves over the columns, forming a rhythm corresponding with the points of support, was reduced to an even size and a delicate scale, running continuously over column and beam, separating rather than joining columns and roof. The horizontal emphasis is further increased by the lateral bracketing pieces attached to the sides of the columns under the tie-beam.

Thus, still with no change in the structural system, a different effect was produced: stiffer, straighter, less dynamic but perhaps more decorative. Since there is no evidence to suggest that the art of heavy structural bracket-

---

* He called it Kinsai, or Quinsai, which A. C. Moule decided meant Hsing Tsai or Hsing Tsai Suo, the 'Temporary Residence' (of the emperor).

** 'The houses in general are very solidly built and richly decorated. The inhabitants take such delight in ornaments, paintings and elaborations that the amount spent on them is something staggering.' *The Travels of Marco Polo*, translation by R. E. Latham. Penguin, 1958.

ing was lost, it is clear that again the change was basically one of aesthetic choice. The emphasis has simply been placed on the roof in a new way by which it now seems to float above the structure rather than to be carried by and flung out by the structure. There also appear to have been other changes: a greater monumentality, a greater use of brick and solid masonry, a greater simplicity and horizontality in overall shape, and probably also a greater symmetry and formality.

Peking is, at once, the 'earliest' example of a town-plan and the source of so many compositions and ensembles, typical of Chinese architecture, where the individual building, however impressive, is never the real object of architecture, but always a mere part in a larger sequence.

Pei-ching, the 'northern capital', has existed since about 2400 B.C., when there was a neolithic settlement on the site. Historically, it was the capital of one of the 'Warring States' in the third and fourth centuries B.C., a provincial town in Han times, lost to the northern invaders during the fourth and fifth centuries A.D., recovered by the T'ang, again held by the barbarians in the tenth to twelfth centuries. In 1215 it fell to Genghis Khan and was rebuilt as Ta-tu or T'ai-du, the 'great capital' of Kublai. This had many resemblances to later Peking, but was more regular.

The Ming emperors first had their capital at Nanking (*Nan-ching*, 'southern capital'), but in 1403 Emperor Yung Lo re-established Peking as the capital and rebuilt it slightly to the south of T'ai-du, and dead on the axis of Coal Hill or Prospect Hill, an artificial hill formed by Kublai out of excavated material from the lakes, which he had enlarged. The walls of the city were faced with brick. By the middle of the sixteenth century the population had grown far beyond the walls, and it was intended to build a complete new wall round the whole city, but in the end only the southern suburbs were enclosed within a (lower) wall, finished in 1552, nine miles round with seven gates, the 'outer city'.

273

263-
269-
277-

The plan of the city is thus clear and easy to grasp. It is composed of four main walled enclosures, the outer city to the south, the inner city to the north, the imperial city within the inner city, (the walls of the imperial city no longer exist) and within that again the palace or 'forbidden' city. The outer and inner and palace city walls were moated as well. Almost all the main imperial buildings were on or immediately about a due north-south axial line running from the south gate of the outer city almost to the north wall of the inner city.

262

The main elements of the plan, considered as a piece of civic design, were, on the one hand, the massive concentric walls with their rhythm of bastions and towers, and cutting across them the straight line of a continuous composition of buildings, spaces and incidents, carefully controlled and related to each other, and forming incidentally a dramatic processional approach to the centre of government.

Two other compositions in the neighbourhood of Peking, basically Ming, should be mentioned. One is the Temple and Altar of Heaven in the outer city, the other the Ming tombs, some twenty miles north-west of the city. The original practices of nature-worship, including open-air altars to the spirits of nature, had been taken over by the

272-

258

259

260

261

258–261 Gardens, Soochow
The Chinese taste for strange shapes and 'natural' forms led to arrangements as artificial in their way as the European formal garden. Curved walls, pierced screens, extravagantly shaped door openings, pools, meandering paths, bridges and water everywhere resulted in a highly romantic sophistication.
These characteristic scenes of Soochow show the relationship between garden, building and water.

258 Hsien Yuan

259 Chuo Ching Yuan

260 Shin Tze Yuan

261 Chuo Ching Yuan

262 Plan of Peking
Mainly Ming dynasty (1368-1644).
Rebuilt on the axis of an
artificial hill in the fifteenth
century, the city grew rapidly, the
population spreading beyond
the southern wall. In the middle
of the sixteenth century,
this southern suburb was enclosed
within another wall, thus forming
the 'outer' city. The 'inner' city
contained the walled
imperial city and within that the
walled palace.

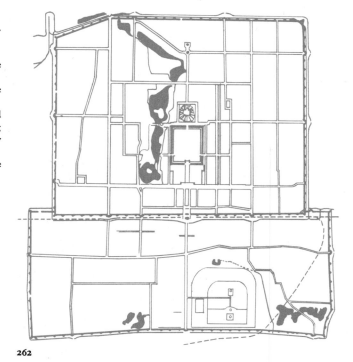

262

**263 Plan of the Fu-ch'eng gate.
Inner city, Peking**
This gate in the west wall of the
inner city is formed of two
buildings on a D-shaped crescent
road. The outer gate building
is a massive loop-holed structure on
top of the wall through which
an arch is pierced.

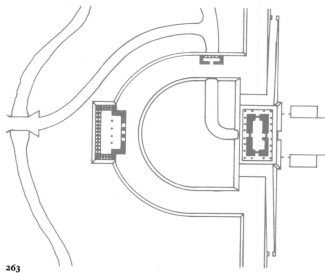

263

**264 Fu-ch'eng Men. Inner city,
Peking**
The inner keep of the gate is a
solid-walled guardhouse with
a verandah.

264

Confucian state and performed by the emperor on behalf
of his people, holding as he did the 'mandate of heaven'.
These altars were outside the gates, and in the fifteenth
century, when the ensemble was begun, the site was in the
suburbs south of the wall. The whole walled, wooded
enclosure, about a mile square with the northern ends
rounded, contains an inner walled and wooded enclosure
nearly three-quarters of a mile from north to south by
just over two-thirds of a mile east to west. Near the
western boundary of this is a square enclosure (but facing
east and west), called Chai Kung or Palace for Fasting,
where the emperor stayed in preparation for the ceremonies.

To the west is the main part of the composition, running
north and south. The whole ensemble is approached from
the side by a ramp. It consists essentially of the circular,
triple-roofed and blue-tiled Temple of Heaven in a
rectangular enclosure to the north, from which a causeway
nearly 400 yards long, raised to the level of the surrounding
tree–tops, leads south, first to a semi–circular enclosure
containing a smaller circular enclosure, within which is
a smaller single–roofed circular temple, and, finally, at the
extreme south, to the circular open triple–terraced Altar of
Heaven set in a square enclosure. The whole composition
from north to south is about half a mile long. The fact of
being raised in level, so that the traverse of the causeway
has been likened to a 'passage through space', the double
climax of the two main centres, one at each end of the
ensemble, the perfect interdependence of the parts of the
whole composition, combine to make it not only a typically
Chinese work of art but one of the outstanding architectural
compositions in the world.

The thirteen Ming tombs, those of Yung Lo to Ch'ung
Cheng (1403-1644), are scattered over a wide area in a
natural amphitheatre, surrounded by montains some twenty
miles north–west of Peking. That of Yung Lo, the
Chang-ling ensemble, forms a kind of centre to the whole
and is approached by a long succession of incidents, a
succession of stone figures of court attendants and animals,
bridges, gateways and so on. Chinese tombs are not   281
mausoleums but mounds containing the coffin in an underground chamber. Until the Ming dynasty, there were no
surface buildings, and these were merely for sacrificial and
ceremonial purposes.

THE MANCHUS: THE LAST FEUDAL DYNASTY

In the latter part of the Ming dynasty, concentrations of
land appeared again, tax irregularities, a dangerous increase
in the power of the eunuchs and in their acts of extortion
and oppression as special agents of the emperor. Once
more peasant wars broke out, and Peking was taken; but
this time it was a northern people, the Manchus, who
profited. The Ming emperor refused to make common
cause with the insurgents against the invading Manchus.
In 1644, first Peking, then the whole empire, fell to them.

The Manchus, like the Mongols before them, merely
operated the state as they found it, and themselves became
'sinofied' to the point of losing their own language, but they
discriminated against the Chinese in various ways (of
which the enforcement of the 'pigtail' was one), and they

were always nervous of national opposition to their rule. However, the Ch'ing dynasty (1644-1911) did provide a long period of peace, during which the population rose to a new level, and cultivation and trade continued to increase. Drama developed, and the novel produced perhaps its greatest masterpiece, usually translated as the *Dream of the Red Chamber* (by Ts'ao Hsueh-ch'in; eighteenth century).

The visual arts rather continued than rose to new developments. Architecturally the Ch'ing carried on Ming styles, rebuilt and added to Ming buildings; there was hardly a break.

THE HOUSE AND FAMILY

Throughout the period of 'bureaucratic feudalism', the family structure remained fairly uniform. The dominant and 'ideal' form, which in practice could be realised only among the better-off, was the large 'joint' family. Based on Confucian principles, this consisted, in its complete form, of parents, their unmarried children, their married sons with their families, all living under one 'roof'. Married daughters left the family and became members of their husbands' families. Any male member might have, besides his principal wife, a secondary wife or wives, whose children were also part of the family. In one house there might be four or five generations and, with servants, several hundred persons.

In the hierarchy of the family the older generation had authority over the younger, and the head of the family was the father of the oldest generation. The position of women was in theory quite secondary to men, and they did not ordinarily have a voice in family councils, but neither was their position that of chattels; it was graded and endowed with definite rights and duties. A woman could have authority over men of a younger generation by virtue of the principle mentioned above, and the head of the joint family could be, and often was, a woman; for a father on his death would be succeeded by his widow and not his son. In the *Dream of the Red Chamber*, which was wholly about a large and wealthy joint family, the head of the family was, in fact, a woman. It was this principle that enabled Tz'u-hsi T'ai Hou, the Empress Dowager of the nineteenth century, and other women in Chinese history, to wield political power. So in practice, women had much influence in the joint family and were often managers of the family's funds and internal arrangements, as Lady Phoenix was for a time in the *Dream of the Red Chamber*.

This general pattern was, of course, subject to exceptions and variations. Poor families tended to be smaller since they could not afford secondary wives, additions to buildings and so on. The traditional courtyard house, however, applied the same general principles already discussed. It was essentially a walled enclosure, composed of one or more courtyards, with a main room or hall facing south and lesser and lower buildings on the east and west sides.

There are some remarkable Ming dynasty houses that have survived, though partly in ruins, in Anhui province. They were exceptional in more than one way: they were all two-storey buildings in the streets of small towns, or sometimes isolated in open ground outside villages.

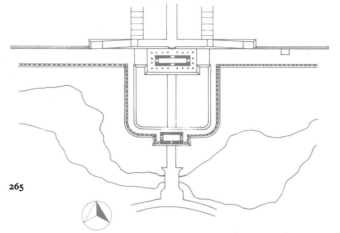

265

265 Plan of the Yung-ting gate. Outer city, Peking
As with the Fu-ch'eng Men, this gate in the south wall of the outer city is marked by an extra length of wall in the form of a U, enclosing a D-shaped space. The Yung-ting Men lies at the very start of the axial line and led to the gate of the inner city.

266

266 T'ien-an Men (Gate of Heavenly Peace). Imperial city, Peking
T'ien-an Men, entrance to the imperial city, faces a huge square which has become the Chinese equivalent of the Red Square in Moscow, Trafalgar Square in London, the Place de la Concorde in Paris or Times Square in New York.

267

267 Wu Men (Meridian Gate). Inner city, Peking
This gate stands astride the great axial way that crosses Peking at the palace enclosure. The red battered base wall is an inverted U on plan. It stands across a moat and is surmounted by white marble balustrades.

268 Peihai Park. Inner city, Peking
The whole area is nearly three and a half miles long with three artificial lakes. In the thirteenth century, when Kublai enlarged the lakes, the material excavated was used to make Coal Hill, on the axis of which Peking was built.

268

269 T'ai-ho Men.
Inner city, Peking
This view of the gate house of
the T'ai-ho Tien (Hall of
Supreme Harmony) is from the
Meridian Gate. A crescent canal
is crossed by five parallel
bridges. The gate house is a
ramped and stepped platform.
The site has a great breadth of
scale typical of Peking.

269

270 Plan of palace city
or 'forbidden' city, Peking
The Meridian Gate is in the lower
centre, above which is the
stream with its five bridges,
and at the centre is the T'ai-ho Tien,
or Hall of Supreme Harmony.

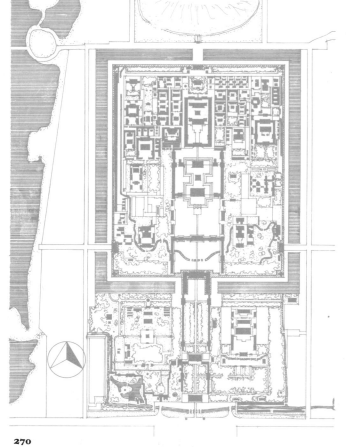

271 T'ai-ho Tien. Palace city,
Peking
The main ceremonial hall of the
Imperial Palace in which the
emperor gave audiences.
It is flanked by two unequal
pavilions, for resting and working.
Here is seen the emperor's
throne on its raised platform.
The coffered ceiling made use of
octagonal binding arches.

270

271

272 The Altar of Heaven.
Outer city, Peking
The altar consists of three
concentric terraces with white
balustrades and steps at the
cardinal points. This in turn stands
within a circular enclosure
which is contained within
a square.

272

Besides not being 'great houses', they were also limited by sumptuary laws to a considerable plainness externally, and also in size. They were not even planned to face south but mostly south-west, for various local reasons. However, the inward-facing arrangement was kept, and though the courtyard was reduced in scale almost to a light well, the plans were arranged around them in a traditional manner.

252 One example must suffice of the plans and sections of a house—that of Fang Hsin-kan's house in Hsi-hsien, Anhui—in a village street. There was a narrow lane to the north-east, from which there was a subsidiary entrance to the house. There were lower buildings to the north-west and south-west (not shown on the plan) but connected to the house; and the entrance, from the south-west, was through a courtyard forming part of these. The kitchen and outbuildings were thus beyond the wall to the bottom of the plan and to the left of the section. Inside the shallow courtyard were two little pools with stone balustrades. At the two sides of the courtyard were two open covered spaces or verandahs (rooms on the first floor), from one of which a door opened on to the street on the north-west, and a service corridor ran connecting it with an entrance to the street on the north-east and with the stairs. The main hall is in the centre of the plan, and the large room above this, not quite central, was probably a ceremonial hall in which family treasures and ancestral tablets were placed. The very small room at the right of the first-floor plan would be a cupboard or store and not a privy, which at that time would never be placed on an upper floor.

The section of the house discloses several points of interest: firstly, the boldly carved roof, whose members were all to be seen (they were not painted but treated with tung oil, as was most of the woodwork, though some ground-floor ceilings and beams were painted with delicate patterns); secondly, the section of the south-west window-wall, with a window-seat on the line of the columns and a curved-out section of the under-window panel, which supported the mullions outside the columns, and these mullions, tied back to the columns, supported quite a considerable eaves overhang by means of a *tou-kung*; thirdly, the free-standing two-storey wall on the north-east (street) side, with its own corbelled capping, entirely for privacy, though the window-wall on that side of the plan was almost entirely circulation space on both floors and only provided light and cross ventilation.

255 A later example from the Ch'ing dynasty of the same tradition is to be found in the same locality. This was an isolated house with two one-storey courtyards. The kitchen, and beyond a lobby, a privy and a pigsty, were on the north of this courtyard, and the entrance to the two-storey house was from the south-west side of the courtyard. The plan followed the usual arrangement, with the principal rooms and halls in the centre of each floor and bedrooms at each side.

253 Two of the illustrations here are the plan and the roof-plan from above of a fairly recent Peking house which is typical enough to serve as a reference to some details of the Chinese house.

The exterior walls were of grey brick, the roof of grey

273 Coal Hill, or Prospect Hill Chung-shan Park, Peking
Looking due north from the palace city, and very much part of the composition, is the artificial hill with a mile-long perimeter, with five pavilions, one set on the top and two on either side.

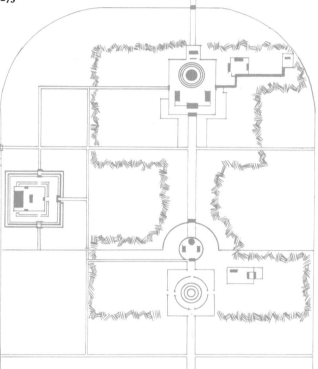

274

274 Plan of the Temple and Altar of Heaven, Peking
The circular temple stands on a triple-tiered platform.
It is linked to the open-air altar by a causeway nearly 400 yards long, raised above ground.
At the far end a three-arched gate gives on to a semi-circular enclosure containing another smaller circular temple.
It is one of the most remarkable architectural compositions in the world, although worked on at different times by different architects.

275

275 Temple and Altar of Heaven, Peking
The three-tiered roof of the temple is covered with blue glazed tiles; the three-tiered ramped platform is granular white marble. The exterior is highly coloured with red columns and brackets of red, blue, green and gold.

276

276 Temple of Heaven cupola, Peking
The carved and painted interior has a coffered ceiling.

277 Drum and Bell Towers. Inner city, Peking
These are the last two northern buildings on the main axis.

277

278 The Drum Tower, Peking
Standing on the intersection of the main axis and the street of Tung Chih Men is the Drum Tower which, though rebuilt, may be the original Drum Tower of Kublai's city.

278

279 The Bell Tower, Peking
The last building north on the axial line. From this point to the south gate of the outer city is about five miles.

279

half-round clay tiles. The entrance gateway, its doors and its roof timbers were bright with colour. These entrances were the only incidents in a street of houses where all rooms looked inwards. Guarded by servants as they were, no-one passed inside without permission. They were also the only point of contact from the inside to the outside world, and here the ladies sometimes used to come out to watch a procession or buy from pedlars.

Just opposite the entrance there was the familiar carved or coloured screen wall. The outer court was paved with stone slabs. A small pool with lotus growing in it was near the centre. A 'date tree' (*Zizyphus vulgaris*) and a crab apple tree grew in the courtyard, and many flowers were set out in pots round the edge. It was not a mere service courtyard; there were guest-rooms and some family-rooms in the side buildings. The kitchen and servants' rooms were in the suite on the south. But the long reception hall between the two courtyards marked a definite division between the outer half of the house, where acquaintances came and parties were held, and the inner half, where only relatives and intimate friends would normally penetrate. It was in the outer that the temporary stage was set up when actors were hired for the owner's birthday celebrations, when the reception hall was also filled with tables and a temporary kitchen was installed in the inner court.

This inner court, encircled by a verandah, was also stone-paved. There was a 'strangely shaped rock' in one corner, and two raised beds of shrub-peonies faced each other in the middle of the two sides. The columns of the buildings and verandah were all painted red, and the beams and other decorated woodwork other bright colours.

In some plans kitchen and service rooms were behind the main room on the north; but here meals were brought all the way from the outer courtyard. In summer the table was set in the open air in the inner court or if it rained on the verandah.

The use of the rooms was, of course, flexible, depending on the tastes and numbers of the family, of guests, dependants and so on. Traditionally the head of the family would occupy the main suite and a married son one of the side suites. The most private places in this very private house were the two little open-air courts surrounded by high walls, one at each end of the main suite. Neither was paved. One had a date tree growing in it; that was the special retreat of the father. The other, that of the mother and daughters, had just bare earth.

The floors of the rooms were stone slabs, and carpets were few. The whole window-wall of a room on the courtyard side was composed of a panel of windows and doors. Windows were of thick translucent paper, which had a certain amount of thermal resistance in winter. In spring they were rolled up, and the rooms opened to the outside air. Unlike the Japanese and the Indians, who continued to make more use of the floor, the Chinese, ever since T'ang times if not earlier, have used tables, chairs and bedsteads of similar heights to those in Europe.

Heating was generally by the portable charcoal brazier, prepared by servants and brought into the rooms in a glowing condition. In the north there was also a form of

280

282

281

283

280 Leng-en Tien, Ming tombs, Peking
Set in groves of pines
and cedars the thirteen Ming tombs
are scattered over a wide area.
The Chang-ling ensemble, tomb of
Emperor Yung Lo (1403-24),
forms a centre to the whole,
and includes the p'ai-lou, a three-
arched stone bridge, a three-arched
gateway, a long avenue lined
by stone figures and animals in
pairs, another gate and two
more bridges before
the tomb is actually reached.
This – the Leng-en Tien – is the
principal hall in the ensemble and
stands on a triple terrace in the
middle courtyard.

**281 Five-arched marble
platform (1522-66),
Ming tombs, Peking**
The p'ai-lou is a Chinese triumphal
arch, leading to the principal
tomb, with parallels in India and
elsewhere.
This example is of white marble,
roofed with blue glazed tiles.

**282 Fang Ch'eng Ming Lou,
Ming tombs, Peking**
At the end of the court beyond
the main hall is a brick wall
about nineteen feet high, topped
with a double-roofed
tower building.

**283 Wan Li tomb (1573-1620),
Ming tombs, Peking**
An isolated walled grove with a
stone tower. The tumulus is about
250 yards across; the tomb is
an axial arrangement of
five vaulted rectangular chambers.
In the end chamber lay the
bodies of the emperor and his two
wives behind a series of
self-locking doors.

284 Plan of Summer Palace
Ch'ing dynasty (1644–1911).
Lying six miles north-west
of Peking, the Summer Palace
extends over 832 acres (inset).
Lakes, hills, islands and woods, all
carefully landscaped, are the setting
for more than 100 buildings.
The main buildings are in the
northern quarter, on a peninsula
(large illustration).

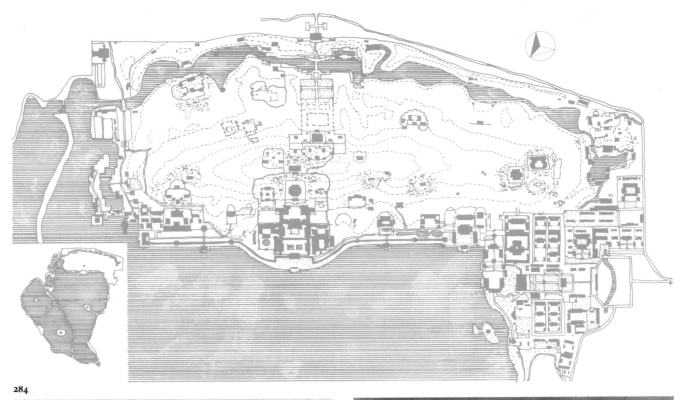

284

285 Summer Palace lake
The lake is surrounded by
an embankment and has
a system of causeways
and islands; it is based
on the West Lake at Hangchow.

**286 Fo Hsiang Ko,
Summer Palace**
The main group of buildings is
dominated by this octagonal tower.

285

**287 The long gallery,
Summer Palace**
Extends as a covered way from a
group of courtyard buildings
near the entrance, on the east,
all the way along the south shore
of the promontory.
The beams of each bay of this
gallery are painted with scenes of
the palace.

286

**288 White marble bridge,
Summer Palace**

287   288

underfloor heating, the *k'ang* or raised heated dais extending over part of the room. Solid fuel was shovelled in at one end and at the other the products of combustion extracted by a short flue taken above the eaves. There were never chimneys in Chinese houses. The *k'ang* served as a sitting area by day and a sleeping area at night, without a bedstead.

Clothes, however, were an important part of the heating system. Reversing the modern practice of light clothes and full heating, the Chinese in winter wore fur-lined or quilted and thick felt-soled shoes in a slightly warmed house. This, at least, had the advantage of greater adaptability to going constantly in and out of doors. Artificial lighting was generally by oil lamps and candles. The Chinese lantern was for decorative and ceremonial purposes.

The kitchen, the privy and the bathroom were more casually treated than in Europe and do not always appear on plans at all. The kitchen was sometimes in the open air, on a verandah or in an outhouse. The privy, consisting of a narrow-lined rectangular pit about two feet deep, with a narrow seat built over one end, was often built as a separate little shed in some convenient corner. Sewage disposal was by a system of carts, often run by private enterprise, which emptied the privies at night in a door-to-door collection and delivered the sewage outside the walls to the surrounding farms, where it was composted and used for fertiliser. As to the bathroom, it must be emphasised that all toilet arrangements in the houses of the better-off, including bathing and washing, were *mainly* provided for by means of basins, bath-tubs, commodes, etc., brought to private rooms by servants. As in all civilizations until the industrial age, domestic comfort, even that of a comparatively modest house such as this example, let alone the luxury of a palace, depended not only on the buildings and equipment but on the cheap labour of servants. In this house there would be at least six men servants and three maidservants living in, besides servants living outside. The men slept in the servants' rooms in the outer courtyard, the maids in the rooms of the females in their charge.

The conventional plan often was adapted to the needs of a special site. In a house on high ground near Hangchow, with views on to the surrounding hills on the west, north and east, the entrance is from the south. The whole plan is turned outwards instead of inwards. The south-facing orientation is dropped; the main hall is turned to face west and east. One side room, perhaps for a guest, is twisted round to face south on to the entrance courtyard. The second hall takes the form of a garden room with a loggia, looking west and north on to the view. One internal space has been created; the study or library has no external view and faces inward on to a pool in a tiny court open to the air and across it to the back wall of a covered space on the other side.

THE CHINESE GARDEN AND ARTIFICIAL LANDSCAPE

In a Chinese house, the garden and the artificial landscape were based upon principles startlingly different from all architecture. We have noticed the dual influence of Confucianism and Taoism on Chinese thought. This duality of opposites is clearly expressed in the relationship, both contradictory and complementary, between the Chinese

289

289 The Empress Dowager's marble boat, Summer Palace
At the extreme western end of the gallery is a group of buildings including the fantastic marble boat built by the nineteenth-century Empress Dowager who was also responsible for many of the other buildings.

290

290 Bridge of Seventeen Arches, Summer Palace
This elegant piece of engineering connects the eastern shore of the lake to one of the principal islands.

291

291 Confucian temple, Ch'u-fu, Shantung
This shows the Pei Ting pavilion in the temple group, the focal point of which was the library (K'uei Wen Ko) containing Confucian tablets. Nearby were stables for visitors to keep their horses, all axially planned. The foundation dates from A.D. 153.

292

292 P'u-tuo Tsung-cheng temple, Jehol. 1767
This temple, one of several Tibetan-style temples built at Jehol by Ch'ien Lung, is dramatically placed on a hillside, adapting itself to the contours.

house and the Chinese garden, and their extensions, the city and the artificial landscape.

The house and the city were formed by Confucian ideas: formality, symmetry, straight lines, a hierarchy of importance, clarity, conventionality, a man-made order. The garden and the landscape were formed by typically Taoist conceptions: irregularity, asymmetry, curvilinear, undulating and zigzag forms, mystery, originality, a deep and persistent feeling for wild nature.

258-261   It was this image of wild nature that the Chinese garden sought to evoke, even on a small scale, and from this derived the principles that came to mould the style of the garden: the avoidance of straightness, of the avenue and the vista, of 'seeing to the end' of anything, the avoidance of 'rules', the modelling of levels, the creation of hills, the placing of rocks and the constant introduction of water. The garden was to be a succession of incidents; it was to re-create the experience of a wandering or rambling in a vaster landscape. Yet man was to be present too, just as in the wildest of the landscape paintings there was almost always some figure, hut, path or bridge. There was to be no dichotomy between architecture and nature. There were more architectural elements in the Chinese garden than in those of Europe, and this integration of the two things was one of the great achievements of the Chinese tradition.

The natural elements of the garden were: the earth itself and its modelling; water; rocks, stone and sand; trees and shrubs, flowers and moss. Grass played little or no part, and the lawn was never used at all. The cult of the strangely shaped rock was a special Chinese tradition. Its original function was to suggest in miniature the dizzy crags of the Chinese landscape, but the search for rocks of more and more remarkable shape became a sort of collectors' cult, as if for natural pieces of abstract sculpture.

The architectural elements of the garden, apart from the buildings surrounding it, were: walls (of course); gateways or openings; lattice work; balustrades; paths and pavings; covered ways; bridges and pavilions. Walls, with their usual and subdividing functions, were freer in form than elsewhere, curving or zigzag on plan, rolling to the contours, serpentine in elevation. Shaped openings into gardens were another specially Chinese tradition: oval, circular, fan-shaped, hexagonal and many other forms. The object was to frame a view or some special aspect of the garden by means of the shape. Decorative lattice work, always a feature of windows, was lavished in garden buildings. The designs for open-work wooden balustrades, for paths and paving, were endless in variety. Open-sided covered ways connecting parts of a building or of a garden were often meandering in plan, rose and fell in level and sometimes added touches of bright colour to the grey-greens of rocks, water and plants. Bridges also were built across the perpetual pools or streams.

Pavilions, of a surprising variety of plan-forms, were specially important as centres of interest and also for use, for they were outdoor rooms, on an island in the middle of a lotus-covered lake, or on a hilltop.

The principles of the garden, from their very nature, were applicable to landscaping on a large scale and made

possible the remarkable synthesis of the artificial landscape, a landscape which was purely a work of art, but not something formal or urbane, which had the qualities of wild nature and yet was a composition of buildings too. While it was based on the natural topography of the place, large elements could be purely artificial.

The area of the West Lake at Hangchow has already been mentioned. The lake itself, the causeways and the islands were all artificial. The ring of mountains on three sides of the lake was brought into the landscape, and groups of monastery buildings and pagodas were dramatically placed on the slopes of some of them. The city itself on the east with its wall completed the vast composition, which in the main is still there to impress the visitor as it impressed Marco Polo.

Two other famous pieces of landscaping are worth mentioning: first, the area of the present Peihai Park in Peking. The three artificial lakes lie to the west of the palace in 268 the imperial city. There was a fourth lake to the north. Landscaping of this area began in the twelfth century and was developed by Kublai in the thirteenth. When the Ming city was built on the axis of Coal Hill, this area remained an imperial pleasure-ground, with romantically placed buildings, libraries, theatres, temples, studios, boathouses, residences of princes, built around the shores. The Ch'ing emperors greatly added to all this. It was here that Emperor Kuang Hsu was virtually imprisoned in enforced seclusion by the Empress Dowager until his death, after she had crushed his effort to introduce reforms in 1898.

The second example is the Summer Palace, which lies 284-29 close to the Western Hills about six miles north-west of the city walls of Peking. The composition extends over 823 acres, the greater part of which is lake; the rest is a 285 composition of artificial hills, causeways, islands and woods. The entrance is from the east, which leads into groups of south-facing courtyards where the imperial living quarters and court buildings were. From here, all along the south shore of the peninsula, runs a long brightly coloured cov- 287 ered way, the beams of each bay decorated with paintings (by craftsmen) of scenes from the Summer Palace itself. At the centre of the peninsula, rising to the top of the hill, is an ensemble of buildings and courts dominated by a high octagonal tower, called the Fo Hsiang Ko. The 286 covered way passes along the shore beyond this to the group at the west end of the peninsula, containing a fantastic marble boat built by the Empress Dowager. She was, 289 in fact, responsible for many of the buildings of the Summer Palace, which was her favourite residence, initiating works of great vigour and charm.

In 1911 the Manchu dynasty were finally overwhelmed by their own obstinate refusal to reform or modernise the state, by which means alone the threat of the Western economic systems, now so much superior to theirs (including that of Japan, who had not refused to reform), could have been met. Sun Yat-sen took office in 1912: in 1949 there culminated a more complete social revolution, but the fascinating problems of modern Chinese architecture, which the aims of industrialisation and the expanding building programmes have put before the Chinese, are outside the scope of this survey.

Stone Lantern, Katsura Imperial Palace gardens

JAPANESE

293 Imperial palace, Kyoto
Begun eighth century.

294 Sairyo-den, imperial palace, Kyoto
The imperial Japanese capital was moved to Kyoto in the eighth century.
From then on, the imperial palace has been continually rebuilt and restored owing to the perishable nature of the building materials, mainly wood. The Japanese house and palace alike favoured the courtyard plan.
Presenting a blank exterior to the outside world, a miniature world within was built of verandahed apartments ranged round carefully laid-out gardens. Japanese building tends to be rectangular on account of the timber post and light infilling panel construction used.
The roof construction was of composite bracketed and corbelled beams.

293

294

295 Sand garden, imperial palace, Kyoto

295

296 Stone garden, Ryoan-ji monastery, Kyoto
Fifteenth century.
These Japanese gardens, where nothing grows or dies, have an air of timelessness about them.
They are a tangible result of the teaching of Zen Buddhism. Rigidly formal on one hand in their use of raked sand, stepping stones and their careful design, they depend too on the curious fortuitous shapes of strange rocks and selected twisted trees. This cult of the contrast between disciplined design and the accident of nature is called 'sharawagi' by the Japanese, and has had some influence on modern architecture in the West.

296

The usual historical and chronological methods are not entirely suited to dealing with Japanese architecture and the history of its development.

The reasons for this are due to the immunity of Japan, over very long periods, from external interference or influences. Those influences which have operated, such as that of Chinese civilization and the neighbouring culture of Korea, have been of themselves continuous and only gradually developing, assimilating new elements.

The same is consequently true of religious and philosophical development, and of social and economic changes. Even after the great and immensely influential eruption of Buddhism (after A.D. 538) into Japanese life, the original and age-old beliefs and traditions of Shinto survived alongside the new beliefs, and are current today relatively unchanged.

Complementary to this steady and strong tradition of thought was the highly organised structure of a medieval society based on an industrious and skilled peasantry bound to their lands.

The whole was reinforced by a highly developed craftsmanship using the available indigenous building materials of timber, metal, clay and fibre.

One can only compare such a culture to that of the Nile valley; in which the overall forms are constant, and changes can only be observed after close examination.

In complete contrast to this immunity from external disturbance and the stability of the social structure, there has been throughout Japanese life the constant threat and actuality of physical disaster, on a gigantic scale, from the natural forces of earthquake and storm, to which these islands are subject. For they are situated on the edge of the Pacific hurricane belt and also in an area where earthquakes are of regular and frequent occurrence.

To live with these great natural forces, men have been compelled to restrict themselves to the continued and universal use of timber for building right up to the advent of Western influence in the last eighty years, which brought them steel and reinforced concrete and engineering techniques to counter the effects of nature. This choice of materials was made easier by the variety and quantity of local forest products and of the general-purpose bamboo.

Stone, though available in plenty, has in consequence been practically eliminated as a building material, except for some store houses and in a few rural areas, and for the defences of the great feudal castles.

A side effect of great influence on Japanese architecture, resulting from the impermanent and temporary nature of so many materials used for construction, has been the replacement of ancient buildings by exact replicas, as illustrated by the earliest Shinto shrines (A.D. 478) which, though probably identical with the original design, have, in fact, been reconstructed many times—as frequently as every twenty years.

Another vitally important feature to bear in mind is the effect that the use of timber always has on form and plan —as a result of the basic use of common units of length, a rectilinear character becomes universal and all-pervading, even in asymmetrical lay-outs.

This natural formality has been used as a contrast by the

297

XVI

XVII

Japanese to the extreme and sometimes hyper-self-conscious irregularity of their gardens; this is also related to the contrast between their society's extreme rigidity and the universality and 'nature consciousness' of their religious or philosophic outlook.

RACE

That these cultural traditions should have been preserved, with all their attendant crafts practically intact, up to 1868, is of unique value, as it is possible to see a highly developed medieval society and its arts at comparatively close quarters. A study of that society makes more clear the enormous losses in individual skills and values that have occurred in the course of the Western industrial revolution.

The Japanese and where they came from can best be deduced from the map. It is clear that the early races forming the population of these islands were not Chinese. They came by sea both from the south, from Indonesia and Indo-China, and from Mongolia via Korea and Manchuria—an admixture of landmen and seamen arriving in successive waves of invasion, driving the native population of primitive tribes and early arrivals, such as the Ainu, steadily northwards. These invaders probably brought with them knowledge of metals and the primitive crafts. Subsequently, in historic times, more immigrants came in from Korea, often craftsmen especially encouraged to settle for the skills which they could impart.

GEOGRAPHY AND CLIMATE

Geographically Japan is a curving line of rocky islands of volcanic origin following the main outline of eastern Asia and mountain heights running roughly north and south. It has, therefore, as one would expect, a high rainfall governed by seasonal trade-winds, which is greatest in the early summer and autumn and least in mid-winter. Average annual rainfall in Tokyo is 63 inches as against, say, 24 inches in London. Also owing to the difference in latitude there is great variation in temperature between the climate of the north and south of the islands.

The high humidity of the summers has dominated the design of buildings, public and domestic, and on the whole the rigours of the cold, dry winters seem to have been met by stoicism and the wearing of additional clothes.

To meet these summer conditions, buildings have been raised on open wooden platforms, which remind one of traditions of southern Asia. They can be thrown open by systems of screens to allow free circulation of air. The roofs have considerable overhang to throw off the rains and give shade in summer while allowing winter sun to penetrate. Being of timber, they are relatively safe against earthquake but highly vulnerable to fire.

MATERIALS

The building materials available, as has already been mentioned, are mainly forest products: paper, tiles and metals.
297 Roofs were, in early days, always thatched or of bark
301 shingles, but elaborate tile roofs were introduced later for large buildings. Sometimes they were finished with copper ridges, spirals and other decoration for temples, town houses, etc., while the earlier materials were still in use.

297 The inner shrine of the sun goddess, Ise
Fifth century.
This shrine has been continuously rebuilt without alteration every twenty years. Its steeply pitched thatched roof is a developed form of the indigenous tent-shaped thatched Japanese hut on stilts. The thatch is laid on a framework of closely lashed bamboo poles.

297

298 Kumesu Shinto shrine, Matsue. Built 1346
Heavy rain and humidity dictated the steeply pitched roof and overhanging eaves of Japanese buildings, and also made it necessary to raise the floor to become a platform on stilts.

298

**299 Kasuga shrine.
Founded A.D. 768**
One of the oldest existing Shinto shrines. Japanese architecture is one of timber frame structure with light infilling panels for protection.
Solid load-bearing walls are rare. This shrine is painted bright vermilion. The numerous lanterns are votive offerings from worshippers, some dating back to 1323.

299

300 Traditional farmhouse, Kansai area
Seventeenth century onwards. Outer walls of country houses are generally filled in with cob, mud bound by chopped straw. In the courtyard walls full advantage is taken of the frame to use panels of lightweight material such as oiled paper. These are often made to slide so that sides of rooms may be opened up in fine weather.

300

XVI *Palace of the Shoguns, Kyoto* XVII *Ninomaru Palace Hall within the Nijo Castle, Kyoto*

301 Nagoya castle. Completed 1611
The pagoda-like form and the curvilinear tiled roofs are imported influences from China. The tiered galleries are supported by a diminishing series of bracketed beams.

301

302 Osaka castle. 1587
Japanese castles are built on a heavy stone platform. The heavy curved battering is protection against earthquake as well as siege. The stone courses are cut to slope inwards towards the rubble core.

302

303 Nijo castle, Kyoto. 1603
This interior of the kuro-shoin chamber clearly shows the framed structure with a beamed and coffered ceiling. The panel proportions are worked out with great care. The wall paintings are sophisticated and elegant.

303

The Japanese use of wood is unique, as has been their craft approach in other fields. The wood is seldom painted or treated, but is carefully selected and used so as to exploit its natural characteristics of texture and colour.

Stone was available; some particularly suitable for building, such as the soft volcanic rock from Tochigi, used for fire-proof buildings, is in general use today. But apart from fortifications, it was not used on a large scale except for the bases of posts, platforms and steps, for garden pavings and in the form of natural boulders, an essential feature of Japanese gardens. Wattle and daub is in frequent use for walling in country districts.

THE PRE-BUDDHIST PERIOD

This period starts with the Jomon neolithic culture related to the Asiatic mainland, and is associated with worship of the mother goddess. As a culture it stretches back into the second millennium B.C., without records or historical landmarks.

Early dwellings appear to be of two main types, often interchanged: pit dwellings of rectangular or oval plan and the hut type usually, with the floor raised on a platform, of southern Asiatic origin. The latest examples of Jomon pottery have been found in Honshu and date from about 1000 B.C.   327-3

The Yayoi culture, centred in Kyushu, marked an advance in craft techniques owing much to influences from the mainland, particularly from China and Korea.

The culmination of these developments was seen during the third and fourth centuries, when the precepts of the Shinto religion were being established and the central imperial government was being formed from the conflicting principalities and kingdoms of earlier times. The main monuments surviving are the great tumuli and tombs centring round the plain of Yamato, south-east of Osaka.

These tumuli are of Korean style, and probably are related to the *stupas* of China and Buddhist India. Their sides were strengthened with baked clay cylinders; the tops were later ornamented with heads and figures of a striking and strongly local character called *Haniwa*. Some of these memorial mounds cover an immense area.

It is from this period, too, that the traditional forms of the Shinto shirnes, such as those at Ise, were developed and have survived relatively unchanged to the present day. The form of these shrines has had more influence on the outlook and methods of Japanese architects than any other group of buildings, until the advent of Western influence.

There are literally thousands of such shrines throughout the country, but the groups at Ise retain the original ancient form, construction and lay-out most closely; this in spite of repeated reconstructions, as well as of being the most venerated.

The two chief shrines are the Ise Naiku, dedicated to the grain goddess, and the Ise Geku, dating from A.D. 478 and associated with the sun goddess. In them are combined all the essential and constantly recurring features of thatched roof with spreading eaves, platform for the main rooms and light timber partitions and walls.   297

They stand inside fenced enclosures and with subsidiary buildings and store house—very much on the lines that

304

304 Matsumoto castle.
Founded sixteenth century.
The surprisingly light-looking
structure seems to float above the
sloping stone base surrounded
by a wide moat.
The shuttered galleries were
constructed for use of and defence
against archers.
Archery reached a very high
standard in Japan, and was still
favoured for silence and
surprise long after the introduction
of firearms.

305

305 Osaka castle
The main weapon against the
Japanese castle or palace was fire.
The upper storeys were of
heavy timber, built in log cabin
style and rendered externally.
The lookout towers or keeps
contained living quarters and
store houses, often on a palatial
scale in both size and elegance.

306-310 Horyu-ji temple, Nara. A.D. c. 607

This, the oldest existing temple in Japan, was built by Prince Shotoku, an early convert to Buddhism. The temple plan was intended to be a complete world in miniature. The principal shrines, the hall for prayer and teaching, and the tope, the sacred tower, are four square to the quarters of the earth, and have the four cardinal entrances up flights of steps.

The pagoda, which in China was sometimes almost solid, is a complete framed structure.

The introduction of Buddhism to Japan opened the way to strong Chinese influences in philosophy and all the arts as well as in architecture. The curved, tiled roofs and bracketed pillars are from China, but the lightness of the structure, which makes the roofs appear to float above the buildings, is Japanese.

306

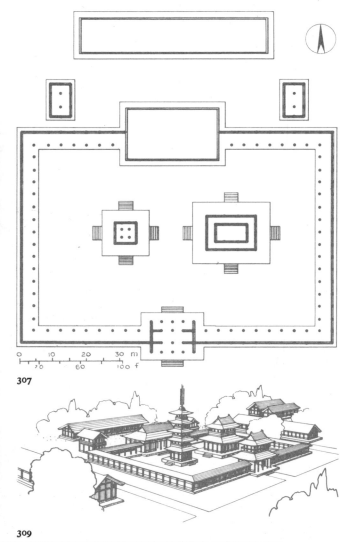

307

308

309

310

must have been followed in the lay-out of the imperial residences of those days.

The lay-out of these groups of buildings and their enclosures is basically symmetrical, though no attempt is made to carry this symmetry beyond the immediate boundaries and into the relation of one building with another.

Even the early buildings demonstrate the constant theme of Japanese thought and planning, in which extreme formality is contrasted and surrounded by the almost self-conscious awareness of nature and natural forms.

Undoubtedly, the royal palaces were large and comparatively elaborate, modelled, no doubt, on ideas from the mainland, acquired through contact with Korea. But none of these or their sites has survived, largely due to the tradition of the moving of the seat of the imperial court at the death of each emperor.

Asuka Period (538-645)

By this time the imperial house was established at Yamato and had close associations with the Korean Three Kingdoms, and through them with the Wei dynasty of north China. From Korea were introduced the first Buddhist scriptures, writings and teachers in 538. By the end of the sixth century, Prince Shotoku Taishi, regent in the name of his aunt the empress, was converted to Buddhism.

The effect of the introduction of Buddhism, apart from the religious and philosophical aspects of its teaching, immediately increased the country's cultural and political ties with China, and brought with it ideas of building on a much grander scale than before. This growth of outside contact with the highly developed and already ancient civilization of China introduced, at one leap, a fully grown and sophisticated art tradition.

Chief among Prince Shotoku's works was the foundation of the Haiyu-ji temple. Other temples, such as the Shitenno-ji, Hokyi, Hamji and Horyu-ji, were established, the last named being built in 607. It still preserves some of its original buildings: the pagoda, the gatehouse and the *kondo* (the main sanctuary).

Much of the work of the period was done by Chinese and Korean artists and craftsmen who had been invited to settle in Yamato, and who brought with them the models for sculptures, such as the great gilded bronze statue of the Sakyamuni trinity in the *kondo* of Horiyu-ji, executed by Tari, the grandson of a Chinese immigrant, and dedicated in 625. Many such bronzes with their symmetrical stylised draperies and archaic smiles must have been derived from small portable figures, and are typical of the Asuka period.

Nara Period (645-793)

The seventh century saw a further increase in influences from the mainland. Relations were established directly with the T'ang dynasty at its capital Ch'ang-an, and emissaries, travellers and scholars passed between the two countries.

The climax of this influence was reached with the founding in 710 of a new capital at Nara. Having a symmetrical, rectilinear city-plan, with the imperial palace as the focus, it was a close copy of the lay-out of the capital city of Ch'ang-an.

Buddhism was all powerful, and Emperor Shomu ordered

311

312

313

311 **Todai-ji temple, Nara**
Eighth century onwards.
Another early temple at Nara.
The Daibutsuden seen here, the cella or hall of the Great Buddha, is of wood with a tile roof.
It is 160 feet high, 187 feet long and 166 feet wide.

312 **Todai-ji temple, Nara**
This corner of a wooden store house shows the traditional log cabin type of construction.
It was from this half-lapped joint, combined with corbelling outwards to form an inverted pyramid in order that the notches should be staggered, that the Sino-Japanese bracket grew.

313 **Todai-ji temple, Nara. Negasu-do**
The Todai-ji group is one of the largest in Japan, the space taken equalling that of the imperial palace. It is Chinese rather than Japanese and has been rebuilt several times since the eighth century. The whole group was extremely impressive as can be judged by the magnificent south gate, the Negasu-do, built in the twelfth century and is influenced by Indian building.

**314 Daibutsuden.
Todai-ji temple, Nara**
The high upswept eaves and the
portico over the main entrance are
strongly reminiscent of the
Japanese torii or free-standing
sun gates. This is the
largest wooden building,
under one roof, in the world.

314

**315 Pagoda of the Yakushi-ji
temple, Nara**
Eighth century.
The tiered roofs do not taper
evenly but show freedom in design
which gives the elevation of
this pagoda something of the
character of Japanese calligraphy.

315

**316 Pagoda of Horyu-ji
temple, Nara**
Eighth century.
In this and the previous pagoda
the spire is an adaptation
of Buddha's many-tiered canopy
or umbrella.

316

that a temple be built in each province, all of them subordinate to the Todai-ji imperial temple near Nara.   311-3

It is claimed that twenty buildings of the eighth century survived. The temple-monasteries, for example the
imperial Todai-ji and the Toshodai-ji, are magnificent
groups of buildings, of which sufficient original structures
remain, in spite of destruction and rebuilding, to illustrate
their scale and style and to allow for fairly detailed reconstructions.

Elaborate roofs of glazed tiles, external woodwork and
columns painted red, with overhanging eaves and gilded
and painted decorations in full colour in the interiors made
them glorious in colour and form.

The central feature was the low Buddha hall, or *kondo*,
contrasted with the pagoda, which had superseded the
stupa, a lecture hall and other monastic buildings.

One of the buildings of particular interest surviving is
the magnificent Shosoin, the imperial treasure-house, built
about 752, of triangular timbers laid horizontally, like the
logs of a log cabin, and supported on a platform and huge   312
timber columns.

All this new and elaborate building activity did not prevent traditional Japanese structures from being built for
everyday purposes, with their traditional forms hardly
changed in any way.

HEIAN PERIOD (794-1185)

The period commences with the removal of the capital
from Nara to Heian-Kyo (City of Tranquil Peace), the
present site of Kyoto.

The new city was built on the lines of a Chinese city-   293
plan as at Nara. Chinese influence was as strong as ever,
and in some ways was increased by the contacts made with
the Chinese court by the nobility and by traders, in addition to that of the Buddhist monks and missionaries who
had provided the original channel between the court and
the outside world.

In this period the new Buddhist sects of Shingon and
Tendai were introduced to Japan, and they brought with
them a mass of minor divinities and a desire for greater
elaboration in buildings and decoration. Their influence
even affected the ancient simplicity of the native Shinto
religion, whose symbols were, for the first time, supplemented by representations of its gods. The two religions,
in fact, began to draw together.

During this period began the system of the peasantry
paying their dues to landowners or their agents instead of
to the imperial government, and this gradually developed
into the feudal system, which gave power to the *samurai*.

Towards the end of the tenth century, the decline of
the T'ang empire accelerated the development of an independent Japanese culture. Scholars ceased to travel between
the two capitals, and finally diplomatic contact between
them ceased. Even contact with Korea was diminished.

From about 898, a far greater independence from foreign ideas began to develop among the nobility, who
ruled the country in the emperor's name. This is often
referred to as the Fujiwara period, the name of the famous clan who effectively governed Japan up to the middle of the twelfth century. It was the first prolonged period

317

317 Itsukushima shrine, western Japan
Thirteenth century.
The Japanese loved contrast, the refined artificiality of man-made objects with natural freedom. Buildings connected by bridges, corridors and covered ways are irregularly dispersed among rocks, wood and water.

318

318 Kinkaku-ji (Golden Pavilion), Kyoto
Fourteenth century.
The elaborate care with which a site was chosen was not a matter of aesthetics – feelings – alone, but a principle of Buddhist doctrine, which constantly refers to the lessons to be learned from the observation of nature itself.

319-321 Saimyo-ji main hall
Fourteenth century. Sketch, plan
and section.
The bracketed capital and
composite beams are similar to
those of China.
Although the basic form is the
rectangular bay, these bays are
capable of independent
development, and a strict symmetry
is not necessarily imposed.
The frame structure carrying its
load upon posts and the raising of
the floor into a platform make
Japanese buildings independent of
the limitations of a sloping
or irregular site.

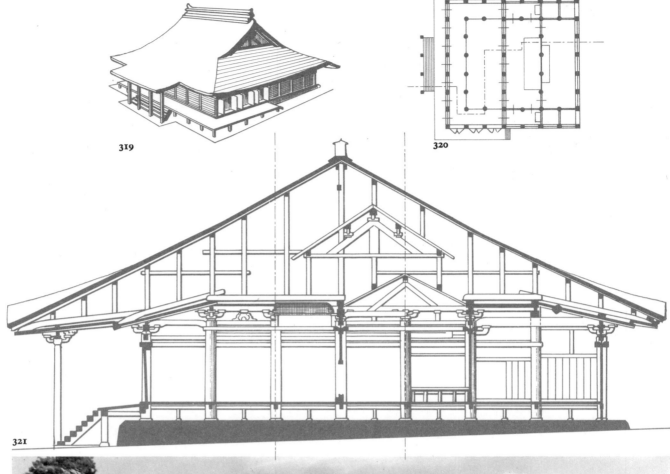

319

320

321

**322 Kiyomizu-dera temple,
Kyoto**
Reconstructed 1633.
The shrines and halls are carefully
distributed over a sloping
wooded site.

322

**323 Shitenno-ji monastery,
Osaka**
Sixth century onwards.
Reconstructed plan.
The early monastery and temple
plans adhered to the strict
symmetry of their Chinese models.
This reconstructed plan is of
the earliest monastery of which
remains are still visible.

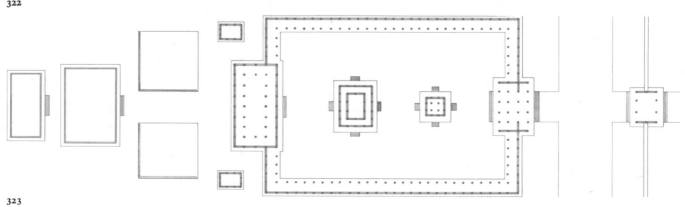

323

of almost complete and deliberate national isolationism.

In opposition to the earlier esoteric Buddhist sects, the aristocracy favoured the cult of Amida (Jodo), in which salvation is open to all who invoke the Buddha's name.

Many temples were built by emperors and nobles. Surviving examples of the period are the pagoda of Daigoji, the Sangen-in, and the lecture halls of the Koryu-ji and Horyu-ji monasteries. All these were elaborately decorated In the temples the difference between inner and outer sanctuaries was eliminated, bringing all the images together in one crowded enclosure.

The palaces and, particularly, the homes of the nobility grew more elaborate, in a style known as *shinden-zukuri*. Here we see the early development, on a large scale, of a style of domestic building which has come to be looked on as one of the typical features of Japan's architecture.

It is characterised by the irregular dispersal of rectangular buildings sometimes linked with covered ways or corridors, and passing through and carefully related to a whole scheme of naturalistic and romantic gardening with rocks, trees, water-ways or ponds, creating a self-contained artificial world of its own. The design aims at personal and social appreciation and recreation, rather than public advertisement or prestige.

KAMAKURA PERIOD (1185-1337)

The middle of the twelfth century was a time of rebellion and civil war, following the decline of the Fujiwara administration. In this conflict the party of the Minamoto family was finally victorious and established a military government of the *samurai* warrior-class at Kamakura, just south of Tokyo, under Yoritomo—about 240 miles west of the ancient imperial capitals.

This revolutionary change in the ruling class and the establishment of a government on military lines (the *bakufu*), which was to be characteristic of Japanese administrations right up to the re-establishment of imperial rule in the nineteenth century, was reflected in many other ways.

The Zen sect of Buddhism, which was brought from China together with influences from the Sung, was particularly suited to the outlook of the *samurai*, and was adopted by them.

The main characteristics of Zen was that it stressed extreme simplicity in ritual and was based on a belief in personal meditation and self-discipline.

Its effects on temple buildings was to eliminate the multitude of minor statues, the Buddha figure now being alone on the altar and not in an inner sanctuary. The temple hall itself was increased in height, and woodwork and other materials were left plain and undecorated. The planning followed the Chinese traditions of symmetry, which, however, the native Japanese planner always tended to transform into a consciously picturesque asymmetry.

It is in this period that the *buke* style of *samurai* house developed, as distinct from the earlier *shinden-zukuri* style of the aristocracy and imperial palaces, based on separate buildings linked with covered ways.

The *samurai* enclosed their homes with a ditch and fence. The rooms were grouped under one roof, or a group of connected roofs inside this enclosure. Materials used were

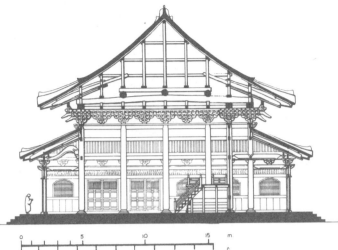

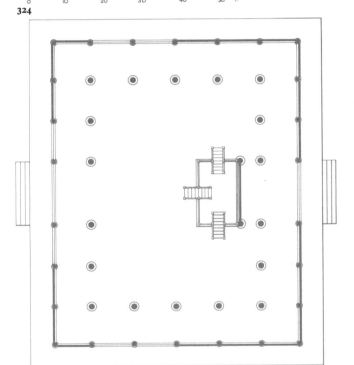

324, 325

326

324, 325 Zen hall, reconstructed from Daitokuji Hatto, Kyoto
Seventeenth century.
Zen teaching demanded a large clear hall with a platform for the lecturer, and a minimum of distraction in the form of images and decoration as an aid to contemplation.
The main load-bearing columns are set well within a light curtain wall.

326 Hoodo (Phoenix Hall), Byodoin temple, Kyoto
Bronze ridge ornament.
Eleventh century.
This type of ornament was developed from the crossed ridge poles of the thatched roof.
The phoenix and cockerel were both sacred to the sun.
The torii or gates were often used as cockerel roosts, for the birds gave warning of daybreak.

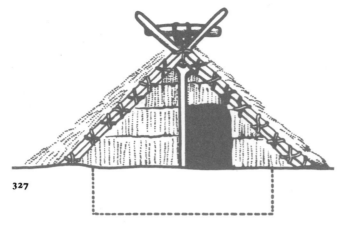

327

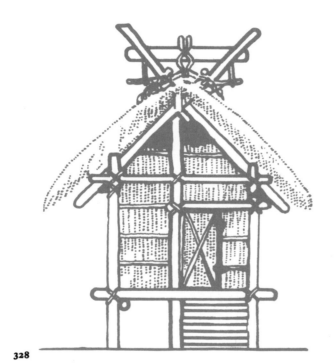

328

329

simple wood and plaster, and roofs were thatched or shingled. Floors were raised on platforms.

The plan provided for public reception rooms, entirely separated from the domestic accommodation of the family; behind, there was provision for servants' quarters, stables and store houses.

The planning only varied in scale, but not in principle, between the houses of the *daimyo* (feudal lords) and the *samurai*. This plan-form, developing in the next period, became the basis on which the Japanese house has been built up to the present day.

In 1274 and 1281 Japan faced the danger of invasion and complete subjugation to the Mongol emperor Kublai Khan. Great military preparations were made to meet these attacks, the second of which might well have succeeded if the invading fleet had not been destroyed in a typhoon.

The disruption and strain of these preparations no doubt weakened the regime, in which the Minamoto had already dropped into second place, surrendering power to the Hojo family, who ruled as their regents.

MUROMACHI PERIOD (1338-1573)

The fourteenth century witnessed another period of internal conflict and civil war involving both the emperor and the ruling class of *samurai*. The re-appearance of the emperor in the political field was short-lived, and Ashikaga Takauji, of the house of Minamoto, became *shogun* (commander-in-chief), and finally established his government in 1339, in the Kyoto district known as Muromachi.

This government was also wholly run on military lines, in the name of the emperor, who remained an isolated figurehead, the powerless captive of an elaborate court ritual.

While the court of the *shogun* lived in the height of luxury, and arts were encouraged and flourished, the countryside and provinces were in a state of constant conflict and poverty, in which old families disappeared and self-made men appeared as local lords.

The Ashikagas continued the support of the Japanese Zen sect of Buddhism and drew many of their advisers and officials from among the monks of the sect.

They were given charge of various foreign trading expeditions, which renewed contact with China, and they returned from these expeditions with manuscripts and many fine examples of south Sung paintings for the *shogun's* collection.

These influences, together with the importance given by the Zen sect to individual meditative exercises and the discipline of self-knowledge, did away with elaborate ritual and stressed the need for quiet natural surroundings, with profound effects on Japanese architecture.

It reinforced and gave full philosophical and official authority for the tendencies we have seen recurring throughout their history; for a studied simplicity and irregularity based on a special approach to natural forms and ways of living. This found its fullest expression in the tea ceremony which has preserved this attitude unchanged to this day.

This ceremony, the *cha-no-yu*, has an elegant and carefully laid-down ritual and equipment of extreme simplicity,

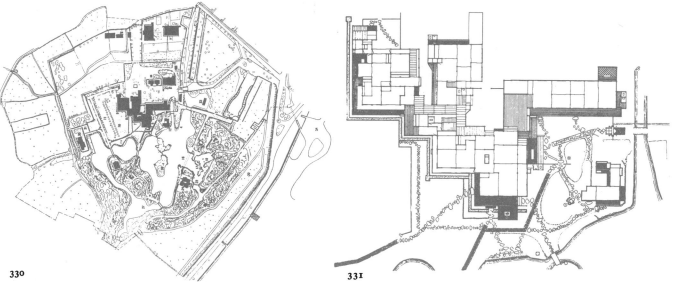

330 Plan of the Katsura imperial palace and its gardens. Kyoto. c. 1620

331 Plan of the shoin and gepparo, Katsura imperial palace
The main complex.

330

331

332

332 The Katsura imperial palace
Aerial view.
This great house epitomises the essentially Japanese form at its highest peak.
The keynote is one of deceptive simplicity which on closer inspection reveals luxurious refinement. The main apartments and small pavilions, summer houses and store rooms are carefully sited in a highly romantic natural garden. The apartments are planned to a module, the controlling factor being the standard straw floor mat, the tatami, whose dimensions are six by three feet. This early use of modular planning, with the consequent standardisation of door and wall panel sizes, together with the use of lightweight panel walling independent of the structure, has been much studied by modern Western architects.

333 Katsura imperial palace, Kyoto
Main entrance.
Japanese gardening and landscaping too has growing influence in the West. There is a great simplicity here which best expresses Japanese taste.

333

334 Shugakuin imperial villa, Kyoto. Built 1655
This apartment was set aside for the important tea ceremony, which may be regarded as a form of symposium under the host, who would direct the topic. The alcove and shelves were intended to display single works of art, a wall scroll or small statue, or a flower arrangement. Tatami are on the floor.

334

335 The shokin-tei, Katsura imperial palace, Kyoto
Instead of doors, whole wall panels could slide back. These panels were often translucent to admit daylight when all openings were closed in cold or wet weather.
The far overhanging eaves of Japanese buildings cut off most direct light, and the interiors were dependent on reflected light from the ground round about.

335

held usually in a room or little house designed especially for this purpose. The members taking part are few; all, irrespective of rank, are equal, and the purpose of the meeting is to converse. The whole is directed by the 'tea-master' who supervises the ritual.

Important elements in this ceremony are the materials and lay-out of the room. The equipment is of the most studied and traditional simplicity, and the focus is the *tokonoma*, a recess for the exhibition of paintings, usually ink and brush, and flower arrangements.

In the palaces, great houses and temples, the painting of the screen partitions assumed a new importance, and beautiful work was done on a large scale, often with brilliant colours, by the school of Kano Momoyama.

The *shoguns* themselves built houses such as the Kinkaku-ji (Golden Pavilion) and the Ginkaku-ji (the Silver Pavilion), set in beautiful gardens for their retirement. 318

One feature of this extraordinarily varied period was the development of the Japanese at sea. Trade developed all down the China coast to the Pearl River, and they were notorious pirates.

As trade increased with the outside world, the ports and harbours assumed a new importance, developing independent and wealthy merchant communities. Through this trade came the first influences from Europe, Portuguese muskets from Macao and the great Christian missionary Francis Xavier.

MOMOYAMA PERIOD (1573-1638)

The Ashikaga *shoguns* failed to keep their control of the provincial *daimyo*, particularly after these had adopted the use of the musket for their foot soldiers. They were driven from power and were followed by three outstanding figures of Japanese history, Oda **Nobunaga**, Toyotomi Hideyoshi and Tokugawa Ieyasu. All were brilliant soldiers, statesmen and splendid patrons of the arts.

Hideyoshi built the palace of **Motonobu** on the outskirts of Kyoto after which this period is named. These three great soldiers and administrators, of whom Hideyoshi is the most colourful personality, between them achieved the unification and pacification of Japan under a strong central government, after years of continuous civil war.

Hideyoshi, who had risen from being a plain peasant-soldier to an all-powerful ruler of the country, initiated much more stringent regulations governing class distinctions and precedence, and based the government on the *samurai*, who were forbidden to enter trade or mix with the merchant class. He also tried, ineffectively, to limit the growing economic power of the merchants.

There was no policy of isolation, and during this period sea-going trade expanded. Europeans, particularly Portuguese, both traders and missionaries, frequented the ports and traded silks and European goods from Macao.

Contact was maintained with China and two great expeditions in 1592 and 1597 were launched through Korea, intended to establish bases for the conquest of mainland territory and an attack on China. Both these expeditions failed.

Europeans at this time, and for nearly fifty years, were on the whole encouraged, and a considerable number of

336

336 The ko-shoin, Katsura imperial palace, Kyoto
The approach to the landing place from the lake and islet.

337

337 The shokin-tei, Katsura imperial palace, Kyoto
The villa in its rich setting of carefully placed rocks, trees and water. The whole ambience of the Katsura group reminds one of the elaborate and graceful tea ceremony, with rooms of varying mood, vistas of charming, simple gardens, lakes, ponds and plants.
The shoin (336), a place for study and contemplation, had the advantage of improved light by the addition of a bay window, a feature introduced during the Kamakura period.

Japanese (more than 300,000), particularly in Kyushu, were converted to Christianity. In this area substantial remains of these foreign missions still survive.

The period ends with the establishment by Ieyasu of himself and his successors as *shoguns* ruling through the *bakufu*. At this time steps were gradually taken to suppress Christianity, and increasing restrictions were placed on foreigners and their entry into the country.

A characteristic activity of all these great rulers, as a part of their policy of stabilisation, was the careful and large-scale reconstruction and repair of the ancient temples and palaces, which had fallen into disrepair, or been damaged in civil war.

302, 305   The most characteristic feature of their building were the great feudal castles of the period, such as those at Osaka, built by Hideyoshi in 1587, Yedo, now a part of the imperial palace at Tokyo, Himeji, Shibata, Matsumoto, founded

304
301   early in the sixteenth century, Nagoya, completed in 1611 and many others.

All these consist of great defensive walls of polygonal dressed stone or granite, with a curious curved batter to resist earthquakes, surrounded by a deep ditch or moat.

These walls are crowned by timber watch towers and dominated by picturesque look-out towers or keeps, built of timber with prominent tiled roofs, several storeys high, to provide living quarters. Within these great enclosures,

303   complete palaces were often built, as at Nijo castle, Kyoto, which contains the palace of Ninomaru.

Important buildings of the period include the temple of Nishi-Hongwanji with its Chamber of Stalks, built by Hideyoshi, the Samboin temple of Daigo and the Kanchi-in of the Toji temple, Kyoto.

YEDO PERIOD (1615-1867)

Ieyesu, by the defeat and deaths of all the surviving descendants of Hideyoshi at the fall of Osaka castle in 1616, achieved complete control for his family, establishing what is known as the Tokugawa Shogunate.

He moved his capital, the *bakufu* headquarters, to Yedo, a village on the site of modern Tokyo, and constructed the great castle there which forms part of the present imperial palace.

The tendency to exclude external influences and foreigners was carried further for fear that internal discontent might become allied with foreign intervention. This policy was hastened by the Christian Shimabara revolt of 1637,

which was put down at once with complete ruthlessness.

Steadily, the Tokugawa regime elaborated its system of controls, including laying down a complete building code based on social position and precedence.

In spite of these restrictions, interest in foreign learning continued to increase, and with the growing use of money in place of rice as the means of exchange the merchant-class continued to grow in wealth and influence. Towards the end of the period many *samurai* were, in fact, hopelessly in their debt.

Official building continued on a large scale—of temples and pagodas at Yasaka and Bessho in 1618, and of elaborate tombs such as those of Nikko to commemorate deceased *shoguns*, built between 1616 and 1636.

The earlier official buildings have much greater interest, for later they became steadily more repetitive and elaborate.

In contrast, the domestic buildings closely related to the tea-houses, and governed by the traditional scale set by the six-by-three foot size of the *tatami* (straw mats) used as floor covering, continued to develop the native style of building and gardening.

The most influential and notable building, which epitomises this essentially Japanese form, is the Katsura imperial palace, built about 1620. This lovely group of buildings with entrance gates, and tea-houses surrounded by a garden and lake of studied informality, was the result, if not actually built under the direction, of the most influential tea-masters of the time. The form continued as the inspiration of domestic building to 1867 and beyond, to our own time.   330-33

Interest also centres on the buildings of merchant town houses, shops, warehouses and bridges. They all show a high degree of skill in design and the simple use of local materials in structure and in details such as screens, trellis and shutters and roof details.

In fact, it is in the popular arts such as these, the Kabuki theatre, and the enormous output of the woodcut artists, that the best and most typical work of the period is to be found.

So that it was from these, the most lively and active elements, rather than from the *samurai*, that the changes under the Meiji restoration were carried out.

The Shogunate was, actually, in a state of internal decay when the increased pressure from European nations, culminating in Commander Perry's forcible intervention in 1857, exposed its weakness. From then onwards its policy was discredited and the isolation of Japan was doomed.

Wheel, Black Pagoda, Orissa

INDIAN

THE CITIES OF THE INDUS VALLEY

The history of Indian architecture must begin with the buildings of the great cities which flourished in the Indus valley between about 3000 and 1500 B.C. There are two chief sites, Harappa and Mohenjo-Daro, lying some 600 miles apart. The mound of Harappa was largely spoiled before it was possible to excavate; most of our information concerning these cities, therefore, comes from the scientific excavation of Mohenjo-Daro.

Both these cities were originally extremely large. They were most carefully planned on a grid system, with main boulevards running right across the city, and the buildings themselves forming rectangular blocks. Both cities were constructed mainly of fired bricks in the English bond. Each contained a high platform which accommodated the walled citadel, and this, in turn, contained a number of large buildings, presumably connected with the functions of government, of most interesting character. The whole city was drained by a system of culverts, the largest of them some eight feet deep. Corbelled arches were used for these culverts, and for some doorways.

The Indus valley house was conceived as a self-contained unit turned in upon itself. Its external walls were battered and were not pierced by any openings. A single passage-way led through from the exterior to the inner court, and in the larger houses this passage-way was guarded by a small keeper's lodge. All windows and doors to the interior opened from the inner court, and access to the upper storeys, of which there may have been at least two plus an open flat roof, was gained by external staircases. Floors and roofs, lintels and stair-treads were made of wood; pieces of charred pine have, in fact, been recovered from the ruins of Harappa, and the walls bear ample evidence in the form of sockets for joists. It is interesting that this part of India, which now is largely semi-desert, or at least cultivated with great difficulty, must at that time have been both exceptionally fertile and contained large areas of forest. The supplies of available timber for roofing and floors, and for firing the colossal quantity of brick, as well as for providing the inhabitants with most of their necessary equipment, must have been enormous.

The buildings on the citadel contained an extraordinary complex which can only be compared with a collegiate building. At Mohenjo-Daro the ground plan of a structure, 230 by 78 feet, shows many cells and small rooms surrounding a court; another contains a bathing pool consisting of a brick-lined and bitumened tank, 39 by 29 by 8 feet, with steps down to the floor, and itself surrounded by a perimeter wall lined with small cells on three sides. It is a generally accepted guess that this complex originally housed the ruling caste of the city, perhaps a college of priests similar to Egyptian institutions. Another building was a hall eighty feet square, with twenty rectangular piers to support the roof. Appended to the citadel was a large granary, the floor of which still survives and contains a well-designed series of air-flues under the floor for drying and preserving the grain. The citadel itself was approached by a long, wandering ramp, which seems, from its calculated avoidance of direct and easy access, to have

served as a processional path, perhaps also playing its part in the defence of the citadel.

A most extraordinary feature of the architecture of these Indus valley cities is that there is no trace of their having been ornamented with plaster work or painting. We know that the visual arts were indeed practised in these cities, and some interesting fragments have been discovered, although all are small. But the buildings themselves, from the largest government palaces, to the meanest artisans' cottages huddled in rows beneath the shadow of the citadel, appear to have been as bleak in appearance as a Lancashire mill town. There may have been coloured mud-facings, but there is another possibility. At the bottom of one of the large domestic storage jars, which were used for clothes and other possessions, as well as for food and liquid, there are traces of a material identified as woven cotton cloth. It may be that ornamental hangings were made of this cloth to cover the bare walls of interiors, just as they are in western India at the present day.

The Indus valley appears to have been immune from the threat of invasion for a very long time. However, the economy may have been subject to some strain, such as a great increase of population in the cities. For, although during their 1500 years of existence these cities retained the original lay-out of their planned grid system, in later times the houses themselves were much subdivided by parti-walls, and conditions of life seem to have become cramped.

Both of these cities suffered a sudden and complete eclipse round about 1500 B.C., by the invasion of a barbarian people sometimes identified with the Aryans. At Mohenjo-Daro, on the circular brick terrace of a well, were found the skeletons of three women lying with their broken pots where they had been struck down, and unburied bodies were lying in the streets. Thereafter, the Indus valley civilization and its architecture disappear from history.

The earliest true structural architecture of India, for which we have evidence, has left no remains, for it was executed entirely in wood. However, in stone-relief carvings of the second century B.C. to the first century A.D., there are many representations of buildings; there are rock-cut caves which imitate the forms of wooden architecture, and there are literary descriptions. Together these enable us to gain a fairly precise idea of the architecture of the time.

The characteristic method of construction was by vertical posts and horizontal beams socketed and pegged with bamboo, with walls of wattle and plaster or brick. The posts may have been set into pots to protect their bases from decay. Large areas were often roofed with a type of barrel vault constructed out of a series of curved wooden members springing from a wooden architrave supported on rows of columns, across which were laid joists supporting most probably a thatch. Railed verandahs, and dormer windows framed in ogival hood mouldings, were characteristic of this form of architecture. One special feature is the kind of railing employed, which consisted of squared-off posts supporting an architrave, and each joined by three railings of lenticular section socketed into

338

XVIII *Kandariya Mahadevo temple, Khajuraho*

the posts. It is probable that these lenticular railings were formed from a pair of the convex-faced first planks, sawn from a circular trunk in the course of squaring it. Railings of exactly this pattern were closely imitated in stone.

THE EARLY FORMS OF ARCHITECTURE

The earliest surviving architecture of India, mainly Buddhist, takes three forms: the first consists of rock-cut preaching caves; the second, of living caves (*viharas*); the third, of *stupas*.

In the hot climate of India, innumerable caves have served generations of religious men as shrines and meditation retreats. Many of the small early caves closely imitate the patterns of conventional structural huts, and have domed or barrel-vaulted interiors (e.g., the third-century B.C. Lomas Rishi and Milkmaid caves in the Barabar hills).

By far the most important type of early cave is the Buddhist preaching hall. This consists of an apsidal basilica-like excavation, with two aisles and a barrel vault springing from a series of columns with pot-shaped bases; it has an ambulatory surrounding a rock-cut *stupa*, and the façade is pierced by a great horse-shoe-shaped window, set in an ogival hood moulding. In the earliest caves of this type at Bhaja (second century B.C.) and Pitalkhora (*c.* 100 B.C.), the rock was intended to be supported and supplemented by an actual wooden construction of roof ribs and external balconies. Later, as at Karle (first century A.D.) and Ajanta caves (first century A.D.), separate wooden members were dispensed with and reproduced entirely in the carved stone. In this series, a great deal of sculpture was employed, much of it figurative, on the column capitals and on panels of the façade. The earlier figures nearly always represent opulently sensuous human couples, sometimes dancing, sometimes riding animals; the later, iconic images of the Buddha and attendant deities. Especially common in the early decorative carving are the rosette and stepped crenellation, while bead and reel mouldings occur. The last of the preaching halls to be cut was at Ellora in the seventh century, and here the ornament shares in the Indian tradition by then developed.

Beside the entrance to these caves was usually placed a monolithic pillar supporting an animal emblem or a Buddhist symbol. These were derived from the well-known Asokan columns, set up during the third century, probably by the emperor Asoka. They were polished monolithic shafts with no base or footings, with bell capitals in the form of a lotus with down-turned petals, supporting on the pericarp an abacus holding a carved animal emblem: bull, elephant, horse or triple lion. These carvings are the earliest works of Indian art of the historical period to survive, and the stone was polished to a mirror-like smoothness which has endured to the present day.

The second type of building, much employed in early India, was the *vihara*. This consists of a courtyard surrounded by small single rooms opening from it. In Gandhara the bases of such *viharas* built of stone have been excavated. They accommodated the monks who lived in the monastery to which the *stupas* belonged, and the courtyards were open in the manner of the typical Asiatic *sarai*. The only examples of such *viharas* to survive are caves cut entirely

338

339

340

341

338 Street in Mohenjo-Daro, Pakistan. Before 1500 B.C.
Brick buildings were laid out on a rectangular grid town plan. The houses may have had corbelled domes. The city was supplied with fresh water and well drained. The whole system has a strong affinity with Sumerian cities.

339 Stupa I, Sanchi
Second century B.C.
The stupa or tope was originally a mound grave, later erected also over sites or relics sacred to Buddha.
The dome later symbolised the universe, the four gates the winds. The dome was surmounted by a many-tiered and gilded umbrella canopy, a form of pagoda.

340 Chaitya hall, Karle
First century A.D.
The original Buddhist chapel was a simple wooden shed with an arched, thatched roof containing a small stupa in an ambulatory. The rows of columns divided the interior into a nave and two aisles.
The nave was lit and ventilated by a horseshoe-shaped window over the main entrance.
None of these early buildings is left, but after the third century B.C. Indian builders began cutting chapels into rock in close imitation of the wooden chapel.

341 Preaching hall, Ajanta. Cave XIX
First century A.D.
In the rock-cut temples the roof follows the horsehoe shape in a simulated barrel vault.
The frescoes of the earlier Ajanta school are here developed into coloured bas-reliefs.
The stupa has a canopy spire reaching almost to the chapel roof.

342 Cave XIX, Ajanta
First century A.D.
At the Buddhist university of
Ajanta there was a series of
twenty-six chapels and schools cut
into the cliff of the ravine,
a secluded site for meditation and
prayer. These halls date from
about the first and second
centuries B.C., to the seventh
century A.D., or later.
The typical entrance with its
horseshoe window and columned
portico shows its timber
technological origin as clearly as
the Greek stone temple.

342

343 Plan of vihara, Elephanta
Seventh century.
The vihara was the living
accommodation for the monks,
based on a cloister and cell
system. It had its origin in the
Aryan family house which is still
the form of the well-to-do
Indian home.
Three or more sets of
apartments are arranged round a
central courtyard. The front
verandah is a great feature.
Here the men of the family sit,
talk and hold council.

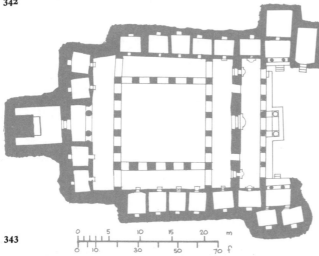

343

344 Buddhist vihara, Ellora
Seventh century.
This cave, known as the Tin Thal,
has the monks' cells arranged
on three storeys.
The central court has become
a pillared hall in order to support
the floors above.

344

in the rock. The earliest of these is probably the small cave, number XIII, at Ajanta, which has polished walls. Most of the great cave-sites of western India have such rock-cut *viharas*, and the evolution of this type during the first seven centuries A.D. represents a leading architectural development on Indian soil. At Ajanta and Ellora especially *viharas* were cut to accommodate the expanding communities of monks. As the size of these *viharas* increased, and upper storeys were added, so it became necessary to support the weight of rock over the large central court by ranges of piers and columns.

During these centuries the façades of the *viharas*, their balconies and the interiors, were increasingly ornamented with relief sculpture and painting, both decorative and figurative. The extremely elaborate decoration was derived mainly from a few basic motifs—the floral garlands, strings of jewels, and rich cloths, with which early custom had, in fact, invested the simple shrines of ancient India. The figurative sculpture was based on iconographic developments that took place during these centuries. A particular feature of importance for later architecture was the adoption of one of the cells in the centre of the back wall of the *vihara* as the shrine for a large cult image—itself usually cut from the rock. As time went on these cells came to be encircled by an ambulatory to allow for *pradakshina*, and then completely detached from the wall.

The third type of early Indian architecture was centred on the *stupa*—a domed structure derived by a process of evolution from the burial tumulus. Old *stupas* formed the focus of the great Buddhist pilgrimage sites. A few feet below the apex is usually placed a small chamber containing relics of the Buddha or of Buddhist saints. The normal Indian mode of paying reverence consisted of walking round sacred objects, keeping them to the right-hand side. This rite is known as *pradakshina*. The earliest architectural development of the *stupas* consisted of facing the dome with stone, and adding a raised terrace with railings and staircases for the performance of this rite. The circular *stupa*, with its terrace, was then enclosed in a larger railing at ground level, which frequently had one or four highly ornamented gateways. Such terraces, railings and gates, either complete or fragmentary and of dates between *c.* 120 B.C. and A.D. 100, have been found at Barhut, Sanchi, Bodh-Gaya and Mathura.

The railing posts were often carved with relief figures of local deities, with elaborate vegetation ornament and narrative reliefs representing Buddhist legends. The ornamentally carved gateways themselves consisted of a series of three separate curved architraves, carried high on solid pillars. There was generally a column near the *stupa*. At Amaravati and other sites in the eastern Deccan have been found the remains of exceptionally fine *stupas*, whose facing slabs and railings of white laminated limestone were carved with a profusion of narrative and decorative reliefs (first to third centuries).

At some of the Buddhist sites the ground plan of an ancient preaching hall has been traced, aligned along an east-west axis with the main *stupa*. This was presumably originally a timber structure, perhaps with brick facings, and it followed the pattern of the apsidal basilica with

345

346

347

345 Side chapel of vihara, Ajanta. Cave XXIII
Seventh century.
Side chapels for private devotional purposes exist for exactly the same reasons as those in Western churches.

346 Vihara, Ajanta. Cave XII
Second century B.C.
This teaching hall is in one of the earliest Buddhist rock-cut monasteries. It has curved architraves, derived from the cross section of the stupa-house, decorated doors and window heads.

347 Preaching hall, Ajanta. Cave XIX
First century A.D.
This chapter house or preaching hall is one of the finest examples of Buddhist architectural design. It is well proportioned, elegant, and the relief decoration is restrained.
Carved bands on the columns have their prototype in the metal bands used to strengthen columns in an earlier timber technology.

348 Gupta temple, Sanchi
Early fifth century.
The earlier form of Hindu
temple consisted of a single cell
with a small, columned portico
attached, an exact parallel
to the cella of Asia Minor and the
Mediterranean.
This is actually a Buddhist shrine,
the earliest example left
in stone.

348

349 Durga temple, Aihole
Late fifth century.
The Hindu development included
a great stone tower over the
shrine. The Durga temple clearly
follows the stupa-house plan,
with an ambulatory round the
shrine. Walking round the
shrine is an important part of the
Hindu rite.

349

colonnade and ambulatory. The ground plan of an enigmatic circular shrine, with interior colonnade, has been
found at Bairat.

Further developments in *stupa* design took place in the
north-western region known as Gandhara, centred on the
valley of the Kabul river. Here *stupas* were constructed
raised high on square plinths, and crowned by enormous
tiers of honorific umbrellas. The most famous of these,
that built at Shah-ji-ki-Dheri, was some 400 feet high.

As time went on, the Buddhist *stupa* evolved a taller
form, and its plinths were contracted into elaborate base-
mouldings. The sixth-century Dhamekh *stupa* at Sarnath is
really a single-domed brick pillar, faced with stone, with
lightly moulded base and bands of incised foliate ornament.

THE HINDU TEMPLE

The evolution of the Hindu temple begins with the village shrine. At the present day, the various stages of evolution may be observed still in progress at different places.
The Indian villager has always been prepared to recognise
the divine in natural objects, whenever it manifests itself.
Thus, an ancient tree with snake-holes at its foot, an
ant-hill or a spring will be recognised as sacred. Gradually
people of substance will provide a carved stone slab to
receive offerings, a railing to keep away cattle, and
sanctify the ground as an enclosure and ultimately a
built shelter for the hallows. Later, this shelter and the
hallows-chamber may be adorned with sculpture, and
an image of the deity may be installed. The earliest
form of Hindu structural temple consisted, thus, of a single
cell with a small portico attached, supported by one or
two pairs of columns. This remained the fundamental
pattern for the temple, although it was subject to considerable expansion and decoration.

The earliest example of this type in stone is actually a
348 Buddhist shrine reconstructed on the hill at Sanchi (c. 420).
By the end of the fifth century, it had become conventional
to add to the roof of the cell a solid superstructure of stone
in the form of a buttressed pyramid with either straight
or curvilinear sides. The early variations (late fifth century)
of this fundamental type are represented by two temples
at Aihole in the Deccan, one of which, the Ladh Khan,
has an enclosed, slab-roofed ambulatory of square plan
349 around the cell. The other, the Durga temple, has an
open verandah-like ambulatory on an elongated plan;
and the great temple at Deogarh in central India (c. 600)
had its central shrine surrounded by four porticoes, and
was raised on a square plinth with four access staircases.
One characteristic and constant feature of the Indian
temple, from the earliest times, was an ornate frame on
the exterior of the cell door bearing sculptured figures
of the purifying river goddesses Ganga and Yamuna at
the base of the jambs, an ornate lintel usually with the
figure of the goddess of good fortune in the centre, and
a series of small panels of amorous couples ranged up the
jambs. From about 600 onwards, it also became conventional to employ a great deal of figure sculpture, chiefly
in panels of narrative or iconic relief, ceiling ornament,
friezes of flying celestials, and vegetation and water deities
on the brackets of the column capitals.

350

351

352   353

**350 Stupa I gate, Sanchi.
c. A.D. 50**
The railings and four triumphal
arches at Sanchi were originally
of plain wood.
This was replaced by elaborately
carved stone as the wood
eventually decayed away.
Names of donors occur at various
sections in both fences and
gates. The original timber form
was therefore followed for
reasons of sacred tradition.
This, the northern gate, is the
finest, the work of a single
master mason possessing unity
which the other, earlier gates lack.
There is only one donor's name
on this gate.

351 Base of stupa, Rajgir
Fifth century.
The stone facings to the stupa
were often carved with relief
figures of local deities, with
elaborate vegetation ornament and
narrative reliefs representing
Buddhist legends.

**352, 353 Stupa I, Sanchi.
c. A.D. 50**
Sculptural details.
Early Buddhist sculpture already
shows the sinuous linear
element associated with India.
The favourite figure pose is the
counterpoised shoulder to hip
with the weight on one leg,
giving a frontal S shape to the
centre line.
The stupa sculptures were
originally covered with a thin skin
of plaster, gilded and coloured.

354 Mullikarjuna temple, Pattadakal
Seventh century.
Sculptural detail.
A great deal of figure sculpture, often telling a story, occurs in relief panels.
They are inextricably woven with architectural ornament and detail.

354

355 Plan of shore temple, Conjiveram
Eighth century.
Under the Pallavan dynasty a more elaborate development of shrine and portico took place.
A hall for ritual dances was added to the portico, and the whole was set in a walled courtyard.
The ambulatory to the shrine was preserved, and the shrine itself was crowned by a massive stone pyramid.

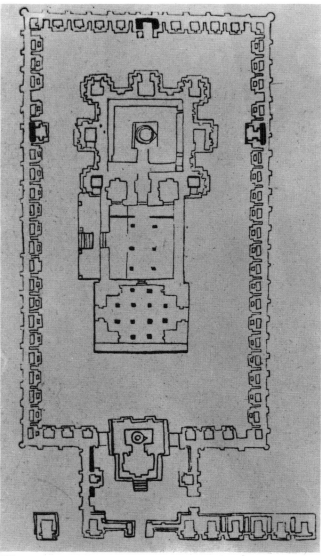

355

On the eastern coast of southern peninsular India, a type of structural temple developed which played an important part in the evolution of Hindu building. This appeared under a dynasty called the Pallavas. The chief characteristics of these temples are that the ground plan of shrine and portico was extended by the addition of a large pillared hall employed as a dance pavilion, sometimes attached to the portico, but sometimes separate. The exterior was adorned with ranges of pilasters, with characteristic round moulded capitals; and at the same time, the mouldings of the plinths on which the temple stood, and of the architrave above the pilasters, were very much developed, the latter with a prominent curved drip moulding. The tower (*shikhara*), above the central shrine, was usually of a regular pyramidal form, and was developed as a series of tiers, each with a prominent curved drip-moulding, and later with a series of miniature blind pavilions.

Opinions are divided as to the origins of this particular temple type, but it seems likely that it originated, actually, at Badami in the Deccan, some time before 600. The most famous examples of this Pallavan style of architecture are the shore temple at Mamallapuram and the shore temple at Conjiveram, *c*. 715. These buildings are elaborated by the addition of a perimeter wall, faced with pilasters and mouldings, ambulatory corridors around the main shrine incorporated into the pyramidal structure, and an entrance hall aligned with the shrine and a dance pavilion. The figure sculpture is of a characteristic restrained style, representing iconic figures of single deities on narrow panels between pilasters; sheer decoration is little in evidence. A characteristic Pallavan pillar is employed on the porticos and on the cloisters inside the perimeter wall, which consists of a caryatid lion, supporting a stump of fluted column crowned by a capital in the form of a fluted circular cushion, supporting a fluted widely expanding abacus. A number of temples in this style are also to be found at Pattadakal in the Deccan, dating from the seventh century. These are mostly of relatively modest size but exhibit the same structural characteristics. They are probably derived directly from the Badami originals.

Before continuing with the discussion of local styles of structural temple it is necessary to consider Hindu cave temples cut in the western Deccan. The earliest of these were a group of small caves at Badami, *c*. 578. These are remarkable chiefly for their extremely fine figure and iconic sculpture cut in very deep relief, but also for the elaboration of pillar types and their profiling. One of the points to which Hindu architects have always devoted the greatest attention is the supporting column. Far from attempting to establish a single formally perfect type, they have applied a great deal of invention and ingenuity to the multiplication of shapes of the capital, its decoration and profiling. Later, the pillar is even developed into a complex of figure sculpture.

The two main groups of Hindu caves are at Ellora and at Elephanta. At Ellora in the western Ghats, there is a large number of caves cut over a period of centuries; sixteen are Hindu. They are characterised by the extreme development of dramatic and vigorously *mouvementé* figure

355, 356

356

357

358

356 Kailasanatha temple, Ellora
Eighth century.
Sculptural detail.
The Ellora style of detailing
– curvilinear decorative elements
and small cartouches –
is evident here.

357 Shore temple, Conjiveram
Eighth century.
The shikhara, or tower over the
shrine, an elaborate
heavy tiered mass of masonry, is
ultimately developed from the
many-tiered umbrella crowning
the stupa, in turn a sign of
respect derived from the badge of
rank over an Aryan
king's tumulus.

358 Kailasanatha temple, Ellora
Eighth century.
The temple was begun by
Krishna I in about 760 to the
glory of his name-god to
whom he attributed his unifying
victory over south India.
It is a technical tour-de-force.
A rock-cut temple, the masons
quarried down into the hill from
above, cutting out a pit varying
in depth from 50 to 160 feet
and leaving in the middle a
detached mass of rock from
which they sculpted a full-sized,
double-storeyed temple.
The plan is symmetrical, of the
Pallavan type. Courtyards and
sanctuaries surround the
central shrine, capped by its
pyramidal tower.

359 Indrani cave, Ellora
Seventh-eighth centuries.
This is the view from one of the
chapels lining the courtyard
towards the seated
figure of Indrani placed
in a sculptured niche.
The elaborate pillars have capitals
of corbelled appearance.

359

**360 Elephant frieze,
Kailasanatha temple, Ellora**
Eighth century.
From the inner courtyard the
temple rests upon a solid plinth
about twenty-seven feet high,
with a sculpture frieze of a
herd of elephants who thus appear
to carry the whole temple on
their backs.
The elephants symbolised the
monsoon rain clouds as well as
strength and fortitude.

360

**361 Sculpture at Elephanta.
The Trimurti**
Eighth century.
The threefold nature of divinity
occurs in both Hindu
and Buddhist doctrine. It is often
portrayed in the latter,
rarely in the former as in this
Trimurti at the temple of Shiva,
Elephanta.
The heads of this colossal bust are
identified as the supreme form
of Shiva in the centre
of the three faces; on the right is
Shiva the destroyer, and balancing
it on the left is the face of
Uma the beautiful wife, or Sakti.

361

sculpture. The first group, the Dasavatara (early seventh century), has two storeys, both planned on the lines of the Buddhist *vihara* with cell at the rear. There are, of course, no living cells around the courts. The second group, on a similar plan, but with a processional path around the shrine, comprises the Ravana-ka-Khai and the Ramesvara (late seventh century) with magnificent figure sculpture. The third is the Dhumar Lena (early eighth century), constructed on a cruciform plan, largely anticipating Elephanta. Ellora is dominated, however, by the great Kailasanatha (300 by 109 by 96 ft), which is a monolithic temple cut from a hillside. Its centre is an originally natural cleft in the rock containing a natural phallic emblem of stone, which had been a subject of reverence for centuries. The upper storeys consist of a single sculpture of a temple of Pallava-Pattadakal type, of the eighth century. The bottom storey with its gigantic figure sculptures was added some hundred years later by the deepening of the floor of the quarry in which the temple stands. Around the walls of the quarry are some of the other caves, in which is represented a vast range of the complex Hindu iconography which was being elaborated during the early Middle Ages. It is clear from many surviving fragments and patches that these works were originally intended to be white-plastered and/or painted as—indeed nearly all Hindu architecture was. The Ellora style of detailing is particularly evident in the curvilinear efflorescence of decorative elements — e.g., brackets, hood mouldings, and small cartouches—which had earlier been kept within rectilinear bounds. Also characteristic are the very numerous panels and bands of miniature figure sculptures representing genre scenes. Again in the Kailasanatha and its attendant caves the columns are splendidly elaborated.

356, 3
360

At Elephanta, an island adjacent to Bombay, the great Shiva temple of the eighth century is well known. This is laid out on a cruciform plan with the centre occupied by a free-standing shrine for a phallic emblem set about with colossal guardian figures, while the rear wall is occupied by the well-known Trimurti, a colossal bust representing three aspects of the god Shiva, and several large panels representing Shiva's legends. Purely decorative carving is almost entirely absent, and the pillars follow a single type with fluted shafts and circular, fluted cushion captials of a contour deeply *bombé*.

361

Of the later forms of Hindu structural temples, so many survive that only the major types can be indicated here. At Somapura (Paharpur) in east-central India, there have been discovered the remains of a colossal, brick-built temple (c. 700) with a high plinth of cruciform plan. It was faced with many large terra cotta panels of relief sculpture. It is most likely that this was a common type in this region up until the tenth century, and influenced architectural ideas in south-east Asia. Other remains of similar design survive at Ahichatra and Nalanda (Buddhist). At Bhitargaon, a large brick pyramidal temple stood on a square, terraced plinth.

Buildings in north-western and central India suffered great devastation at the hands of Moslem invaders. Among the groups of temples that remain is the famous complex

362

362 Alampur temple
Twelfth century.
Door carving.
This façade of a temple in the
south-western Deccan illustrates
certain features which are
characteristic both of the period
and the region, in particular
the pyramidal structures with
deeply incised ornament above the
windows and doorways.

364

363

365

363 Cave XXIX, Ellora
Seventh–eighth centuries.
The caves at Ellora were cut
along the hillside for one and a
quarter miles, and date from
the fourth to the twelfth centuries.
Caves XVI - XXIX
date from the seventh to eighth
centuries, and were mainly
dedicated to Shiva.

364 Alampur temple
Twelfth century. Detail of pillar.
The ornamentation at Alampur is
of a high quality.
The bands of decoration in which
a single motif is repeated
are of varying widths and weight,
yet they combine together
in a totally satisfactory way.

365 Cave XXIX, Ellora
Seventh–eighth centuries.
In the Kailasanatha and its
attendant caves the columns were
splendidly elaborated.

**366 Khandariya (Shiva) temple,
Khajuraho. c. A.D. 1000**
The cella or shrine is crowned
with a massive buttressed
spire. There is no intention of
searching for structural economy.
The spire is an emotional
symbol, a vehicle for displaying
deep homage to the gods in
the form of elaborate
craftsmanship.

366

**367 Khandariya temple,
Khajuraho**
Sculptural detail.
Few surfaces of this giant
man-made stone pinnacle are left
without ritual carving.

367

**368 Muktesvara temple at
Bhuvanesvara, Orissa. c. 900**
The undercut crown
of the deeply gadrooned pinnacle
derives from the original
reed-built shrine.
Tall reeds set vertically were bent
inwards towards the top, their
heads tied together in a bunch.
This knot would be
protected against weathering by
an upturned pot, later the pot or
jar of immortality, the Kalasha.
In Hindu architecture this
is the equivalent of the Buddhist
many-tiered umbrella.

368

of Hindu and Jain structures (tenth to twelfth centuries)
at Khajuraho, in central India. Three of the twenty-five 366, 3
temples that survive of an original eighty may be specially
mentioned: the Khandariya Mahadeva, the Lakshmana
and the Chaunshat Yogini. The two former epitomise the
highest achievement of the Candella architects, and combine features noted in earlier work. The *cella* containing
a phallus or an image, and its porch, together with an
assembly hall aligned with the *cella* door, are enclosed
in a broad, pillared, verandah-like ambulatory. The
whole area comes under the shelter of a vast, many-tiered
roof, which visually preserves the basic form of *cella*
with portico. The *cella* with its ambulatory is surmounted
by a massive buttressed spire, of square plan, with a curvilinear contour, covered with elaborately carved rhythmic
devices, and crowned with the deeply gadrooned, flat
circular cushion, known as the *amalaka* and the pot.
Against the spire the buttresses are developed as smaller
spires, and similarly crowned. Over the area of the assembly
hall rises a less lofty pyramidal roof, terraced and carved.
The long main portico, and three projecting verandahs
at the other cardinal points, are covered by subsidiary
pyramids. The plan is based upon two squares whose
corners are cut off by a diagonal flight of four deeply
stepped-in recessions, thus offering on the exterior several
series of receding profiles.

This exterior is elaborately carved; the plinth with
highly developed and varied horizontal mouldings, consisting of as many as sixteen members, and the rest with a
variety of motifs, including figures framed between
moulded pilasters. From the level of the cell floor, above
the plinth, to one tier above the projecting eaves—which
have an elaborately carved drip-moulding—are four bands
of superb figure sculpture, representing the inhabitants of
the heavens. For the temple itself represents the cosmic
mountain, rising up from earth, through the heavens,
into the beyond. The exterior, in fact, was the prime concern
of the architect offering its elaborate sets of interlocked
rhythmical elements. At Khajuraho the interiors have
finely chiselled ceilings. It is characteristic of Indian architecture that such buildings were not erected as engineered
works from previously cut and shaped stone members,
but were constructed as piles of fitted and roughed-out
blocks that were afterwards finished by stone-carvers.
As only corbelled arches were known in pre-Moslem
India, all walls are massive, and internal volumes are very 370
small compared with external. Various standard symbolic
features are the carved curvilinear brackets between the
entrance pillars, and the lavishly carved jambs and lintel
of the *cella* doorway.

The Chaunshat Yogini temple at Khajuraho is one of
a number of its type known, consisting of sixty-four small
spire-crowned cells arranged around a square (elsewhere
circular), open court. Each cell is dedicated to one of the
Yoginis, feminine divinities whose images each occupy a
cell. The type is derived from the Gandharan *stupa-*
court, and reflects a meditative cult employing a ground-
mandala.

In Orissa, mainly at the great temple-cities of Bhuvanesvara and Puri, with their hundreds of shrines, the

Hindu temple developed more conservatively. Relatively small early shrines, like the Parasuramesvara (*c.* 800) and 368 Muktesvara (*c.* 900, at Bhuvanesvara), preserved the *cella*-portico form, with the portico consisting of a long rectangular chamber, the spire curvilinear and characteristically high-shouldered. External rhythmic decoration was mainly on the spire, the portico-chamber having pierced stone lattices, some formed with figures in relief. The Muktesvara has an interesting stone arched *torana*. The faces of the spires bear cartouches of decorative and figure carving. As usual in Orissan temples, pillars are absent. The series at Bhuvanesvara includes: the eccentric Vaital Deul in which the cell-spire is replaced by a strange transverse pavilion, imitated from a south Indian motif; 9-371 the Rajarani with its multiplicity of buttress-spires, its fine figure carving and perhaps the world's finest foliate relief panels; and the great Lingaraja (A.D. 1000). This has, in addition to the *cella* and portico-chamber, a dance-hall (for ritual dancing) and a large offering hall, all aligned in a continuous structure.

2, 385 The most famous Orissan temple is that at Konarak (the Black Pagoda, early thirteenth century), a huge ruin, never completed. It was conceived on an ambitious plan, the whole building in the form of a chariot dedicated to the sun god, with six ornamental wheels and colossal 386 carved draught horses and elephants to pull it. Its upper terraces bear colossal free-standing sculptures of musicians, its walls a vast number of figural reliefs, mostly of an extravagantly erotic character.

In western India and Rajasthan, medieval temple forms were derived from the same type as appears at Khajuraho. Characteristic developments were: the treatment of the many pillars of the interior with tiers of relief figure , 384 sculpture (Kiradu, Udayaswara, Udaipur, Modhera); 388 the multiplication of verandahs (Larger Sas Bahu, Gwalior); the treatment of the outside of the spire with a regularly banded multiplicity of miniature spires (Udayeswara, Kiradu); and the elaboration of the interior with a multi-386 tude of bracket figures and panels of relief (Mount Abu). In general the evolution here in time tended towards greater decorative elaboration by repetition of identical motifs, and a stiffening both of the ornament and the technique of the figure sculpture.

In the Deccan during the earlier Middle Ages, the temples bore many close resemblances to those of western India, especially in the use of banded spirelets around the main spire. These were arranged one above the other in such a way as to give the appearance of a bundle of punctuated ribs running the whole way up the structure from plinth level (Sinnar, Jhogda).

374 Further south, in Mysore, between *c.* 1050 and 1300, a highly indiosyncratic architecture was developed under the Hoyshala dynasty, built in a greenish choritic schist, somewhat squat in proportions. The plans and ornament display 'rococo' features: stellate plans for the spires; a vast multiplicity of mouldings, e. g., even under the eaves; monolithic polished pillars of great complexity; the whole temple and its polished, sensuous figure sculpture enveloped in lush foliate ornament, undercut often to a depth of eighteen inches.

369

369 Lingaraja temple, Bhuvanesvara. A.D. 1000
According to Brahmanical tradition, this temple was built in the seventh century, but archaeologists have dated it later. The main shikhara is over 180 feet high, a masterpiece of dry stone masonry. It still shows the vestigial form of the primitive reed-built shrine. As Indian architecture slowly evolved from the reed and timber building to the cave, and thence to the free-standing stone building, it never lost its strong conservative backward-looking tradition.

370

370 Lingaraja temple, Bhuvanesvara
Section and plan.
The plan of Lingaraja is an axial grouping of hall, antechamber and cella in one architectural unity, though this is marred today by the later piecemeal addition of shrines and kiosks at its base. Note also the small interior volumes relative to exterior bulk of masonry.

371

371 Lingaraja temple, Bhuvanesvara
Free-standing buildings.
These in turn are as massive as the caves or carved natural pinnacles. They were built as great stone mounds, shaped and carved in situ.
The enclosed spaces, the chapels and chambers, are tiny in proportion to the mass of stone surrounding them.
Not only manpower, but highly skilled manpower, must have been very cheap.

372 Brihadisvarasvamin temple, Tanjore. 985-1018
Like the Kailasanatha at Ellora, the Brihadisvarasvamin is built after a unified plan. The Chola emperor Rajaraja I commissioned it to commemorate further victories of unification in southern India. The principal shrine is on an enormous scale, being 82 feet square, and surmounted by a stupa tower of thirteen storeys, 190 feet high.

373 Great temple, Madura
Seventeenth century.
The great shrine itself tends to be dwarfed at Madura by the massive subsidiary buildings in the temple precinct. The temple grounds are surrounded by a high boundary wall surmounted by towers.

374 Sri Ranganatha temple, Mysore
Between 1100 and 1350, old and new temples received the addition of huge pyramidal gateway towers, or gopurams, arranged in tiers and built first of stone and later of brick rendered with plaster.

375 Plan of the Great temple, Madura
Seventeenth century.
The great temples of southern India are the cities of the gods. They reproduce in their plans the main features of the ancient Aryan sacred town lay-outs. The inner temple is the equivalent of the god-king's palace. The chapter house is the council chamber. They are approached on two main axes, the Rajah's way and the south way, the south being the abode of the spirits of the dead, and therefore sacred as an exit. The plan contains a bathing tank for purification, bazaars, debating and teaching halls and pavilions, law courts and gardens.

376 South gopuram, Great temple, Madura
Sculptural detail.
The smothering of the towers with deep carved relief must be seen as having its function as an act of worship in itself, in the effort and expense of its creation. Its actual content as doctrinal storytelling is secondary.

377 Hypostyle pavilion, Great temple, Madura
One of the flat-roofed pavilions in the main compound surrounding the central shrine.

372

373

374

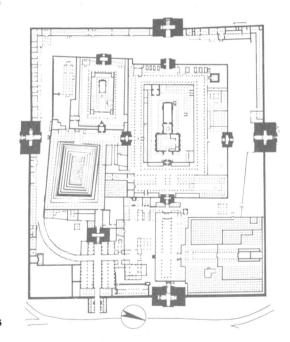

375

376

377

Under the Vijaynagar empire (1350-1565), much architecture was made, related to but a little less ornate than the Hoyshala. The greatest work at the capital was, however, destroyed by the Moslems, who put an army of men to work for a full year on the wrecking. The ruins at Hampi are a famous tourist spot, and the few remains, such as the 'elephant stables' and one or two small shrines, have a romantic appeal. Specially characteristic is the evolution of huge halls (e.g., Vellur, Vitthela, Hampi), with pillars composed of bundles of shafts, or of complex groups of figure sculpture cut in the round.

In the far south, on the Tamil plains, yet another distinct architectural tradition evolved, which is not yet extinct. 372 Its greatest earlier work is the Brihadisvarasvamin temple at Tanjore (985-1018), of stupendous dimensions. It consists of a square *cella*, with purely pyramidal spire, hall, portico and Nandi-pavilion, all aligned within a court. The Nandi-pavilion is a feature of Shiva temples, and contains a monolithic sculpture of Shiva's bull facing the shrine. The *cella* is surrounded, under its tower, by a dark, recessed corridor in which are some of the best surviving medieval wall-paintings. The roofs are tiered pyramids crowned by bulbous domes, and the sculpture between the pilasters, on the relatively plain exterior, is mostly much over life-size. A characteristic moulding consists of a row of gryphon-heads. The abacus of the pillars spreads wide, and combines with the lotus-form beneath it. Pure ornament is at a discount; the decor is composed from purely architectural features and figure sculpture.

Between 1100 and 1350, a new building-type emerged: the *gopuram* (Chidambaram, Srirangam). Old and new temples received the addition of the colossal pyramidal gateway-towers to their surrounding courts, usually at the cardinal points. The tiers of the pyramid above the basic rectangular volume were of stone only on the earlier examples. The later *gopurams* had these upper storeys composed of brick with plaster facings; the well-known external painted figure sculptures crowded onto these upper tiers are, thus, usually modern refurbishings. The basic volume was pierced by a huge tunnel, treated with relief sculpture; the exterior panels between the pillars bore a set of iconic figures embracing the whole *Saiva* system. The *gopuram* was crowned by a transverse barrel, often treated with ornamental projections.

The further development of south Indian architecture took place in the sphere of the temple court, and reached its apogee in the seventeenth century. The concentric rectangular enclosures were multiplied, the *gopurams* of each succeeding enclosure increasing in size to nearly 200 feet in height. Srirangam has five such enclosures. The main shrine, usually an old temple of great sanctity, lay in the centre, and the innermost courts were gradually roofed in, while hundreds of subsidiary shrines and buildings came to occupy the others. The main features of the flat-roofed courts were the colossal hypostyle halls 381 (Madura, Ramesvaram) and corridors up to 500 feet long, lined with pillars. The pillars themselves, or rather piers, were derived from the Vijaynagar columns, and were treated as enormous complexes of figure sculpture,

378 **Vidyashankara temple, Sringeri**
Twelfth century.
The portico is stretched into a long rectangular chamber. The tower is more domical than usual and the curves are echoed by the walls and their engaged columns.

378

379 **Hypostyle hall, Great temple, Madura**
Seventeenth century.
The colossal hypostyle hall has corridors up to 500 feet long. The pillars, or piers were treated as enormous complexes of figure sculpture in the round, with leaping horses, lions, royal retinues, often painted and gilded.

379

380 **Pillared corridor, Ramesvaram**
Seventeenth century.
Contemporary with Madura, this colonnade is a further example of the intricate stone carving of the period.

380

381 **Great temple, Madura**
Entrance to the Sundaresvar shrine. This doorway gives access to the shrine of Sundaresvar, an incarnation of Shiva, and is guarded on each side by huge figures of dwarapalagas or demons.

381

382 The Black Pagoda, Konarak
Temple of the sun god, or Surya Deul. Erected in the reign of Narasimhadeva (1238–64), the whole building was intended to represent a gigantic triumphal car. The tiered pyramid is covered with sculptured figures, often of a highly erotic nature.

383 Sun temple at Modhera, Gujarat, western India
The Gujarat shrines, dating from 1025 to 1298, are of particular richness and delicacy. Built of soft golden sandstone, the carving is at once restrained and luxuriant.

384 Plan of Modhera temple
Eleventh century.
The temple consists of an open pillared porch connected by a narrow passage to the assembly building and thence to the sanctum. The plan is entirely organic with each part of the shrine related logically to the whole.

385 Ornamental wheel, Black Pagoda, Konarak
The wheel did not only represent one of the chariot wheels. It served from early Aryan times as a sacred symbol of the sun, whose daily course was analogous to the course of divine law.

386 Interior of the Dilwara shrine, Mount Abu
Tenth century.
The famous Jian shrines at Mount Abu represent the final culmination of the Gujarat syle. Built entirely of white marble, the Dilwara can be considered among the architectural wonders of the world.

387 Tower of Fame, Chitorgarh. c. 1200
These Hindu towers of victory are the lineal descendants of the pillars of victory. The form here is almost completely obscured by carving.

388 Great Sas Bahu temple, Gwalior Fort, Gwalior. 1093
The temple is divided into three storeys with open loggias separated by heavy architraves. The deep balconies penetrate the mass of the building to render it elegant and light.

382

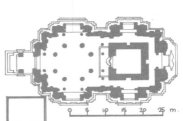

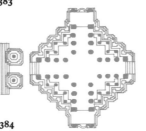
383

384

385

386

387

388

389

390

391

392

389 Kesava temple, Somnathpur. 1050-1300
The Mysore temples of this period have certain characteristics which separate them from the mainstream of Indian architectural development.
Among these is the star-shaped ground plan with temples grouped round a central shrine.
Also characteristic is the high podium and the intricate grill windows with polished pillars, and in particular
the unbelievable richness of the decoration.

390 Sibsagar temple, Assam
Eighteenth century.
This temple, built to the Bengali pattern, consists of a small shrine with a single tower above it.
The stone imitates the form of thatch, and the top is surmounted by the ceremonial umbrella.

391 Temple at Nizambad, in the Deccan
Thirteenth century.
Although partly ruined, the features of the building can still be clearly recognised:
the monumental form, the absence of soft decoration, the massive base.

392 Panchachura temple, Vishampur, Bengal
Eighteenth century.
This temple takes its name from its five-domed towers – the five jewels.
These are arranged over a shallow corbelled 'domed' roof on a central plan.

393 Temple at Palampet, east Deccan
Early thirteenth century.
As at Nizambad the base of the building is deep and heavy, elaborately divided into horizontal tiers.

393

394 Surya temple, Pathan, Nepal. c. A.D. 1000
Typical of the period is the triangular form above the window, and the heavy architrave.

394

395 Angkor Wat, Cambodia. 1112–52
The grandest and most famous monument of the Kmer civilisation.
It was designed like Versailles to celebrate the power of its Roi Soleil, Deveraja.
Rising from the jungle, this vast temple-mausoleum is nearly two and a half miles in circumference.

395

396 Angkor Wat
Ascent to the main shrine and attendant buildings.
The main entrance is along a balustraded causeway leading to a great gateway, beyond which is a gallery richly decorated with reliefs.
A stairway leads up to a square crossed by galleries, and a further staircase leads up again to the turreted pyramid that supports the innermost shrine.
Thus the whole temple is a vast step pyramid.

396

397 Mingalazedi, Pagan. A.D. 1274
The shrine resembles certain Javanese buildings in its relationship of square terraces to circular superstructures.

ultimately completely in the round, with leaping horses, lions, royal retinues, and often painted. The courts contain enormous stepped tanks, surrounded by cloisters, with small island pavilions (Srirangam, Suchendram). Temples like these bring into their orbit many facets of life; some of their corridors are used as bazaars, workshops, meeting-places for religious men, etc. One interesting fact is that modern craftsmen in the south have developed great skill in imitating old styles for the purposes of restoration and development.

Three further local styles must be mentioned. In Kashmir, during the early Middle Ages, stone temples were made (Martand, eighth century; Avantipur, ninth century), related perhaps to central Indian types and close to wooden prototypes. They consisted of plain, tall stone shrines on moulded plinths. Rudimentary porticos supported on pilasters, with high triangular hood-moulded pediments, adorned the four faces. One framed a door, the others, relief panels. The high-pitched stone roofs had a step in them, recalling the tiers of originally wooden gables. They stood in a cloistered court with a single gateway building that was almost an exact replica of the shrine.

In Bengal, a large number of small shrines that consist simply of cells with curvilinear, moulded towers above them were, and still are, built. But the most characteristic Bengali building is the square brick temple, with a high pitched brick roof of curvilinear contour imitating the form of a thatch (Jor Bangla, eighteenth century). The faces of these buildings bear many terra cotta relief sculptured panels, often humorous or propaganda stories.

392

The last type to be mentioned is the post-Moslem architecture of the Rajput palaces and related buildings. Many of these are of enormous size and have been little studied. The most famous monuments are the group executed in the 1730's at Jaipur by the then maharaja. His famous concrete and marble observatory consists of enlargements, to a monumental scale, of the dials of astronomical instruments. His famous palace, Hawa Mahal, presents a façade of five diminishing tiers of hooded balconies with stone lattices.

397

Fretted window in the Medersa Ye'-Khan, Shiraz

ISLAMIC

**398–400 Great mosque,
Damascus. Begun 707**
Exterior, interior, and plan.
The oldest congregational mosque
to survive.
It contains converted Syrian
and Hellenistic temple buildings,
both the hall and the corner
towers becoming minarets.
The interior clearly shows the
deviation from the aisled basilica,
with a triangulated truss-beamed
wooden roof.
A mosque which was used only
for services and meetings was
a large simple hall.
These halls ran along one side of
a courtyard, and were usually
entered by doors in their
long sides.

398

399

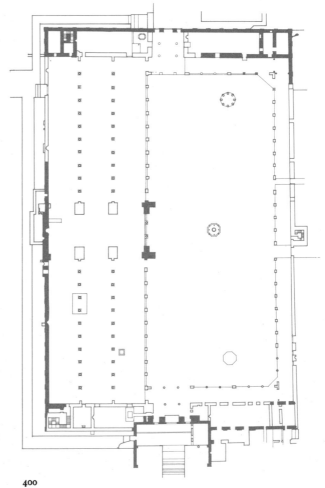

400

THE TYPES OF BUILDING

The earliest major work of Moslem architecture was undertaken in the lifetime of Mohammed (d. 632). This was the rebuilding of the primitive sanctuary of the Ka'ba at Mekka—since replaced. It was carried out by a carpenter, probably an Abyssinian from a wrecked ship, in his native style. For Arabia had then nothing worthy of the name of architecture. The walls were decorated with paintings of Mary, Jesus, Abraham, prophets, angels and trees, as the anti-iconic bias of Islam only arose during the eighth century, and was enshrined in the *Hadith*, not in the *Koran*.

The principal architectural types of Islam are the mosque, the tomb, the fort and the palace. Public baths, fountains and lesser domestic architecture above peasant level employed features drawn from the major types. The mosque is fundamentally an enclosure for prayer, and the focal point for the brotherhood of Islam. It need not necessarily be roofed, as it was not in early times or later in India. Along one or more walls may run roofed or vaulted colonnades, which attracted architectural invention. The entrance gate and doors were also subject to architectural elaboration, and the form of many of the Islamic tombs (e.g., the Taj Mahal) is derived from the type of the gate pavilion.

415 Inside the mosque are five principal features: the *mihrab*, the *minbar*, the screen, the massive desk to support the *Koran*, the fountain for ablution. The *mihrab* is a niche in the wall marking the direction of Mekka (introduced first at Madina, 707), toward which Moslems direct their prayer; it was most frequently adorned with bands and panels of ornament. The *minbar* is a raised pulpit, often canopied, with a staircase. A screen may form an enclosure round the *mihrab*, and is said to provide protection, while he is at prayer, to the sultan or governor, whose official residence is frequently appended outside on to one wall of the mosque. The *Koran* desk is frequently a stone structure supported on pillars, and the fountain may have its arcaded canopy.

The earliest great mosques were built in Iraq, at Basra and Kufa, by native craftsmen, as were most of the early mosques in conquered territories. They were roofed, with archless colonnades whose columns were taken from pre-Islamic buildings—another very common practice in Islam. It was in Egypt, however, about 673, that the four corner minarets seem to have been first added to the complex. They may well have been derived from the corner towers of the Syrian Hellenistic temple *temenoi* which had been converted into mosques, as in the case of the great mosque of Damascus, the oldest congregational mosque to survive. Elsewhere (e.g., the mosque at Qairawan), a single huge minaret towered in the centre of one of the enclosing walls.

The earliest existing monument of Moslem architecture (begun 643), the work of craftsmen from all over the Islamic empire, is the Dome of the Rock at Jerusalem, said to be on the site from which Mohammed made his night journey to heaven. It is of the 'rotunda' form followed by Christian churches in Jerusalem, the outer lower storey of octagonal plan, the inner circular colonnade around the Rock supporting, on four piers and twelve columns, a clerestory with sixteen windows, domed originally with a wooden dome. It is remarkable both for the extreme clarity

401

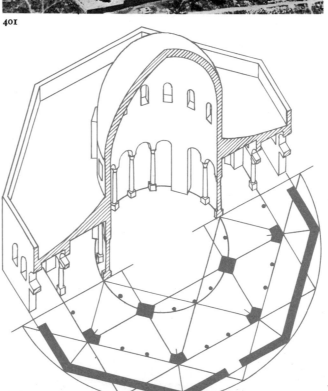

402

403

3-400
406

-404

401-403 **Dome of the Rock, Jerusalem. Begun 643**
The earliest existing monument of Moslem architecture stands on the site from which Mohammed is said to have made his night journey to heaven.
It is also the legendary site of Abraham's sacrifice, and of the Great Temple.
It is one of the oldest sacred sites in the world, Judaic, Christian, as well as Moslem.
It is one of the finest compositions, too. The great golden dome is set over an octagonal rotunda, echoing Graeco-Byzantine form and technique.
The site is distinguished by a well, sheltered by a small domed cupola. The relation of fresh water to any holy site, both for refreshment and purification, is an essential factor in Middle Eastern architecture.

404 Dome of the Rock, Jerusalem. Begun 643
The well-proportioned
exterior was originally covered
with rich mosaic.
A dome signified either a tomb
or a shrine, and only occurred in a
mosque which was or
intended to be a burial place.

405 Desert palace, Mschatta
Ornamental frieze. Eighth century.
The zigzag trace ornament is
balanced by symmetrically
placed rosettes and covered with
finely worked floral scrolls.
The line and rosette motifs
have their origin back in Persian
Archaemenid times.

406 Qairawan tower, Tunis. Begun 670
A single huge minaret tower
occupies the centre of one of the
enclosing walls,
a development of the fortress
gate combined with a landmark
that indicated the sheltered
enclosure for travellers,
the 'caravanserai', the basic form
of Moslem plan.

404

405

406

of its proportions and for the richness of its ornament. Originally the exterior, like the interior, was covered with mosaic. Capitals were carved with typical formalised acanthus scrollwork; there was marble 'veneer' work; the mosaic inside followed a wide variety of abstract and scrolled patterns; under the tie-beams of the semi-circular arches were metal plates worked in *repoussé* in the same manner. Sassanian and Coptic, as well as Syrian, elements can be recognised in the ornament.

The Dome of the Rock was a 'shrine'. The earliest stone mosque extant, that of Damascus (begun 707) on the rectangular plan of the *temenos*, preserves traces of a similar rich internal decor. Here, however, survive the first known examples of what was to become one of the greatest ornamental glories of Islamic architecture, the pierced stone window-grilles, laid out on complex geometrical schemata—another extension of an older Roman-Byzantine conception.

The earliest group of Syrian desert palaces lays the foundation for further developments. Quasayr'Amra, the earliest (*c.* 715), was a modest complex of buildings with low stone pointed arches, vaulted and domed with pendentives, not squinches, in stone, ornamented with figurative frescoes and a glass mosaic paving. This was a type of palace much repeated, on various scales, in Syria. The most impressive of them is Mschatta. This is a square, walled enclosure of brick (eighth century), with corner towers and five half-round towers to each side. Interior building, including a three-apsed hall, remained in various stages of completion. The most striking feature is its luxuriant bands of highly formalised relief ornament.

Under the 'Abbasid dynasty in Baghdad the most influential patterns for later architecture were laid down. Baghdad was itself originally a city planned from scratch. In 762, thousands of workmen were assembled and the work began. The plan is said to have been first traced with lines of ashes on the ground, so that Khalif Al Mansur might see it clearly. It was circular, some 2,638 metres in diameter, with four gates named after the provinces towards which they opened. The brick walls bonded with reed matting at least were finished within four years. Each of the gates —with bent entries—had an audience hall above it, roofed with a gilt dome. Isfahan was also said to have been founded originally on such a circular plan, approximately 3,000 metres across. At the centre were the palace and the great mosque. The palace, with its huge tunnel-vaulted hall and green dome, was built under the influence of lingering Sassanian conceptions of regal glory. These were probably responsible for the 'Abbasid fondness for palaces with such great audience chambers, usually domed, and ranges of public rooms.

Under the 'Abbasids, the form of the mosque varied widely. The older archless type was common. At Raqqa and elsewhere, roofs rested on arcades. Some, like the great mosque at Susa, were vaulted, with a dome crowning the area before the *mihrab*. The exterior wall of the colossal brick mosque at Samarra (842), like that at Raqqa, is punctuated with half-round towers resembling the fortifications of a city. Samarra is also notable for its stucco relief ornament. Some are in a style clearly derived from that of

Margin references: 47, 407 · 405 · 409

407

408

409

407 **Blue mosque, Isfahan**
Eighth century.
Fretted and inlaid window.
The fretted window has functional advantages in a scorching, arid climate.
The intricate decoration carries on from the Byzantine tradition. This was given added impetus by the strict observance of Mosaic law forbidding iconographic reference to men and animals. Instead, floral and geometric patterns were developed to the ultimate degree.

408 **Mihrab of Sultan Oljeitu, Masjid-i-Jami, Isfahan**
The niche with its decorative arches and non-structural pilasters is yet another variation on the symbolic door or gate to heaven.

409 **Gate section, Baghdad. Begun 762**
Baghdad was built on a circular plan with four gates at the cardinal points, a form which occurs again and again, as the Temple of Heaven, from Asia Minor to China. The gates had a bent entry for defensive purposes, a device adopted by the Crusaders. Over the Baghdad gates were audience halls for customs and credential examination.

410 Ibn Tulun mosque, Cairo. 878

The driving force behind Islam was the nomad, and nomadic influence is clear in later development. The form becomes non-urban, based on the walled, fortified enclosure round a well — oasis architecture.

410

411 Qairawan mosque. Begun 670

The earliest of the North African mosques outside Egypt.
Being desert architecture, the mosque is essentially an arcaded courtyard, blank to the outside, elegant and well proportioned within.
The aisles use antique columns.

411

412 Ibn Tulun mosque, Cairo. 878

The pointed Moslem arch and dome derive from the use of brick rather than stone.
The brick is corbelled rather than segmented as a true arch.
The opposing sides of the arch or dome 'lean' one against the other. The thrust is quicker converted into downward dead weight, and less massive buttressing is needed to take side thrust than with the semi-circular arch.

413 Ibn Tulun, the minaret

The minaret is developed from the watch tower and landmark for the traveller's shelter.
The crenellations, vestigial fortifications, are more decorative than functional.

412   413

Mschatta, with its rosettes and triangles filled with floral scrolls. Some exhibit features (stepped crenellation with rosettes) that hark back to Achaemenid times.

An especially important development that took place in the eighth and ninth centuries, during the 'Abbasid Khalifate, was the evolution of ranges of roofed arcades at right angles to the wall in which the *mihrab* was set, thus producing the effect of an aisled sanctuary. The Aqsa mosque in Jerusalem is an outstanding example (c. 760). This can be traced westwards through the mosques of Ibn Tulun (Cairo) and Qairawan (Tunis) to Cordova. The square minaret of Qairawan was likewise carried to Cordova to become the pattern for western Islam.

EGYPT

The mosque of Ibn Tulun contains the most important early construction (878). The arcades of the enclosure and of the east end, which are in brick, are of 'Abbasid date. They consist of extremely elegant pointed arches that spring from pairs of round pillars engaged in broad, plain and strong piers. The arcade is united by bands of stucco palmettes that run as dados, and continue around the arches. On the soffits of the arches appear sophisticated geometrical designs. Into the spandrels of the arcade are set small arched windows. As is characteristic of all the early Egyptian mosques, the brick construction was given sumptuousness by surface treatment with stucco, paint and gold, whereas in Syria, the Byzantine tradition of precious marbles, ornate metal panels on walls, arches, doors, and mosaic prevailed. In both regions, however, antique columns with their capitals were re-used. In Cairo, the mosques of Amrou, El-Azhar and others employ them.

El-Azhar is of the greatest interest; begun in 971, it was frequently restored or rebuilt. Here was set up in 974 what is now the oldest university in the world. Attached to the mosque, whose sanctuary was used for teaching, were many auxiliary rooms to accommodate the students. Two especially important features are found here, which became the basis for much later development. First, below the oldest pointed dome—slightly ogival—above the entrance, the transition from the square volume to the octagon is treated neither with true squinches nor pendentives. The diagonal faces of the octagon are opened by deep arched niches, which have their ends standing in space like stalactites. Second, there are long continuous bands of Kufic inscription in stucco relief which follow the architecture.

The last Fatimid monument, the small, stone-built mosque of El-Akhmar in Cairo (begun 1125), exhibits a later stage of these features. Flanking its arched pediments are panels of inset stalactite ornament, and beneath the projecting balcony of the minaret are similar forms derived from the false squinches; the stone-cut Kufic is superb. Here is introduced a new ornamental feature—the filling of deeply inset pediment-arches with shell-like angular fluting which radiates from a circular cartouche. This is connected with the fluted squinch-arches of the dome at Qairawan. The unusual stone construction, like the contemporary fortifications of Cairo, is derived from Syrian examples, through the intermediacy of Syrian architects, who employed Byzantine methods.

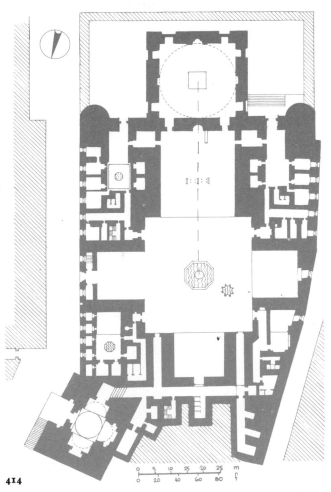

414

415

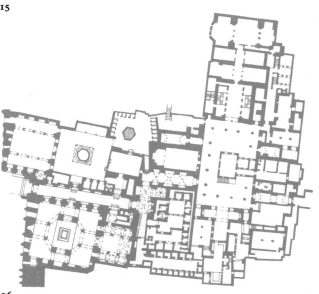

416

414 Plan of Sultan Hassan mosque, Cairo. 1362
The cruciform mosque was introduced into Egypt by Saladin. The four arms were related to the four rites of orthodox Islam.

415 Ibn Tulun, Cairo. Mihrab and minbar
The mihrab is a niche in the wall directed towards Mekka. The minbar is a raised pulpit with staircase, often canopied. In the Ibn Tulun mosque, the mihrab was set in a system of arcades which gave the effect of an aisled sanctuary.

416 Qalawun complex of buildings, Cairo. Begun 1284
The site contained two mosques, two mausoleums and a hospital. All the buildings correspond to one form or another of the cruciform plan.

**417 Qait Bey mosque, Cairo.
1436-80**
This funerary mosque for
Qait Bey uses two-toned materials
in horizontal bands.
This technique became typically
Cairene.
The minaret has three concentric
tiered galleries.
The jutting out machicolations
developed in Byzantine
fortifications are their prototypes.

417

**418 Qalawun mosque, Cairo.
Begun 1284**
Detail of columns and window.
The numerous Roman ruins provided columns, capitals and
ready-made building materials.
Roman capitals were adapted
to their own use by Arab
craftsmen, sometimes in a
rough and ready or structurally
incongruous way.

418

The next era of Egyptian history was marked by the introduction, under Saladin, of the mosque of cruciform plan, to accommodate the four rites of orthodox Islam. At the same time, the development of the centrally planned mausoleum of the ruler took place. The complex of two mosques, two tombs and a hospital, built by Qalawun in Cairo (begun 1284), is an outstanding work. All the buildings correspond to the cruciform plan.   416, 4

The crowning architectural achievement of Islam in Egypt, however, is the work carried out for Qait Bey (1436-80). Some was devoted to refurbishing El-Azhar, but the most distinctive was the construction of his palace and funerary mosque. The latter, another banded structure, is dominated by the huge pointed horseshoe-arch of banded stonework before the *mihrab*. The interior contains a number of the arched niches lined with stalactite; the exterior of the dome and part of the towering minaret bear relief geometrical surface ornament. The great use made of two-toned material and the double arch are both strongly reminiscent of Spanish Moresque. The former technique later evolved into the typical Cairene black-and-white geometrical design (e.g., Bordeini mosque, 1628).   417

NORTH AFRICA AND SPAIN

The great mosque of Qairawan (begun 670) is the earliest   406, 4
building of this school. Its external walls are plain, with   419-4
rectangular buttressing. All its external members are of massive proportions, the square minaret, as well. Just under half the length of the plan is occupied by the sixteen-aisled sanctuary. The colonnades that support the sanctuary roof are of superb and delicate proportions, resting on antique, cylindrical columns, and the arches are the round horseshoe kind characteristic of this region, resting on deep dies above the capitals. The earliest known Islamic glazed faïence tiles—imported, no doubt, from Persia—are set in the wall around the front of the *mihrab*, and on either side of its doorway stands a unique pair of columns of red and yellow porphyry from Carthage.

In several later mosques are found colonnades of similar design to those at Qairawan, though of less elegant pro-portions—for example, at Sfax (ninth century), in the great mosque of Algiers (1018) and Tlemcen (1240). At the last two places, however, there occurs, as well, the extraordinary Moslem invention, related aesthetically to stalactite ornament: the deeply scalloped arch—here the   420
horseshoe. One finds both arch types of the structure combined to frame the head of the *mihrab* at Tlemcen mosque. In the actual arcades of Sidi Bou-Medina, also at Tlemcen, there is a yet later adaptation in the use of the scalloped arch as a moulded enclosure for the horseshoe, both set in a flat rectangle of ornament. In fact the colon-nade became exceptionally important in western Islam, because the roofed areas of sanctuary and cloister came to predominate much in size over the area of the open court. At Tlemcen, for example, the court occupies less than one-quarter of the area of the whole. The rest, typically, bears on the flat frieze above its arcades a flat timbered roof, with low domes incorporated at salient points, e.g., over the bays before the *mihrab*, the entrance, occasionally elsewhere. An especially characteristic feature

419

420

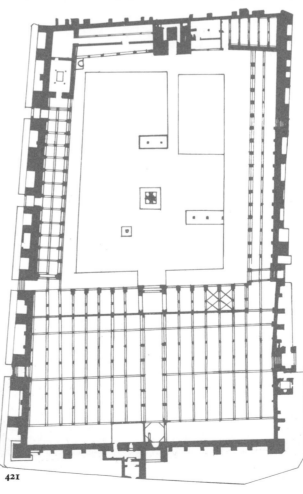

421

419, 421 Qairawan mosque, North Africa. Begun 670
Interior and plan.
Nearly half the plan is taken up by the sixteen-aisled sanctuary. The brick arches rest on antique columns. The tie bars are part of the original structure.

420 Qairawan mosque, late scalloped arches
This type of arch represents a complex idea. Elements are the closing roots of the horseshoe arch, and stalactite ornament. The form as such may have been suggested by the exposed elevation of the scallop-moulded lining of a headed niche, e.g. the mihrab.

422 Gate at Chella, North Africa
Twelfth century.
The octagonal towers were built with obtuse angles to deflect bombardment and battering. They are capped with square platforms which overhang as a form of machicolation.

422

423 Buttress tower, Marrakech
The enormous walls are buttressed by equally massive towers. The decoration may be compared with European Gothic interlacing and tracery. The lower arch is an interlaced form of the reverse curve or ogee arch.

423

of North African work, perhaps originating in Spain, is the small, flat porch-like roof projecting from the uppermost part of the door-setting, high above the entrance. Its underside is treated ornamentally (e.g., Sidi Bou-Medina, thirteenth century). This form is still found carried out modestly in wood on houses (e.g., the Kasbah, Algiers).

A number of first-class medieval secular structures survive in North Africa. Among them are the massive walls of Marrakech, with their colossal rectangular buttress-towers; the bridge and dam at Tebourba, Tunisia; the fortified gate of Mehedia, Morocco; and the superb gate at Chella, whose plain octagonal flanking towers support rectangular summits, the projecting angles being underslung with stalactite niches.   423   422

In Spain, the Arabs were able to employ not only architectural fragments from the Visigothic buildings they destroyed for their purposes, but also their techniques. The earliest surviving great monument, the mosque at Cordova (begun 786), is full of actual fragments and technical reminiscences. Here the arcades resemble in design those of Qairawan and Sfax; their stonework is banded with two tones. An interesting technical resource that harks back to Rome (e.g., aqueduct at Merida) was adopted to give the necessary height to the vast expanse of flat roof. The arcades were doubled, a second arcade standing clear above the first. Only the *mihrab* chamber was vaulted, with an octagon based on intersecting horseshoe-arches. Exceptionally interesting is the structure of the enclosure before the *mihrab*. Its colonnades are not only doubled, but the lower arches are scalloped, and the spaces of the upper arcade are occupied by scalloped half-arches springing from the centres of the lower arches. The ornament is lavish: blind arcades, some interlaced, of scalloped arches, geometrical window grilles, areas of lively if formalised floral invention, and some areas of Spanish repeat-pattern.   425, 427

The Alcazar of Seville was originally the palace of the Umayyid commander, and reached a peak of finish in the twelfth century. It has, however, been repeatedly reworked since. The oldest part is probably the Hall of Ambassadors. This architecture preserves the relatively simple general forms of older North Africa: antique columns supporting plain horseshoe-arches. The whole interior, however, is lined with an enormous variety of polychrome tiles. Some fragments of old carved stucco are preserved. The exterior exhibits high projecting porches with stalactite ornament.   428,

The Alhambra, Granada (begun 1230), the palace of the rulers of Granada, is perhaps the most famous of the works of classical Moslem architecture in Spain. Externally it resembles an imposing fortress; internally it displays the most sumptuous design, laid out with gardens and enclosed courts, with luxurious chambers and a mosque. The whole interior is incrusted with painted plaster ornaments, and with stretches of glazed and lustred tiles. The structure, however, is light, of mud-brick with burnt-brick facings, and the roofs are of wood with plaster revetments. The delicate arcades follow several arch-patterns: some are horseshoe, some are high, slightly pointed round arches; the most characteristic, however, are flat, almost triangular, pointed arches, from which depends an extraordinary efflorescence of plaster stalactites. The upper corners of rooms   430-4

424

425

424-427 Mosque at Cordova. Begun 786
The great arcaded hall is based on that of Qairawan.
The structure before the mihrab not only has double arcading but the arches are scalloped.
The second tier of arches springs from the crest of the first.
The dome over the enclosure before the mihrab is carried on two intersecting vaults, square in plan.
They complement each other as binding arches and produce an octagonal centre.
Structure and decoration are combined in exceptional comity.

426

427

428 Alcazar, Seville, Hall of Ambassadors
Twelfth century.
Parts of the structure of the Hall of the Ambassadors are the oldest part of the Alcazar.
It is lined with later polychromed tilework in rich geometrical patterns.
The most complicated interlaced patterns were built up from simple repeating units.

428

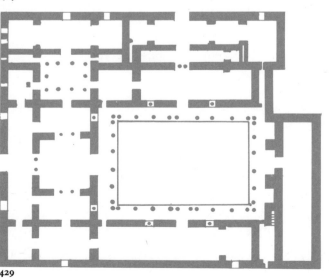

429

429 Plan of the Alcazar, Seville
The plan is simple.
Chambers are arranged round an arcaded, lined courtyard with the inevitable running water.
The whole is inward looking.

430 Court of the Lions, Alhambra, Granada
Second half of fourteenth century.
Shelter from hot sun by day and cold winds by night,
with fresh running water nearby, was the desert dwellers' idea of Heaven.
Mosques and palaces were built round this theme.

430

431 Court of the Lions, Alhambra
'Stalactite' detail.
The so-called 'stalactite' detail is derived from the corbelled squinch made up of successive layers of brick.
The individual layers were first scalloped out for lightness both in weight and space.

431

432 Salon de los Ajimeces, Alhambra
Detail of ceiling.
The Islamic dome was built up of successive layers of flat brick courses laid concentrically and gradually closing in.
The inside of the dome was therefore stepped in appearance, but these tiers were usually filled up and smoothed out in plaster.
It later became the practice to leave these steps of brick which were fancifully carved and scalloped. The squinches or corners where the dome is married to the right-angled walls were first treated in this manner; eventually the technique spread to the whole dome.
The resulting patterns form diminishing spirals, similar to the surfaces of fir cones or pineapples.

432

are similarly incrusted, as are the brackets of beams. Some of the flat ornamental panels of plaster work give evidence of substantial invention. By far the larger part of the ornament, however, consists of hundreds of identical repetitions of a single motif.

Spanish traditions, in fact, lingered on in North Africa, especially in Morocco. Such buildings as the Sultan's palace in Tunis reveal their Spanish Moresque origins. Down into the fifteenth and sixteenth centuries the tradition remained alive. The ornamental style, however, stiffened, and design was subjected to stricter geometrical restraints. Outstanding buildings are the palace of Hussein, Tunis, the palace of Arsat-ben-Abd-Akath, Fez, and many large private houses. Even in these later buildings one finds arcades sporting superb ancient pillars, Byzantine or classical, complete with their Corinthian capitals.

MESOPOTAMIA AND PERSIA

In this region, a generally consistent architectural style developed for the mosque. This was marked by a fondness for large areas of plain surface. Domes are smooth and pointed, arcades favour the pointed arch with massive plain piers, minarets are round and tapering, with a single ornamented balcony. Punctuation by columns and capitals is discountenanced, and huge continuous stretches of ornament —shallow stucco relief, brilliant glazed tiles, ceramic *opus sectile*, etc.—came to be applied to walls, domes and arches, both inside and out. Following the techniques of pure brick construction, each bay of arcades is frequently roofed with its own small, shallow dome; indeed Persian builders developed a virtuosic facility in the construction of brick domes and vaults. The mosque entrances are set under colossal arches framed in a plain rectangular façade, which is often flanked by a pair of circular minarets. However, the virtuosity of Persian building in its pursuit of exotic patterns was essentially ornamental though carried out in structure. Complex vaults or domes following stellate plans, tiered squinches developed after complex curves, so as decoratively to fill a colossal arch, were, in fact, subject to a drastic quadratic simplicity. A harmonious proportion of simply faced masses was the basis of the design.

In the Masjid-i-'Ali Shah of Tabriz (fourteenth century), the stupendous faces of bare brick reveal the fundamental power and simplicity of Persian invention. The extravagant and fantastically varied polychrome ceramic ornament, with which the sixteenth- and seventeenth-century work at, say, the Blue Mosque at Tabriz, or the Masjid-i-Jami at Isfahan, is covered inside and out, is never allowed to disturb the tenor of the main features.

The mosques of Persia were so repeatedly reconstructed that there is little really early work intact. The Tarik Khana at Damghan (eighth to ninth centuries) shows the earliest form of arcade—squat, round pier and pointed arch. Mosque plans varied a great deal. Some were broader than long, with as many vaulted aisles along the side walls as at the sanctuary end (Nayin, tenth century). Others may have emphasised the tunnel-like approach to the *mihrab*. (Nayriz, also tenth century.) The court of the Masjid-i-Malik at Kirman is vast in proportion to its arcades, while the great Masjid-i-Jami at Isfahan (tenth century and

433–4

433

434

435

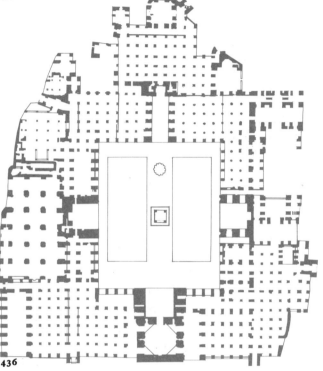

436

437

438

433 Entrance to the Masjid-i-Jami, Isfahan
Tenth century and later.
Persian Moslem architecture
is noted for its elaborate ornament
which spreads everywhere.
The exotic patterns, however, are
never allowed to dominate
the structure, but are subordinated
to it. In the entrance to the
Masjid-i-Jami, tiered squinches are
used one above the other to
fill the arch and transform it into
an enormous geometric apse.

434, 436 Masjid-i-Jami, Isfahan
Entrance gateway and plan.
The sheltered courtyard and
ceremonial gate are still
the essence of this complex plan,
much rebuilt and added to over
nine centuries.

435 Masjid-i-Jami, Isfahan
Detail of apse.
The Moslem use of architectural
inscriptions both in cursive
and the very geometric Kufic
scripts have never been paralleled
in Western architecture.

437 Vault detail
A further example of Persian
vaulting, showing the elaborately
devised frets to the windows.

**438 Gowhar Shad mosque,
Meshed. 1418**
The shrine of Imam Riza,
an Islamic martyr, was built
continuously from the eleventh to
the nineteenth centuries.
This mosque built at the order
of Queen Gowhar Shad, with its
intense colour, is one of the
finest buildings in the Imam Riza
complex, which consists of
several mosques, colleges, libraries
and offices.

439 Masjid-i-Jami, Yezd, Persia. 1362
This finely proportioned entrance is based on a geometrical pattern three squares high. Arch and pinnacle height, and other elements, are based on the 'golden section'.

440 Tomb of Chah Chiragh, Shiraz
Fourteenth-fifteenth centuries. The dome is of a flamboyant bombé shape, covered in tiles. The basic angular unit of these tiles produces a design matching that of the stepped patterns of the Shiraz carpet.

441 Door of mosque. Indjeminareli, Konya, Turkey. 1251
Interlaced and palmette designs fill the arcade above a range of engaged columns like those flanking Western church porches. Both may derive from early Syrian and Armenian church architecture.

442 Tomb of Timur (Tamerlane), Samarkand. 1405
Persian and central Asian domes resemble the Cairene but with an additional slight swell at the base. In section they are of the shape of a Saracen helmet. They were sometimes gadrooned, ribbed or fluted like giant melons.

443 Portico, Chihil Sutun palace, Isfahan. c. 1700
This porch with its trabeated construction comes directly from the Graeco-Persian tradition.

439

440

441

442

443

later) is on a cruciform plan, extended into a vast series of domed and vaulted arcades. The shrine of the Imam Riza at Meshed, perhaps the best-revered spot in Persia, contains more than one mosque. It is a vast complex of courts, buildings and corridors of such extreme lavishness of ornament with a huge gold dome and minarets, gold gateways, silver and gilt doors, as to transcend description. It was built from the eleventh to the nineteenth centuries.

In Persia, there survives a great deal of architecture apart from the mosques. There are, for example, many mausolea of the great, which display exuberant invention in their design. The early mausoleum of Ismail the Samanid (907) at Bukhara is a battered cuboid, with pillars at the corners, and a low dome, whose wall is geometrically rusticated. Similar types were frequently made for several centuries. Especially interesting, however, are certain funeral towers with conical domes. These are gadrooned, fluted, or triangularly buttressed cylinders with various solutions applied to the ends of the vertical features (Gurgan, Gunbad-i-Iabus, 1006; Varamin, Ala-ad-din, 1289; towers at Ghazna, e.g., Masud III, 1114). The tomb of Timur (1405), which follows the general pattern of the mosque, is dominated by a massive circular tower crowned by a gadrooned dome of slightly *bombé* contour.

There, is however, one type of building which employs entirely different structural principles from those of vaulting and brick arcades. This is the peristyle portico or cloister of wooden pillar and architrave construction, with projecting eaves and flat roof. The pillars are narrow and tapering, and stand usually on tall carved bases. The ancestry of this type is ancient, reflecting the pattern of the Achaemenid hypostyle hall, carried down the ages at the level of humble domestic design. It was a method much used in Turkestan, but known in Samarkand (Koh-Tach) and in Isfahan, for example, the palace of Chihil Sutun (rebuilt *c.* 1700).

TURKEY

Turkish architecture proper begins in the fourteenth century, with the establishment of the Ottoman empire. It owes its origins to Persian types, but it was subject to strong influences from Byzantium. Indeed, as their penetration of previously Byzantine provinces progressed, the Ottoman empire took over for its mosques the pattern of Christian St Sophia, with its variants. The chief Turkish elements of design can be found on the Seljuk monuments of Konya, which otherwise follow Persian traditions. These elements are: plans showing several parallel arcades, which tend to reduce their number as time goes on; pairs of tall, circular minarets flanking the portal; porches with flanking niches; triangular arches with slightly scalloped sides; rectilinear or prismatically faceted stalactite ornament; and faceted columns with stalactite capitals. The Persian sense of superbly proportioned massive volumes is absent, and the ornamental motifs take on a plastic emphasis which they were never permitted in Persia.

The gateway of the Indjeminareli (1251) at Konya, shows this tendency most clearly. Here, massively projecting though clearly laid out, interlace and palmette designs fill the arcade and its frame above a range of engaged columns, like those flanking the portals of western churches.

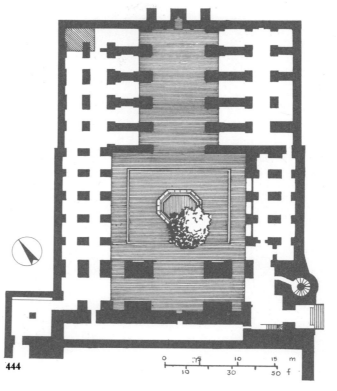

444 Plan of Masjid-i-Jami, Nayriz
Tenth century.
The entrance to the forecourt is insignificant.
On an axis, with the well at the centre, the great aisled hall leads to the mihrab at the far end.
The enormous piers of the arcade almost form a tunnel to the niche.

444

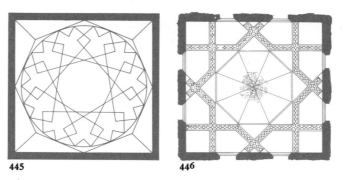

445, 446 Masjid-i-Jami, Isfahan
Vault plans.
Placing a dome over a square plan was always a problem.
The original Islamic solution was to use intersecting arches to reduce the square to an octagon and then corbel inwards from that.
Examples can be found from Spain to Persia.

445   446

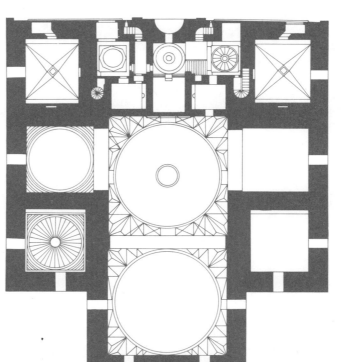

447 Plan of the Green mosque at Bursa. 1414-24
The Turkish solution to the vaulting problem was taken from the Byzantine, and this is hardly surprising with such an example as St Sophia ready to hand.
The corners of the square were filled in with corbelled brick or masonry to give a warped plane.
A circle was eventually reached whose diameter was the same as the side of the square.
The dome itself really springs from this ring, and is generally shallow.

447

448-450 Suleiman mosque, Constantinople. 1557
Exterior, interior and plan.
After the conquest
of Constantinople in 1453 many
great buildings of Byzantine
design were erected.
The Suleiman mosque is square in
plan, crowned by a central
dome flanked by four half domes,
and capped at all corners
by smaller domes.
The great central dome is carried
on four huge piers.
The courtyard has become a
forecourt rather than an integral
part of the plan.
Ornament is sparingly used,
consisting of two-toned stone
bands in the Cairene manner.
The rest is mainly inscriptional.
One of the most interesting
things about this great building is
that a purely Byzantine structure
of a vast scale should
be erected as late as
the mid-sixteenth century.

448

449

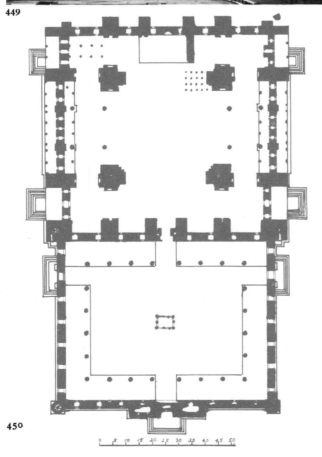

450

Occasionally in early work in Armenia, the small niches of the stalactite contain the shell-like striations noted on certain Egyptian buildings. The entire framed arcade of the north portal of the great mosque of Divrigui (1228) could be called a symmetrical stone-cut sculpture, so large have the elements of the design grown, many of the curvilinear foliate motifs occurring only once on each side of the frame. This type of decorative treatment seems to be a constant feature of early Turkish work.

The conquest of Constantinople (1453) brought about a sharp change in the design of the mosque. Before this event, mosque sanctuaries, entirely roofed with domes over a rectangular plan, had been built. The Green Mosque at Iznik (1379) had a single dome, and a frontal stone arcade with sparing ornament. The Green Mosque at Bursa (1424) was roofed with two main and six subsidiary domes. After the conquest, however, many great buildings of purely Byzantine design with multiple domes, half-dome squinches and stone arcades were erected in Constantinople and elsewhere.

In these new mosques, the idea of the mosque as an integral enclosure was lost, and the courts became mere forecourts to the sanctuary. From two to six free-standing pencil-like minarets were set out around this forecourt. The most impressive of these earlier mosques is perhaps that of Sultan Bayezid (1497). The flat Byzantine domes rise in tiers; the cloisters of the courtyard are also roofed with domes. The arcades within are supported on cylindrical columns of late classical type with stalactite capitals, and there is a cornice of stalactite. There is little other ornament. Two later mosques of similar plan, the famous Suleiman mosque (1557) at Constantinople, and the Selim mosque at Edirne (1570), show two of the possible ground plans for such structures. Both are square overall and buttressed. The centre dome, however, is carried on four massive compound piers in the Suleiman; on eight smaller octagonal piers in the Selim.

448-4

In the great Suleiman mosque, ornament is not unduly lavish. The round arcades are of banded stonework. The entrance door and the niche of the *mihrab* have tall triangular arches filled with stalactite, which also adorns the pendentives of the domes. Such ornament as there is, stylised foliate or calligraphic, is reserved in cartouches, or carried out in the stained-glass of pointed or circular lights. The tombs of the sultans, on similar but smaller plans, were, however, more lavishly adorned, as were the palaces. Linings of Turkish faïence tiles were exuberantly employed in the private apartments of the rulers, as well as on roofed fountains set up in the cities.

INDIA

The earliest substantial Islamic buildings in India to survive are mosques and tombs of the early thirteenth century —Kutb-ud-Din's mosques at Ajmer and Delhi, and the tapering gadrooned tower known as the Kutb Minar, actually the free-standing minaret to the mosque related to the Ghaznivid funereal towers. These were constructed by Indian craftsmen, of local reddish stone. The straight-sided pointed arcades of five and seven arches, forming the façade of the sanctuary, are constructed by the native

454
452,

XXIII

XXV

XXIV

XXVI

corbelling method. The beauty of these buildings is in their bands of superbly cut relief ornament, and of Kufic and Arabic script. These were cut from Persian patterns by native craftsmen. Islamic architecture in India eschewed the lavish polychrome designs of Persia. Beauties of material and sheer design were expressly sought.

Elsewhere, the use of native resources produced extraordinary results. The Ataladevi mosque in Jaunpur—equipped with early radiating arches—exhibits a doorway flanked by square strongly battered towers, with rows of open arcades within the main arch above the doors. In Ahmedabad, domed mosques were built out of the highly wrought fragments of medieval Hindu temples. Entire colonnades of Hindu columns were deprived of their figure sculpture, or re-vamped. The mosque of Mahafiz Khan (c. 1490) is flanked by a huge pair of exotically wrought minarets, with two projecting balconies in pure Hindu style. Other mosques in Ahmedabad are remarkable for their ornament, among which the fretted stone windows of the Sidi Sayyid are exceptionally beautiful.

Early in the sixteenth century, the first Moghul, Babur, employed an Ottoman architect, who was the first of many foreigners to be called to build in India. To this source is attributed the extraordinary skill of dome-construction exhibited by Indian Islamic architecture. The third Moghul, Akbar (1556-1605), devoted much effort to the construction of a complete city of pink sandstone at Fatehpur Sikri, near Agra. The buildings of this complex display the most extraordinary and extravagant invention.

The mode of construction favoured for the buildings was by pillar and canopy. The long projecting eaves of the earlier sixteenth century are here developed in such structures as the Panch Mahal, of five, unwalled diminishing
455 storeys. The throne of the Diwan-i-Khas is a unique invention. From the lowest level rises a lone central pillar (the *axis mundi*, no doubt) that spreads by thirty-six moulded stalactite brackets to support the throne. Four bridges cross the open space diagonally to the gallery, where stood the courtiers. Many of the buildings are adorned with exquisite pierced grilles, and with elaborate serpentine brackets at the eaves' corners. The Jami mosque is adorned with a colossal doorway 176 feet high, banded with light stone and crowned with canopies and large palmettes. Both within the arch and on its faces it is opened into arched balconies.

Most beautiful of the later mosques is the Moti Masjid,
456 Agra (the Pearl mosque, 1650). The single-storey colonnade around the court supports, on its slender columns, projecting eaves. The façade of the sanctuary shows seven low-pitched scalloped arches on square piers. A long eaves-like drip-moulding runs above the arcade; three onion-domes and nine small arcaded canopies adorn the the roof. Only the scantiest of relief moulding adorns the white stone.

Numerous mosques and palace buildings in India are of high artistic quality, but perhaps the Moslem rulers spent most effort and money on their own tombs. These, for their variety and egomaniac majesty of invention, must certainly be reckoned among the most magnificent tombs in the world.

452

453

454

455

451 Kutb Minar, Delhi.
Detail. Early thirteenth century. The minaret relies on pure form for its effect. The bands of decoration are uncoloured, the ornament being both script and Kufic inscriptions.

452 Kutb Minar, Delhi
One of the earliest surviving Islamic buildings in India. The gadrooned sides and tiered galleries show influence of native tope building.

453 Fatehpur Sikri, Near Agra. 1556-1605
Detail of bracket.
The bracket capital is of the same Hindu design as those at Sanchi, but the human figure has been turned into an abstract arabesque for iconoclastic reasons.

454 Arcades of the Great mosque, Ajmer
Early thirteenth century.
Contemporary with the Kutb Minar, these straight-sided, pointed arches are corbelled.

455 Diwan-i-Khas, Fatehpur Sikri
Sixteenth century.
The mode of building was pillar, lintel and canopy, with heavily bracketed balconies and overhanging roofs in the Indian tradition. The symmetrical four-square building owes much to Hindu palace tradition.

456 Pearl mosque, Agra. 1650
The simple colonnade supports
a low-pitched roof with wide
projecting eaves. The white stone
is unadorned. The scalloped
edge of the arch is really a series
of shaped corbels in tiers.

456

**457 Tomb of Sher Shah,
Sahasram, Bengal. 1545-50**
The Afghan chieftain ruled
Hindustan from 1540 to 1545.
His tomb was built on an island
in an ornamental lake,
the centre of a paradise in which
he and his chief followers
could lie. The giant lotus-shaped
dome derives from the stupa,
but is structural, not a stone
tumulus. Like early stupas, it is
completely symmetrical,
a circle on a square.

457

458 Taj Mahal, Agra. 1632-53
Shah Jehan's tomb for his wife
has become one of the best-
known Indian buildings.
The bulbous dome crowns a
symmetrical building of a type
derived from the characteristic
Indian mosque gateway.

459 Screen at the Taj Mahal
The screen of pierced trellis work in
marble is inlaid with semi-
precious stones. It is strictly
geometrical.
The meandering pattern is
reminiscent of the border
decoration of Moghul
illuminations.

458

The fourteenth-century tombs of the Delhi sultans are
solid structures reminiscent of Persian types. That of Ghi-
yas-ad-Din, is a massive, battered cuboid of red sandstone,
banded with white marble, and crowned with a dome of
white marble, eighty feet high. The tomb of Isa Khan,
Delhi (1547), has an octagonal base beneath the dome and
is surrounded by an arcade with long eaves, and crowned
by eight ogival canopies on pillars—a type that endured
long in northern India. It reached its apogee in the enormous
tomb of Sher Shah, at Sahasram, Bengal (begun 1545). 457

In the Deccan, at Bijapur, tombs displayed the most
extravagant fantasy. The basic Persian pattern of cuboid
and dome was preserved, but the tomb of Ibrahim Rauza
(1615), for example, has a narrow-necked bulb-dome of
small proportions, the neck encircled by everted petal-
like forms. Four ornate minarets with bulb-domes crown
the corners, and a number of small pavilions the flat roof.
Under the eaves, especially around the corner buttresses,
crowd clusters of serpentine stalactite brackets.

The most famous tombs, however, are those of the
Moghuls. Of these the greatest are the tombs of Humayun
(c. 1560) and of Shah Jehan's wife, the Taj Mahal (1632-53); 458
the two share substantially the same pattern. Each of the
four sides presents a towering arch set in a rectangular
surface like the door to a Persian mosque, flanked by tall
octagonal volumes, whose faces are opened by arched
balconies. A huge bulb-dome, raised on a drum, crowns the
central area under which the bodies repose, and canopies
on columns crown the massive octagons. Humayun's
tomb is banded and panelled with two tones of stone, and
is devoid of minarets. The Taj is of overwhelmingly white
marble, and has four, large circular minarets crowned with
canopies standing free at the corners of the plinth.

In building the Taj, the emperor beggared his empire.
According to inscription, it was built by a Turk to the
design of an architect from Lahore (not a Frenchman or
Venetian, as has often been said). The calligraphy was
executed by a Shirazi. Its restrained and elegant floral
inlay, inside and out, contains precious stones, and nowhere obscures the architectural features. The fretting of 459
the screens, especially those around the central area, though
fundamentally geometric, is imbued with the Indian feeling for vegetative life. Although it is certainly a native
Indian production, its architectural success rests on its
fundamentally Persian sense of intelligible and undisturbed
proportions, applied to clean, uncomplicated surfaces.

459

Rose Window, North Transept, West Front, Notre-Dame, Paris

MEDIEVAL

**460 The Pantheon, Rome.
A.D. 120-24**
This temple was erected by
Hadrian on the base of an older
temple of Agrippa.
The plan is circular, covered by a
dome with a height and
diameter each of 142 feet;
the concrete walls were once
marble faced.

460

**461, 463 Sta Costanza, Rome.
c. 350**
Plan and exterior.
Here one finds the development
of a plan based on a double circle,
one inside the other,
with niches in the walls that hint
at an octagonal plan.
The surrounding aisle is roofed by
vaults which also absorb the
thrust of the dome that tops
the columns of the inner circle.

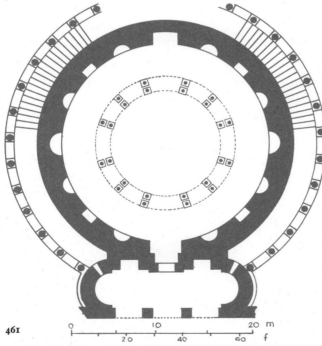

461

462

462, 464 San Lorenzo, Milan
Fifth century (remodelled in the
sixteenth century).
Plan and exterior.
This is one of the most important
early churches. Its plan is an
apsed square of solid walls
enclosing an inner apsed square of
columns supporting the roof,
a groined vault.
It is an organic structure in which
each part supports and balances
some other part –
a truly medieval building.

463

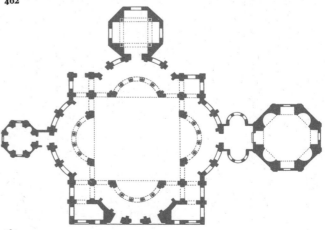

464

ROMAN VAULTED BUILDINGS

There are many branches and many types of architecture that can be considered under the general heading of medieval, but the majority of the buildings we know were churches, and nearly all have in common the feature that their structure is basically one of arches and curves and later of vaults or domes, and it is in this that the principal distinctions from classical architecture are to be found. There, regular plans based on the rectangle and elevations which were universally vertical were the rule, while the horizontal architrave, with triangular pediment above, was the essential feature of the façade. In the medieval style on the other hand, the straight line was the exception rather than the rule, plans were irregular and varied, curved exhedrae or apses were frequent, while in developed medieval buildings the roofs consisted of arches, vaults and domes. Further, the building material also differed, for in the medieval style bricks or small stones set in cement or mortar, itself as hard as the stone and occupying almost as much of the wall space, were well nigh universally employed, whereas in classical building large blocks, carefully squared, were used, almost without mortar. But the most important difference of all lay in the thought behind the work, for in the medieval world thrusts and counterthrusts balanced one another, so that every part of the structure became an essential element in an organic whole, in a way which was never called for, never conceived of, in classical building. In medieval architecture each part lived in relation to every other part; in the classical style the results were achieved by mathematical proportion.

This system of balance characterises all truly medieval work, whether it be Byzantine or Carolingian, Romanesque or Gothic, and whether the dome or the vault, the round or the pointed arch was the characteristic feature. It was important to a degree never dreamt of in any previous style, and hardly ever called for or paralleled since in subsequent styles like that of the Renaissance (though there are countless 'medieval' elements in Renaissance building) or those of today, where modern materials and methods have to some extent removed the necessity for the subtle compensations of thrust and counterthrust that were required if a building made entirely of brick or stone, like St Sophia at Constantinople or Amiens Cathedral, was not to fall to the ground.

To understand the story of medieval architecture one must know something of the origin and earliest development of such essential features as the arch, the vault and the dome, and it is necessary to begin the enquiry with an examination of certain buildings of pre-Christian use and nature, notably the great baths and palaces of Imperial Rome; for it is there that many of the constructional problems that characterise the medieval style were tackled on an extensive scale (see section on Roman architecture, pp. 55-79). This architecture, the characteristic features of which were the vaults above and use of apses or exhedrae on plan, and where the importance of the interior was stressed rather than the outside, had an especial appeal to Christian patrons. Indeed, the whole essence of the architecture seemed to tally with the teaching of the Church, which stressed the importance of the inner man, the soul rather than the body, and which urged man to seek salvation and glory in heaven rather than on earth. It is not surprising therefore that it was soon adopted by patrons of the new faith for the use of the Christian community, even if at first the more conservative form of the basilica, with timber roof, was more usual. Something more will be said of these conservative basilicas later; here the evolution of the new type may be briefly examined, for one of the most important of the early churches that has come down to us in Italy belongs essentially to this new type. It is the San Lorenzo at Milan, which was built in the third quarter of the fifth century. On plan it is an apsed square, similar in form to some of the rooms in Domitian's palace but on a larger scale. Its solid outer walls however enclose an inner apsed square consisting of columns which support the structure on which the roof is poised. Like the roofs of many of the Imperial Roman buildings, this is composed of an intersecting groined vault. The walls and the vaulted roof of the surrounding aisle serve to support and buttress the central area, taking up and subtly compensating for the thrust of its roof. [462, 464]

The derivation of the plan of this building from those of Imperial times is clear, but there has been great advance, for in the first place the building has become an entity, independent and standing in its own right, and in the second, its structure has become organic, in that each part is not only important in itself but also serves to support and balance some other part. It is in fact a truly medieval building, significant not only because it provides adequate, even impressive, housing for a Christian church, but more, because it is architecture in the true sense of the word and not mere building.

But in all these buildings there is one limiting factor; the vaults are of concrete, and their erection was only possible when the correct materials and a knowledge of how to use them were present at one and the same time. And it was only in Rome and the Roman sphere fairly narrowly speaking that this knowledge was available. Elsewhere domes and vaults had to be built of stone or brick, and to stand entirely as a result of the skill of their construction and not primarily because of the strength of the concrete and the massiveness of the buttressing. In the Eastern world structural methods distinct from those of Rome were developed; more will be said of them below.

A similar origin and a similar evolution from pre-Christian prototypes is to be traced with regard to building of octagonal plan. One of the most highly developed examples is the church of San Vitale at Ravenna (526-48). The first stage in the evolution of the plan is to be seen in the circular chambers in Domitian's palace; in the next the simple circle is elaborated by adding or including four semi-circular exhedrae, so that on plan the circle becomes virtually an octagon. In the next the inner circle is included in an outer one. The result of these elaborations is to be seen in Sta Costanza at Rome (c. 350), where the plan consists of two circles, an outer one with niches in the walls which hint at an octagonal plan, and an inner one which is virtually an octagon. The surrounding aisle is roofed by vaults which also serve to support the thrust of [468-470] [461, 463]

465 Church of San Vitale, Ravenna. 526-48
The capitals of this church are of the new Byzantine type known as impost capitals and are remarkable for the delicacy of their carving.

465

466, 467 SS. Sergius and Bacchus, Constantinople. 527
Ground floor plan and interior. The plan is a simple square enclosing an octagon. There is an elementary apse on the eastern wall, and the seventy-foot-high dome is given externally a unique ribbed treatment.

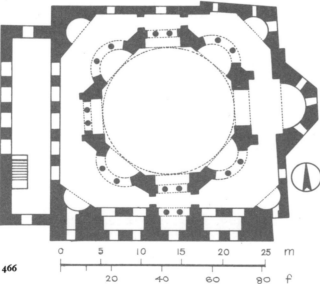

466

467

the dome that tops the columns of the inner circle.

In the next stage, which is represented by Constantine's Church of the Resurrection at Jerusalem (*c.* 350), the inner circle of columns is surrounded by an octagon, and in the final and most elaborate form the inner and outer rings have both become octagons. San Vitale at Ravenna and SS. Sergius and Bacchus at Constantinople represent variations on the theme. The latter has a square plan outside, but inside this is made into an octagon by the inclusion of small niches in the corners and is further elaborated by the addition of an apse which projects from the eastern wall. The former is more elaborate, for the inner octagon is taller and more delicate, and the eastern side is open, to provide a long presbytery; the main portion of this is included within the wall-space of the surrounding outer octagon, though here too there is a small projecting apse.

There is one feature that distinguishes these two churches from their Roman prototypes and from San Lorenzo at Milan; it is that they are roofed with domes, not groined vaults. True, the Pantheon was roofed with a dome, but it was poised over a circle, a plan which offers little possibility for elaboration. It was moreover a colossally heavy affair, with a great mass of concrete at its extremities to act as a counterpoise to its thrust, whereas the domes of SS. Sergius and Bacchus and San Vitale are of brick, or even of hollow vessels. They are light and delicate and are supported not by a great counter-weight but by a subtle system of buttressing, which serves to compensate the thrust and carry it down at an angle to the ground. Here the principles of organic architecture have been developed and thought out to an advanced degree, and San Vitale is not only a wholly organic building but also an outstandingly beautiful one, for its proportions are exceptionally fine and balanced. Here an architect who was also a great artist was at work.

But it was not either in San Vitale or in SS. Sergius and Bacchus that the most important architectural invention of early Christian times was made, but in certain other buildings, where the dome rests not on a circular or nearly circular basis, but is poised over a square. The problem of how to transform the square of a ground plan into a circular base for the dome was probably the most important of all those that confronted the early Christian architects, and here the evidence as to the rôle played by Rome in solving the problem is very much less clear and precise. San Lorenzo at Milan, San Vitale at Ravenna, and the rest, are all buildings which can be explained as being the direct outcome of ideas which were thought of and developed in Rome, and the evidence can be documented by the study of buildings which actually survive. But there are not present in Italy any actual examples of early date that show that the problem of poising a circular dome above a square base was solved there for the first time. For that the surviving evidence is to be found elsewhere, more particularly in the eastern Mediterranean.

THE DOME AND THE EAST

We have already encountered buildings of square plan, both for pre-Christian and Christian usage, as in the great baths and palaces of Imperial Rome or in the church of

468

469

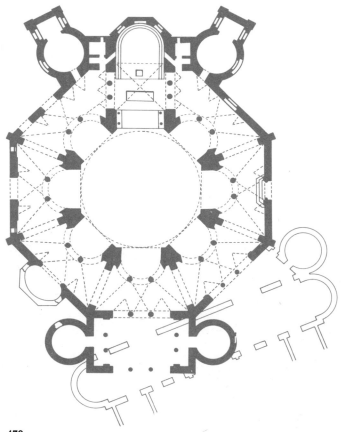

470

468-470 Church of San Vitale, Ravenna. 526-48
Here the plan has developed into a more sophisticated double octagon. The light dome rests on pendentives but is obscured from the outside by a protecting timber and tile roof. Although the church is Roman in inspiration, Byzantine elements are everywhere evident, particularly in the mosaics that adorn the sanctuary, and in the contrast between the richness of the interior and the simple brick exterior.

471 Tomb of Galla Placidia, Ravenna. c. 540
The present structure formed part of a much larger complex which has now disappeared.
It was intended for use as a funerary chapel.
It is cruciform in plan, the crossing roofed by a vault.
The exterior is a plain brick building devoid of all architectural ornament, providing a striking contrast with the highly decorated interior.
All the vaults are covered entirely with mosaic which flows from one surface to another without a break.

471

472 Diagram of squinch
Virtually an arch or arches built across the corners of a square at the upper level, which serves to turn the area into an octagon on which a dome is constructed.

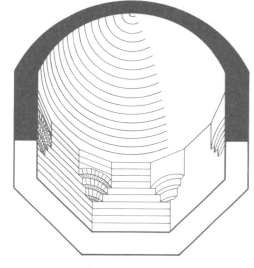

472

473 Squinch in the palace at Firuzabad
Third century. This is one of the earliest examples of the use of a dome to roof a building of square plan. The transition from square to circle is effected by means of a squinch, a series of arches corbelled out from the corner, serving to turn the square into an octagon.

474 Le Puy Cathedral, Auvergne
Twelfth century.
The squinch here takes the form of a semi-dome or conch, as in an apse. The coloured tufas of the region are used to produce a decorative effect.

473

474

San Lorenzo at Milan. These were elaborated in various ways. Sometimes the square was extended by the addition of semi-circular exhedrae on three or even all four of its sides; sometimes square projections were added, so that the building automatically assumed a cruciform plan. This could in turn be elaborated by adding columns at the four corners inside the square, so providing an open square within the closed outer wall, on which the central portion of the roof could rest. An important early example of this elaboration is to be seen in a building at Musmiyah in Syria, known as the Praetorium: it dates from the second century A.D. and shows in embryo the idea of cruciform church with central dome supported on columns. For obvious reasons this plan appealed especially to Christian patrons, and variations on the cruciform plan probably began to become important soon after the official adoption of Christianity early in the fourth century; though it was only during the sixth century that any really serious developments were made. The first problem was to find a satisfactory form of roof for the square base.

We have already encountered instances of the roofing of buildings of rectangular or square plan by means of groined vaults. The evidence suggests that the domical vault over square was also known to the Roman architects: it consists of a vault of which the uniformly curved surfaces reach down into the angles at the four corners without a break. Though it provides a more satisfactory type of roof for a square building than the groined vault, its height is limited in direct relation to the size of the square below, and there are no possibilities of variation. Such a roof exists on the little building at Ravenna known as the Mausoleum of Galla Placidia (c. 540), and though it provides a satisfactory area for decoration with mosaic, it is unduly limited, and moreover makes impossible the inclusion of any windows directly illuminating the central area.

The dome proper, on the other hand, is an independent structure set on a drum, which can be varied in height to form an external as well as an internal feature and into which windows can be inserted, as they were, for example, in Justinian's St Sophia at Constantinople. But in order to make the construction of this drum possible, it was essential to convert the square of the area below into a circle. This was the great problem that confronted the architects of the fifth and sixth centuries, and so far as we know the first solution was not arrived at in Rome but in the East. Two distinct methods were discovered, and curiously enough early examples of both appear side by side in the same building, the church at Abu Mina, near Alexandria in Egypt. It dates from between 400 and 410.

The simplest system is that known as the squinch. This is virtually an arch built across the corners of the square at an upper level, which serves to turn the area into an octagon: by recessing the masonry over the salient points on each side of the square and oversailing the arches at the corners, a more or less adequate circular foundation could be provided for the drum. But it was not a wholly satisfactory solution, for the springing of the squinch arches was set a third or half-way up the main arches that topped the square, and this was a point of weakness rather than

475 a

471

-474

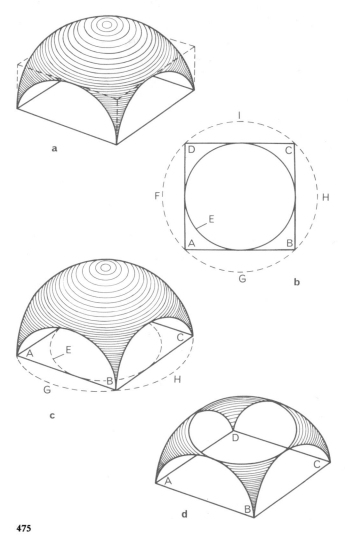

475

475

476

475 **The evolution of the domical vault and the pendentive**
The area that can be roofed by the domical vault (a) is directly limited by the size of the square below. The pendentive (b, c, d) serves as an admirable transition from the square below to the circular base of the dome. Its spherical-triangular shape serves to transfer thrust to the pier below and not on to the arch itself, as in the squinch.

476 **Tomb of Theodoric, Ravenna. c. 530**
This structure is in two storeys, a circle surmounting a decagon 45 feet in diameter.
One enormous convex slab of stone weighing 470 tons forms the roof, like an inverted dish 35 feet across. Its transportation was a remarkable technical feat for its time.

477 Church of the Nativity, Bethlehem. 527-65
Constantine's first church on the traditional site of Christ's birth was rebuilt in the sixth century. It is remarkable for its high Corinthian columns and stately, simple plan.

477

478 St Demetrius, Salonica
Fifth century.
A rare extant example of a five-aisled basilican church in the Greek Orthodox world. It was burnt in 610 and again in 1917, but the west and east ends are original and the rest was faithfully restored on both occasions.

478

479 St John of Studios, Constantinople. 463
Plan.
This church shows probable Oriental influence in the great width in comparison to its length, in contrast to the basilicas of Italy, which are much larger.

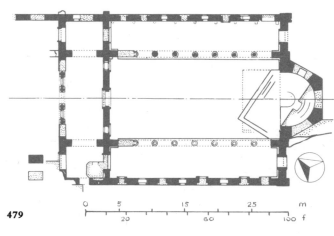

479

of strength. The squinch was however used quite extensively, not only in early times but also at a comparatively late date. We thus see it for example at Abu Mina in Egypt; in the baptistry of Soter at Naples in Italy (465-81); in the fifth century at Kalaat Siman in Syria; and in the tenth and eleventh centuries in churches like Hosios Lukas and Daphni in Greece. The earliest instances of its use are to be found in Sassanian Persia, in the palaces of Firuzabad   473
and Sarvistan: the latter is of the fourth century and the former probably dates from as early as the reign of Ardashir II (234-42). On the basis of this evidence the squinch may be regarded as the Persian solution of the problem.

More ingenious, and also more satisfactory, is the second solution, which is known as the pendentive. It consisted   475 b,
in building in the angles the first stage of a domical vault, but stopping short at the level of the summits of the main arches that top the open square. This provided a completely circular base, on which a separate dome could be built at an independent angle; or, as was more often done, a circular drum with vertical walls could be inserted between the base and the actual dome. The pendentive provided an admirable solution, for its spherical-triangular shape served to convey weight and thrust downwards to the pier or column below it, and not where the squinch tended to impose it, on the arch itself. Further, the vertical drums could be pierced with windows to admit light. Indeed, the pendentive is an admirable example of organic architecture, where weights are conveyed to the ground and thrusts compensated not by mass but by a subtle disposition of counter thrust.

No example of a pendentive that is earlier than that at Abu Mina (400-10) has so far been discovered, but the idea would appear to have been perfected in Syria or Asia Minor, and it seems probable that it was taken from that area to Constantinople by the Anatolian architects who worked for Justinian in the sixth century; it was used by them in most of the buildings done for that emperor. It may be taken as the Hellenistic solution of the problem.

THE BASILICA

Though, as was stated at the outset, the essence of medieval architecture was the organic principle, the experiments with circular and cruciform plans, with vault, dome and means of transition, were long drawn out, and a more conservative type of building, with rectangular ground plan and simple timber roof, remained important, not only throughout the centuries of evolution between the days of Augustus and Justinian but also, especially in the West, until a very much later date. This type was the basilica, and even though it was conservative and unambitious, the influence which its plan exercised is to be found to a greater or lesser degree in practically all the architecture of Christendom.

The simplest form, a rectangular building with three aisles, topped by a timber roof, had been used extensively in pre-Christian times, especially for judiciary purposes. Even before the adoption of Christianity, the custom of extending one end by the addition of a semi-circular apse had become general; there was usually an entrance, preceded by an atrium or forecourt, at the other end. When

480

481

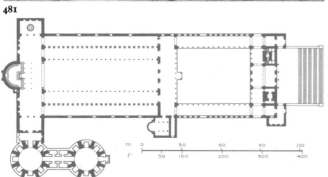

483

482

484

480 St Paul's-without-the-Walls, Rome. 385
Rebuilt 1823.
This was one of the grandest basilicas in Rome, surpassed only by St Peter's; its plan was similar.

481 Sta Sabina, Rome. 422–38
The original character of this church has survived the many alterations. It is austere, with semi-circular arches resting on Corinthian columns.

482 San Lorenzo, Rome. 432
This is a typical Roman Basilica, but at the eastern end a large crypt has been contrived to house the relics of the saint, so that the floor has here been raised.

483 Old St Peter's, Rome. 450
Plan.
Constantine's first basilica must have been the grandest of all the early Roman churches, but it was pulled down to make way for the one we see today.

484 Sta Maria Maggiore, Rome. 432–547
The single-aisled interior with ranges of slender Ionic columns and horizontal entablature faithfully follows the classical basilica on which the church is modelled.

**485, 486 St Eirene,
Constantinople. 532**
A church was built on the site by
Constantine, but the present
structure was built by Justinian.
It was repaired after earthquake
damage in 564 and again in 740.
The present building consists of
an ingenious combination of an
apsed basilica and a domed square.
The dome is set on massive piers,
between which are columns
dividing the aisles and supporting
the gallery rather than the side
walls and roof as in the old basilicas.

485

486

**487 St Sophia, Constantinople.
532-37**
Plan.
The plan shows three apses and
three aisles separated by columns
that also support the side
galleries. The great central dome
rests on spherical pendentives.

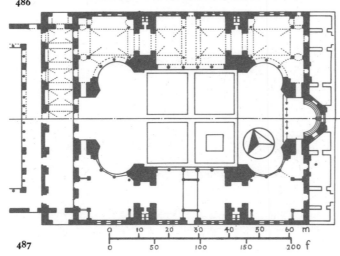

487

Christianity was adopted as the official religion of the
State the plan at once commended itself to the Church,
for it simultaneously provided adequate space for a large
congregation and an axis towards a sanctuary, for the altar
was from the earliest times in the apse, even though at
first the buildings were not by any means always orien-
tated towards the east.

Some of the earliest churches in Rome were actually
pagan buildings, re-used, like Sta Pudenziana; but the
building of churches on a considerable scale began in the
fourth century, and we have virtually a complete example
in St Paul's-without-the-Walls, for though it was burnt
down in 1823 it was restored exactly on the lines of the
original building of 385. Other early examples include
Sta Sabina (422-38) or Sta Maria Maggiore (432-547). Old
St Peter's, set up in 450, was no doubt the grandest of all
of them, but it was destroyed in the fifteenth century to
make way for the present Renaissance structure.

These basilicas belong to two main groups: a more
conservative one, where the columns that separate the
aisles are topped by a horizontal entablature like those of
the old classical temples, and a more progressive one, where
the columns are topped by arches. The earliest ones have
apses at the end of the central aisle only: apsidal termina-
tions to the side aisles appeared at a rather later date, and
were first developed in the East. Transeptal projections to
north and south just in front of the apses were however
quite an early feature in Rome; they produced a T-shaped
plan, as for example in Sta Maria Maggiore. Another
elaboration which appears as early as the fourth century
though it was unusual before the sixth, was the inclusion
of a crypt below the apse. These were used to house the
remains of saints and martyrs and became more common
and more important as the cult of relics was developed.
One of the best examples is in the church of San Lorenzo
in Rome, where the crypt is so large that the eastern end
of the church seems almost to have two storeys. The side
aisles were also invariably lower than the central one, so
that clerestory windows could be inserted to illuminate
the central aisle.

Outside Rome the basilica found favour as the most important church form in numerous cities in Italy; the great
basilicas of Sant'Apollinare Nuovo (c. 540) and Sant'Apollinare in Classe (c. 535) at Ravenna are typical. The plan
was used by Constantine for the churches he founded all
over the Christian world, like the first St Sophia at Constantinople and the Church of the Nativity at Bethlehem; the
latter still survives as a basilica though it was entirely
rebuilt by Justinian in the sixth century. But the form was
never really popular in the eastern part of the Christian
world and today few basilical buildings are to be found
there, for the early ones were mostly pulled down to make
way for structures of another type. The most important
examples now standing in the Orthodox world are the
church of St John of Studios at Constantinople (463) and
the Panaghia Achieropoietou and St Demetrius at Salonica. The last of these is especially fine for it has five
instead of the customary three aisles, and built piers alternate with a series of columns to break the monotony of
the main aisle. The building was almost completely de-

480

481,
483

482

477

479
478

488

489

488 St Sophia, Constantinople. 532-37
In St Sophia a dome was used as a roof over a square for the first time on a really large scale. It is supported on four great piers which inside are so inconspicuous that the dome appears, as a contemporary writer stated, 'to be supported on chains from heaven'.

489 St Mark's, Venice. 1042-85
Interior. The similarity in feeling and construction between this church and St Sophia is clearly demonstrated in a comparison with the previous illustration. The addition of a transept to the north and south of the central dome, however, give it a truly cruciform plan. In this it follows Justinian's Church of the Holy Apostles at Constantinople.

490 St Mark's, Venice. 1042-85
St Mark's ornate façade with five portals faces the splendid square. The central dome is repeated in four smaller domes on the arms of the cross. The interior is richly faced with marble and mosaics.

490

stroyed by fire in 1917, but it has now been entirely reconstructed on the basis of the original plan. The church of St John of Studios is interesting, for it is very much wider in comparison to its length than are the basilicas of Italy, and in this it probably shows the influence of ideas that penetrated from Asia Minor and blended with those brought from Rome by Constantine at an earlier date.

BYZANTINE CHURCH ARCHITECTURE

It has sometimes been said that Byzantine architecture is eclectic, in that it consists of a blend of various ideas that were developed previously and which came from East and West alike. This is no doubt true, but it is also true that all art of quality has always owed an immense debt to the past, and if the Byzantine architects blended ideas from diverse sources to form the basis of their new style, they did so with genius and imagination and succeeded in achieving results of outstanding glory.

If we set aside the various tentative efforts which have been noted so far, most of them more Roman or more Eastern than Byzantine, the story may begin with the series of buildings set up in the second quarter of the sixth century under the patronage of Justinian, more especially at Constantinople. They belong to various types, but all represent variations on a merging of the themes of basilica, cross, and square roofed with a dome. Simplest and most straightforward is the group of which St Eirene at Constantinople (532) may be chosen as the type example. It consists virtually of an ingenious combination of the ideas of an apsed basilica and a domed square. The dome is set on massive built piers, between which are columns which serve to divide the aisles and support a gallery; they no longer support the side walls and roof as they did in the old basilicas, though the idea of the basilica is there on the ground. The resemblance is even more striking if we compare the interior with that of St Demetrius at Salonica, where built piers already alternate with a series of columns, though they have no function other than to strengthen the long aisles; columns were well enough in Rome but hardly sufficiently secure in the East where the shock of earthquakes was from time to time experienced.

In order to give greater length, and so approach more nearly to the conventional basilica, this plan was elaborated by the addition of further bays to the west, sometimes vaulted and sometimes domed; in the latter case a building consisting of two domed squares, one in front of the other, was produced. Similarly the central square was extended in other directions by the addition of a square at the east to form a choir and squares north and south to form transepts. Justinian's famous Church of the Holy Apostles at Constantinople, now destroyed, was of this type; indeed, it may be counted as the type example of the five-domed type, with a large dome at the crossing and smaller ones on the four arms of the cross. Its plan was followed almost exactly in St Mark's at Venice early in the eleventh century, in Cyprus and elsewhere. St John's church at Ephesus, as remodelled by Justinian, represents a further elaboration, for the nave is considerably longer than the other arms of the cross and has two domes, while there is one at the crossing and one each on the other arms.

The most imaginative blend of the ideas of basilica and domed square, however, is that which produced Justinian's greatest foundation, St Sophia at Constantinople, one of the most glorious and original buildings that have ever been set up. It replaced Constantine's church, a basilica which was destroyed by fire in the Nika riots of 532. It was completed in the amazingly short time of five years, ten months and four days, under the direction of the architect Anthemius of Tralles, who was described by his contemporary, Procopius, as 'the man most learned in what are called the mathematical sciences, not only of the men of his own time, but of all men for generations back'. He was helped by another, Isidore of Miletus, who also rebuilt the dome when it fell shortly after as the result of an earthquake.

The proportions of the building are vast, and also unusual. The span of the dome is 104 feet, over a base 250 feet long and 230 feet wide, and the dome, when it was first built, was astonishingly low in comparison to its span, seeming as one contemporary writer said 'to be suspended by golden chains from heaven', so unobtrusive were its means of support. Never was this building surpassed, never even imitated, in the Byzantine world. It remains unique, a building of exceptional genius. And it stands today, little changed but for a few additions made by the Turks when they turned it into a mosque after their conquest of Constantinople in 1453.

The ground plan again represents that of a basilica with three apses and three aisles separated by columns which also support side galleries. But above, to give greater length, there is a vast semi-dome, as it were an immensely enlarged apse, at the eastern and western ends of the main aisle, and these not only give an unprecedented feeling of spaciousness but also add an amazing lightness to the whole building. Between them is the great central dome itself, standing on a low drum pierced by windows to light the central area.

It is however not only thanks to the imaginative conception of its plan and elevation that St Sophia stands supreme but also as a result of the exquisite quality of the interior decoration. The walls up to the level of the galleries are covered with huge marble slabs, chosen for the subtlety of their veining and polished to shine like mirrors; something of the original effect can now be comprehended thanks to cleaning done in recent years by the Byzantine Institute of America. Above, the wall surfaces, the arches, the vaults, the semi-domes, the pendentives and the dome itself were all adorned with glittering mosaics. Some of those of Justinian's day survive on the arches and the vaults of the lower storey; they are now being cleaned. The figural mosaics above the doors, in the galleries and between the windows of the walls that close the north and south arches are later additions, which replaced the earlier work, torn down perhaps during the days of Iconoclast supremacy (726-843), when figural art was forbidden. And, mingling with this, to complete the picture, ran the delicately carved cornices and, supporting it all, the richly decorated capitals with their silhouette-like ornament, in a style wholly new and wholly successful. It was no wonder that contemporaries regarded the building as miraculous,

485, 486

489-492

487,
p. 18

491

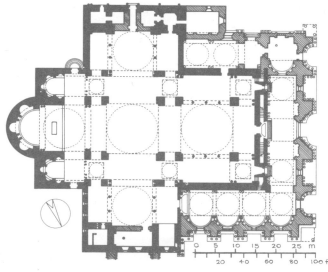

492

**491, 492 St Mark's, Venice.
1042–85**
Roof detail and plan.
The tall timber and metal-sheathed
domes stand clear
of the shallower stone structural
domes and are a weatherproof
shield to them.
Crowns of gold were added to the
timber-built domes
in the thirteenth century.

493

494

493 Kapnikaria, Athens
Tenth century.
An example of a cruciform
basilica, with the prothesis and
the diaconicon as subsidiary
structures which fill up
the corners left between the arms
of the cross.

**494 Kariye Camii,
Constantinople**
Eleventh to early fourteenth
centuries.
A church with two antechambers
or narthices, with the walls
separating the main apse from the
side chapels carried forward
to support the dome.

495 Katholikon, Daphni
Ninth century. This is one of
the few churches with large
domes that survive in Greece. Its
dome is supported on squinches.

495

496 Gračanica, Serbia. 1321
This church represents the final
form of Byzantine building with
domes on high drums
surrounding the central dome.
The exterior is of brick and stone.

496

**497 Hosios Lukas,
Greece. 1000-25**
The principal church, like that
at Daphni, has a large dome
supported on squinches. Beside
it stands a second church with a
dome on a tall drum, of
slightly later date.

497

**498 Virgin Pammakaristos,
Constantinople, funerary
chapel. 1315**
The ornate exterior, with its
blind arcading, is typical of
the last phase of Byzantine
architecture as developed under
the Palaeologue emperors.

498

**499 Church of the Holy
Apostles, Salonica. c. 1312**
In this church decorative
brickwork was used with great
effect. The patterns are either
geometric or in the form of the
Islamic script known as Kufic.

499

or that visitors at a later date were so impressed and over-
awed that more than one was converted to Orthodoxy as
a result of his visit.

St Sophia happily survives, but many of Justinian's other
foundations, at Constantinople and elsewhere, have
perished. Nor is it possible to say much of the architecture
of the next few centuries, for after the vast enterprises of this
great patron the treasury was empty and the spirit to emulate his performances was dead. But if nothing very spectacular was done, it was during the next two or three
centuries that the Byzantine architectural style developed
into an idiom which was to survive conquests, wars and
poverty, and to spread over the greater part of the Orthodox world, from Cyprus in the south to Novgorod in
the north, from Asia Minor in the east to Sicily, Venice
or Moldavia in the west.

The essence of the plan was the cross, of the roof, the
vault and dome, and countless variations on these themes
were rung, mostly, it is true, on a small scale. But even if
the conception of the interior as a huge spatial unity
passed, the later buildings showed great feeling for delicacy,
proportion and balance, and many are extremely attractive. Until the twelfth century or thereabouts, the basilical
idea continued to predominate on plan, but it had been
subtly combined with the cross, so that the exact nature
of the plan varied according to the standpoint; from the
western end it seemed to be basilical; from below the
dome it was cruciform. Above, however, the cross predominated, for the roofs of the main choir, transepts and
central aisle were usually carried up to a higher level than
those of the side aisles or the side chapels, so that they
made the pattern of a cross, with the dome marking the
point of intersection of the arms. Invariably however, soon
after Justinian's time, the side aisles had been made to
terminate in chapels; they were called the *prothesis* and
diaconicon in the Orthodox world, and had an essential
part to play in the liturgy. The dome in such churches was
usually supported on four free-standing columns or piers,
the former topped with finely carved capitals, the latter
with marble impost blocks. But sometimes, especially in
Greece, the walls separating the main apse from the side
chapels were carried forward to support the dome at the
east, though there were still columns to the west. More
often than not, too, transverse aisles or narthices were
added at the western end, to form a sort of ante-chamber
to the church, and at times there were even two such
chambers, as we see, for example, at Kariye Camii at   494
Constantinople; often however the second narthex was a
later addition.

In another variant the cruciform plan predominated,
while the idea of the three-aisled basilica was subordinate.
That is the case, for example, in a church at Athens known
as the Kapnikaria, where the *prothesis* and *diaconicon* to the   493
east, and the corner-areas to the west, are subsidiary structures, set up, as it were, to fill in the four corners left
between the arms of the cross. Other subsidiary buildings,
side chapels, aisles, or whatever it may be, were also often
added as time went on, to provide greater space or
sometimes to serve as funerary chapels, so that the later
churches were often very complicated. Quite frequently,

XXVII

XXVIII

XXIX

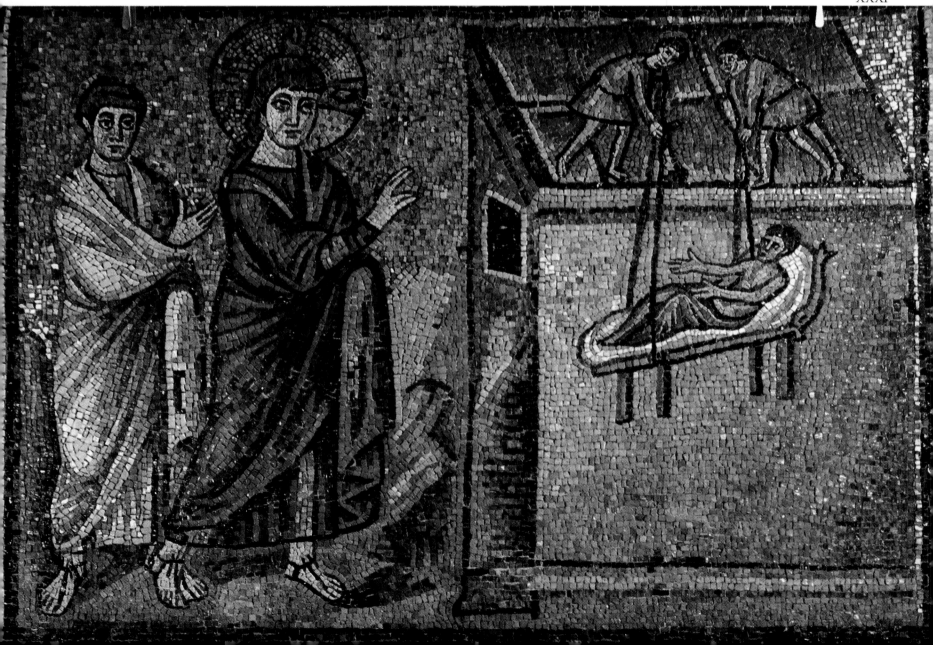

indeed, as in the churches of Constantine Lips and the
Pantocrator at Constantinople, or the monastery of Hosios
Lukas in Greece, complete three-aisled churches were set
up beside and communicating with existing ones, to produce what were virtually double or even triple churches.
A great complexity of plan so far as interior disposition is
concerned thus characterises many of the later buildings,
though this was not usually the initial intention. But the
details remained good till the end, and in the richer
churches there were usually fine capitals and lovely cornices.
The emphasis was always on the interior, but the outsides
of many of the later edifices often have great charm, and
the way that vault rises above vault, dome above dome,
is sometimes truly beautiful. Striking too is the way in
which after about 1300 the exteriors were treated from
the ornamental point of view. Blank arcading thus became
extremely popular, as in the church of the Virgin Pammakaristos at Constantinople, and bricks were also often
set to form decorative patterns, either geometric or imitating the Kufic script of Islamic writing; no better example of this is to be found than in the Church of the
Holy Apostles at Salonica, erected shortly before 1312.
Glazed pottery vessels were also sometimes built into the
walls to add a touch of colour.

Another tendency of this later work was the reduction
in span of the domes and also the elongation of the drums
on which they stood into tower-like structures. Such tall
drums appeared from the thirteenth century onwards, and
were especially popular in Greece and the Balkans. The
most extreme and perhaps also the most attractive example
is to be seen in the monastery church of Gračanica in
Yugoslavia, dating from 1321. The outside of this church
presents a complex of great beauty and charm; the inside
is less successful, for the piers are massive and numerous,
the floor-space confined, and the height exaggerated.

BYZANTINE SECULAR ARCHITECTURE

Very few buildings other than churches survive above
ground, but it has been possible to gather some idea of
domestic buildings from descriptions and as a result of
excavations. The houses, so far as we can tell, were like
Roman ones as we see them at Pompeii, with a central
court and rooms opening off it; often, if not always, they
had two storeys. Of the palaces, the most important was
the Great Palace adjoining St Sophia at Constantinople.
Though it was originally probably similar to Diocletian's
palace at Spalato, it gradually took on a very different
character, for any architectural unity that it had originally
was lost owing to the numerous additions that were made
subsequently. Almost every emperor seems to have added
to it, and by the tenth century, when Constantine Porphy-
rogenitus wrote his famous description of it, it had become
a vast complex of heterogeneous buildings and open spaces,
churches, living quarters, barracks, audience-halls and
so forth; it even included a covered hippodrome similar
to, but smaller than, the great Hippodrome which bounded
it to the west. The nearest parallel is to be found in the
Kremlin at Moscow, which was, indeed, its lineal successor. The proportions and grandeur of some of its halls
are indicated by the massiveness and immensity of certain

497

498

499

496

500

500 City walls, Constantinople
Fifth century.
Built by Theodosius II, these
walls are single in depth
on the seaward side, and double
to the landward with a moat
before them.

501

**501 The so-called Palace
of Constantine Porphyro-
genitus (known to the Turks
as Tekfour Saray), Constantinople**
It is all that remains of the great
Blachernae complex near the
Golden Horn. The present
structure mainly dates from
early Palaeologue times.

502

**502 The Golden Gate,
Constantinople**
Fifth century. Part of the city
walls, where the land walls
join the Marmara. It is a
triple-arched structure with two
flanking towers and represents
a variant of the Roman triumphal
arch. Originally there were
statues on the top.

**503 Propylaeon of the
Golden Gate, Constantinople**
A propylaeon, or outer gate,
was added in front of the great
Golden Gate itself at a slightly
later date. The façades of the
walls on either side were
adorned with sculptures, some of
which survived as recently
as the seventeenth century.

503

XXX Baptistery and cathedral, Pisa XXXI Sant'Apollinare Nuovo, Ravenna

504 The Monastery of the Lavra on Mount Athos, Greece
The monastery was founded in the tenth century, but most of the buildings that are now in it are of a later date. The complex comprises one principal church, a large refectory and numerous chapels in addition to the living quarters.

504

505 Yerebetan Saray, Constantinople
Sixth century. One of many such large underground cisterns built in Constantinople, with brick semi-circular vaults built in two directions supported by marble columns, some of which are obviously taken from antique buildings and others of simple Byzantine origin.

505

of its substructures which have recently been excavated; they date from the time of Justinian or just before. This palace was deserted about the twelfth century for another on the shores of the Golden Horn, called the Blachernae, a part of which still stands to a height of three storeys. The date of this portion has been disputed, but it is probably to be assigned to the end of the thirteenth century. Somewhat similar structures, built by the Comnene emperors of the East (1204-1461), survive at Trebizond.

If we know little of domestic architecture, we know rather more about fortifications, for the walls of several cities, notably those of Nicaea and Constantinople, survive very much in their original state. Those of Constantinople are both impressive and beautiful. They were set up by Theodosius II between 413 and 447. On the sea-front there is a single wall; landward there extends over some four miles a great double line of defence with moat before it. There are ninety-six towers in each wall, spaced alternately and at equidistant intervals along its whole length. At intervals gates were provided, the most important of them being the so-called 'Golden Gate' near where the land-walls join the Marmara, a great triple-arched structure of marble with two flanking towers on either side of the arches. Originally it was topped by statues, and there were bronze letters over the arches. It represents a variant of the Roman triumphal arch, treated as a defensive unit.

Another important aspect of early Byzantine architecture to be seen at Constantinople are the underground cisterns, of which there are a considerable number. Most of them are roofed with vaults or small domes supported on a multiplicity of columns, usually re-used from other sites. But one, the so-called 'Bin-bir-derek' or 'Thousand-and-one columns' is more original, for the columns, each 12.40 m. in height, must have been made especially for it. It has been, with a reasonable degree of probability, assigned to Anthemius of Tralles, one of the architects of St Sophia.

Finally, there are the monasteries, early examples of which survive in Syria and later ones in various parts of the Byzantine world, more especially on Mount Athos. Always they comprise one principal church, which is surrounded by the living quarters, and there are often numerous subsidiary chapels. The rooms are usually small, the only one of significance being the refectory. They do not usually present any very distinctive Byzantine architectural features, though some of the monasteries of Mount Athos are spectacular both as structures and because of the position they occupy.

RUSSIA

The history of architecture in Russia begins in the eleventh century, for nothing of earlier date survives, though the records tell us that wooden churches were set up at Kiev by Vladimir soon after he adopted Orthodox Christianity as the faith of his new empire in 988: no doubt there were wooden houses and pagan temples before that. The first masonry church to be built, however, was St Sophia at Kiev, which was begun in 1018 and finished in 1037. It was apparently a five-aisled structure with central dome, of a purely Byzantine type; the church of St Mary

506

507

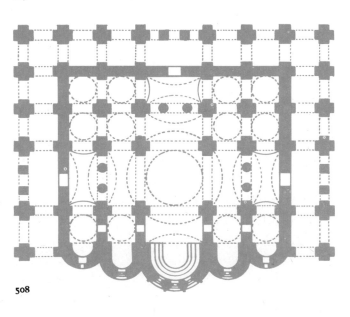

508

506 Church of St Nicholas, Panilov. c. 1600
The main portion of the building represents the first stage in the elaboration of the simplest type of wood construction, indigenous to central Russia. The roof of the porch, in the form of a 'kokoshka', a Russian woman's head-dress, was much developed from the sixteenth century onwards.

507, 508 St Sophia, Kiev. 1018-37
Exterior and plan. The first masonry church to be built after the adoption of Christianity by Vladimir in 988.
Twelve domes surround the central dome, symbolising Christ and the apostles.
The exterior was rebuilt in the seventeenth century and shows a conservative adherence to this use of the dome, for stylistic rather than functional reasons. Although Byzantine in inspiration, the division of the interior into small compartments, so emphasising the vertical, gives it a native Russian feeling.

**509 St Sophia, Novgorod.
1045-62**
The domes were probably
originally of Byzantine type:
the onion-shaped domes
which replaced the original ones
after the Mongol conquests
are of a type which was developed
in Russia and soon became
characteristic of that country.

509

**510 Cathedral of
St Demetrius, Vladimir.
1194-98**
The basic plan is Byzantine,
as is the dome on a tall drum,
but the decoration of the
exterior with sculptures in low
relief is a new feature. The
motifs are oriental and the idea
perhaps came to Russia from the
Caucasus.

510

**511 Church of Our Lady of
Kazan,
Komolskoe, near Moscow.
1649-50**
Exterior. The onion domes, which
probably originated in Novgorod,
the ancient capital, are here
seen applied to two elongated
but basically Byzantine churches,
the Kazan Church and the Church
of the Intercession on the Nerl (512).

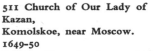

**512 Church of the Intercession
of the Virgin, on the
Nerl. 1166**
This is a three-apsed building
with a single dome on a drum
which is supported on internal
piers. Like many of the churches
of Russia it is extremely high in
proportion to length and breadth.

512

Panachrantos at Constantinople may be compared. Four
further aisles were added soon after, as well as a number of
domes, to make a total of thirteen, symbolising Christ
and the twelve apostles. At first these were probably fairly
low, akin to Byzantine ones, but the church was extensively repaired after the Mongol conquests of the thirteenth
century; the drums were probably elongated and the
domes given a new form at that time. But the division of
the interior into a number of small chambers and the
effect of verticality that this produced must have already
characterised the interior before the nine-aisled plan was
adopted, and it was this impression of verticality that
served to make it a Russian rather than a Byzantine
building.

Byzantine influence, however, was to remain important
until about 1240, when the Mongol advances cut Russia
off from the south, and other churches in Kiev, such as
that of the Virgin of the Dimes (Desyatinnaya), or others
in the region, like the Church of the Transfiguration at
Chernigov (1017), were basically Byzantine. The same
was true even of the earliest churches in the north, like
St Sophia at Novgorod (1045-62), though there the ten-   509
dency to stress the vertical was even more marked. The
same feature was true of other early foundations at Novgorod, like St Nicholas (1113), the Church of the Nativity
of the Virgin (1117), or that of the Monastery of St George
(1119). All were roofed with domes, and it was probably
in Novgorod that the typical Russian onion-shaped domes
on tall drums were first developed, for the city was never
overrun by the Mongols, and architecture could thus develop without interruption. Is was from there that Moscow
drew most of its ideas when it became the capital in the
fourteenth century.

Medieval architecture in Russia was developed finally
in Moscow, where the churches in the Kremlin, that of
the Dormition (1475-79), the Annunciation (1484-89), and
St Michael the Archangel (1505-09) all follow Novgoro-   515
dian prototypes. But the last two of these were built by
Italian architects, and soon the introduction of new ideas
from Italy and the West changed the old medieval forms
into a new Russian Baroque. The development of this
new manner was assisted by the assimilation, in brick and
stone, of ideas which had previously been worked out in
wood; the influence of wooden prototypes was indeed
one of the principal formulative influences of later Russian
church architecture. Defensive architecture, as we see it
exemplified in the towers of the Moscow Kremlin, also   513,
owed quite a debt to what had been done at an earlier
date in wood.

ART IN THE WEST, c. 600-c. 1050

It cannot be claimed that the period of architecture from
about 600 onwards was of great importance in the West,
for such church building as was done was either in a very
conservative style or on a very small scale. But the age
was not quite as dark as has sometimes been held, and
there was quite a lot of activity in spite of wars and barbarian inroads. In Rome, for example, basilicas were erected by nearly all the popes. Many of them were extensive
and quite fine, but not new departures architecturally,

513

514

515

513 The Kremlin and Red Square, Moscow
An expression in brick and stone of ideas originally worked out in wood from native Russian concepts. The conception of the Kremlin, a series of independent churches, palaces, reception halls, etc., within a walled enclosure, was derived from the Great Palace at Constantinople.

514 The Kremlin's Borovitski tower, Moscow
Late sixteenth century. The stepping of this stone tower represents a very popular fashion in Russian architecture. It was probably derived from experience in the use of timber.

515 St Michael the Archangel, Kremlin, Moscow. 1505-09. Alevisio Novi
Built by an Italian architect, this church shows an extraordinary sensitivity to the native style that clothes new ideas from Italy and the West, soon to change the old forms into a new Russian Baroque.

516 Krak des Chevaliers, Syria
Twelfth century.
Described by a Moslem as a bone stuck in the throat of the Saracens, Krak stands today as one of the best-preserved Crusader castles in the East.
It represents the Western European fortress manned with Eastern defensive strategies.
With the advantage of its site Krak is an ordered, scientifically planned, self-supporting citadel with wells, store houses and living quarters.

516

517 Caernarvon Castle, Wales.
1285–1322
Begun by Edward I Caernarvon has a single circuit of walls strengthened by polygonal towers carefully designed to give cross fire at every point.

517

518 Carcassonne, Aude
Thirteenth century (restored by Viollet-le-Duc in the nineteenth century).
The problem of enclosing and defending a town by walls meant the imposition of some sort of external control over a settlement which had grown from haphazard beginnings. The town walls or bulwarks (boulevards) later became places for promenading townspeople.

518

519 Ávila, Spain
Fourteenth century.
Another well-preserved walled town. The circular tower with its obvious advantages over sharp angles when under battering seems to have been brought from the East.

519

520

521

523

525

522

524

526

520 The medieval walls, Jerusalem

Rebuilt in sixteenth century.
The old city of Jerusalem is a
fine example of a completely
walled town of the late Middle
Ages. The walls have at their base
a wide, sloping talus against
mining — a Saracen invention.

521 Keep, Tower of London

Late eleventh century onwards.
The keep was built by
William I as the town citadel
and to maintain a garrison
for police purposes and for
defence. Later additions
turned the keep into a
concentric fortified complex.

522 Keep, castle of the counts of Montfort, Houdan, France

Eleventh century.
This circular keep would have
been the last centre of
resistance for a stronghold.
The semi-circular towers at
the cardinal points were
sited to give cross fire for
mutual defence.

523 Windsor Castle

Eleventh century onwards.
In spite of much accumulated
stone building and restoration,
the motte (mound) enclosed by a
bailey (rampart and ditch)
of the original earthwork and
palisade still dictates the basic plan.

524 Castello Nuovo, Naples. 1279–83

The kingdom of Sicily and
Naples was successively Byzantine,
Saracen and Norman, and
upon this foundation Frederick II
founded the first modern
European autocratic state.
It is well proportioned and of a
highly organised symmetry.

525 Bodiam Castle, Sussex. 1386

Bodiam is an entirely symmetrical
building, almost square in
plan, showing control over
building form generally associated
with axially designed classical
buildings.
The Crusaders brought back from
the East a concept of planning
which had been developed
by the Moslems from the eighth
century, and which influenced
castle building from late Norman
days until the time of Henry VIII.

526 Albi Cathedral, France. 1282–1390

This fortified church is closely
linked to the main defences of the
town itself.
The form of this important
Gothic cathedral is that of the
town gates and walls.
During the internecine wars
of the late Middle Ages Albi was
something of a frontier town,
and the church was intended to
withstand a siege.

527 St Martin de Canigou, France
Early eleventh century.
An example of a tri-apsidal church with stone barrel vaulting in the so-called 'first Romanesque' style.

527

528 San Pietro, Toscanella
Seventh-eleventh centuries.
A church in the style known as Lombard Romanesque, the façade being decorated with blank arcading.
The basilica plan was still adhered to, but invention was shown in the use of barrel vaulting in the interior.

528

529-531 Aachen (Aix-la-Chapelle) Cathedral. 792-805
Plan, interior and exterior. Charlemagne's mausoleum occupies the centre of the complex. It was no doubt modelled on San Vitale at Ravenna. The entrance is flanked by stair turrets and leads into a polygon of sixteen sides 105 feet in diameter.
Every two columns of this polygon converge on one pier to form an internal octagon which supports a dome forty-eight feet in diameter.

529

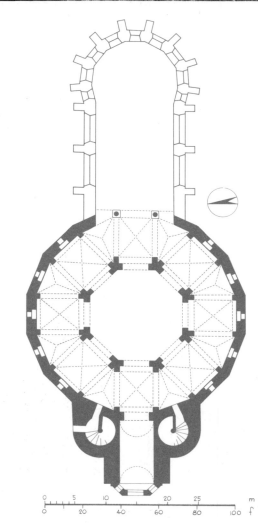

530

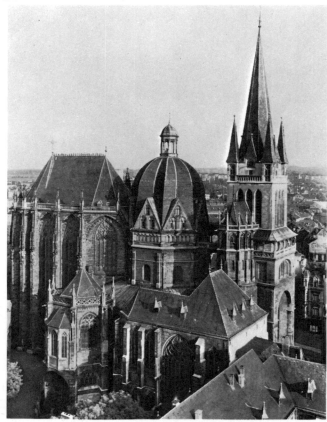

531

being in the main simply reproductions, on a somewhat smaller scale, of the great basilicas of the fifth century. The two main types of basilica which have already been discussed here, namely those where a horizontal architrave or an arcade top the columns, are represented. Similar basilicas were erected elsewhere in Italy (especially in central Italy), and the basilica remained the principal church type until the twelfth century. But in a few places new trends were forthcoming; the most important was the development of the Lombard Romanesque style. There it would seem that new ideas were taking shape, and though the basilical plan was adhered to, barrel vaults began to be used for roofing in the ninth century, and blank arcading probably became popular at much the same time, as a means of decorating the façades. The churches of San Pietro at **528** Agliate near Monza (875) and San Pietro at Toscanella may be noted. The latter was founded in 628, but was considerably altered first in 740 and then again in 1040, and the more elaborate part of its exterior is probably to be assigned to the later date.

Though Lombardy was soon to become quite important as a centre of building, thanks to some extent to the presence of a group of highly skilled workmen whom we know as the Commacene masons, it was probably in Spain that the most interesting developments took place during these centuries, even if the initial ideas were probably transmitted from Lombardy. The churches of the period were all on a very small scale, but they mostly show a number of original features which actually represent in embryo what were to be the principal characteristics of the next great architectural style we shall examine— the Romanesque. So important are these Spanish churches, indeed, that they were distinguished in the 'twenties by the name 'First Romanesque', and the Spanish scholar who coined that name, Puig-i-Cadafalch, claims that the style was more than a purely local one. He traces its manifestation in Italy, in the south of France and even further north in central France, Germany and Switzerland, and maintains that had the tentative experiments that we see in the 'First Romanesque' not been made, the architectural history of western Europe might never have developed in the way that it did.

The churches of this group sometimes have one, sometimes three, aisles, and in the latter case there are three apses, an idea probably adopted from the Byzantine world. Often there is blank arcading on the outside. But the most important feature is the roof, which consisted of a stone vault; it was not the timber structure characteristic of the Italian basilicas. In these rather low, simple, three-aisled tunnel-vaulted churches of the 'First Romanesque' style we see, in fact, the prototypes of the great vaulted cathedrals of the early twelfth century. Of examples on Spanish soil, San Miguel de Liño, founded in 848, is typical. In southern **527** France the style is represented by such a church as St Martin de Canigou, which dates from between 1001 and 1026. There had been little development during the century and a half that separates these two buildings, but in the course of the next century quite amazing strides were to be taken in France, and these are heralded in San Pedro de Casserres (1010); for there the simple barrel vault has

532

533

534

532 Germigny-des-Prés, France. 806
This building is cruciform and seems to be Armenian in inspiration, another example of the eclecticism of the Carolingians. The church was originally part of a large monastery complex.

533 Maria Laach Abbey, Germany. 1093-1156
The idea of a double-ended church was taken by the Ottonian architects from the Carolingians, and became one of the characteristics of German Romanesque.

534 Gatehouse of the abbey, Lorsch, Germany. 810
The lower portion of this structure derives from a Roman arch, but the pointed cornices above may perhaps have been inspired by wooden prototypes.

535 Abbey church, Gernrode, Germany. 961
This Ottonian church has a flat wooden roof, and the crossing is marked by great transverse arches that herald the true diaphragm arches of the next phase of development.

536 Worms Cathedral. Begun 1016
Another double-ended church similar to Maria Laach, with circular towers flanking the apses, and external arcading at high level.

537 Hildesheim Cathedral, Germany. Bronze doors. 1015
The magnificent bronze doors, with scenes of the Creation, Fall and Redemption, were commissioned by Bishop Bernward (993-1022) originally for St Michael's at Hildesheim, but are now in the cathedral.

538 St Michael's, Hildesheim. 1001-33
Interior.
This church with a nave and two aisles also has two apses, two transepts and two chancels. Two squat towers are over the crossings and the nave is divided into three squares which are indicated by larger piers. The design of this church proved an inspiration for other Central European examples.

535

536

537

538

been strengthened by transverse arches, which serve to split it up into a series of bays corresponding to those marked by columns rising from the floor below.

In tracing the origin of Romanesque, however, the small churches of the Mediterranean world do not provide the only evidence that must be considered. Developments in the north under the patronage of the rulers of the only truly developed state of the time, the Carolingian, were more spectacular and more impressive, though they left their descendants in Germany rather than in France.

At its outset, the architecture of the Carolingians was essentially eclectic; ideas were assimilated from various sources, and quite a number of buildings which clearly reflect the various sources of their inspiration still survive. Charlemagne's mausoleum at Aachen (792-805), for example, is a direct copy of San Vitale at Ravenna. Germigny-des-Prés in France (806), originally the church of a considerable monastic complex, is a cruciform building, which would seem to have been inspired from Armenia, while the curious little building of around 810 which survives at Lorsch and which must have been part of the monastery there, was in part inspired by a Roman prototype, though the pointed arcades above perhaps reflect the influence of a type of building proper to wood rather than stone (see below; Earl's Barton Church). Classical inspiration of an even purer type is to be seen in the church of San Agostino del Crocefisso at Spoleto, a most unusual building, which was at one time believed to be late Roman, but which is now usually regarded as mainly Carolingian, while a type of plan which was to become above any other essentially Carolingian was also probably inspired by later Roman architecture. It was that of the basilical church with apse at each end, as we see it around 820 in a manuscript plan of the lay-out of the Monastery of St Gall in what is today Switzerland. This idea of the double-ended church was freely developed in Carolingian times; it passed to the Ottonian architects and became one of the most characteristic features of German Romanesque in the eleventh and twelfth centuries, as for example at Maria Laach (1093-1156), Mainz (978; restored 1036) or Worms (1016 and later).

Another feature which was developed by the Carolingian architects is also apparent in all these buildings, namely, a transept both at east and west and a number of circular towers flanking the apses; there were also usually towers at both crossings, so that many of these buildings had two large and four smaller towers, and at times even more round towers were added. The cathedrals set up in southern and central Germany in the eleventh century differ of course in detail, and they are vaulted in a way unknown in Carolingian times; but apart from that they serve to give a very good idea of what the more important Carolingian buildings were like. Nowhere else in Europe did architecture remain so conservative as here. The massive western ends are termed the *Westwerk* in German.

Nor can it be said that the Ottonian age (863-1024), which in many ways represented a revival of the Carolingian, brought a great deal of change, though there are some notable buildings in Germany that were set up under the patronage of the Ottonian emperors. The most im-

(margin references: 29-531, 532, 534, 540, 533, 536)

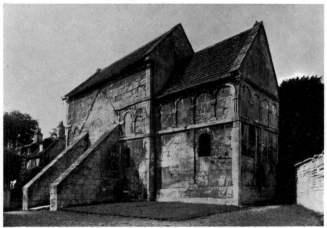

539

539 St Lawrence, Bradford-on-Avon, Gloucestershire. 970
The plan follows a type very usual at the time, with a smaller rectangular choir projecting at the east of a larger rectangular nave. The building is remarkable for the excellent masonry of carefully squared stones. Few other buildings of the period show a similar excellence of craftsmanship.

540

540 Earl's Barton Church, Northamptonshire
Tenth century. This is perhaps the finest example of Anglo-Saxon architecture that has come down to us. It has been suggested that the pilaster strips on the surface derive from wooden prototypes.

541

541 Sompting Church, Sussex
Early eleventh century. An example of the southern style of village church, stone built with a single aisle with apse, that first evolved soon after the arrival in Britain of St Augustine in 597. The unusual form of the tower roof was first developed in Germany.

542, 543 Greenstead Church, Essex. c. 1013

Two views of exterior.
The oldest wooden church that still survives in England, contemporaneous with the stone churches such as Earl's Barton. Built of oak and elm, it reflects the squat, stocky form that these short-baulk timbers favour rather than that of the tall stave-churches found in Scandinavia.

542

543

544 Church at Borgund, Norway. c. 1150

Section.
An example of a tall stave-church built of pine.
The type of roof shown here was used for the early Westminster Palace depicted in the Bayeux tapestry.

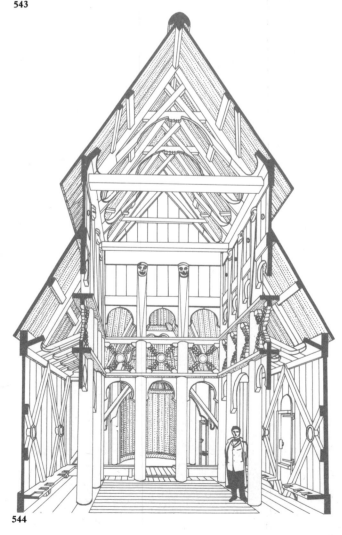

544

portant of them probably are the abbey at Gernrode (961) and the church of St Michael at Hildesheim (1001-33). Both have flat wooden roofs, but the crossings are marked by great transverse arches which herald the true diaphragm arches of the next phase, when the naves were divided up by arches into a series of bays—a very desirable feature when the danger of fire was an ever-present one. It may be noted in passing that St Michael's at Hildesheim is especially remarkable because of the bronze doors and other features which were made for it, thanks to the patronage of Bishop Bernward (993-1022). They are now in Hildesheim Cathedral.

Though it falls outside the main line of continental developments, the early architecture of Britain deserves a mention, for though modest in scale, it was possessed of a very individual style of its own. The first manifestations came soon after the introduction of Christianity by St Augustine in 597, and a few stone-built churches of this age have been excavated. There were two distinct groups: a southern centred on Canterbury, and a northern, around Hexham. Normally the churches had a single aisle with apse; 'porticus', adjoining structures rather like additional aisles, were often added, to give a transeptal or three-aisled appearance. With the cultural Renaissance set on foot by Alfred at the end of the ninth century more ambitious buildings began to be erected, and though most of them were destroyed after the Norman conquest to make way for structures on a larger scale, vestiges of a few larger churches or more or less complete smaller ones survive. They are usually very tall in comparison to the extent of the ground plan, like the church at Bradford-on-Avon (970), which is distinguished by the excellence of its masonry. Usually pilaster strips decorate the outsides, and on the tower of Earl's Barton, these have been very greatly developed (tenth century). It has been suggested that they reflect the idea of wooden prototypes, the pilasters representing the timbers and the stone the plaster of half-timbered construction which was a familiar technique in central England from early times. On balance, however, it is more likely that we see here a local development of the Eastern idea of blank arcading, which we have noted in the Mediterranean world, and especially in Lombardy.

Wood was, however, very important as a building material, and one wooden structure still survives in the little village church of Greenstead in Essex. In view of the nature of the timber available in England at the time—stocky oak and elm rather than slender pine—it is probable that wooden buildings assumed the form of stock work that we see here rather than that of the tall stave-church type usual in Scandinavia. But in areas where pine trees were indigenous, these were very important. Early examples survive at Urnes and at Borgund in Norway (c. 1150), but there are also a number of carved wooden doors from other churches of earlier date; they were probably wooden churches not unlike Borgund (a form probably developed in pagan times). It is also possible that the type of roof seen on these churches was used in England, even if tall stave-churches were not, for the roof of Westminster Palace as depicted on the Bayeux tapestry is closely akin.

535
537, 53

539

540

542, 5

544

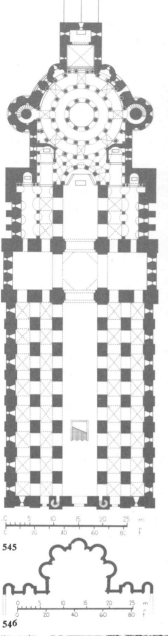

545

546

547

545 St Bénigne, Dijon. c. 1001
Plan.
The plan has a circular structure at the east end with a vaulted roof to the nave.
The development of the east end was a result of the growing interest in pilgrimage and the adoration of relics, and this one suggests the Church of the Holy Sepulchre at Jerusalem.
From these beginnings developed the idea of the apse and the ambulatory plan.

546 St Martin, Tours. 918
Plan.
This is the plan of what remains of the original building, among the earliest of Romanesque churches.

547 St Philibert, Tournus. Begun c. 950
The most interesting feature of this Burgundian church is the roof divided into bays by transverse arches which rise directly from the circular piers. Between each pair of the transverse arches is a barrel vault at right angles to the nave walls.

548

549

548 Frescoes at St Savin-sur-Gartempe, France
Eleventh century.
Noah's ark. Detail of fresco from the vault.
The nave, narthex and crypt of St Savin were designed to take the beautiful frescoes known as the 'Bible of St Savin', one of the finest examples of Romanesque mural painting.
Scenes from the Old Testament occupy the vault.
The New Testament is illustrated in the porch, along with scenes from the Apocalypse.

549 St Savin-sur-Gartempe, France
Eleventh century. The great barrel vault may be conservative from the architectural point of view, but it provides an admirable surface for frescoes.

**550, 551 Bayeux Cathedral,
France**
Interior and exterior. This
building was begun in the
eleventh century and was
added to continually until the
central tower was completed
in the fifteenth century.
It is remarkable for its
twenty-two chapels and the
immense Romanesque crypt
under the sanctuary.

550   551

**552 St Benoît-sur-Loire,
France. Begun c. 1068**
Known also as Fleury, it was one
of the centres of Benedictine
monasticism from 655,
when the relics of the saint were
taken there from Montecassino.

552

ROMANESQUE IN FRANCE

Though the Carolingian and later the Ottonian and Franconian monarchs had been great patrons of architecture, and though important initial developments were made in Lombardy, it was in northern and central France that the greatest strides were made in the development of architecture in the eleventh century, and it was there that the style which we know as Romanesque reached its most brilliant fruition around 1100.

The first beginnings, apart from the initial experiments of the 'First Romanesque', can be traced in the plan of St Martin's at Tours (918), where the bones of the patron saint were enshrined at a lower level, with an ambulatory-like structure around the shrine. A similar disposition was adopted in the crypt of the church of 858 at Chartres, portions of which still remain; while at Auxerre the crypt of the cathedral was remodelled in 859 to permit pilgrims to pay reverence to the bones of St Germain. From these small beginnings there developed the idea of the apse and ambulatory plan, which afforded a suitable setting for relics and also permitted the passage of pilgrims without disturbing the services, which, in a monastic institution, were taking place in the central area at practically every hour of the day.

In addition to the development of the eastern end, which was the direct outcome of the growing interest in pilgrimage and the adoration of relics, experiments were also being made in the elaboration of ground plans in other respects, as well as in the problems of roofing. Charlieu was thus rebuilt about 940 with a barrel vault, while St Bénigne at Dijon was erected around 1001 with a circular structure at the east end and with a vaulted roof to the nave. The east end suggests the plan of the Church of the Holy Sepulchre at Jerusalem and precedes a more general adoption of the circular plan a century or so later as a result of the Crusades. But perhaps the most interesting of all the experiments of the period is illustrated by the church at Tournus, which was rebuilt in various phases from about 950 onwards. Its east end as rebuilt at that time was of an ambulatory plan, with radiating chapels, and was a three-aisled structure, the division between the aisles being effected by great circular piers. The most interesting feature however is the roof, which is divided into bays by great transverse arches springing from the piers; and each bay is roofed by a transverse barrel vault. At the ends of these are windows which permit light to be provided at the very summit of the building in a way quite impossible with the longitudinal barrel vaults usual in these buildings, such as that at Charlieu or that set up later at St Savin. Though the latter is extremely impressive and provides an admirable surface for a frescoed decoration, it is architecturally less progressive than the roof at Tournus, which in many ways heralds the groined vault and ribbed vault. These were to be the great glory of the fully developed Romanesque, for there also it was possible to insert a window high up without weakening the support afforded by the side walls; though when seen from the east or west the effect was produced of a continuous vault not broken up in the way it is at Tournus.

553

554

555

553 La Trinité
(Abbaye aux Dames),
Caen. 1062-1140
Founded by the wife
of William the Conqueror, it has
a fine western façade flanked by
two towers. A square tower
over the crossing completes this
homogeneous design.

554 St Etienne (Abbaye aux
Hommes), Caen. 1066-77
An illustration of the remarkable
intersecting sexpartite ribbed
vault, with two bays included in
each vaulting compartment.

555 St Benoît-sur-Loire.
Begun c. 1068
The nave wall, weakened by the
clerestory windows below the
barrel vault, is strengthened
again by the abutting vaults
of the side aisles and by the blind
arcade below the clerestory
windows.

556

**556, 557 St Etienne.
Nevers. 1083-97**
This pilgrimage-style church
has a three-storey nave elevation,
with a gallery above the
aisles and a clerestory above
the gallery. The barrel vault
over the nave, with its transverse
arches, has its thrust partially
counteracted by the half barrel
vault of the gallery, which
abuts against the nave wall.

557

558 Neuvy-St-Sépulcre. 1045
The plan of this church
reproduces closely that of the
Church of the Holy Sepulchre at
Jerusalem,
but it remains wholly
French in expression.

558

There was, however, still to be much trial and experiment before this important architectural feature was fully developed, for though some Romanesque churches were roofed with barrel vaults, many of the great eleventh-century buildings of France still had wooden roofs, in any case over the main aisles. But they were, in many cases, divided into a series of bays by great spanning arches —diaphragm arches they are called—sometimes above each corresponding pair of piers and sometimes only at every other pair. Before discussing later developments of the vaulting system it will be well to note a few of the monuments.

The earliest are to be found in Normandy, and Bernay (1017-49), Jumièges (1037-66), Bayeux (1049-77), Domfront (c. 1050), and the churches of St Nicholas (1062-83), La Trinité (also called the Abbaye aux Dames, 1062-72) and St Etienne (or the Abbaye aux Hommes, 1066-77) at Caen may be noted. All are distinguished by their large size, by the presence of two western towers and usually of one at the crossing and by the absence of decoration; the capitals are either quite plain or perhaps have the volutes indicated in very low relief, while the doorways are adorned at most with dog-tooth or similar conventionalised pattern. It was from Normandy that the Romanesque style came to Britain, first introduced by Edward the Confessor at Westminster and not by William the Conqueror. 550, 553 554

As one proceeds southwards through France the style changes, and the tendency to include a sculptured decoration becomes more marked. A number of regional groups are to be distinguished, both with regard to plan and decoration. Along the Loire, for instance, the churches were often aisleless, and the naves were often wide, even when aisles were present. The great abbey churches of Lessay (1080-1178), St Benoît-sur-Loire (from c. 1068), La Charité-sur-Loire (1059-1107), St Etienne at Nevers (1083-97) and Neuvy-St-Sépulcre (1045) may be noted. 552, 556, 558

All are important, but for different reasons. St Benoît-sur-Loire, also known as Fleury, had been one of the chief centres of Benedictine monasticism since 655, when the relics of St Benoît had been taken there from Montecassino. Nevers was a double church of somewhat unusual plan, recalling those of Ottonian Germany, though from the architectural point of view its greatest interest lies in the way the galleries over the side aisles are roofed with half arches, springing from the summit of the outer wall and resting against the high wall of the central aisle. They constitute what are virtually flying buttresses in embryo. La Charité-sur-Loire is remarkable, again, because of the obvious Islamic influence that is to be seen in the architectural detail; the arches of the east end are trilobe, and there are sculptured plaques of a wholly oriental character inserted into the walls above them. Finally Neuvy-St-Sépulcre is of particular interest. Its plan reproduces closely that of the Church of the Holy Sepulchre at Jerusalem, though the building methods and the detail are, of course, wholly French, as similar plans were often adopted after the twelfth century as a result of the Crusades.

The next distinctive region is Burgundy, and it is perhaps the most important of all, for it was there that the great mother church of the Benedictine order, Cluny, was situated. The first great church, dating from 927, was pulled 562

down to make way for a second in 955; the second made way for a third, which was begun in 1088 and finished about 1118. It was on a far grander scale than any other, with five instead of three aisles and no less than seven towers. The apse was of the ambulatory type, the side aisles separated from the central choir by columns topped with elaborately sculptured capitals. The interior was apparently roofed with a pointed barrel vault, and there were frescoes, with a great figure of Christ in Glory at the eastern end. All this stood till the early days of the nineteenth century; today no more than one transept, itself a church of no mean proportions, survives *in situ*, though the choir capitals, works of the greatest beauty, are preserved in the local museum. There is perhaps no greater tragedy in the history of architecture than that of the pointless destruction of this superb building early in the nineteenth century.

The other churches of Burgundy, such as Saulieu (1119), Beaune (1120-40), Paray-le-Monial (1109), Vézelay (1104), and Autun (second quarter of the twelfth century), all owe a direct debt to Cluny, and so do many of the churches which marked the staging points along the pilgrimage routes to Santiago de Compostela in Spain, for the abbey of Cluny, to a great extent, afforded the inspiration for the pilgrimage traffic which played so important a rôle in the religious life and thought of the age. St Sernin at Toulouse (1060-80) and the church of Ste Foy at Conques, for instance, are essentially 'Cluniac' in character. A word will be said about both of them in connection with the regions where they are located.

All these Cluniac churches follow a similar plan. There was usually an apse and ambulatory at the eastern end, with chapels radiating from it; the interiors were usually roofed with barrel vaults, and there was usually a clerestory with triforium below it. The side aisles were roofed with groin vaults. There was often a tower at the crossing and two more at the west end. But only in St Sernin at Toulouse was the five-aisled plan of Cluny repeated; the other churches of Burgundy and the pilgrimage routes had three aisles. Often, however, there was sculpture, and this was centred on the capitals of the choir and the tympana of the west doors. Some of the finest sculpture of all times is to be found on these churches; the capitals of Cluny, Vézelay and Autun, and the tympana of Vézelay, Autun and Conques are perhaps the most outstanding, though they are equalled, even perhaps surpassed, by the more ornate style of the south, as seen at Moissac or Souillac.

In the Poitou, with Poitiers at its centre, sculpture played a rather different rôle from that in Burgundy, for it was less monumental but more universal, and sometimes spread from the tympana to cover the whole west front, as, for example, in Notre-Dame-la-Grande at Poitiers. A profusion of ornamental sculpture is one of the characteristics that distinguish the churches of this region. In dimensions they were generally less impressive than those of Burgundy and the Loire; the interiors were often rather dark, for usually the churches were roofed with barrel vaults, and there was no clerestory and no direct lighting in the naves. The outsides were ornate but less impressive from a distance, because western towers were rare; their place was usually taken by small circular turrets, built in

559

560

561

559 Abbey church, Cluny. 1088-1118
The one transept that remains of the original church, which was destroyed in the early nineteenth century. It makes a church of no mean proportions on its own (see 562).

560 Paray-le-Monial, Burgundy. 1109
Exterior.
The extent to which the 'Cluniac' churches followed the design and appearance of the great central abbey of the Benedictine order can be seen by comparing the exterior of Paray-le-Monial with the remaining transept of the parent church (559).

561 Paray-le-Monial, Burgundy. 1109
Interior.
One of the many churches deriving from Cluny, the nave is roofed with a barrel vault with a clerestory and triforium below. The side aisles are roofed with groin vaults.

**562 Abbey church, Cluny.
1088–1118**
Plan and elevation.
Now destroyed, this church was
the longest in France, 443 feet.
It was the mother
church of the Benedictine order
and influenced many
Burgundian churches such as those
at Saulieu, Beaune,
Paray-le-Monial, Vézelay and
Autun – all 'Cluniac' churches.
The apse had an ambulatory with
side aisles and was separated
from the choir by columns
with finely sculptured capitals.
The church was on a grand scale,
with five aisles and seven towers.
Today no more than one transept
survives (559).

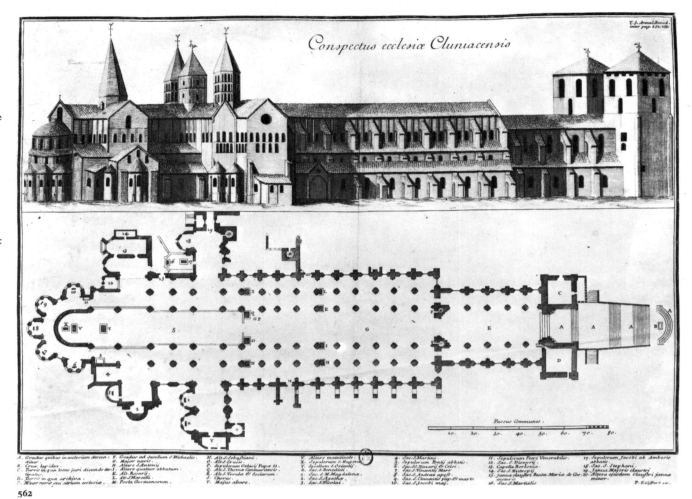

Conspectus ecclesiæ Cluniacensis

562

**563, 565 Notre-Dame-la-
Grande, Poitiers. 1130–45**
Façade and detail.
An illustration of the finely
carved west front. A profusion
of ornamental sculpture, often
wittily grotesque, marks the
churches of Poitou. The small
circular turrets with their conical
roofs of scale-like tiles
are also distinctive.

563

**564 Ste Madeleine, Vézelay.
Begun 1104**
The nave (1120–40) of this
splendid Burgundian church
is roofed by a groined vault with
transverse arches – a form
of vaulting which, through
canalising much of the thrust
to the piers, facilitated
the cutting of clerestory
windows in the nave wall.

564   565

566

567

568

569

566 Ste Madeleine, Vézelay. Tympanum, c. 1125-30
The central tympanum of the narthex, with its remarkable figure of Christ in Glory, surrounded by Apostles, his garments swirling restlessly about his feet, is one of the crowning achievements of the Romanesque sculptors.

567, 569 Abbey church, Souillac. 1130-40
Sculptural details. The carved pillar or trumeau and the figure below it, with its 'dancing' movement, are excellent examples of the sculptural style of the Toulouse regions. The figure (569) is of the prophet Isaiah.

568 Tympanum, Autun Cathedral. 1130-40
This detail from the tympanum shows Christ in Glory; the whole illustrates the Last Judgment. Autun Cathedral, with its tympanum and its beautiful sculptured capitals, contains some of the finest examples of fully fledged Romanesque sculpture.

570 Pilgrimage routes to Santiago de Compostela
Many of the churches which marked the staging points on the route to Santiago de Compostela (the burial place of St James, to which pilgrims flocked to pay reverence and to obtain absolution) owe their inspiration to Cluny.

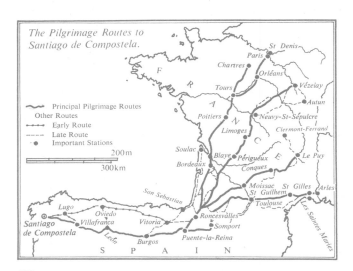

570

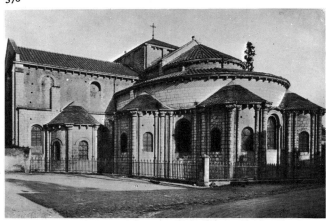

571

571, 572 St Hilaire, Poitiers
Mid-eleventh to early twelfth centuries. Exterior and interior. Although the churches of the Poitou are usually roofed with a barrel vault, the nave of this church is in fact covered by octagonal domes on squinches – a device which relates it to the domed churches of Périgord (574-76).

572

a curious scale-like masonry. The plans too were distinct from those usually followed in Burgundy, for there were usually three apses instead of the apse and ambulatory with radiating chapels.

There are several fine churches in Poitiers itself—St Hilaire (1049 and early twelfth century), Ste Radegonde (1090) and Notre-Dame-la-Grande (1130-45) are the most important—and the region also is very rich. Aulnay (1125-40), Chauvigny (c. 1100), St Savin (1060-1115) and Melle, where there are three fine churches, may be noted. That at Chauvigny, standing on the top of a hill, is especially impressive, while the great barrel-vaulted nave of St Savin is distinguished by its magnificent series of paintings with scenes from the Old Testament.

The Poitiers style, with its abundance of sculpture and its turrets, exercised a considerable influence on Périgord, the province immediately to the south, and that region was in turn linked with the Toulouse area; though in this case any influence that was exercised was in the opposite direction, for most of the churches of the Toulouse area are earlier in date that those of Périgord. The churches are nearly all profusely adorned. In the north the sculptures are in the main decorative, though the region shares with the western Poitou a love of large equestrian figures on the tympana; Angoulême (1105) and Ste Marie-des-Dames at Saintes (c. 1150) are noteworthy. In the south, the very expressive, almost tortured, though superbly fine, sculptural style of the Toulouse region was adopted, and some of the finest examples of the school are to be found in Périgord, notably at Souillac (1130-40) and Beaulieu (c. 1130).

The most interesting architectural feature of the region, however, is the presence of a large number of domed churches. As many as seventy-seven examples have been noted, most of them in Périgord, though they extend to neighbouring areas, as for example to the north, at Fontevrault (1119-25), on the banks of the Loire, and as far south as Spain, for example San Vicente de Cordona. The domes vary in number, some churches having only one, at the crossing, while others have two, three, four or five. At Angoulême (1105) there are four; at Périgueux there are five, one at the crossing and one on each of the arms of the cross. The latter follows the typical Byzantine five-domed plan, as conceived by Justinian in his Church of the Holy Apostles at Constantinople and copied early in the eleventh century in St Mark's at Venice.

The question as to why this essentially Byzantine form of roof became popular in south-western France has never been satisfactorily answered. It has been suggested that the idea was brought back from Constantinople by the Crusaders, that it was introduced through Greek traders, of whom there was a large colony at Marseilles, and perhaps also at Bordeaux, that it was adopted from Venice, or brought by way of Cyprus. All these explanations are possible, but none serves to explain why the dome was so popular in this region and not elsewhere, especially when other areas were nearer to the Byzantine world or in closer touch with ports having Greek colonies.

The region between Périgord and the Pyrenees was, after Burgundy, the most important as regards sculpture. We know rather less about its architecture, for more of its

573

576

577

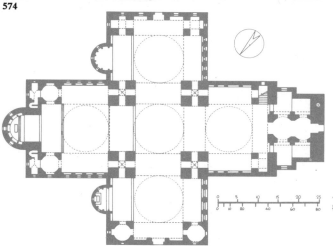

574

575

578

573, 576 Ste Radegonde, Poitiers. 1090
Exterior and interior. Only the apse, crypt and ambulatory of this church are Romanesque; the rest of the church is Gothic. The Romanesque capitals of the choir apse are particularly fine.

574, 575, 578 St Front, Périgueux. 1120
Exterior, plan and interior. One of the best of the domed Périgord churches, having five domes, one at the crossing and one on each arm of the cross. This follows a Byzantine model and the plan is almost identical to that of St Mark's, Venice (492). The interior shows clearly the pure form of the Byzantine use of arches and domes. It was probably originally intended to cover these with plaster and to paint them with frescoes.

577 Ste Foy, Conques, Aveyron. 1045-1119
A pure example of the pilgrimage style, on one of the main routes to Santiago de Compostela. This narrow building possesses fine carved capitals and a striking tympanum of the Last Judgment. The church has preserved its medieval treasure, which includes the richly decorated reliquary statue of Ste Foy.

**579 St Gilles, near Arles.
1140-60**
The west front of this Provençal
church is adorned with fluted
columns and pilasters, Corinthian
capitals and architraves which
might almost have formed
part of a classical temple.
But the Burgundian influence
can be seen in the sculptures
of the tympana.

579

580 St Trophîme, Arles
Twelfth century.
Similar to St Gilles. The central
aisle has a wooden roof.
Note the pure classical
flavour of the main doorway.

581, 583 St Pierre, Moissac
Twelfth century onwards.
Exterior and detail.
The tympanum on the southern
portal shows Christ in Glory
surrounded by the four and twenty
Elders and the symbols
of the four Evangelists.
Like many of the churches in this
area, St Pierre has been
greatly restored, and little remains
of the original building.
Only the cloister and porch
are truly Romanesque,
the latter containing some of the
finest Romanesque sculpture.

580

581

**582 St Gilles, near Arles.
1140-60**
Detail of façade.
This detail shows a Corinthian
capital and fluted column typical
of these Provençal churches.

582

583

churches have either perished or been restored, so that the old structures have vanished even if the plans have been retained. This is the case of St Sernin at Toulouse, after Cluny the largest of the pilgrimage churches, and it is also true of Moissac, for there only the cloister and porch survive from Romanesque times, the church being later. But the porch (1115-20) is perhaps the greatest Romanesque sculpture that we have. The lovely church at Conques (1045-1119) stands on the fringe of the region; it has already been noted as an outstanding example of the pilgrimage style, and it remains as one of the purest and most inspiring, though by no means one of the largest, examples of the type. It is very tall, contains a mass of fine capitals, and there is an elaborate tympanum depicting the Last Judgement over the western doors.

Two other regions remain: the Auvergne and Provence. The former is mountainous and was in medieval times secluded, less prosperous and more independent than the others; its character is attested by the nature of its architecture. Its churches are mostly on a comparatively small scale: they are tall and rather dark inside, with barrel-vaulted naves. There are sometimes western towers; the most distinctive feature is the raising of the inner part of the transepts to a level higher than that of choir or nave, so that on the outsides there is a curious box-like projection at the centre. The most striking example of this type is probably the church at Issoire. Churches at St Nectaire and St Saturnin in the mountains nearby are akin, as is that of Notre-Dame-du-Port at Clermont-Ferrand (late eleventh century). Indeed, this is perhaps the key example of the group, though today it is less attractive and impressive than the others, for it is in the midst of a noisy, crowded town, whereas St Nectaire and St Saturnin stand on the hill tops in secluded villages. There are fine capitals in the choirs of many of these buildings, but not much other sculpture.

On the fringe of this region and the next is the mountain city of Le Puy, with its cathedral, a large three-aisled structure, adorned with sculpture of a very Islamic character. It is however something of an isolated phenomenon, and the buildings of Provence, which is the next region towards the south, are quite distinct, for there classical ideas seem to have survived, to appear anew in churches like St Gilles (1140-60), and St Trophîme at Arles (twelfth century). Their west fronts are adorned with fluted columns, Corinthian capitals and architraves which might almost have formed part of a classical temple. Some buildings show Burgundian influence; they are three-aisled and have barrel vaults in the side aisles, even if the central aisles usually have wooden roofs of the type usual in early Italian basilicas.

ROMANESQUE IN SPAIN

Much of the work in northern Spain is really to be regarded as allied to that of France, for the Pyrenees hardly constituted an effective barrier, and the pilgrimage traffic to Santiago de Compostela carried the pilgrimage style to that place and to churches along the route. Santiago itself (1078-1126) is at first glance hardly distinguishable from a French church, though closer attention shows that there are certain Spanish elements. The eastern apse, for example, is set within a square external mass, and the sculptures that

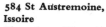

584

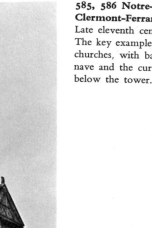

585

586

584 St Austremoine, Issoire
Eleventh-twelfth centuries. The characteristic Auvergnat tower is seen here, with the projecting rectangle caused by the raising of that portion of the transepts. These churches are often decorated on the outside with inlaid coloured stone.

585, 586 Notre-Dame-du-Port, Clermont-Ferrand
Late eleventh century. The key example of Auvergnat churches, with barrel-vaulted nave and the curious projection below the tower.

587, 589 Zamora Cathedral, Spain. 1151-74
Exteriors.
The larger churches of Spain often contained distinctively
Spanish sculpture, and in the region of Salamanca a high ribbed dome of Islamic influence. The cathedral at Zamora is a good example of this type. The smaller churches are even more Islamic, built of brick in the style known as 'Mudéjar'.

587

588

589

588, 590 Santiago de Compostela. 1078-1126
Interior and sculptural detail.
At first glance this cathedral could be in France, though closer examination reveals
Spanish elements.
The sculptures are of a very Spanish expressiveness
as is here shown on the Portico de la Gloria (c. 1180) with its statues of apostles, prophets and elders.

590

591, 592 Salamanca Cathedral. 1160
Exterior and doorway.
The dome is perhaps the most notable feature of this church, and is treated with considerable ingenuity. It has stone ribs, a high drum and an octagonal spire.

591

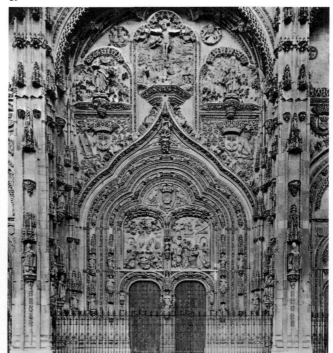

592

adorn two of its doors are essentially Spanish; those of the famous Portico de la Gloria (*c.* 1180) are of an exuberance quite foreign to French work, whether Romanesque or Gothic.

In Catalonia and the north-east there is a great deal of Romanesque work, but it is mostly on a comparatively small scale and represents a local development of the 'First Romanesque' style rather than a branch of the progressive Romanesque architecture of France. In the centre, however, French influence penetrated to some extent as a result of wars against the Moors in which the French were associated with the Spaniards. But as a whole the architecture of this area took on a Spanish garb. The larger churches were adorned with sculptures of a Spanish type, and in the region of Salamanca they were often roofed with high ribbed domes on pointed arches, which attest Islamic influence; the cathedrals of Salamanca (1160) and Zamora (1151–74) are the most important examples. The small churches, which are often of brick, show even more marked Islamic influence. This half-Islamic style is know as the *Mudéjar*.

ROMANESQUE IN BRITAIN

Though Edward the Confessor's church at Westminster was in the new Norman and not the old Saxon style, it was really as a result of the Conquest of 1066 that the new manner spread rapidly through the country. During the thirty years or so between then and the turn of the century a surprising number of new cathedrals and great abbey churches were begun, even if most were not finished till after 1100. The most important of these foundations were Canterbury (1070), Lincoln (1072), Old Sarum (1076), Rochester (1077), St Albans (1077), Ely (1090) and Durham (1093), all of which were of tri-apsidal plan; and Winchester (1079), Tewkesbury (1088), Gloucester (1089), St Paul's, London (1087) and Norwich (1096), all of which followed the apse and ambulatory plan so popular in the great pilgrimage churches of France. Indeed, the early Norman churches of consequence were all built on one or other of these plans; only rather later was the square east end, which had been a characteristic of Saxon architecture, revived. But when it was revived, towards the end of the Norman period, it became extremely popular and almost supplanted the other systems adopted from the continent.

All these great Norman churches are characterised by their plain massive dignity. At Durham, where stone vaults over the main aisle were used for the first time, the great stone-built piers are adorned with shallow-incised patterns, as were those of a few other buildings in the north, but the capitals are quite plain. At Hereford (1107–50) and a few other places the *voussoirs* of the arches are adorned with chevron or dog-tooth mouldings, and the door arches of later Norman churches were also often decorated in a similar manner. But it was usually only in the small country churches where the Saxon tradition was still alive that the tympana of the doors were decorated with figure sculpture, and only very rarely are sculptured capitals found at all; the most important are some of very early Norman date in the castle chapel at Durham and others a little later, in the crypt at Canterbury. Where elaborate sculptures appear on the larger buildings, as in the Prior's Door at Ely.

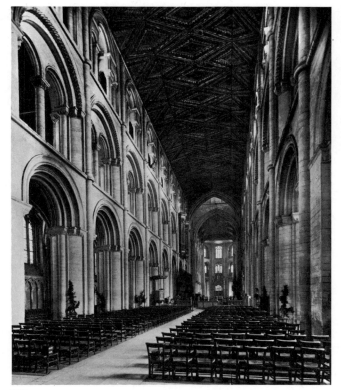

593

594

595

593 Peterborough Cathedral. 1118–94
A great number of Romanesque and Gothic churches were timber roofed. Though that at Peterborough has been continually repaired and restored, it probably gives a fairly accurate picture of what a great number of these churches which have since been vaulted were like originally.

594 Abbey church, Tewkesbury. 1088
One of the great number of new churches that sprang up immediately after the Norman Conquest, in the new manner that rapidly displaced the old Saxon style. It is characterised by its massive dignity and simplicity. The columns were originally plastered and painted with bold geometric patterns.

595 Hereford Cathedral. 1107–50
Detail of pillar and arch.
The voussoirs of an arch adorned with chevron mouldings, a typical decorative form found in Norman churches.
The intricate carving on the capital bears witness to Celtic influence.

596, 597

596, 597 Malmesbury Abbey. 1164
Doorway and sculptural detail.
These sculptures are later
than the church itself,
and show the influence of
central or southern France
rather than that
of the more austere Normandy.

596

597

598, 599 Rievaulx Abbey, Yorkshire. 1132
Exteriors.
A Cistercian foundation, one of a
large group, of which only
the ruins remain.
It was distinguished by plainness
and absence of carving,
though fastidiously elegant in its
severity. This was the second of
the monasteries to be built, the
first being at Waverley in Surrey.

598

599

(c. 1150) or the great south porch of Malmesbury Abbey (1164), the work is always later and the style shows the influence of central or southern France and not that of Normandy.

596, 5

Though it was at Durham that the first attempt was made to roof the main aisle with stone, the stone vault was not at once universally adopted in England. In a few instances the builders seem to have intended to use it, but when the time came they did not dare. In others timber roofs were part of the original design, and this was true of the later Norman cathedrals, like Peterborough (1118-94), as it was of the earlier ones. Perhaps the builders were deterred not only by the span but also by the amount to be done, for the English churches were characterised by very long naves, as, for example, at Peterborough and St Albans.

593

These major buildings all show great variety. Sometimes the piers that separate the aisles are immensely tall and dwarf the triforium, as at Gloucester; sometimes they are short and squat and the triforium is large, as at Southwell; sometimes all three registers, lower tier, triforium and clerestory, are of the same height, as at Norwich. In later work the triforium is sometimes included below the arch of the main bay, as at Christ Church, Oxford (1180). Sometimes again arches are plain, sometimes decorated, while capitals vary in shape and type. But apart from the fact that the later buildings were more profusely decorated than the earlier ones, there seem to be no rules that governed these factors, and regional groups are much less marked than they are in France. It is only in the smaller churches that variations of style can be attributed to the influence of the locality, and in the regions where good stone was available, they were often delightfully decorated, often reflecting the cultural nature of the area. In Kent and Sussex the influence of France is thus to the fore; in Gloucestershire and the neighbouring counties the work is mostly in an old, near-Saxon tradition; on the fringe of Wales 'Celtic' motifs were popular; and in Scotland and on the borders, the old interlacing patterns of 'Northumbrian' art re-appear. Architecturally the smaller buildings reflect, often with a delay of a quarter of a century, the ideas that were earlier developed in the cathedrals and great abbey churches.

602

One distinct group of larger buildings must, however, be noted—that of the Cistercian foundations, which are all distinguished by plainness and an absence of carving, though they are also characterised by what is almost a fastidious elegance. In these the square east end is universal, and in the earlier ones the triforium storey was usually absent. No less than sixty-three Cistercian foundations were made; many have disappeared and of those that survive all are ruins. The most important are Rievaulx (1132), Fountains (1135), Kirkstall (1152), Buildwas (1155), Byland (1175), Furness (1175) and Jervaulx (1175).

598, 5

ROMANESQUE IN ITALY

Romanesque architecture is hardly represented in the parts of Italy that were to become famous as a result of the Renaissance, but it was in Lombardy and Emilia in the north that many of the developments which were to make the style distinctive first took place. The cruciform pier, which could support arches in four directions at its summit

600

601

600, 601 Durham Cathedral. Begun 1093
Durham cathedral is magnificently sited on a rocky promontory, dominating the town like an acropolis. Durham is noteworthy as the earliest example of large-scale use of vaulting. Its decorated columns are a northern feature; similar ones are found on Holy Island (Lindisfarne) and at Dunfermline in Scotland.

602

603

602 Southwell Minster, Nottinghamshire
Eleventh century.
The Norman nave is distinctive because of the great size of the triforium storey.

603 Gloucester Cathedral. 1089
The nave, choir and transepts are Norman, although the choir was refaced in the Perpendicular style. The nave vault is of Early English rib and panel.

604

605

606

604-606 Canterbury Cathedral. Capitals
Early twelfth century.
The first Norman church was destroyed by fire in 1170; it was then enlarged and rebuilt. The carved capitals are of that date and follow the attractive style of Provence and Périgord.

**607, 608 Modena Cathedral.
1099-1120**
Exterior and interior.
An Emilian church having a
porch with elaborate columns
supported on animals.
The interior has three storeys.

607

608

609 Parma Cathedral. 1058
Another church of Emilia akin to
the churches of Lombardy.
They constitute a clearly defined
group.

609

610, 611 San Zeno, Verona. 1070
Exterior and interior.
A striking feature of this church is
the wheel window which provides
the illumination for the nave and is
rare in Italy at this time.
The façade is sternly simple, with
a projecting porch with two
columns resting on the backs of
crouching beasts.
There are low-relief
sculptures on either side.
The nave arcade of compound
piers has intermediate piers
and semi-circular arches.

610

611

was thus first used there. Some authorities would also hold that ribbed vaults were developed in those regions at an earlier date than in France, though there has been some dispute as to the exact date of the first building in which they appear—the church of Sannazzaro near Novara— which Kingsley Porter believes to be as early as 1040. Ribbed vaults were, however, used in Sannazzaro at Milan (1075-93), San Michele at Pavia (c. 1100) and elsewhere, and groin vaults, without the ribs, were of course in use well before that. One of the most important examples is at Mazzone, dated about 1030.

These Lombard churches mostly had two-storeyed interiors, and a system of open arcaded galleries round the apse was developed, as in St Giacomo at Como (1095-1117), perhaps as a derivative of the blank arcading which had been a popular feature in the region from early times. Central towers were normal, but bell towers were usually independent structures; their popularity became universal in the twelfth century, though they were used as early as the seventh. There are, for example, large numbers of them in Rome, though otherwise the architecture of that city and its region was hardly touched by Romanesque ideas.

Closely akin to the churches of Lombardy were those of Emilia, of which the cathedrals at Modena (1099-1120) and Parma (1058) are two of the most important. There were also many fine churches in the region to the north, such as San Zeno at Verona (1070). They were usually built of brick rather than stone, and were entered by way of elaborate porches with columns supported on recumbent animals. Here the interiors were usually of three rather than two storeys, though the roofs were mostly of timber. They constitute a clearly defined group, but though many of the churches are impressive, they are hardly of the same outstanding quality from the architectural point of view as those of France. More impressive is the group of which Pisa Cathedral (1063) is the most outstanding example; for though timber roofs remained more or less universal, a very elaborate form of external arcading was there developed which gives to examples of the group a very impressive appearance. The group was widely distributed, for not only are churches at Lucca, like the cathedral (1204), San Frediano (1112), and San Michele (twelfth century) to be assigned to it, but also a few buildings in Apulia, like the cathedral at Troia (1093-1127).

There is little that can be called Romanesque in Florence and central Italy, though San Miniato at Florence (1013) may be noted, for its nave is divided into compartments by great transverse arches. But in southern Italy there were flourishing developments of the Romanesque; in Apulia on the one hand and in Sicily on the other. In Apulia the main centre was Bari, and though some of the churches attest links with Normandy, most of them, with San Nicolas at Bari (1087-1197) as the type example, bear witness to a local development of the style. The cathedrals at Trani (1098), Bari (late twelfth century) and Bitonto (1175) are perhaps the most important examples. But here again, though the buildings are fine, they did not lead the way to greater subsequent developments as did those of France. The same is true of Sicily, though many of the

612

613

614

612 The Duomo, Assisi
Eleventh century.
An example of late Italian Romanesque, also interesting with its attached campanile and façade decorated with pilaster strips.

613, 614 San Miniato, Florence. 1013
Exterior and interior
The nave of this church is split up into compartments by great transverse arches,
and the eastern portion has a crypt open to the nave and containing the tomb of the saint. Interior and exterior are notable for the introduction of banding in alternate black and white marble, which was to become very popular in Italy in Gothic times.

615, 616 The Pisan Complex
Cathedral 1063-92
Campanile 1174
Baptistery 1153-1278
Here is seen the whole Pisan group
– baptistery, cathedral and tower.
The siting and relationship of
the buildings and the famous
peculiarity of the campanile,
inclining at an angle, combine to
make this group one of the most
famous architectural complexes in
the world.

615

616

617, 620 Monreale Cathedral,
Sicily 1174-1232.
Aerial and exterior views.
The exterior is exotic and
charmingly decorated, but the
interior is of a quiet dignity,
the result of the basilican plan
imposing a simple directional unity.
All the wall space is, however,
covered with mosaics in a
wholly Byzantine style.

617

618

618 Cefalù Cathedral, Sicily.
1131
The building shows the same
richness of decorative
detailing as in Monreale Cathedral,
but it is more irregular.
Here again there are Byzantine
mosaics, finer and earlier
than those at Monreale.

619 San Nicolas, Bari. 1087
The façade is severe and plain,
in contrast to those of the
later buildings of Sicily.

619

620

buildings there have a strange, exotic charm. The cathedral at Cefalù (1131) and the larger but perhaps somewhat ostentatious church of Monreale (1174-1232) are the most important of them.

ROMANESQUE IN GERMANY

Developments in the early eleventh century represent on the one hand a natural growth from the architecture of Carolingian and Ottonian times, with its typical characteristic of the double-ended church, and show on the other the effects of changes that had been taking place elsewhere. In the region of Trier, for example, certain Lombardic features are to be observed, notably blind arcading on the cathedral there (1016-78). Much more important, however, was the influence of France, first in the adoption of the cruciform aisled plan, which was first used at Hessau around 1100, and resulted in the departure from the old two-ended plan in many buildings of the twelfth century, and secondly in a rise from the end of the twelfth century in the popularity of ribbed vaulting. It first appeared at Trier and Worms, and was thereafter adopted more or less universally. But these innovations only penetrated slowly, and the architecture of the lower Rhine remained on the whole a very conservative one. The double-ended plan also remained popular in north Germany, though cruciform buildings were perhaps more usual there than in the Rhineland. Towers were also less popular, and most of the churches have two at the western end rather than the massing of small round towers which accompanied many of the double transept churches of the Rhineland. The architecture of Germany is also characterised by a love of plans of unusual form like the trefoil, as in St Maria im Kapitol at Cologne (1065), and round and octagonal churches, following Carolingian prototypes, were also popular.

PROBLEMS OF VAULTING

Though the Romanesque churches of central and southern France, with their rich sculptures, provide us with some of the finest buildings in the world, it was in the plainer structures of the north, or, as some would think, in Lombardy, that the most important architectural developments were taking place, for there, through the last quarter of the eleventh century, the architects were tackling the problem of vaulting the nave and choir with something more flexible than the barrel vault. The groined vault, over a square bay, which consists virtually of four barrel vaults intersecting at right angles, was used in the side aisles at Fontevrault and elsewhere quite early in the century, but attempts to use this on a large scale over the main aisle had been confronted by three problems: firstly, that of sagging when the area to be spanned was considerable; second, that of adequate support to counter the thrust at the sides; and third, that of coping with the problem of elevation, for if the round form was used, the diagonal section of the vault was automatically of greater height than the transverse one which spanned the nave. This could be compensated for, to some extent, by springing the transverse arches at a higher level, but the result was awkward and unattractive. It was only by using a pointed arch for the diagonal vault, in association with the round transverse

621

621 The Capella Palatina, Palermo. 1132-40
The church consists of a sanctuary in the form of a Greek domed church, but with a long nave of Latin character. The walls are covered with mosaics; those at the east are the work of Greeks, those in the nave by Sicilians. The nave roof was done by Islamic craftsmen and is a fine example of Fatimid art.

622

622 Monreale Cathedral, Sicily. 1174-1232
The mosaics on the walls present the most complete cycle of scenes from the Old and New Testaments that is known to us.

623–625 Perspectives of Canterbury Cathedral
These diagrams show a groin vault (623), a sexpartite ribbed vault (625) and a quadripartite ribbed vault (624).

623

624

625

626 Autun Cathedral, Burgundy
Second quarter of the twelfth century.
This interior shows the pointed barrel vault roofing the nave, with clerestory lighting.
The side aisles are roofed with groin vaults.

626

627 Perspective showing cathedral construction
This diagram indicates the functional character of ribbed vaulting and flying buttresses. The ribs play much the same rôle as the steel frame of an umbrella.

627

arch of the nave, that the problem could be adequately solved. The solution was reached around 1090, but whether it was in Lombardy, in Normandy or in England that it was first arrived at it is hard to say; indeed the solution may have been reached independently in the different regions. It was certainly in the Anglo-Norman area that the idea was most fully exploited, and Durham is the earliest example of its large-scale use. Once the ribbed vault had been invented, a whole series of developments followed as a natural consequence.

First of these was the use of the ribbed vault itself, for it greatly facilitated the problem of actually building a vault and also made it stronger and more efficient. It consisted of building simple arches both transversally and diagonally over each bay, so that they formed a frame rather like the metal of an umbrella, onto which the filling of the vault could be laid. In this way the mass of wooden centring or scaffolding necessary for the groin vault could be eliminated. If wood was scarce, each arch could be built in turn, so that a minimum quantity was required, and further, the ribs could be multiplied in number, so giving greater strength and variety. The earliest example of ribbed vaulting over the main aisle that survives is at Durham, where work was begun in 1093. The ribs vary in number and arrangement. The simplest form producing what is known as the quadripartite vault, was most usual in early times; examples of this are to be seen at Durham and at Caen (c. 1125); such vaults were usually employed above a double bay. As time went on the number of ribs was multiplied until, in Tudor times, they constituted a riotous decorative pattern on the roof.

The other development to which these experiments led was that of the pointed arch, though there is some doubt as to whether its employment was due to indigenous evolution or to its introduction from the East, where it had been known to Islamic architects for many centuries. It might well have been brought back from Syria or Palestine by the Crusaders. But there can be little doubt that it was as a result of their own experiments that the Norman architects were tempted to use it, and we see it appearing in quite a number of buildings of the first half of the twelfth century which are otherwise Romanesque in character, not only as a roofing feature but also over the arcades between the aisles; Autun is perhaps the most striking example. At   626 the same time the idea of tall multiple piers stretching from floor to roof was developed.

The transition from Romanesque to Gothic was a gradual one, and it is sometimes not easy to say whether a building and its decoration is to be included under the one head or the other. At Sens (1144–68) round and pointed arches are used together, and it is truly transitional. At Autun the sculpture is wholly Romanesque in spite of the pointed arches. In the west front of Chartres (c. 1160) the sculpture   636 is already perhaps Gothic rather than Romanesque, and as noted above, the flying buttress appears in embryo in a completely Romanesque form at Nevers. If a decision had to be made, it would probably be in favour of regarding Abbot Suger's cathedral at St Denis near Paris as the   628 first truly Gothic structure in France. Its western portals were built between 1135 and 1140, with pointed arches

and a profusion of sculpture in which tall elegant figures like those of the west doors at Chartres predominated, and it was roofed with a fine ribbed vault of pointed form shortly before its consecration in 1144. It was followed by Chartres in the third quarter of the century, but only the sculptures of the west portal of this building survive, for it was destroyed by fire in 1194.

GOTHIC IN FRANCE

If Abbot Suger's foundation at St Denis and the closely similar work in the earlier cathedral at Chartres, both dating from around 1144, are still to be classed as transitional, they nevertheless show many features that are already wholly Gothic, namely great height, pointed arches and pointed ribbed vaults. These features were further developed in a number of churches founded soon after the middle of the century; most important are those of Notre-Dame at Senlis (1156) and at Soissons (1160-1212), but there are numerous other examples, for it was an age of great building activity. The development of the new style was carried even further at Laon, begun about 1160, for there are to be seen many of the features which were soon to become hallmarks of the style, namely three western portals, all adorned with sculptures, and flying buttresses above the aisles to support the walls of the main aisle. The cathedral is, however, unsual in some respects, for it has a square east end instead of the buttressed apse or chevet usual in France, and seven towers were allowed for in the plan, which suggests the influence of German Romanesque. In the developed Gothic style in France, where height became almost an obsession, it was thereafter found hardly possible to include one at the crossing. Though the idea of towers at the ends of the transepts is to be seen sometimes in embryo, they were seldom built elsewhere than at the west end, where their lower stages formed a vital part of the complex of the west front; the upper stages were not always completed.

Next in date is Notre-Dame at Paris, which was begun in 1163; the nave and the lower part of the west front were finished about 1200, and the western towers about 1240. The great rose windows of the transepts date from about 1225. Here already the ideas which were to dominate the whole of Gothic architecture in France are already well developed and the chevet at the east end is one of the most glorious in France; it is like some sort of fairy vision of a forest of stone. The plan was conceived as a rectangle, but transepts were added to make it a cruciform church, with portals at the end of the transepts which are nearly as important as the western one. Inside there are three more or less equal storeys, and the vaulting is sexpartite. The whole building is carried up to an immense height, and the wall-space has already been reduced to a minimum by the enlargement of the windows, so that there is a blaze of light inside. The wall that remains consists of little more than piers between the windows, and these are made strong enough to support the roof by means of the flying buttresses which take up the thrust of the ribs of the vault at a high level and convey it downwards at an angle by means of a subtle system of supports, until it is taken up by the outer walls of the aisles. In the short

630

-635
199

628

628 St Denis, Paris. 1144
This early Gothic church has the pointed arches and pointed ribbed vaults that came to characterise the style. This burial place of the French kings is one of the earliest truly Gothic structures.

629

629, 630 Laon Cathedral. 1160
Exteriors. The new Gothic style is here further elaborated, with flying buttresses to support the walls of the nave. Sculpture has spread from the tympana to other parts of the building, for example the upper part of the towers.

630

631-635 Notre-Dame, Paris. Begun 1163

Plan, exterior views and interior. The plan of this cathedral was conceived as a great rectangle, but transepts were added to make it a cruciform church. It has three portals at the west end, and transept façades which are nearly as important as the western one. Inside there are three equal storeys, and the vaulting is sexpartite. The flying buttresses between the windows take the thrust of the ribs down to the outer walls of the aisles. The miracle of the lightness of stone skeleton and glowing glass, which was the genius of Gothic architecture, is seen here to perfection, only a few decades after the earliest essay in this style. The large windows in a Gothic cathedral should be regarded as glass walls, not as big windows. They are a translation into mural transparencies of the mosaics and frescoes of earlier times.

631 West façade
632 View along nave towards west end
633 Ground plan
634 Flying buttresses
635 North window, exterior

631

632

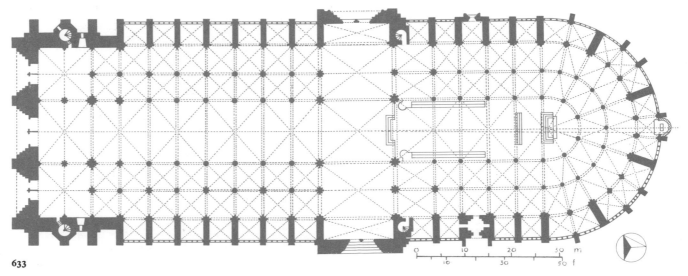

633

634

635

space of time which separates the embryonic half-arch, which was used for instance at Nevers (*c.* 1097), from Notre-Dame at Paris, the flying buttress had reached virtual perfection. Its development went hand in hand with that of the ribbed vault, for thanks to the ribs the weight of the roof could be concentrated above the piers, where it was met by the buttresses. With a barrel or groined vault, where the weight was more equally distributed, this would not have been so, and the great windows which form so essential a part of Gothic church building would not have been practicable. The piers, the ribs of the vault, and the flying buttress are the bones of the building, the glass and the light-screening walls below the windows no more than its skin. Once again we have an example of the organic character of medieval architecture. Indeed it was in Gothic as a whole and most of all perhaps in the Gothic of France, that these ideas were carried out to their fullest extent.

The form of the buttresses at Notre-Dame is comparatively simple: at Chartres, where rebuilding probably began almost immediately after the fire of 1194, they are more elaborate and more varied, even if they approach more closely to forms proper to Romanesque rather than to Gothic architecture. But many of them are things of great beauty and delight in themselves.

The nave and choir of Chartres as we now know them were finished about 1230; the north and south porches, with their famous sculptures, were completed soon after the middle of the century, and the building was consecrated in 1260. The plan of Chartres was to a considerable extent conditioned by previous structures, for the earlier western end was re-used, as was a crypt, perhaps as early as the tenth century, at the eastern end, and it is probably because of this that the transepts are large and the choir of unusual width, so that the more elaborate services could be accommodated. The choir was later separated from the nave by an extensive screen. Altogether Chartres presents one of the grandest and most impressive of all the great Gothic cathedrals of France, though its plan is unconventional and hardly typical of that normal to the Ile-de-France as we see it in such cathedrals as Paris (Notre-Dame), Rheims or Amiens.

But Chartres is typical in another way, and shares with almost all the others one very distinctive feature: it is a cathedral church in the middle of a town, not a monastic church within an enclosure of cells and cloisters, set in the countryside. Like the others it was built with the aid of funds provided by the laity and to a great extent as the result of a communal effort, for which rich and poor alike provided their support. These churches represent the result of intense general enthusiasm. They were churches for the people to worship in, not places of pilgrimage or monastic seclusion. As such their sculptures and their glass had to encourage, help and instruct the worshipper, so that there grew up a new system of decoration, more universal, more humane, which directed the beholder's thoughts to life rather than death. Scenes from Christ's life, which represented the ideal to be emulated, or from the lives of saints, who would help the man of the world along his course, or figures of the Virgin, stressing her more tender, human character, thus took the place of the more

636

637

638

639

640

641

636-641 Chartres Cathedral. 1194-1260
Exterior, plan and sculptural details.
The plan of Chartres was conditioned by previous structures on the site, for the earlier west end was re-used, as was a crypt at the eastern end. It was built with funds provided by rich and poor alike, the result of intense general enthusiasm, a church for people to worship in rather than a place of pilgrimage. The brilliant sculptures and glass transform the church. Here the decoration looks towards life with great exuberance, rather than a preoccupation with the Last Judgment characteristic of Romanesque churches. The figures of the saints and Christ are tender and sympathetic, rather than awesome and judging, and the whole is a powerful hymn to man's perfectability.
636 West façade
637 Ground plan

638 Flying buttresses
639 Sculpture on the Royal Portal. c. 1150

640 Window, west façade
641 Capital detail

642 'Saint Barbara' by Jan van Eyck (d. 1441)
This Renaissance monochrome painting shows all the medieval building trades in the background. The surveyors and architect, the masons and scaffold-builders are seen, and on top of the tower there is a wooden crane operated by a manpowered treadmill.

642

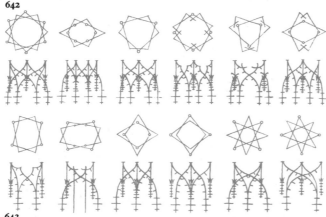

643

643 Medieval mason's working drawings
This page from the notebook of a medieval master mason shows the geometrical setting-out of columns and tracery. The medieval architect worked entirely by taking his measurement from such geometrical constructions, not from any specified series of dimensions.

644 Le Mans Cathedral. Begun c. 1218
Flying buttresses.
A detail of the tall, elegant flying buttresses that are so light they no longer seem made of stone.

644

alarming themes of Romanesque art, where stress was laid on the perils of the Last Judgement and the tortures that awaited the wicked. Christ too, as we see Him at the outset on the west front of Chartres, was no longer the aloof judge, divine and awesome, but human and sympathetic, the Man of Sorrows, who could understand, help and comfort the sinner. We see the full realisation of this trend in the famous figure at Amiens, done about 1220, known as 'Le Beau Dieu'.

More characteristic of this new universal style than Chartres was the great coronation church of Rheims, begun in 1211 and finished about the middle of the century. It is one of the very few churches of the age to be completed as designed. Usually the plans were too ambitious, and when the first enthusiasm, engendered by the religious revival of the twelfth century which we see manifested in another way in the Crusades, came to an end, many of the buildings were left incomplete. One of Chartres's west towers is thus a later addition, dating from 1506; the west front of Amiens was never finished; the nave of Beauvais was never even begun; and Bourges was vaulted at a lower level and in a more economical manner than planned. But Rheims was finished and decorated down to the minutest detail, though even there changes were made as building progressed; rose windows took the place of the conventional sculptured tympana over the western portals, and sculptures in a newer more up-to-date style were substituted about 1240 for some of those which had originally been made about 1220 for the lower registers of the west front. The old ones were transferred to two doors on the north side, the so-called Judgement porch and the porch of St Sixtus.

In many ways Rheims represents the culmination of French Gothic, with its cruciform plan, its great height, its vast area of window space, its multiple piers, which have here replaced the more conservative round pillars, and with its tall, elegant flying buttresses and the mass of sculpture that decorates the whole exterior. It would have seemed impossible to go further than this, and at Amiens, begun in 1218, there is rather less profusion of exterior decoration. But the height is even greater—140 feet from floor to the springing of the vault and 200 feet to the ridge—and the proportions are perhaps more satisfactory. There are, moreover, exceptionally fine carved wooden choir stalls, and sculpture of unequalled quality on the west doors and, of a rather later date, at the end of the south transept. At Beauvais (1225-71) the choir and transepts were taken up to an even greater height, with a glorious forest of buttresses at the chevet. But the new nave was never begun, and the old one, the 'Basse Oeuvre' as it is called, dating in part from Carolingian times, still remains. At Bourges (1190-1275) the plan was even more ambitious, for it comprised five instead of the customary three aisles, with five western portals. But the scheme was too ambitious, and the roof was hurriedly completed at a lower level than originally intended.

Bourges is a five-aisled church without transepts, and as such is unique in France. The other cathedrals are all variations on the transeptal theme that we saw in Notre-Dame at Paris, at Rheims or at Amiens. Rouen Cathedral

645, 6

648, 6
652

645

**645, 646 Rheims Cathedral.
Begun 1211**
Exterior and interior.
This church is the culmination
of French Gothic, owing
its arrangement to its purpose
as the coronation church of
the kings of France.
Its cruciform plan is developed
to a height of 267 feet in
the western towers, and
above the central portal is a
rose window 40 feet in diameter.
A sense of immensity has been
achieved within,
both solemn and regal.
The clustered piers supporting
the arches over the nave
arcade rise up to intersecting
vaults 125 feet above the floor.

646

647

**647 Amiens Cathedral.
Begun 1218**
There is less profusion of
sculptural decoration in this church
than at Rheims,
but the vaults are even higher
– 140 feet from the floor to the
springing of the vaults.

**648, 649, 652 Bourges Cathedral.
Begun 1190**
Plan, interior and exterior.
The original lines along which
the church was planned proved
too ambitious, and the roof was
completed at a lower level than
was intended.
The church has five aisles
but no transepts, and as such is
unique in France.
Inside, the double aisles at
different heights resemble Milan
Cathedral. The east end has
double flying buttresses
and pinnacles.

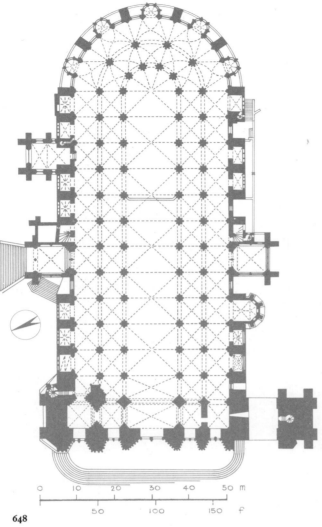

648

649

**650 Le Mans Cathedral.
Begun c. 1218**
The chevet, or east end, of this
church is remarkable for the
thirteen radiating chapels
which project from it.

650

**651 Palace of the Popes,
Avignon**
Fourteenth century.
An example of secular architecture
that accompanied the great spurt
of church building.

651

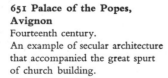

652

dates from the first quarter of the thirteenth century; it has three fine towers and a double-storeyed nave arcade. The rebuilding of Le Mans was set in hand about 1218; its chevet is again of exceptional beauty. Strasbourg, begun in 1290, represents the Rheims style, modified by German taste. St Ouen at Rouen, begun after 1300, represents one of the last great enterprises of this astonishing phase. In the fourteenth century a series of disastrous wars put a stop to nearly all activity, and it was not until the fifteenth century that work was resumed, as for instance in St Maclou at Rouen (1432-1520) and at Abbeville (1480-1539). Both are in the somewhat exaggerated flamboyant style which characterised later French Gothic; the gentle progression from tentative efforts to the final style we know as perpendicular, which characterised Gothic architecture in Britain, was never seen in France. There the best work was nearly all produced in the thirteenth century. Its glories are unequalled, but when that age was over, subsequent developments were less interesting, less progressive, than in England.

Very considerable developments in secular architecture ran parallel with this amazing burst of church building, and a number of castles, some of them almost cities in themselves, were set up in the fourteenth century. Just as the churches were monuments to a great age of piety, so these were monuments to a great age of chivalry. But they were mainly for defensive purposes, and it is in their planning, with the elaborate double entrances, flanking towers, barbicans and so forth, that they are most interesting from a purely architectural point of view; problems of vaulting, support and proportion were a good deal less important. In the thirteenth century Carcassonne is perhaps the most outstanding example; in the fourteenth the Papal palace at Avignon. The transition from defensive castle to grand dwelling place was here well on the way.

GOTHIC IN GERMANY AND THE NETHERLANDS

These countries are really only of local importance, for they added little to the basic nature of Gothic, even though distinctive styles were developed in a number of areas. German Gothic thus does not represent an independent evolution from the Romanesque architecture of the region; rather, it was imported as a developed style from France about the middle of the thirteenth century. To this developed style were added certain local features, such as the open-work spires so popular in the Rhineland and the centre of the country—one of the finest is that at Ulm (1377-1417). The most imposing of all the German cathedrals is that of Cologne (begun 1248), but it tells by size rather than detail, for it is really little more than an enlarged but coarse copy of the cathedral at Amiens. It was completed, following the thirteenth-century design, only in 1880.

In the north, brick was often substituted for stone, and this was also the case in Belgium and Holland. In Holland a very individual type of building, a great hall-church, of great height and with long narrow windows but with little in the way of towers, was developed. Belgium on the other hand was in closer contact with France, and churches like Ste Gudule's at Brussels or St Bavon at Ghent have little to distinguish them from those of northern

(margin numbers: 4-650, 518, 651, 653, 655, 656)

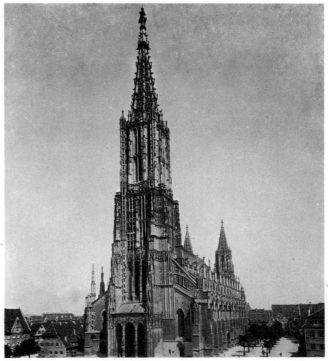

653

654

655

653 Ulm Cathedral, Germany. 1377-1417
An example of the open-work spire of local inspiration added to the imported French Gothic model. The spire is 529 feet in height.

654 St Elizabeth, Marburg. Begun 1257
The nave and aisles of equal height make this typical of the hall church and dispense with the necessity of introducing flying buttresses. A continuous walk, piercing the buttresses, extends round the building.

655 Cologne Cathedral. Begun 1248
The most imposing of all German cathedrals, by size rather than detail. Its towers are over 500 feet high, but its proportions are clumsy and monotonous, and the tracery detail is repetitious. It was completed, following the original design, in the late nineteenth century.

656 St Bavon, Ghent
Thirteenth century.
These Belgian churches have little
to distinguish them from those of
northern France, though here the
sexpartite vaulting is carried
out in brickwork.

656

**657 Grand' Place
belfry and town hall,
Bruges**
Fourteenth century. One of the
great Flemish civic groups
with towering belfries, in a
magnificent and ornate style,
which were popular in this
period. These huge belfries are a
curious and distinctive feature
of Belgian Gothic.

657

**658 Antwerp Cathedral.
Begun 1352**
The largest church in Belgium,
work on which was continued
into the sixteenth century.
It is in the mature Flemish style
with many slender pier shafts and
huge clerestory windows.

658

France. The most distinctive features of Belgium are the
great belfries which are hardly found elsewhere, and the
civic buildings, of which there is a very imposing series
built in the fourteenth century, are scattered over the
country. That at Bruges is one of the finest.   657

GOTHIC IN ITALY

The Gothic style as developed in northern Europe was
foreign to Italy and Italian taste, and the few wholly
Gothic buildings to be found there seem somehow completely out of place. The most important is, of course,
the vast cathedral at Milan (1386), akin in some ways to   661
Bourges, but over-scaled and over-ornate in its decoration. More restrained is the abbey at Fossanova (c. 1200),   663
near Rome, a more or less direct copy of a late Burgundian
abbey church. The church of St Francis at Assisi (1228-
53) also owes something to northern Gothic, though it is
unusual in that it has two storeys. The lower is divided
into vaulted compartments; the upper is vaulted in one
great span.

As opposed to these and a few other 'northern Gothic'
churches, a completely independent and indigenous type
of Gothic was developed in Italy, which probably owed
more to the old early Christian basilicas than to influence
from north of the Alps or to that of Lombard Romanesque.
In these buildings pointed arches were used, but the piers
more often than not imitated the circular columns of
classical times, and vaulting problems were avoided, the
old wooden form of roof usual on the basilicas being
adhered to. In central Italy, especially at Florence and
Siena, the buildings were usually of brick, and the façades
were adorned with elaborate marble revetment. The most
important examples of the style are the cathedrals at Siena   659, 6
(1245-1380), Orvieto (begun 1290) and Florence (begun   662
1296); there are numerous other churches in the style in
Florence and elsewhere.

Italy was also distinctive with regard to its secular
buildings, town halls, castles, palaces and houses, nearly
all of which are distinguished by Gothic features such as
the pointed arch or the multiple column, even if most of
them are proto-Renaissance rather than Gothic.

GOTHIC IN BRITAIN

The Gothic cathedrals of Britain belong in the main to
an indigenous architectural style, different in many ways
from that of France. Unlike the architecture of Germany
and the Netherlands, it represents a local evolution from
Romanesque, and many of the features that characterise
France are absent. The plans are thus much longer in
comparison to width; the eastern chevet, often the crowning glory of France, is absent; there is never the same interest in height for its own sake; flying buttresses were never
used with the same bravado as in France; nor do the interiors
present anything like the same unity. Again, the great
French cathedrals were mostly conceived as a whole, even
if they were not always completed; the English were
conceived piecemeal, and it is only in one instance, at Salis-   665-66
bury (1220-58), that the nave, choir and transepts are
all of one period or indeed of one style. But if something
of the brilliance and perfection of French Gothic is lacking,

659

660

**659, 660 Siena Cathedral.
1245-1380**
Exterior and interior.
This church is of brick with
elaborate marble revetments.
The plan is cruciform, covered by
a dome and lantern.
The interior is remarkable for the
elaborate striping of light
and dark marble, covering walls
and piers, and for the inlaid
floor done by skilled Sienese
craftsmen. Even the campanile is
decorated in the same striking
way.

662

661

**661 Milan Cathedral.
1385-1485**
The façade is of shining white
marble. The work is very florid
and ornate, but it finds its
closest parallels in Northern
Europe rather than in Italy.

**662 Orvieto Cathedral.
Begun 1290**
Like Siena, this church is elaborately
decorated with many-coloured
marbles. There is
some fine sculpture in the
building and attractive alabaster
windows. Standing on a hill, the
cathedral dominates the town.

663

664

**663 Abbey, Fossanova.
c. 1200**
This is a more or less direct copy
of a late Burgundian abbey church,
and is more restrained in style than
many Italian Gothic structures.

**664 Burgos Cathedral, Spain.
1221-1457**
Burgos Cathedral is of outstanding
elaboration and delicacy. The spires
are entirely of openwork, and
are richly ornamented.
A particular feature is the
central lantern or 'cimborio'.

**665 Salisbury Cathedral.
1220-58**
The majority of the great English
cathedrals were monastic
foundations with all the ancillary
buildings. They are therefore
usually found on the edge,
rather than in the centre,
of a town. Their plans are not so
compact or restricted as those of
the great French cathedrals such
as Chartres, situated in the centre
of the town. A feature of
the English cathedral is its
multiplicity of chapels and
chambers, branching from either
side of a long, narrow axis.
These were necessary because
of the building's double
function as secular and monastic
church. The English builders could
afford to spread over the
neighbouring ground to meet
all these various requirements.
Salisbury Cathedral is mainly
in the Early English style.

665

666 Salisbury Cathedral
View along nave looking east.
The nave is characteristic
of Early English.
It has sexpartite vaulting, circular
piers with attached shafts,
a large triforium and little carved
decoration.

667 Salisbury Cathedral
The chapter house (c. 1263)
is octagonal; the central pier
is a cluster of very slender
columns which branch out into
the vaults overhead like the
ribs of an umbrella.

666

667

there is a deep sincerity about the English churches which is unequalled. Outside, the lower roof-lines give a point to the towers or spires which is lacking in France, and the placing of the cathedrals in a secluded close seems to offer an admirable compromise between the rural seclusion of the French Romanesque abbeys and the hemmed-in bustle of the setting of their cathedrals.

Again, there is a greater diversity of styles in English Gothic, and whereas in France there are broadly but two, that of the great thirteenth-century churches of the Ile-de-France and that of their successors in the fifteenth century, which are sometimes over-flamboyant, in England there was a continuous progression from the style we know as Early English, with its narrow slender arches and restrained tracery, through the elaboration of the Decorated, to the logic of the Perpendicular, where the tracery rises in one continuous line from floor to roof. And it was only in England that the evolution of ribbed vaulting was carried to its logical conclusion to produce the form we know as fan vaulting. Again, the mass of material in Britain is also unique, for there are probably more small parish churches of quality than in any comparable area on the continent.

Of the great buildings of the Early English phase (c. 1190-1300) the transepts at York (1227-70), with the great window at the northern end known as the 'Five Sisters', and the cathedral of Salisbury (1220-58) are perhaps the most outstanding. They represent the culmination of a style which was evolved directly from the Norman, by way of a few preliminary stages, as for example in the Temple church in London (commenced 1185) and the cathedral at Ripon (c. 1180). It reaches its highest perfection perhaps in the Chapter House at Salisbury (c. 1263).

These local developments, which were well-nigh universal, may be contrasted with those in a more limited series of buildings which took place as a result of the penetration of new ideas from France. Canterbury Cathedral, for example, which was almost entirely rebuilt after the fire of 1170, was the work of a French architect, William of Sens, and it represents a development of ideas which had already been formulated between 1144 and 1168 in the cathedral at that place. Albeit, the English developments were very considerable and produced ultimate solutions of great originality and very great beauty, especially at the east end of Canterbury, the 'Corona', as it is called. Westminster Abbey (1245-69), again, is a church of French type, with chevet at the eastern end and flying buttresses to support the central aisle; it too was the work of a French architect.

But these, both of them buildings of the greatest quality, are exceptions, and the evolution which can be traced from Ripon through the transepts of York and at Salisbury was carried forward at Wells (1220-42) and in the nave and two choirs at Lincoln (1230-80), to produce the style we term Decorated (c. 1300 to c. 1380). The arches tended to become wider and less lancet-like, the proportions somewhat less elegant but perhaps sounder and more lasting, while the buildings were enlivened with tracery of greater elaboration, and the doors and capitals were adorned with a greater profusion and with a new type of decorative sculpture in which figures played an important part.

670

669
667

671

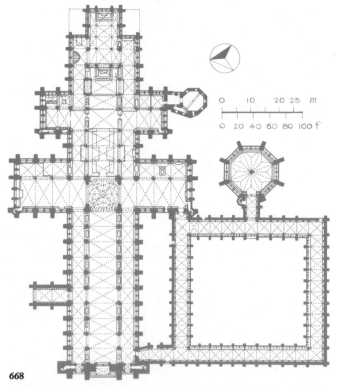

668

668 Salisbury Cathedral. 1220-58
Plan.
The plan shows double transepts with a central tower.
The octagonal chapter house (c. 1263) is on the south side, together with a cloister.

669

669 Ripon Cathedral. c. 1180
Even in such an example of early Gothic as Ripon the façade is composed of more open space than solid stone.
It is austere and undecorated, and relies upon its structural unity for its aesthetic effect.

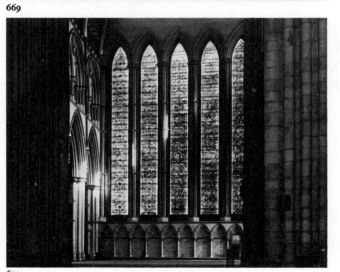

670

670 York Minster. 1227-70. The 'Five Sisters' window
The lancets of the north transept are attenuated to a marked degree. Their calculated slenderness frames the stained glass in rather unusual grisaille tones.

671 Lincoln Cathedral. Angel Choir. c. 1260
An example of the Decorated style with the arches wide and the proportions less elegant than solid. The tracery is of great elaboration, and figures appear in the profuse sculpture.

671

672 Winchester Cathedral. 1079-1235
The longest medieval cathedral in Europe. The Perpendicular superimpositions (the vaulting is of 1394-1450) entirely disguise the Norman nave and choir.

672

673 Westminster Abbey. 1245-69
More French than English, Westminster has flying buttresses and a chevet at the east end. Designed originally by French architects it has been much altered, rebuilt and extended from Norman to Tudor times. This photograph shows Henry VII's chapel, added in the early sixteenth century.

673

Figure sculpture, it is true, was never as extensive as in France, but on occasions, as at Wells and in the Angel choir at Lincoln, it was of a quality in no way inferior to that of France, though it was usually more reticent and more linear. The tracery of the windows showed great variety, the earlier forms being based on geometric designs—we know them as reticulated—the later on freehand curves, and these we term flamboyant. This was the style used in the later Gothic of France, and there is reason to believe that it was first introduced from England. It was however developed in France to a fuller degree than in Britain.

The next phase, the Perpendicular, was first employed at Gloucester soon after 1330, while buildings elsewhere were still being erected in the Decorated style; only later, about 1380, did the style become a universal one. At first it was confined to tracery, for the Norman choir at Gloucester was simply re-faced, and a new, great east window was inserted. The result was an amazing *tour de force*, and also a surprising achievement, if one remembers that the terrible Black Death decimated the population in 1349. But the choir, together with its elaborate ribbed vault, was finished in 1357, and the cloisters, where developed fan vaulting was used for the first time, in 1407. The tower dates from 1450 to 1457. It is one of a series of very beautiful structures set up in the fifteenth century; the central tower at Canterbury (*c.* 1495) is probably the most lovely of them.

The fullest development of the Perpendicular style, however, was due to the patronage of the Tudor kings, and the last phase of it (*c.* 1480-1600) is sometimes called Tudor. Henry VII's chapel at Westminster (*c.* 1512), St George's chapel at Windsor (1460-1510) and a number of churches in various parts of the country serve to represent the style, but its crowning glory is without doubt King's College chapel at Cambridge (1446-1515). It is beyond question one of the world's most glorious buildings; there, perpendicular tracery and fan vaulting combine with superb proportions of plan and elevation to produce an interior which is surely unsurpassed.

Much of the secular architecture of the Gothic phase was of considerable importance, for it saw the transformation of the defensive castle into the more or less wholly domestic house. Many architectural problems were similar in secular and ecclesiastical work; thus the windows of banqueting halls, guard rooms and so forth are closely akin to those of churches, and similar vaulting systems were used for roofing. But the exteriors of the castles called for special treatment, and the details of defensive lay-out and such features as machicolation, were greatly developed by the Gothic builders, even if some of them were originally brought back from the Near East by the Crusaders. The castles were often of great beauty as well as of practical efficiency. By the sixteenth century, however, the castle had virtually become a thing of the past, though in colleges and similar buildings Gothic mannerisms survived till the new Renaissance style penetrated under the influence of Inigo Jones. The last wholly Gothic building is probably the hall stair of Christ Church, Oxford, which dates from 1638.

679

675

683
680

682, 6

685

674

675

676

677

678

679

674 Ely Cathedral
Eleventh-fourteenth centuries.
The original Norman crossing
of the nave and transept was
covered by an octagonal lantern,
seventy feet across, in the
fourteenth century.
This structure is mainly of wood
and uses cross-binding arches
with warped planes.

675 Canterbury Cathedral
The Perpendicular central
tower (c. 1495)
was added by the Tudors to the
original design of the French
architect William of Sens.

676, 678 Exeter Cathedral
Fourteenth century. An impressive
example of the Decorated style,
it has striking twin towers
over the transepts. The west
façade is completely dominated
by the enormous arched opening
the full width of the nave.
In fact it is simply the vaulted
nave brought to a sudden end,
filled in with glass and held
in a delicate lattice screen.
At a lower level a solid stone
screen of figural sculpture
provides a break similar to that
of the narthex of a basilica.

677 Hereford Cathedral
Eleventh-fourteenth centuries.
This church has a Decorated
central tower added
to the Norman nave and choir.
It was completely restored
and refaced in the nineteenth
century.

**679 Gloucester Cathedral.
The Cloisters. 1407**
Fan vaulting was here first
used on an extensive scale.
The fan vaulting appears
to be very complicated at first
glance because the purely
decorative ribbing is given as
much importance as the central
ribs of the vault.
The system is based on a
very wide arch with a flattened
top and this can be
distinguished both in the
window openings and
cross-section of the cloisters.

680 St George's chapel, Windsor. 1460-1510
A large west window with Perpendicular mullions and transoms filled with stained glass of the Tudor period.

681 Westminster Hall roof, London. 1397-99
This hammerbeam roof is a fine example of engineering in timber. It is the method of building up compound beams out of comparatively short and strong pieces of timber to span a very wide opening; in fact it is a form of corbelling in timber.

682, 684 King's College chapel, Cambridge. 1446-1515
Roof and interior.
In this building Perpendicular tracery and fan vaulting combine with superb proportion of plan to produce a magnificent interior. It is undoubtedly the finest example of this style in Britain.

683 Henry VII's, chapel, Westminster Abbey. c. 1512
The final development of fan vaulting was the dropping of pendants from the centres of the circular vaults in the higher ceiling. Here the structure is almost completely hidden by the elaborate carving and piercing; in the last phase of the Gothic arch the Gothic principles are already being turned into a decorative form much closer to the Renaissance than to Gothic.

685 Christ Church, Oxford. Roof of Hall stair. 1638
An example of Gothic fan vaulting executed at a date when the Renaissance style was already to the fore elsewhere.

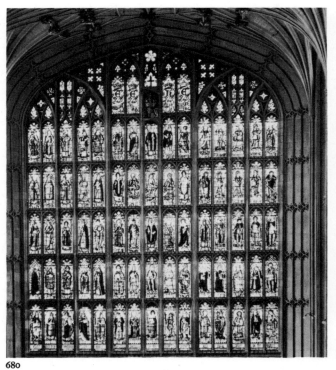

680

681

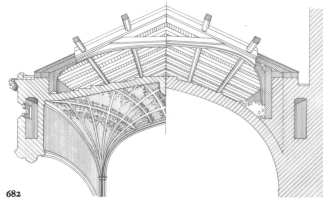

682

683

684

685

Vitruvian man – drawing by Leonardo da Vinci

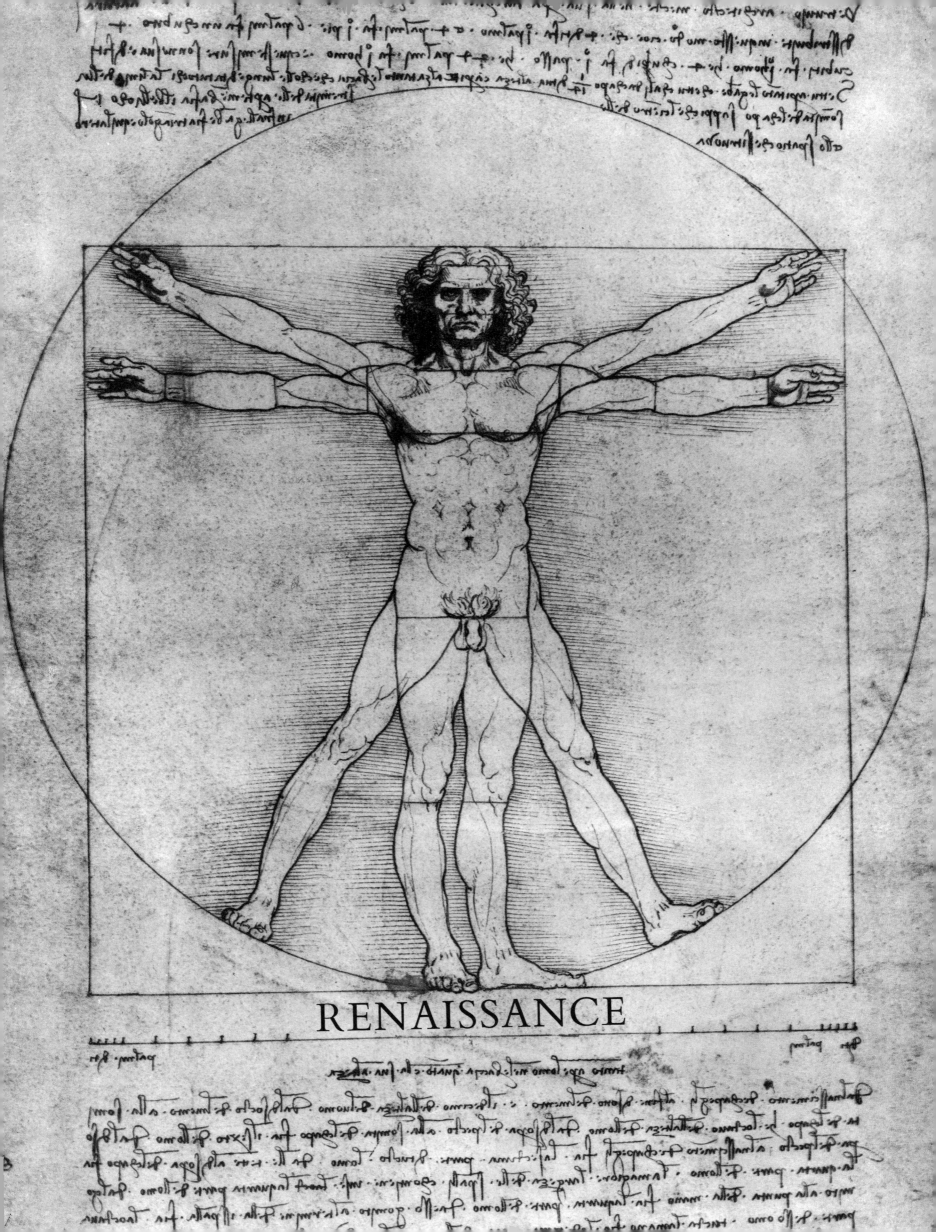

RENAISSANCE

686 Foundling Hospital, Florence. 1419.
Filippo Brunelleschi
Although there is no direct connection between classical architecture and Brunelleschi's loggia this is the first true Renaissance building in spirit. The columns and vaults are light and clear, and the upper portion is clearly separated by the line of the entablature.

686

687, 688 San Lorenzo, Florence, 1420.
Brunelleschi
Interior and plan.
The plan, derived from the basilica, is traditional.
The feeling of spaciousness has been achieved, partly by the slender proportions of the columns, partly by the arcade line of chapels acting as extensions to each of the aisles.

687

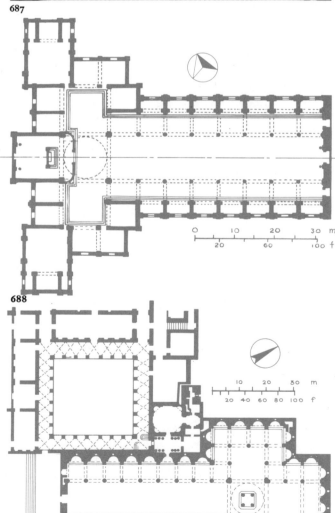

688

689 Plan of S. Spirito, Florence, 1436.
Brunelleschi
Brunelleschi's S. Spirito retains the Latin cross shape of a Gothic church, but the unit of composition is the Renaissance square.

689

ITALY IN THE FIFTEENTH CENTURY: THE EARLY RENAISSANCE

It is significant that the invention of Renaissance perspective should be credited to Filippo Brunelleschi (1377-1446). To him and his fellow-artists order was an essential basis of art, and not merely order but demonstrable, recognisable order. It is this that lies behind Renaissance architects' desire for symmetrical planning and carefully proportioned spaces, and their ideally patterned town plans, as also the artists' study of the anatomy of nature in general and man in particular, of light and dark, of movement, and of the relative proportions of the parts of bodies as first investigated by the Greeks. The study of the interrelationship of parts of objects (systematised as proportion) and of objects to other objects (systematised as perspective) provided the framework necessary for the Renaissance to express itself in terms of ideals of beauty inherited from the ancients and the scientific examination of physical environment; and as such was as important to architects as to artists.

Brunelleschi learnt design as a goldsmith and is known to have done painting and sculpture. Although he derived his classicism primarily from Tuscan Romanesque buildings, he did add to this by studying Roman ruins and incorporated in his work Roman techniques of construction and planning. From this time on, until the recent past, a study of Roman architecture was a valued if not always an essential part of an architect's training. In 1419 Brunelleschi designed the loggia of the Foundling Hospital, a harmoniously proportioned and detailed composition of arches on columns and terminal bays framed by pilasters. Similar elements appear in the church of San Lorenzo (begun 1420), traditional in plan, but serenely proportioned. The columns, pilasters, arches, cornices, etc. are constructed of dark stone (*pietra serena*), while the remaining surfaces are whitewashed. This is a traditional Florentine method, used here to underline the ease and clarity of the interior. The church of S. Spirito (begun 1436) is very similar, but shows a great gain in solemnity from its modular plan, each portion of the plan being a multiple of the square bay of the aisles, and the vertical dimensions, too, being controlled by the same measurement. Transepts and chancel are identical; the nave is an extended version of one of these.

The central plan, in which all sections are in fact equal and focus on to a central point, is the clearest expression of this demonstrable order which the Renaissance valued so highly. The aesthetic pleasure to be found in such an arrangement is partly an intellectual one, but the central plan tends to bring with it a quality of complete homogeneity which is apprehended sensually and appeals as much to our age as to the *quattrocento*. In the little oratory of Sta Maria degli Angioli (begun 1434), Brunelleschi created the first Renaissance central plan: a central octagon surrounded by a ring of eight chapels. In 1444 Michelozzo began a ten-sided addition to the church of SS. Annunziata, with large niches opening off each side—a plan derived from the ruins of the Roman temple of Minerva Medica, and thus one of the first examples of architectural borrowing

686

687, 6

689, 6

XXXVI *Casas y Novoa: Baroque façade of Cathedral, Santiago de Compostela*

from antiquity. Brunelleschi's church may have been based on the same prototype.

The Renaissance is often characterised as the rebirth of the antique spirit of classicism and the revival of antique forms. Such a description hardly fits the work of Brunelleschi and his generation, although it may approximate to their intentions. The first designer whose work goes far towards a re-creation of Roman architecture was Alberti (1404-72), a man peculiarly suited by his training in the liberal arts, mathematics, music and law, and by his close acquaintance with the writings and the monuments of antiquity, to lay the foundations of Renaissance classicism in precept and practice. He wrote, among other things, treatises on painting, sculpture and architecture. The last was published in Florence in 1485, but written in the 1450s and known to many in manuscript. The best-known English version is that of James Leoni (1726). More than any other *quattrocento* production, it contains the essence of fifteenth- and of early sixteenth-century architectural thought, and it remained the starting point for many later treatises. Alberti's own starting point is the book by Vitruvius, using it with great independence of mind and discarding it whenever it runs counter to his own experience and sense. Nevertheless, Alberti accepts Vitruvius's valuation of the architecture of ancient times: architecture as an art began in Asia, was developed in Greece and perfected by the Romans—an article of faith not seriously challenged until the middle of the eighteenth century. As he had already done for the painter, Alberti in this treatise elevates the designer of buildings from his lowly connection with the mason's craft. From now on, for better or worse, the architect is the white-collared professional he remains to this day. 'Him I call Architect, who, by sure and wonderfull Art and Method, is able, both with Thought and Invention, to devise, and, with Execution, to compleat all those works, which ... can with the greatest Beauty, be adapted to the Uses of Mankind: And to be able to do this, he must have a thorough Insight into the noblest and most curious Sciences.' Beauty comes from proportioning and, secondarily, from the use of classifical forms such as the orders which have ornamental value; the simplest geometrical forms, the square and the circle, and their immediately related shapes, are the most perfect and symbolise the perfection of God and His universe.

Of Alberti's five most important works, two are additions to and alterations of earlier structures, two were left substantially incomplete, and two were considerably altered since his time. But each of them is an important part of architectural history. The Palazzo Rucellai, designed about 1446 for a rich Florentine merchant, shows the first Renaissance use of a system so familiar to later centuries: the articulation of a façade by superimposed orders. Since the dimensions of the parts of the orders are interrelated by a module (half the width of column or pilaster), their use provided Alberti with a controlling system for the measurements of the whole façade. For the same patron he completed the Gothic façade of Sta Maria Novella, proportioning the whole and its parts on the ratio 1:2, and linking the narrower upper storey to the broad lower storey by the insertion of scrolls, a device much copied in succeeding

690

691

692

690 S. Spirito, Florence, 1436. Brunelleschi
In this church the same system of proportion runs through all its parts, achieving harmony and spaciousness.
The vertical measurements, for instance, the height of columns, are proportional to the ground plan. The ease and clarity of the interior, as in San Lorenzo, is underlined by the dark stone of columns, arches, cornice, etc., against whitewashed walls.

691 Sta Maria Novella, Florence. c. 1456. Leone Battista Alberti
This is a façade added to an already existing Gothic church. The small doorways under pointed arches and the rose window are parts of the older building, and the problem was to harmonise new with old.
The upper storey has been connected with the lower by scrolls, a device much copied later.

692 Palazzo Rucellai, Florence. c. 1446. Alberti
The great Renaissance townhouses had to be semi-fortified because of the violent and unstable political climate of the time. The ground floor was a heavily defended yard, surrounded by guardrooms, quarters for men at arms, and stabling. The family and household proper lived on the first and upper floors. The few windows on the ground floor are high and heavily barred. Alberti here used the Roman Orders in very shallow relief, one above the other, as they were used on the Colosseum, with the Doric on the ground floor, the curious form of Ionic on the first, and the Corinthian on the second.

XXXVII *Michelangelo and Rainaldi: Palazzo del Senatore, Rome* XXXVIII *Juan Bautista de Toledo and Juan de Herrera: Escorial, Madrid*

**693 'Ideal City'. c. 1475.
Piero della Francesca (attrib.)**
Gallery of the Marches, Urbino.
This tempera painting may
be a theatre design. The use of
parallel perspective makes the
picture valid for one observation
point only.
Here we have a centrally
planned building on a central
axis directly related to the
spectator through use of a
natural eye-level. The spectator can identify himself
with the scale of the buildings and become a part of
the picture.

**694 Palazzo Medici-Riccardi,
Florence. 1440-60.
Michelozzi**
The first of the fifteenth-century
Renaissance Florentine palazzos.
Its descent from the medieval
fortresses can be seen in the solid
stonework of the lower wall
and the living space confined to
the upper storeys.
The rustication is graded in
each storey.

**695 Palazzo Strozzi, Florence.
Begun by Benedetto da Maiano,
1489**
The typically Renaissance
articulation of each part of a
building is here clearly shown.
The straight lines of
entablature and rows of windows
mark out the stages which
mount to a crowning cornice.
The use of rusticated stone as
ornament is also typical.

**696 Palazzo Pitti,
Florence. Begun 1458.
Brunelleschi or Alberti**
The middle portion of this
palace has been attributed to
both Brunelleschi and Alberti.
From 1550 to 1859 it was the
residence of the Grand Dukes
of Tuscany and during this
period it was greatly enlarged.
Typically Florentine in its use
of rusticated masonry and arched
window recesses, the Palazzo
Pitti far exceeds the other palaces
in its massiveness and scale.

693

694

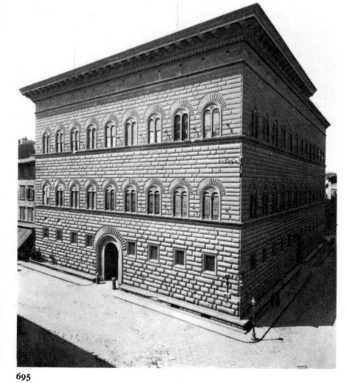

695

696

697

698

699 700

701

697 San Francesco, Rimini. 1450. Alberti
Alberti's task was to modernise an existing church, turning it into a monument to the local ruler, Sigismondo Malatesta, his mistress and his following of humanists. Alberti clad the Gothic church in a layer of Roman antiquity, more truly classical than anything achieved by the Renaissance hitherto. The front of the church was left incomplete and an enormous hemispherical dome was to have covered the east end of the church.

698 San Francesco, Rimini. 1450. Alberti
Side wall.
Along the flank wall, Alberti arranged a series of arches and recesses containing the sarcophagi of scholars and poets prominent in the Ducal court.

699, 700 San Francesco, Rimini. 1450. Alberti
Arch and column details.
These details show Alberti's careful use of classical motifs in his architectural detailing.

701 Sant'Andrea, Mantua. 1470. Alberti
This is deliberately based on the classical Roman temple front, with columns, entablature and pediment. The columns are changed into pilasters, appropriate to the character of the wall. The single-bay triumphal arch is reminiscent of the Arch of Titus.

702 Sant'Andrea, Mantua. 1470. Alberti
The side walls have been broken by recessed chapels, but there are no side aisles to take away from the expanse of the Roman hall with its barrel roof and coffered ceiling.

702

703, 704 San Sebastiano, Mantua. 1460. Alberti
Exterior and plan.
The basic form of San Sebastiano is square and shows clearly the porportion 1:2, which appears so much in Renaissance building. (The width of the chapels equals half one of the sides of the square.)
It is the first Renaissance church to be designed on the Greek cross plan. The building has not been well preserved.

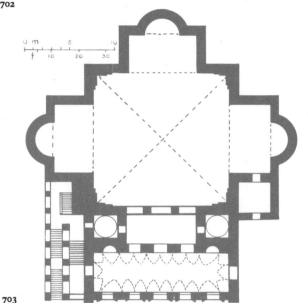

703

704

705 Church of the Certosa, Pavia. 1481. Giovanni Antonio Amadeo
Amadeo, one of the first Renaissance architects to appear in northern Italy, gave his churches an elaborate veneer of Renaissance ornament which was soon imitated by architects in Germany and France.

705

centuries. In three other churches, San Francesco in Rimini, and San Sebastiano and Sant'Andrea in Mantua, Alberti struggled with the problem of how to find a satisfactory classical external form for a building that internally combines a lofty nave with low aisles or chapels. In Rimini (1450) 697-7 he remodelled a Gothic church into a classical monument to Sigismondo Malatesta, ruler of Rimini, his mistress Isotta and the humanist scholars at his court. For the façade Alberti adapted the three-bay form of the Roman triumphal arch; along the side of the church he arranged a series of massive arches containing sarcophagi to commemorate the scholars. Over the east end of the church Alberti intended a semi-spherical dome, comparable to that of the Pantheon. Clearly he was trying to achieve an effect of Roman solemnity by basing himself on Roman prototypes, yet, significantly, he uses these prototypes freely and does not hesitate to use original detail. There is a fundamentally different attitude here from that of the Neo-classicist who is more likely to aim at archaeological correctness.

This inventive use of antiquity appears also in the two Mantuan churches. San Sebastiano (designed 1460) is cen- 703, 7 trally planned; Sant'Andrea (designed 1470) longitudinally. 701, 7 Both have façades based on the form of the Roman temple front, and in both cases the temple front is remodelled in terms of the triumphal arch. The break in the base of the crowning pediment on San Sebastiano is derived from the side of the triumphal arch at Orange in France. In the façade of Sant'Andrea the narrow-wide-narrow rhythm of the triumphal arch dominates over the static frame of all pilasters carrying a broad pediment. The same design (minus the pediment) at the same level and on the same scale reappears as the internal elevation: the big, arched opening becomes the chapel, three of which either side of the nave create strong cross accents in a longitudinally planned church. With their deep coffering, repeated in the feigned coffering of the nave vault, and in the broad spaciousness of the interior, this church carries a strong character of *Romanità*.

It is part of Alberti's significance that these buildings should have been commissioned and erected outside Florence. Other buildings, in Rome, Naples and Ferrara, have been attributed to him. We witness here a gradual change of taste in art and architecture which is happening at various speeds in different parts of Italy and will soon be echoed beyond the Alps. From the republican merchant city of Florence, a new art spreads to the courts of petty tyrants, princes, kings, popes and emperors. A real understanding was more slow to spread than were its outward forms. Where, as in northern Italy, a Gothic style still flourished, the Renaissance style could be adopted as a source for new decorative motifs to be incorporated in Gothic architecture. Examples of coherent Renaissance architecture are not to be found in northern Italy until the 1480s and 90s, except for those buildings commissioned from Florentine designers, of which Alberti's are the most important. Others include the Portinari Chapel, added by Michelozzo to the Milanese church of Sant'Eustorgio (*c.* 1462) and, in the same city, Filarete's Great Hospital (1456–65). A leading local architect, Guiniforte Solari, added a third storey to Filarete's two, using Gothic windows and

706

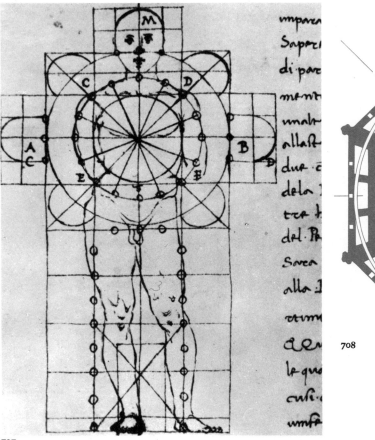

707

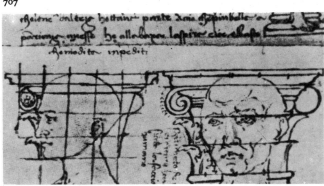

709

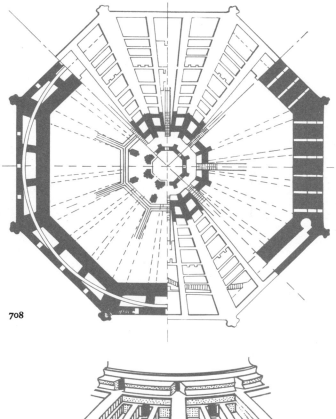

708

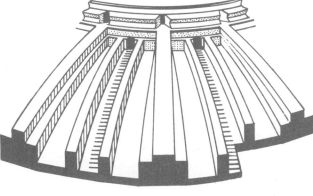

710

**706 Florence Cathedral.
Begun 1296, finished 1461**
This cathedral took so long to
build that it spanned the transition
from Gothic to Renaissance.
The body of the church
shows the calm and spacious
Gothic style typical of Tuscany:
the dome, by the Renaissance
architect Brunelleschi, is
Gothic in form but Renaissance
in detail.

**707 Francesco di Giorgio:
study of proportion. c. 1482**
One of several studies
of proportion in an architectural
treatise by di Giorgio.
Ideal proportion can be taken
from the human body and
applied to architecture.
This follows the philosophical
conception of man being the centre
of creation and all else
being in harmony with him.

**708, 710 Florence Cathedral
dome. 1420-34.
Brunelleschi**
Sectional and construction
diagram.
Brunelleschi's dome is oval and
was designed in the medieval
manner with an inner and outer
shell, to be erected without
scaffolding. It is a great feat of
construction as well as design and
was thought to be impossible
to erect.

**709 Francesco di Giorgio:
column capital with head
of man c. 1482**
Another study from
di Giorgio's treatise on proportion.
There is scholarly punning
on the words 'capital' and 'capita'
(head).

711 Plan of Sta Maria delle Grazie, Milan. 1472-85
This Milanese church was designed in the Gothic style by Giovanni and Guiniforte Solari, and Bramante later added the choir and chancel in singular juxtaposition.

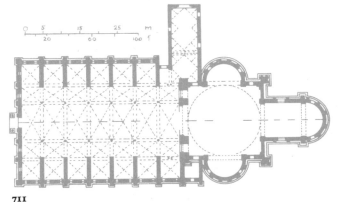

711

712, 713 Tempietto, Rome, Begun 1503.
Donato Bramante
Exterior and plan.
A chapel in the cloisters of St Peter in Montorio which interprets the ancient Roman circular temple.
The Renaissance saw no essential conflict between pagan past and modern Christianity.
This is a perfect example of what Alberti thought a Christian church should be, in circular shape, in the dome which could elevate the thoughts, and in the free-standing which raises it out of its surroundings.

712

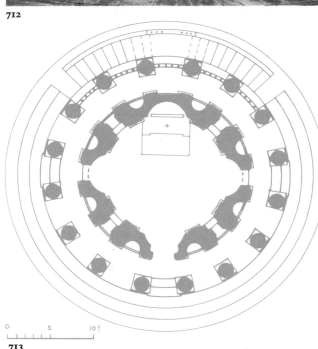

713

spacing them without regard to the spacing of the lower bays. The first Renaissance architects to appear in northern Italy were born in the 1440s and range from Giovanni Antonio Amadeo, whose Colleoni Chapel in Bergamo (1470) and Church of the Certosa in Pavia (1481) are particularly rich anthologies of Renaissance ornament and soon became fruitful hunting-grounds for designers from France and Germany, to Donato Bramante who is one of the greatest figures of Renaissance architecture.

705

ITALY IN THE SIXTEENTH CENTURY: HIGH RENAISSANCE AND MANNERISM

With Bramante (1444-1514) we move into the High Renaissance, a brief period of utterly harmonious architecture based on the research and performance of *quattrocento* architects. More particularly, it is the fruit of Alberti's efforts, who died thirty years before the first High Renaissance building was designed.

Bramante was born in Urbino and was a successful painter before he turned to architecture. It is likely that he knew Piero della Francesca, the Umbrian painter who worked in San Francesco in Rimini, and whose painted architectural settings are firmly Albertian. In 1485 Bramante designed the east portion of Sta Maria delle Grazie in Milan, a Gothic church begun by Giovanni and Guiniforte Solari in 1472. In plan he based himself on Alberti's San Sebastiano, and there is something Albertian also about the sharp detailing that unambiguously defines the internal space. To move from the Gothic nave into Bramante's choir and chancel is to recapture something of the excitement the building must have caused in its day. Leonardo da Vinci was in Milan in the 1480s and 90s, and one would wish to know more about the relationship that developed between him and Bramante, six years his senior. Certainly Leonardo was much concerned with architectural problems. His drawing of a man in a square and a circle is an interpretation of Vitruvius's influential passage relating the proportions of the human figure to the proportions of temples. During his stay in Milan, Leonardo made several sketches for centrally planned churches which hint at Bramante's subsequent masterpiece, his design for the church of St Peter's in Rome.

693
711
p. 233

In 1499 the invading forces of Louis XII of France captured Milan. Leonardo went home to Florence; Bramante went to Rome. There he studied ancient ruins, and there he designed the most important buildings of the High Renaissance. This phase belongs to Rome, in the way that the early Renaissance belongs to Florence, but with one significant difference: Rome attracted and patronised great artists and architects; she did not bear them herself — and both statements remain true for subsequent phases of the Renaissance. In the fifteenth century some efforts had been made to rescue Rome from her medieval impoverishment, and the rebuilding of St Peter's was considered. Alberti played some part in both; the courtyard of the Palazzo Venezia (begun 1455), if not designed by him, must have been influenced by his spirit. This and other palace buildings, such as the Cancelleria (1486-98; often, in defiance of its dates, attributed to Bramante), are the swallows that herald the summer of the High Renaissance.

714

716

719

715

717

718

720

**714, 716 Tempietto, Rome.
Begun 1503. Bramante**
Dome and cornice.

**715 St Peter's, Rome.
Bramante's plan. 1506**
The original plan passed by
Pope Julius II was never executed.
The symbol of the cross
combines with the symbolism of
centralised geometry.
The dominating Greek cross
with its dome is accompanied by
small repetitions of the same
figure in the diagonal axes.
The whole fits into a large square
from which the four apses project.

**717 St Peter's, Rome.
1506-1626**
Aerial view.
The work of many architects,
from Bramante in 1506
to Bernini, who finally erected in
1667 the entrance piazza
surrounded by 284 columns.
It incorporates designs
by Sangallo, Raphael, Peruzzi,
Michelangelo, Fontana, Vignola
and Maderna, who added the
rather inept long nave to
Michelangelo's central plan.
But despite the resulting
somewhat confused plan it is
undoubtedly one of the most
impressive buildings in the world,
certainly the most
important building of the period.

**718 St Peter's, Rome.
1506-1626**
West view.
This photograph indicates
what Michelangelo's church
would have looked like had
Maderna's nave not been added.
Seen without Maderna's
façade its massiveness and fluid
outline has an almost sculptural
quality as if it was hewn
in one piece from some gigantic
rock.

**719 Raphael, 'The Marriage
of the Virgin'. 1504.
Brera, Milan.**
This painting is contemporary
with the Tempietto by Bramante,
which was greatly admired for
its simplicity and perfection.
Raphael's painted church shows
his generation's interest in the
central plan but lacks Bramante's
feeling for the solemnity
of Roman classicism.

720 St Peter's, Rome
Interior of dome.
The construction of the present
dome was planned by
Michelangelo, who set himself
the problem of supporting it
250 feet from the ground on four
piers rather than on a circular
wall. With its lantern
the dome is 452 feet in height.

721 Raphael, School of Athens'. 1511. Vatican Palace.

Bramante, who was commissioned to rebuild St Peter's in Rome, designed a building involving a central plan.

Nine years before his death the foundation stone was laid, and although the crossing piers and arches had been constructed in the next thirty years there was much altering of his original design.

Raphael's setting for the great philosophers of antiquity is closely related to Bramante's intentions. Arms forming a Greek cross meet under a large dome. The architecture is severe, with statues and massive coffering setting off the simplicity of the structural framework.

721

722 St Peter's, Rome. 1506-1626

View from east.

Maderna's façade (1606-12) at the east end of the lengthened nave serves to obscure the effect of the dome.

722

12-714
716
Bramante's Tempietto, a little chapel in the cloisters of
St Peter in Montorio, was begun in 1503. An original
interpretation of the ancient circular temple, it is at once
an act of homage to the great past and, in its function and
symbolism, a Christian monument. The Renaissance saw no
essential conflict between the pagan past and modern
Christianity: Botticelli's Madonna is the sister of his Venus;
Michelangelo's Christ of the *Last Judgement* is a synthesis
721 of Apollo and Hercules; in Raphael's frescoes *The School
of Athens* and the *Disputà*, Plato and Aristotle, and Christ
and His apostles face each other across the papal apartment.
Contemporaries hailed the Tempietto as a masterpiece
capable of holding its own against the great buildings of
the ancients. Small in size, it is monumental in scale and
could be enlarged without loss of coherence.

Pope Julius II (1503-13) should have some of the credit
for the magnificent creations of the High Renaissance on
account of his enthusiastic patronage of Bramante, Michelangelo and Raphael. He entrusted Bramante with the
greatest commission Christianity had to offer: the rebuilding
5, 722 of St Peter's. It almost goes without saying that Bramante's
design should have involved a central plan. Combining
planning ideas sketched by Leonardo with stylistic elements from Alberti, it is the fullest expression of the aspirations of the High Renaissance. The basic form of the plan
is a square. Inscribed in it and projecting beyond it are
the arms of a great Greek cross, meeting under a large
dome. Between these arms lie smaller Greek crosses; diagonally beyond them, in the four corners of the square,
stand four towers. These elements coalesce to form one
composition without losing their integrity. Similarly Bramante's elevation shows a building divided vertically into
storeys; the vast building is broken down into humanly
accessible units. The crown of the whole composition was
to be a semi-spherical dome similar to that of the Pantheon,
resting on a uniform ring of columns. The foundation
stone was laid in 1506, and work proceeded swiftly, but
when Bramante died in 1514, although the crossing piers
and arches had been constructed, there followed about
thirty years of much redesigning and little progress.
What the interior of Bramante's cathedral might have
been like is shown best in the architectural setting Raphael
721 gave his ancient philosophers in *The School of Athens*.

One domestic building by Bramante must be mentioned
as of great historical importance: the house of Raphael
(acquired by the painter in 1517). It consisted of two storeys: the lower was rusticated and massive, and acted,
aesthetically as well as physically, as a base for the upper
storey with its columns, pedimented windows and balustrades. Here we meet for the first time the concept of the
piano nobile, the first floor which contains the most important rooms and is given the greatest aesthetic importance.★ This invention was soon imitated, by Raphael
723 himself in the Palazzo Vidoni Caffarelli (*c.* 1515-20), and
by Renaissance architects everywhere.

Raphael was responsible for other buildings, such as the
little Greek cross church of Sant'Eligio degli Orefici which
'in its pure whiteness, its austerity of forms, and the abstract
clarity of its geometrical scheme epitomises the religious

★ Throughout, the first floor or storey is that above ground level.

723 **Palazzo Vidoni Caffarelli,
Rome. c. 1515-20. Raphael**
The two-storey palazzo, as in the
original design, must have
appealed to Raphael, since
he designed another, in Florence,
for the Pandolfini family.
This one is similar to his own in
Rome, the façade echoing the
importance of the 'piano nobile'.

724 **Palazzo Farnese,
Rome. 1534-45.
Antonio da Sangallo and
Michelangelo**
A patrician family's city house
with coat of arms in the centre.
Its dignified opulence later became
the accepted style in Europe
for clubs and banks.
The ground floor windows are
larger than in the past,
but this floor was still occupied by
stables, outdoor offices and
servants only. The top storey
and entrance were designed
by Michelangelo.

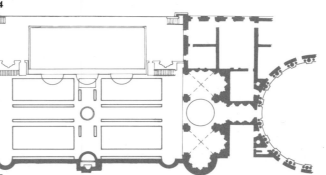

725 **Plan of Villa Madama,
Rome. c. 1516. Raphael**
The first of the great
Renaissance villas to be planned
with a garden lay-out.
Gardens were treated formally,
in geometric shapes,
rather like outdoor extensions of
the houses.
The villa itself, with circular
courtyard and apsed and niched
rooms, is reminiscent of
the grandeur of Roman baths.

726 **Villa Madama, Rome.
c. 1516. Raphael**
Painted decoration was used
extensively by the ancient
Romans. Raphael studied it in
detail, and the decoration of the
Villa Madama is taken directly
from Nero's 'Golden House'.
the remains of which had been
discovered below ground. For this
reason this type of decoration
was known as 'Grottesche', and
was used extensively.

727, 728 Laurentian Library, Florence. Begun 1524. Michelangelo

Interior, section and plan.
The library is long and comparatively low; the anteroom is tall and narrow.
Instead of a Renaissance balance between the two rooms there is a deliberate contrast heightened by the different levels.
Decorative elements are used in an entirely new way.
The coupled columns in the anteroom (see 730) do not support the cornice for instance.

727

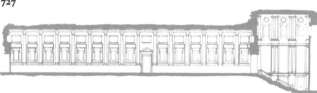

728

729 Medici chapel, Florence. 1521-34. Michelangelo

The New Sacristy in the church of San Lorenzo.
Michelangelo designed this building to correspond with Brunelleschi's Old Sacristy in the same church. Here is the first manifestation of Mannerism, the interior treated sculpturally with the main features being the tombs of Giuliano de' Medici (seen here) and Lorenzo de' Medici.
The recumbent nudes under the sculptured figure of Giuliano represent Night and Day.

729

feeling of the Renaissance' (Wittkower), and the Villa Madama on the Monte Mario near the Vatican—only a small part of what should have been the first great building-and-garden lay-out, formally planned and embodying some of Raphael's considerable archaeological knowledge.

Climaxes are brief; complete harmony may end in boredom. Political events in Italy were soon to shatter the shining image of High Renaissance Rome, but even before that the arts were turning away from harmony as an ideal. The period that followed used to be described as the beginning of a long process of cultural decay. More recently, labelled Mannerism, it has been studied with great interest, not least because its conditions and modes of expression are in some cases comparable with our own. It is not possible to do justice to a complex movement by defining it briefly. Perhaps the best way to describe Mannerism is first in negative terms, as a denial of the qualities of the High Renaissance by means of inverting many of its characteristics. The positive corollary of this is that this attitude was consciously adopted in order to create an art more expressive and personal, that brought with it freedom from classical canons and bred inventiveness. The resulting investigation into expressive means led to a greater awareness of the affective potentialities of space, of the quality of surfaces, of light and dark (all echoed in the painting of the period), that provides the basis for seventeenth-century artistic communication. Freedom may be dangerous to the creative artist, and there is no doubt that much Mannerist work is little more than capricious, while the idiosyncratic creations of one artist could become the cliché of another. Towards the end of the century Mannerist architecture turned into a dry, impersonal exercise in classical design, as though architects sought self-protection in discipline.

Generally speaking, there was a retreat from fundamental, timeless principles of design, such as clarity and visible stability of structure, subjugation of ornament to structure, and the shaping of environment to accord with man's natural requirements. The new freedom could be used for frivolous and for serious ends, and two outstanding examples may serve as illustrations of both categories: the vestibule and library of the monastery of San Lorenzo in Florence, by that most serious of all artists, Michelangelo (1475-1564), and the Duke of Mantua's pleasure-house, the Palazzo del Tè near Mantua, designed by Raphael's chief assistant Giulio Romano (1492 or 1499-1546).

Michelangelo designed the Laurentian Library in 1542. It had to fit into a long wing, and it had to be reached from a vestibule on a lower level. The long shape of the library being given, Michelangelo decided to underline it dramatically by prefacing it with the contrasting form of the anteroom: square in plan and uncomfortably tall, and all the more emphatically vertical for being lit by windows near the ceiling (Michelangelo had intended to use roof lights). Its walls are treated in storeys, with niches and decorative panels suggesting windows, and columns rising from what could be the first floor, i.e. the *piano nobile*. But the niches are not windows, and their detailing is designed to contradict the conventional equilibrium of pilasters and pediments; the columns are recessed into the

725, 72

727, 72
730

731-73

730 Laurentian Library
Interior of anteroom.
Columns and corbels have no
functional significance whatever.
They are recessed into the wall.
But this is Mannerism in a
sublime form, a highly artificial
system upheld by the severest
discipline.

730

**731 Palazzo del Tè, Mantua.
1526–1531. Giulio Romano**
Classical Mannerism applied to the
great palazzo.
The house comprises four long
low wings surrounding a court, and
with its garden it suggests
the beginning of a more open
ground plan.
Classical canons have been flouted,
for instance baseless pediments on
the court side, and on the garden –
the alteration of the a, b, c,
motif to bring forward the three
centre bays. Rustication,
instead of denoting structural
strength as in the fortress-palazzo,
is used as background ornament
behind the order.

731

**732 Palazzo del Tè, Mantua.
1526-31. Romano**
Detail of courtyard.
The absence of logic and the
earthbound quality of the building
are apparent on this courtyard wall.
The large, weighty keystones,
the different sized block stones and
columns and the pointless
niches, arched and square,
are all infringements of the
classical· order.

732

733 Palazzo del Tè, Mantua
Main entrance.
This triple archway leads to the
courtyard, its smooth façade
belying the irregularity of the rest.
It is like an unadorned Roman
temple.

733

734 Palazzo del Tè, Mantua
Interior.
The rooms of the palace have been
executed with more
symmetry of plan than the
façade, but here too there
are details of illogicality – the short
square doors in high, vaulted
rooms, for example.
The ornaments and paintings are
by Romano and his pupils.

734

wall in denial of their aesthetic function of appearing to carry the building; the floor space is almost filled by a strange and entirely original form of stairs (not finished until 1552) that flow heavily from the library door. The library itself is comparatively harmonious, but here too is found the quaint device (so familiar to us from subsequent architecture that we hardly notice it) of treating the inner surface of a wall as though it were the outside of a building. Above a dado the same height as the reading desks (which thus provide the visual base) are windows with architraves and cornices, and above them, panels suggesting mezzanine windows, flanked by pilasters. The effect of the anteroom and library together is strange and disquieting, austere and unaccommodating.

The Palazzo del Tè, built between 1526 and 1531, consists of four long, low wings forming a square court. The earthbound quality of the house is emphasised by the use of surprisingly large details, such as enormously weighty keystones that come into conflict with pediments and other adjacent items, and oversized fireplaces. Rustication is used almost everywhere with wild illogicality, so that a surface treatment conceived to suggest strength comes to suggest decay and unreliability. In the Doric entablature on one side of the court, some of the triglyphs have slipped a few inches downwards as though disintegration was imminent. There are different sized columns of the same order placed side by side, baseless pediments, and many other similar infringements of classical canons. The elegant garden side demonstrates a more sophisticated Mannerism. It is based on the repetition of a design motif found throughout the history of man, but particularly favoured by the Renaissance (we have seen it already in Alberti; Bramante used it frequently): the three-part unit consisting of a small, a large and a small element, often called the 'a b a' motif, or, more obscurely, the 'rhythmic *travée*'. But the effect of this façade arises from the architect's refusal to repeat the motif: he gives the impression of repeating it, but changes it continually, and thus, so to speak, forces the various sections of the façade out of step with each other. The three centre bays of the façade seem to project far in front of the side-bays because of the use of much larger 'a b a' motifs: it is more or less on the same plane.

Mannerism can be sober or playful, obvious or latent; it tends always to be disquieting. It is better, perhaps, to think of it as an attitude rather than a style, and of its varying productions as the creations of differing personalities working in a period of collapsing conventions. Other outstanding Mannerist buildings are Vasari's Uffizi (originally offices, now a museum) in Florence (1550-74), forming three sides of a street-like court and using simplified classical elements in shallow, brittle forms; Ammanati's courtyard of the Palazzo Pitti, Florence (1558-70), where rustication, changing from storey to storey, impartially covers walls and columns; Vignola's Villa Farnese at Caprarola (1547-59), a pentagonal castle around a circular court, approached by elaborate steps and ramps and decorated internally in a sub-Raphael manner; the same architect's Villa Giulia near Rome (1550-52), with its elaborate court and garden buildings; and Pierro Ligorio's Logetta of the Casino of Pius IV in the Vatican gardens (1560-61),

732

737
738

735

736

735

737

736

738

735 Villa Farnese at Caprarola. 1547–59. Giacomo da Vignola
A Mannerist fantasy.
A pentagonal fortress built round a circular court with, outside, a complicated system of ramps and flights of steps.
The walls of the inner court are decorated with balconies and figures inside niches.

736 Courtyard of Pius IV's Casino, Vatican gardens, Rome. 1560–61
Designed by Pierro Ligorio, this small paved courtyard is simple in plan, but the loggetta on the right is Mannerist in its addition of irrelevant relief sculpture to the adjoining walls.

737 Jacopo da Pontormo, 'Descent from the Cross'. c. 1525
Church of Sta Felicità, Florence. This deposition by the Florentine Mannerist painter shows the development in painting which runs parallel to the Mannerism which influenced architecture.
With its fluidity of movement and ambiguity of space it contrasts sharply with the classicism of, for example, Raphael's 'School of Athens' (721).

738 Uffizi court, Florence. 1550–74. Giorgio Vasari
Mannerism was concerned much with the treatment of space. These two tall wings lead the eye down the length of the narrow court, through the pierced loggia to the Arno beyond. The contrast between mass and lightness is deliberate, and in the original design, where the first floor of the loggia was colonnaded, it was even more marked.

739 Palazzo Bevilacqua, Verona. 1530.
Michele Sanmicheli
One of the palaces which Sanmicheli built in Venice and Verona under the Mannerist influence of Rome.

739

740 Teatro Olimpico, Vicenza. Begun 1580.
Andrea Palladio and Vicenzo Scamozzi
The seating was like a classical Roman or Greek theatre, arranged in a tiered horseshoe, the whole roofed in.
On the stage a permanent scene was built in false perspective.
It is the prototype for all theatres and opera houses since.

740

741 Interior of Villa Giacomelli at Maser
Frescoes of Veronese.
This is no longer just wall decoration but pictorial art of a highly organised kind.
The figures have been made to appear part of
the room by various illusionist tricks. In its way it is as stylised as 'Grottesche,' but it has the additional aim of representing to the owner and his guests the sort of idyllic pastoral life of the villa countryside.

741

simple enough in form, but almost covered with discordant relief sculpture.

This same period saw Michelangelo's greatest architectural achievements, the laying-out of the Piazza del Campidoglio in Rome (from 1536) and the continuation of work on St Peter's (from 1545). These belong to the world of Mannerism in some of their details, but in other respects foreshadow the Baroque (as does Michelangelo's *Last Judgment* fresco, 1536-41). The perspective effect of the trapezium plan of the piazza, and the consideration of the changing views of buildings and sculpture on the piazza as one mounts the ramp leading up to it—the sculptural, concentrated plan of St Peter's, its meandering outline and energetic dome and lantern—prepare the ground for Bernini and the High Baroque. Highly original in general form as well as in detail (notice particularly the use of a giant order, running through two or more storeys, both on the piazza and on St Peter's), these buildings lack the anguished note of his earlier works and sound instead a note of vigour which was echoed by the next century.

No mention has so far been made of Venice, but it would be surprising if the city and state that produced Bellini, Giorgione, Titian, Veronese and Tintoretto were to be found lacking in fine architecture. With her economy based on Oriental trade and her oligarchical republic, Venice in many respects stood aside from the rest of Italy, but could not fail to be affected by all the creative activity further south. The sack of Rome in 1527 resulted in a dispersal of artists and architects, many of whom travelled north. The architecture of Venice, until then somewhat parochial, now received the imprint of High Renaissance grandeur and converted it into a richer and more joyous style. Jacopo Sansovino (1486-1570) arrived in Venice in 1527 to work as sculptor and architect. He gave High Renaissance form to the traditional Venetian palaces (e.g. Palazzo Corner della Ca' Grande, 1532), and in the Logetta at the foot of the tower of San Marco (1537-40) and the adjacent library of San Marco (1532-54), he fused Roman monumentality with Venetian sensuality: coloured marbles, sculpture in relief and free-standing, lacy balustrades, deep mouldings and arches to set shadow against light—these are the counterpart of Titian's painting. Sanmicheli (1484-1559) also came to Venice from Rome in 1527, but he had been born in the Veneto, at Verona. In 1535 he was placed in charge of all Venetian fortifications, and from then on built a fine series of city gates for Verona— the earliest of them much fortified, the later ones more symbolical than functional in their massiveness. He also designed some noble palaces for the cities of Verona and Venice, among which the Palazzo Bevilacqua, Verona (1530), is particularly important for its introduction of Mannerist tendencies into north Italian architecture.

The most important architect of northern Italy in the sixteenth century, however, is Andrea Palladio, not only for the quality of his work but also for the influence which his buildings, his treatise and his drawings had on other countries and other centuries. Palladio (1508-80) is in many respects Alberti's successor: he too was a serious student of classical learning and of Vitruvius and Roman architecture in particular, and he too leavened his antiquarian

717, 7
720, 7

739

knowledge with practical intelligence and sensibility. His
work includes all kinds of buildings—civic (he remodelled
the basilica in Vicenza in 1545, clothing the medieval town
hall with a two-storey frill of 'a b a' arcading; this motif
is sometimes known as the 'Palladian motif' as a result of
his frequent use of it); domestic, both as palaces and villas;
and ecclesiastical. His larger churches, San Giorgio Mag-
743   giore and Il Redentore, are in Venice; his domestic architecture is in and around Vicenza. The fame of his town
and country houses is such that it has tended to overshadow
that of his churches, but these were so highly regarded by
later generations of Venetian architects as to inhibit the
spread of Baroque expressionism there, and they greatly
impressed the Neo-classicists of the eighteenth century.
Their façades are adaptations of what Palladio believed
was an ancient Roman device, the interpenetration of two
or more orders and pediments. In this way he continued
the researches of Alberti, and if there is something Mannerist about the very coolness of his designs (disguising
the passionate desire to comprehend fully the architecture
of the ancients that must have impelled his studies), Palladio, like Michelangelo, and unlike any other architect
of the middle of the sixteenth century, stands as much outside
his time as in it, reaching back to Alberti and to antiquity,
and forward to the legions of architects (most of them
outside Italy) who were to be guided by him in the future.

Behind his domestic buildings, even more than behind
his churches, lay his archaeological studies. In so far as he
had to interpret the evidence he collected in his reading
and travels, he tended inevitably to give them original sixteenth-century qualities, but no one in his time, nor for
some time after him, had as profound an understanding of
Roman design, nor, more important, as fine a gift for
translating that understanding into a practical basis for
modern design. Thus the palaces are similar in many ways
to his reconstruction of the Roman town house, as shown,
for example, in the plan of a Roman house he drew for
his friend Daniele Barbaro's edition of Vitruvius. The Pa-
746   lazzo Chiericati (1550) has its superimposed open colonnades because Palladio believed that the Romans had surrounded their squares with such covered walks. His villas
usually have temple fronts framing their main entrances,
projecting as porticoes or flush with the façade (again, so
familiar a feature that one takes its existence for granted,
but the product of Palladio's decision that Roman temple
design must have been derived ultimately from Roman
house design). The most famous of these villas is the Villa
, 747   Capra (or Rotonda, 1567) on a hill near Vicenza. This
has a remarkable central plan, so harmonious that one
almost omits to question the necessity for the four porticoes and flights of steps. More typical, however, are the
winged villas in which Palladio gives intelligent and monumental form to complex functions. The villas were both
weekend retreats and farm houses to their wealthy merchant owners, and it is clear from the existing buildings
and from Palladio's writings that he gave careful consideration to the practical problems this duality raised. Hence
the noble, sometimes richly decorated, always symmetrically planned houses, and hence the extensive low wings
of many of them, sweeping symmetrically away from the

742

743

744

742 **Palazzo Massimi, Rome.
Begun 1535. Baldassare Peruzzi**
The architect plays off flatness
against curve and hollow,
small scale against larger scale,
light elements against heavy,
in a way that seems to mock
the classical appearance of
the ground storey.

743 **Il Redentore, Venice.
1577-92. Palladio**
One of Palladio's larger churches,
Palladio's churches were
highly regarded by generations of
Venetian architects,
although his fame rests mainly on
his country houses.
Il Redentore is cruciform with
side chapels; as with all his buildings,
there are the principal and
subsidiary orders and pediments
used on the façade.

744 **San Zaccaria, Venice.
1458-1515. Pietro Lombardo**
Lombardo was one of a family of
architects who worked in
Venice. This church is an example
of his early work and still
shows traces of medieval planning.
Renaissance forms appeared later
in Venice than they did in Florence.

745 Villa Capra (or Rotonda), near Vicenza. Begun 1567. Palladio
Palladio always designed his villas with reference to their setting. This one on a hill is built to command views from each of its sides. The flight of steps and temple front are taken from ancient Roman building, but their context is entirely original. They are not used merely as a single frontage, as in English Palladian, but repeat on all four sides.

745

746 Palazzo Chiericati, Vicenza. 1550. Palladio
Palladio introduced the colonnaded loggia into the palazzo façade, a link between the house and the outside.
He based it on researches into ancient Roman domestic architecture, from which he thought their temple architecture derived.
The coolness and serenity are offset by the sculptures on the roof, a favourite theme of Palladio's, seen to great effect against a Mediterranean sky.

746

main approach to accommodate horses, stores, etc. Palladio designed these houses with the care and high idealism architects had previously reserved for churches. Not only within their simple forms are they laid out symmetrically (sometimes symmetrically about both axes), but the proportions of each room are calculated on a simple mathematical ratio, and the different rooms of the house are interrelated by these ratios. 'Those proportional relationships which other architects had harnessed for the two dimensions of a façade or the three dimensions of a single room were employed by him to integrate a whole structure' (R. Wittkower, *Architectural Principles in the Age of Humanism*, London 1949, p. 113).

Vincenzo Scamozzi (1552-1616), Palladio's pupil, carried his master's classicising style into the seventeenth century. His book *Idea del'Architettura Universale* (1615), together with Palladio's *Quattro Libri di Architettura* (1570), brought their designs to the drawing tables and libraries of architects and patrons all over Europe and in the New World.

Genoa and Milan flourished architecturally in the sixteenth century, particularly at the hands of Galeazzo Alessi (1512-72), who knew Roman sixteenth-century architecture at first hand and built some fine palaces in both cities. He also designed the centrally planned church of Sta Maria di Carignano, Genoa (designed 1552, begun 1577), basing himself on Bramante's plan for St Peter's. Pellegrino Tibaldi's façade of San Fedele in Milan is a good example of northern Italian late Mannerism: a little disquieting, a little boring, with a dryness that tended to affect Mannerism everywhere before the upsurge of Baroque vitality swept it aside.

THE SIXTEENTH CENTURY OUTSIDE ITALY

Fifteenth-century Europe, outside Italy, allows only occasional glimpses of Renaissance design as slow corollaries to the spreading of Renaissance literary concepts, and it is not until the sixteenth century that one can speak of native attempts at Renaissance design in these countries. Spain, France, the Low Countries, Germany and England differed considerably in their receptivity to the Renaissance. Geographical position, political and religious conditions, the strength or weakness of medieval traditions, these and other factors gave great variety to the adaptations and transformations to which the rest of Europe subjected the Italian Renaissance.

One common element, however: everywhere the Renaissance was received at first as little more than a stylistic novelty to be worn lightly without consideration of the principles and ideology involved. Late Gothic design delighted in rich decoration on simple structures: Italy offered a treasure-chest of new and fascinating ornaments. This produced a fashion-consciousness that one does not expect to find before the end of the eighteenth century. For example, Charles V was worried in 1528 by the stylistic conflict between Diego de Siloë's Italianate design for Granada Cathedral and its recently built Royal Chapel. In 1529-30 the cathedral authorities of Seville received from the architect Diego de Riaño designs for three rooms in three different styles, Gothic, Plateresque, and more or less High Renaissance. Charles's son and heir Philip II

748

750

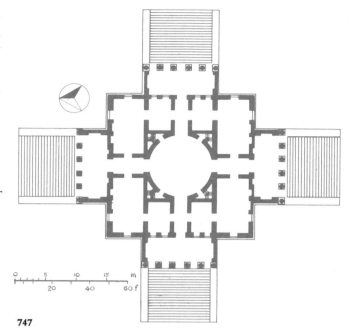

747

747 **Plan of Villa Capra, near Vicenza. Begun 1567. Palladio**
The house was designed essentially as a cube.
Palladio brought to domestic architecture the idealism that his predecessors had brought to church design. Internal as well as external symmetry is common to his houses, which also tend to be cubic or at least very compact.

748

748 San Fedele, Milan. Pellegrino Tibaldi. 1569-1652
This façade is a good example of northern Italian late Mannerism. It represents a last stage before the arrival of the Baroque.

749

749 Colegio de San Gregorio, Valladolid. 1488-96.
Plateresque decoration.
In Spain this type of decoration, Plateresque (silversmith-like), was used extensively.
It is a curious mixture of Gothic, Mohammedan and early Renaissance, and was spread over walls with little relation to what was underneath.

**750 Granada Cathedral.
Begun 1528.
Diego de Siloë**
This cathedral, one of the great
Spanish churches, has elements
of Gothic, Renaissance and even
Baroque, but is mainly an
extremely good example of the
Plateresque style of decoration.
Siloë's Italianate design
for the interior is a Renaissance
adaptation of the medieval
cathedral at Seville.

750

**751 Château of Blois.
East wing. 1498-1503**
The château of Blois was begun
in the thirteenth century
and was continued by Louis XII
who added the east wing,
which shows remarkably little
Renaissance influence.
The building now forms an
irregular quadrangle, the north side
being commissioned and
the south embellished (1515-24)
by Francis I
and the west built (1635-38)
by François Mansart for
Gaston d'Orléans.

751

**752 Château of Blois.
Court façade. 1515-24**
The court façade,
with its famous spiral staircase
in its open tower, was Francis I's
addition to the château.
The windows here have panelled
instead of moulded mullions,
and the dormers and chimney
stacks are attractively carved.

752

at first patronised Plateresque design and then demanded
a more ascetic classicism. Plateresque means silversmith-
like, and the name indicates what has been called the
'adjectival' quality of the style—ornament only loosely related to the structure. Riaño's town hall in Seville (begun
1527) illustrates this to some extent, but both his work
and that of Siloë show a firmer grasp of Renaissance design
than that of their colleagues. Charles V's palace at Granada
(designed 1527 by Pedro Machuca, who had studied painting in Italy) is unique at this time for its mature handling
of High Renaissance forms.

The beginnings of Renaissance design in France are similar. A wave of château building in the Loire area was
carried out in basically traditional terms, but with ornament learnt from north Italian buildings. During the first
decades of the sixteenth century, the French were involved
in wars in northern Italy and took the opportunity to
borrow stylistic ideas as well as Renaissance objects and a
few Renaissance artists. But at first it was the more facile
versions of the Renaissance they appreciated—the Certosa
at Pavia rather than Alberti's Mantuan churches. The court
front of Francis I's wing (1515-24) of the château of Blois,
for example, though different in ornamental detail and
more neatly organised with its grid of shallow pilasters
and entablatures, is in its essentials not only the same as
Louis XII's wing (1498-1503) but also as the unequivo-
cally late Gothic château of Josselin (1490). The delight
with which the masons of the château of Chambord heaped
north Italian ornament on to its elaborate roofscape belongs
to the late Gothic spirit of ornamental *largesse*. In the
1530s progress was fast. Important Italian designers came
to France, worked for the king and established a court
style. The Florentine painter Rosso Fiorentino arrived in
1530; two years later came the young Primaticcio, who
had worked under Giulio Romano on the decorations of
the Palazzo del Té. Rosso died in 1540; Primaticcio worked
in France until his death in 1570. They and the assistants
they collected and instructed evolved for the royal château
of Fontainebleau a novel decoration known as strapwork
(interior of gallery of Francis I, about 1533-40). Later,
Primaticcio was responsible for projects and buildings of
considerable importance, such as the wing 'de la Belle
Cheminée' at Fontainebleau (1568).

Elsewhere, the first stages of the Renaissance were complicated further by a variety of cross-influences. Countries
such as England, the Low Countries (i.e. the modern
Belgium and Netherlands, united by Charles V), and Germany (meaning the German-speaking middle of Europe),
are geographically more remote from Italy and, as the
century progressed, raised at least partial barriers against
direct Italian influence through the rise of Protestantism,
and thus tended to use Italianate ideas and motifs at second or third hand. In England, for example, the late
Gothic style known as Perpendicular (see p. 232) was still
very much alive, and produced in Tudor architecture a style
which owed nothing to the Renaissance but was in many
ways concordant with it. A handful of Italians worked
for the English court in the second and third decades
of the sixteenth century, adding touches of Renaissance
ornament to Tudor buildings, as at Wolsey's Hampton

749

701-7

751, 7

753
754

760

757

762, 7

753

754

756

755

757

753 Chambord. Begun 1519. Pierre Nepveu
This vast château is entirely symmetrical. It also shows the beginning of the Renaissance idea of façade, and a terrace is included. The round turrets are still feudal, and the roof is a mixture of feudal shapes and Renaissance decorative detail.

754 Chambord. Roof detail. 1519-40
Chambord's roof is a proliferation of turrets and chimneys, romantic and Gothic-looking, the detailed Renaissance decoration of which was all carried out by north Italian masons.

755, 756 Convent of Christ, Tomar, Portugal
Main cloister, interior and exterior. The main cloister of the Convent Palace of the Knights of Christ was built by Diego de Torralva in 1557. A Portuguese example of High Renaissance architecture, it shows a marked Italian influence.

757 Fontainebleau. Aile de la Belle Cheminée. 1568. Primaticcio
This late example of Primaticcio's work is more strictly architectural, less picturesque than earlier designs. The general lay-out with its double flight of steps is impressive but lacks his usual bravura.

758 São Vicente de Fora, Lisbon. 1582–1605. Filippo Terzi
This church was
the first Portuguese design of
the Italian architect Filippo Terzi.
In its restraint and austerity
can be seen the influence of the
Escorial on Portuguese building.

759 Fontainebleau. Cour de l'Ovale. 1528 onwards
The Cour de l'Ovale is the
court of the medieval castle
to which Gilles le Breton
added a Renaissance gateway
(the Porte Dorée)
and a portico and external
staircase (seen here in its
present fragmentary state).
This indicates a command
of classical details and form
new to France but spreading
rapidly in the 1530s.

760 Fontainebleau. Gallery of Francis I. 1533–40. Rosso and Primaticcio
After the successful Italian wars
Francis I called over to France
many Italian painters and designers,
chief among them Rosso and
Primaticcio.
The decoration of this gallery is a
mixture of painting and stucco,
reminiscent of the Vatican Loggia
and the Palazzo del Tè.
The fine carved woodwork is
probably French or Flemish.
This gallery besides being a great
reception room was to house
the classical antiquities Francis I
brought back from the wars.

758

759

760

Court (begun 1515), where Giovanni da Maiano contributed the relief busts of Roman emperors and probably the panel of Wolsey's arms, all in terra cotta. Already in the middle of the 1530s, when the wooden screen in King's College chapel, Cambridge was made, the credit must go to French or possibly Dutch workmen, not to Italians, and when Henry VIII built his bombastic new Nonsuch Palace in Surrey (begun 1538), he employed 'the most outstanding artificers, architects, carvers and sculptors of diverse nations, Italians, Frenchmen, Dutch and men of his own country' (George Braun, *Urbium Praecipuarum Mundi Theatrum Quintum*, 1582). Little wonder if the result, in so far as we know it, is quite un-Italian in character and hardly Italian in detail.

The middle of the century shows in many places a much firmer grasp of Italian design, often fused with traditional elements rather than haphazardly imposed on them. In Spain an extreme form of Italian classicism was required by Philip II—a style, in fact, almost devoid of national traits, unless its austerity may be taken to be as natural an expression of the Spanish character as is prolific ornamentation. The chief monument of this phase is the Escorial, one of the first great palace complexes of the Renaissance. It was not strictly a palace: on a slag-heap (*escorial*) near Madrid, Philip constructed a building to be a monastery with a large abbey church, a mausoleum for Charles V, and a palace for the king and his court, all in one. He commanded Juan Bautista de Toledo to leave Naples for Madrid in order to draw up his plans. In lay-out the Escorial derives ultimately from late Roman palace planning, as in Diocletian's palaces at Spalato, but its many straight wings and rectangular courts focus on a magnificent centrally planned church. Work began in 1563, and the building was completed in 1584; meanwhile Juan Bautista died. His place was taken in 1572 by Juan de Herrera (c. 1530-97) who made some alterations to the original design and almost completely redesigned the church, slightly ameliorating the palace's intended austerity without loss of dignity. Stylistically the finished building belongs to the High Renaissance for most of its details and to Mannerism for its dry use of the classical canon.

In France too this was a period of climax. In fact, the classical buildings of the 1540s to 1570s mark the establishment of a tradition of classicism which continues through French architecture into the twentieth century, and which is never lost sight of for long. This tradition was created by two architects, Philibert de l'Orme and Pierre Lescot, but its establishment was aided by the arrival in France in 1541 of another Italian, Sebastiano Serlio. Serlio, who had worked in High Renaissance Rome, is best remembered for an architectural treatise, brief in text and rich in illustrations, which became one of the most fruitful (because one of the most easily assimilable) sources of information and ideas for architects all over Europe during the next 150 years. Serlio also left some buildings, among which the château of Ancy-le-Franc (begun 1546), with four equal wings around a square court and four taller corner pavilions, all with steeply pitched roofs, best showed how the language of the High Renaissance could be adapted to French usage.

761

761

764

p. 236

759
6, 767

761 **King's College chapel, Cambridge. Screen. c. 1530**
The Renaissance reached England first in the decorative arts of sculpture and carving. This wooden screen was the work of French or possibly Dutch workmen.

762

762, 763 **Hampton Court. Entrance front, after 1515; interior of Great Hall, 1533**
Renaissance ornament was added by Wolsey to a Tudor building in the relief busts of Roman emperors by Giovanni de Maiano and the terra cotta arms.
The Great Hall is entirely Gothic but with Renaissance putti and foliage in the roof spandrels.
In England the influence of the Renaissance was still confined to ornament; building construction remained unchanged.

763

764 Nonsuch Palace. Begun 1538
The English version of the ideal
Renaissance palace commissioned
by Henry VIII.
A curiously mongrel building,
quite un-Italian in feeling
despite the lavish use of external
Italianate decoration. Workmen
were employed from Italy, France,
Holland, as well as from England.

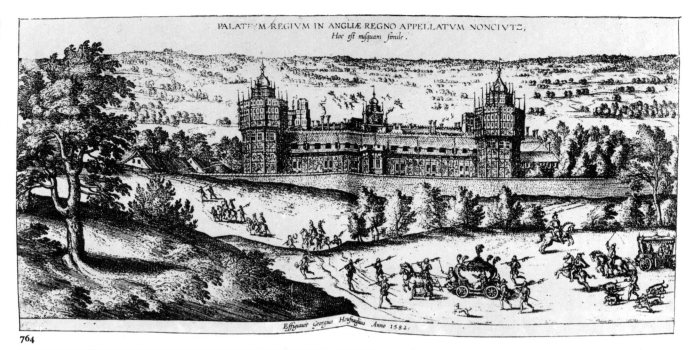

764

765 Louvre, Paris.
Pierre Lescot's wing, 1546
Lescot's work on the medieval
palace established a classical
tradition in French architecture
which lasted until the twentieth
century. Its derivation
from the Italian palazzo is obvious,
but it has French
characteristics of its own: the
balance between the verticals and
horizontals, the steep-pitched
roof and the dwarf order for the
lower top storey.

765

766 Ancy-le-Franc, Bourgogne.
Begun 1546.
Sebastiano Serlio
Serlio, coming from the Italy
of the High Renaissance,
imposed a more rigorous
concept of symmetry and
order on a building that
in other respects continues
the traditions of
French château architecture.

766

Lescot began in 1546 to rebuild the medieval royal palace in Paris, the Louvre. The three-storey wing that he completed shows an astonishing grasp of Renaissance detail and, perhaps even more astonishing, a completely French mode of expression that shows through the southern vocabulary. This judgment may be based in part on the debt that later French classicism owes to this building, but a comparison between Lescot's Louvre and any Italian palace shows a different sense of form and composition (in Lescot an intricate play of many verticals against a few strong but broken horizontals, as against the usually relaxed, undynamic balance of Italian Renaissance palaces), and there is the northern steep roof as well as Lescot's useful invention, the dwarf order for the low top storey.

Philibert de l'Orme (c. 1510-70) is an even more impressive figure, partly because he left behind more buildings of varying character, as well as two treatises, *Nouvelles Inventions pour bien bâtir et à petits frais*, 1561, and *Premier Livre de l'Architecture*, 1569. The attachment to common sense implied in the first title is evident also in the second book where it is combined with a real understanding of ancient and Renaissance theory. The quality of his work is very high. Offspring of generations of skilled masons, and adding to his native training a period of study in Rome, de l'Orme became chief architect to Henry II, to Henry's mistress Diane de Poitiers and to Henry's wife and widow Catherine de Médicis. In 1547 he designed the sepulchral monument to Francis I, erected in the cathedral of Saint Denis, a free adaptation of the classical triumphal arch, wonderfully detailed in finely cut marble. In the same year he began the château of Anet for Diane de Poitiers, making particularly free use of Renaissance forms in the projecting entrance pavilion, and attaching to the right wing a centrally planned chapel that not only proves him to be fully conversant with latest developments in Italian design but also, in the four main arches curving three-dimensionally through space, anticipates Baroque space modelling. The house is laid out in three wings forming a court with the stepped wing of the entrance pavilion closing the fourth side. The main entrance to the house is marked by a projecting bay, a frontispiece (now in the courtyard of the Ecole des Beaux-Arts in Paris) that is one of the most fruitful motifs invented in the sixteenth century; it reappears, copied or adapted, in most areas of Europe. In 1563 de l'Orme began the palace of the Tuileries, near the Louvre but outside the city walls. We know little of what he intended, but it seems likely that he designed the palace as a building of four wings around a court, one of which greatly dominates over the others—the prototype of the early seventeenth-century Luxembourg Palace. Typical of his attitude to classical canons, and typical also of his generation in France (which included the literary group called the Pléiade, fed on the classics but insisting on the equal value of the French language as a vehicle for high art—see Du Bellay's *Deffense et Illustration de la langue francoyse*, 1549) is his invention of a specifically French order of columns, used on the Tuileries, their vertical fluting interrupted by horizontal bands of decoration. The ancients, he argued, invented different orders as they seemed necessary: France lacks the marble quarries to produce

765

68, 769

767

768

769

767 Ancy-le-Franc, Bourgogne. Begun 1546. Courtyard. Sebastiano Serlio

768, 769 Château of Anet. Begun 1547. Entrance and chapel cupola. Philibert de l'Orme
Anet was begun in 1547 by Philibert de l'Orme for Diane de Poitiers. He makes personal use of Renaissance forms in the projecting entrance pavilion and on the house itself. The chapel is centrally planned, with four main arches curving three-dimensionally through space.

773

770

771

775, 77

770 Bruges Palais de Justice. 1520
In the early part of the century Renaissance influence in the Low Countries shows itself in the imposition of Renaissance ideas on a late Gothic form.

770

771 The Hague town hall. 1564-65
On a less imposing scale than Antwerp town hall, this equally shows the fusion of Renaissance elements brought from France with the native tradition of building.
An outburst of public and commercial building took place in the Low Countries at this time of great prosperity.

771

772 Cologne town hall. 1569-73. Wilhelm Vernukken
A two-storey Renaissance addition with arcade by a designer imported from the Low Countries. Decoration was lavished on the adjacent walls.

772

monolithic shafts, so that columns have to be constructed out of several drums of stone leaving visible horizontal joints, therefore it is only reasonable to design a column that makes positive use of these divisions instead of ignoring them. De l'Orme considered it essential to view classical traditions by the light of reason, and in this he set the tone of French architectural thought for centuries.

In the Low Countries this period produced one outstanding building, and this, with symbolic rightness, is the town hall of Antwerp. Antwerp had recently become one of the most flourishing cities of Europe through her port and extensive continental trade. The government of the country was centred on Brussels, but the economic life of the provinces focused on Antwerp, in the same way as, fifty years later, the northern provinces were to look to The Hague for government and to Amsterdam for trade. Compare the town hall of 1561-65 with the Bruges Palais de Justice of 1520, and you have the contrast not only between the first imposition of Renaissance ideas on a late Gothic form and the later absorption of Renaissance ideas into the body of local tradition, but also between the comparatively aristocratic and ecclesiastical atmosphere of Bruges and the busy materialism of Antwerp. Formally not unlike the earlier town halls of the Low Countries (e. g., Bruges, fourteenth century, and Middelburg, fifteenth century), that of Antwerp is so coherently conceived in terms of Renaissance elements received from France rather than from Italy that there remains little sign of stylistic duality. On a much less imposing scale, the town hall of The Hague (1564-65) shows a similar stylistic fusion. The town hall in Leipzig (1556) is a comparable German example. It is reasonable, then, to speak of a northern Renaissance style in architecture that belongs to both the old and the new worlds and which must be assessed in terms of its own inherent qualities and not in terms of Italian classicism.

In England the position was much the same. After the flamboyance of Henry VIII came the cooler cultural atmosphere of the Protectorate, Edward VI and Mary I. Here too the middle of the century was a moment of relative classicism, seen in Old Somerset House in London (begun 1547; in partial use 1557; destroyed in the eighteenth century) and even more in Longleat House, Wiltshire, built by Sir John Thynne (begun 1553), although only a limited use was made of Renaissance elements.

During the last third of the sixteenth century France and the northern countries experienced an architectural phase often described as Mannerism. In some senses it is Mannerist, but in so far as Mannerism presupposes the prior establishment of a classical canon, only in places where the canon was sufficiently firmly established for the breaking of it to be meaningful can Mannerism in the Italian sense be said to have obtained. Otherwise Mannerist phenomena in these countries should be explained by such facts as that at this time, when northern designers were looking more and more intently to Italy for ideas, Italian architects were developing their Mannerist idioms; that a playful use of Italian motifs, fundamentally akin to the previous use of Gothic motifs, can produce an appearance of Mannerism without involving the anti-classical attitude essential to true Mannerism; and also that the atmosphere

773

773 Antwerp town hall. 1561-65. Cornelius Floris (or de Vriendt)
By now Renaissance ideas were absorbed into the body of local tradition. The inspiration in this building is French rather than Italian, but the result is something new and indigenous, as at Longleat in Wiltshire.

774

774 Amsterdam town hall (now the Royal Palace). Begun 1648. Jacob van Campen
The Netherlands' equivalent to the classical royal palaces of the rest of Europe.
Dutch architects excelled not in buildings like this but in the merchants' houses of small proportions. This building was the original town hall, becoming the royal palace in 1804.

775, 776 Longleat House, Wiltshire. Begun 1554, burnt down 1567, rebuilt 1568 onwards.
Sir John Thynne
Exterior and plan.
Longleat represents a more indigenous achievement.
It is symmetrical in plan, with Renaissance elements
in the balustrades and subdued portico. The type of large flat-looking window has a curiously modern look, as does
the four-squareness of the building.

775

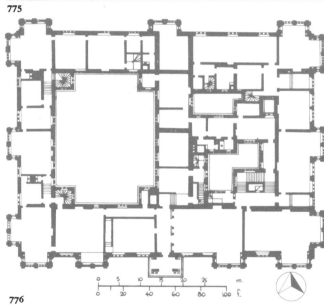

776

777 Hardwick Hall gallery, Derbyshire. 1590-97
The idea of the gallery as chief reception room was taken from Italy. Hardwick gallery
is 166 feet long, with Italian coffered ceiling. It runs the full length of the building and
is lighted here by a continuous row of enormous mullioned windows which are typically English.

777

778 Hatfield House, Hertfordshire. 1607-11
Hatfield is E-shaped, and although strong influence from the continent can be seen in the cupola and stonework decoration,
the structure, with its turrets, reminds one of its descent from medieval architecture.

779 Plan of Hardwick Hall, Derbyshire. 1590-97
The hall is placed on the axis of the main entrance
and in that marks a departure from other country houses.
Off the hall was the pantry and buttery, and from the latter one reached the chapel.

778

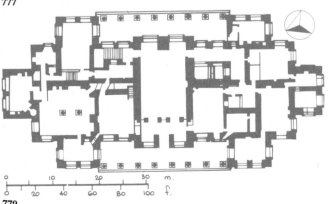

779

of political and religious strife in these decades was liable to find expression through discordant architectural gestures, superficially akin to Mannerism. The Protestant northern provinces of the Low Countries fought for and achieved independence from the southern provinces and their Spanish rulers; France suffered the disaster of civil war between Protestants and Catholics; England was faced with the threat of invasion by the forces of the Counter Reformation, headed by Spain, and stood in a state of emergency. In Germany too forces were grouping, and there the actual conflict came at the beginning of the seventeenth century, from 1618 until 1648.

France was the country to come closest to real Mannerism, and in Jean Bullant (c. 1520-78) she produced a major Mannerist architect. He studied in Rome and contributed a treatise, *Reigle Générale d'Architecture* (1563), and a more technical work, *Petit Traicté de Géometrie et d'Horologiegraphie* (1564), to the growing flood of architectural literature coming out of western Europe. History was against him, in that the almost continual strife that racked France from 1560 until 1598 left more opportunity for paper work than for the execution of large buildings, and it is noticeable that Bullant's projects, as well as those of his contemporary Jacques Androuet du Cerceau the Elder, contain an increasing element of fantasy, as though practical considerations were at a discount in this period of political chaos. His scheme for the enlargement of the château of

780 Chenonceaux for Catherine de Médicis (1576; original château 1515; bridge added by de l'Orme for Diane de Poitiers) is vast in extent and includes colossal elements such as the hemicycles forming a courtyard in front of the old château and the triumphal arches leading into it. The gallery he added to de l'Orme's bridge is decorated externally with a system of overlapping panels and pediments very close to the recent framing of paintings in the Sala Regia in the Vatican, by Daniele da Volterra.

Du Cerceau was responsible for the publication of several books of architectural engravings, among them two volumes recording the most important French buildings of his century. He also designed and began two influential châteaux, at Verneuil (c. 1565) and Charleval (1573). Verneuil was of the kind initiated by Anet: three wings plus an entrance screen and gateway. Charleval was intended to be far bigger. The main part of the château is of four wings around a square court, but this is preceded by an enormous enclosed court flanked by more wings forming subsidiary courts complete with two large churches. If executed, this would have been considerably larger in area than the Escorial, and the formal planning of the château would have been extended by means of a vast garden laid out in formally patterned *parterres*. In so far as we know du Cerceau's intentions for the château's elevations; they were to have been rather restless compositions involving large sculptures, giant pilasters, strips of rustication and vertically linked windows.

In the Low Countries, the late Gothic emphasis on decoration overshadowed developments in architectural form, and the greatest efforts were put into the publication of ornamental pattern-books by Frans Floris, Vredeman de Vries and others (and again others in Germany, such as

780

781

782

780 Chenonceaux.
Begun 1515.
Bridge (1556-59) and gallery (1576)
Philibert de l'Orme added a bridge to the earlier structure on which, a few years later, Jean Bullant built the gallery. Together they form an almost separate wing and Bullant s elaboration of detailing is different in character from the main château.

781 Heidelberg castle, Ottheinrichsbau.
Between 1556 and 1559
Successive Electors Palatine added their own sections to a late-medieval keep. Ottheinrich's wing is generally held to be the first German Renaissance palace building. It was executed largely by foreign artists, particularly men from the Netherlands. The façade is covered with a wealth of symbolical carvings, including mythological heroes, virtues, and over the entrance, the patron himself. The castle has been in ruins since the late seventeenth century.

782 Town hall at Krems, Austria
Oriel window, c. 1560.
In the Low Countries, late Gothic emphasis on decoration overshadowed developments in architectural form, and this tendency spread to Germany, Austria and Scandinavia. The oriel window at Krems is an example of this, and may well have been a result of the successful publication of ornamental pattern-books in these countries.

**783-786 Wollaton Hall,
Nottinghamshire. 1580-88.
Robert Smythson**
Exterior, plan and details.
The architecture of Elizabeth I
at its most vigorous.
It is intentionally castle-like, and
makes self-conscious use of
medieval motifs.
It is nearly square and no longer
inward-looking, which marks
a departure from the
building tradition of the time.
There is no courtyard, the centre
of the house being occupied by a
large windowless hall,
light for which comes from a
clerestory. Above that is a huge
chamber with turrets.
Renaissance decoration is by
Flemish and Dutch craftsmen,
the Dutch gable (785) and
strapwork (786) being
typical of the period.

783

**787 Burghley House,
Northamptonshire. 1585**
Courtyard.
Another adaptation of the Roman
classical arch as it reached
England via France. The niches
between the columns are typically
French. The three orders are
correctly used, but the bay window
looks incongruous, and
the style changes again with
the Flemish
decoration at the top.

784

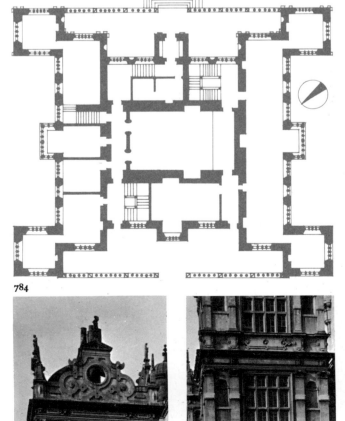

785   786

787

that of Wendel Dietterlin). Here too is found a strong element of fantasy and extravagance (in Dietterlin's case so extreme as to suggest a psychotic origin), and the success of these books was great throughout northern Europe. Decorators from the Low Countries were in great demand in England, Germany and Scandinavia. Already the castle at Heidelberg in Germany, to which the Elector Palatine Frederick II (1544-56) added an arcaded block, and his successor Ottheinrich (1556-69) a three-storey wing, owes more to the busy ornament of such craftsmen than to the basic architectural form, which may well have been given by the electors themselves. Wilhelm Vernukken came to Cologne from the Low Countries to add a two-storey arcaded loggia of classical character to the town hall and lavished a wealth of novel decoration on the adjacent walls (1569-73). The same ornament appears on the gables of Antwerp, Deventer (in the northern province of Over-ijssel), Wollaton (England) and as far east as Danzig; it is based on the Italian-French invention 'strapwork', transforming it into a more geometrical and flatter motif.

Wollaton, near Nottingham, may be taken to represent the architecture of Elizabeth I's England at its most vigorous. Aggressive, intentionally castle-like and making self-conscious use of medievalising motifs, Wollaton exhibits a rough strength, a quality of barbarian rhetoric, that fits well into one's picture of the period (1580-88). External and internal decorative details tell of the employment of Flemish or Dutch craftsmen.

ITALY IN THE SEVENTEENTH CENTURY

The decline of Mannerism into academicism coincided with the Council of Trent and the organisation of the Counter Reformation. It was a period of austerity in which the function of the arts in religion was questioned and defined. The period of art that followed, known as Baroque, seems far removed from the severe note struck by the Council, but it is more directly religious than art had been since the Middle Ages, and it fulfils the Council's demand for an art which will make real and comprehensible the doctrines of the Church. In painting and sculpture it is an art of miracles, martyrdoms, ecstasies and apotheoses; in architecture it is an art of glorification and transcendence. More perhaps than in any other period, the architect concerns himself with the symbolical and affective content of his building, within its surroundings. The adjective 'theatrical', used without its note of puritanical aversion, fits many aspects of Baroque architecture: it is an architecture of presentation—the presentation of doctrine and mystery in the Church, and in the palace, the presentation of taste and wealth and the mystery of the divine right of kings. The language used by international Baroque architecture continued to be that of ancient Rome, but Mannerism had shown the expressive potential residing in deviations from strict observance of grammar and syntax. Since architecture was now used to create a transcendental rather than a humanist environment, the continued use of classical forms was accompanied by a tendency, consciously or unconsciously, to abandon the classical premise of a man-centred architecture, varying in degree with different architects and places. Thus there is

some truth in the familiar remark that Baroque architecture is Gothic architecture made out of classical elements, but it would be more exact to say that the Baroque architect deploys classical elements to achieve ends comparable with those of Gothic architecture. The pioneering of the Baroque style and the creation of many of its finest monuments happened in seventeenth-century Rome, but it was the work, significantly enough, of architects, painters and sculptors from other parts of Italy and from other countries.

We have already met Vignola as a Mannerist architect. We have also seen that Michelangelo's later architectural works, the Piazza del Campidoglio and his contribution to St Peter's went beyond Mannerism to a more vigorous style. The building that marks most completely the transition from Mannerism to Baroque is the church built by Vignola to be the mother-church of that strong arm of the Counter Reformation, the Society of Jesus. The plan of the Gesù (begun 1568) is based on a plan prepared by Michelangelo and derived from Alberti's Sant'Andrea in Mantua: nave and chapels (no aisles), a domed crossing and short transepts and chancel, the same width as the nave. The internal effect of the Gesù is different from that of Sant'Andrea: there, the size and windows of the chapels created strong cross-currents counteracting the axis of nave and chancel; here the chapels are smaller and dark, and the lines of the building lead the eye to the crossing and to the light that falls from the drum into the chancel. Later decorations inhibit this internal focus, but the contrast with the calm balance sought by Alberti and the High Renaissance is clear enough. The façade of the church was the work of other architects departing from Vignola's design, but both the design and the façade have elements which the Baroque develops and transmits to Baroque church design everywhere: the façade steps forward and increases in plasticity from sides to centre, and scrolls, derived from Alberti's façade of Sta Maria Novella in Florence, link the two storeys of the façade. So many Roman Catholic churches built during the next 100 or 150 years derive from the Gesù that it would be difficult to exaggerate its importance, but it still belongs in part to the world of Mannerism. In subsequent Roman churches based on the Gesù model, such as Sant'Andrea della Valle (begun 1591) and Sant'Ignazio (begun 1626), Mannerist elements are gradually dropped or given new meaning. The further development of the Gesù façade can be outlined by mention of a few important examples. The façade of Sta Susanna (1596-1603, by Carlo Maderna), although small, makes full use of the plastic innovations of the Gesù, emphasising vertical elements and adding a balustrade to the top of the pediment, as though reluctant to end with a hard line or even to end at all. That of SS. Vincenzo e Anastasio (1646-50; by Martino Longhi the Younger) makes a powerful crescendo of free-standing columns, overlapping pediments and sculpture, almost independent of the structure of the west end of the church. The façade of Sta Maria in Campitelli (1636-37; Carlo Rainaldi) is stepped violently forwards and back and emphasises this sculptural gesture by continuing the recesses through the broad pediment, with the effect, again, of making inde-

781

83-786

788-790

691

791

794

795

788–790 Church of the Gesù, Rome. Begun 1568.
Vignola
Façade (1584), plan and interior.
The plan is based on one by
Michelangelo, a domed crossing
with short transepts and nave
and chapels (no aisles).
The cross between the Gothic and
Renaissance set the pattern
for churches until the present day.
The interior is lit by windows
above the chapels, and
light concentrated on the altar
by windows in the dome.
For the first time the architect
has treated lighting as a
dramatic problem. The internal
decoration is of later date.
The façade is later also but based
on Vignola's design.
The same problem arises as always
with this type of church:
how to combine a classical two-
tiered façade with the tall nave
and lower aisles behind it.
The tiers are linked with Alberti's
device of the scrolls at
Sta Maria Novella, but here they
are more clumsy. Decoration has
begun to smother form.

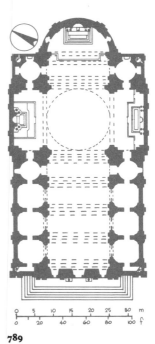

789

788

790

791

**791 Sta Susanna, Rome.
1596-1603.
Carlo Maderna**
This makes full use of the plastic
innovations of the Gesù.
The verticals are emphasised.
The heavy roof line used
by Renaissance architects has gone,
and the building ends in a
balustrade on top of the pediment.

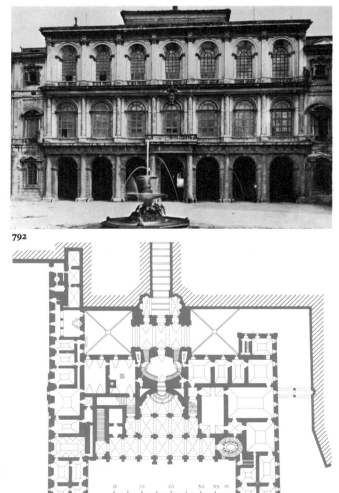

792

793 794

**792, 793 Palazzo Barberini.
Begun 1628**
Entrance and plan.
A break-away from the block-like
palazzo. The plan has opened up.
Two wings jut forward each side
of the front, and the centre
is opened in wide loggias.
There is a Palladian elegance
which hitherto had only appeared
in country villa architecture.
The entrance front
is by Gianlorenzo Bernini, and the
plan by Carlo Maderna.

**794 SS. Vincenzo e Anastasio,
Rome. 1646-50.
Martino Longhi the Younger**
The Baroque church façade
tended increasingly to become a
piece of theatre.
The architect has exercised his
imagination in terms of
free-standing pillars and sculptural
effects, like the overlapping
pediments.

795 Sta Maria in Campitelli, Rome. Façade. 1636-37. Carlo Rainaldi
Stepped violently forwards and back, this façade has an even more sculptural quality. The recesses are continued through the broad pediment, breaking the skyline, and conveying again the impression of the façade growing upwards into space.

795

796, 797 Sant'Andrea al Quirinale, Rome. 1658-70. Gianlorenzo Bernini
Façade and plan.
The concave half-oval screen-wall leading up to the portico gives a scenic effect, reminiscent of Bernini's far larger colonnade at St Peter's.
It counterpoints the convex oval of the building.
The Baroque made great use of pilasters rather than columns. Here they help to lead the eye upwards inside to dome and lantern.

796

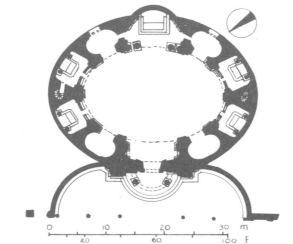

797

cisive what would have been a strong concluding line.

Churches such as these, however, represent only one development within the rich field of Roman Baroque. Other architects, often starting from the time-honoured concept of the central plan, gave entirely original forms to their churches, and to their internal spaces an expressive power that has seldom been matched. The springtime of the Baroque, marked by the joyousness and virility of Sta Susanna, is followed by the rich summer, the High Baroque period, lasting roughly from 1625 to 1675, and dominated by three great architects: Bernini, Pietro da Cortona and Borromini. Bernini (1598-1680) was the son of a Florentine sculptor working in Naples; he achieved international fame as sculptor and architect and was also an accomplished painter. Cortona (1596-1669) came to Rome from Florence in 1612 or 1613; he achieved equal fame as architect and as painter. Borromini (1599-1667) arrived in Rome from Lake Lugano about 1614 to work under his uncle Maderna, primarily as a carver of decorative detail but more and more as draughtsman; as such, and occasionally as designer, he was employed by Bernini until he began his independent work in 1634. The coinciding, in time and place, of these three men is part of the reason for Rome's architectural splendour and influence in this period. To this we must add the enthusiasm and lavish expenditure of a succession of popes (at a time when the papal authority in Europe was fast declining), and the mounting wave of religious activity and enthusiasm, producing new saints to whom new churches were dedicated and new religious imagery and modes of expression.

800

The finest churches of the High Baroque are comparatively small buildings. Bernini's Sant'Andrea al Quirinale (1658-70) is planned on an oval lying across the door altar axis. A concave half-oval screen-wall outside the church leads to a majestic portico and plays counterpoint to the convex oval form of the church itself. Inside, the strong cross-axis of the oval is counteracted by blocking it with pilasters at either end, part of a series of pilasters carrying a broad entablature which leads the eye to the chancel where St Andrew suffers martyrdom in the painting over the altar and, in sculptural form, floats heavenward in the pediment of the chancel screen; in the dome and lantern, sculptured *putti* and cherubs await him. The architectural elements are severely classical. In the lower part of the church dark marble glows warmly, but in the dome, the heavenly sphere, all is white and gold. Bernini modelled his church of Sta Maria dell'Assunzione in Ariccia near Rome (1662-64) on the Roman Pantheon. Hence the severity of the exterior (particularly the use, on the body of the church, of vertical and horizontal strips suggesting pilasters and entablature reduced to diagrammatic terms), and the bold juxtaposition of geometrical volumes. In another church, San Tomaso di Villanova at Castelgandolfo, also near Rome (1658-61), Bernini used the Greek cross plan first used in 1485, but gave it much taller proportions.

796, 7

Cortona rebuilt the church and crypt of SS. Martina e Luca (1635-50), built the façade and piazza of Sta Maria della Pace (1656-57) and also designed the façade of Sta Maria in Via Lata (built 1658-62). Each work is quite different from the others: the first owes much to Cortona's

798
799

XXXIX *Longhena: Sta Maria della Salute, Venice*

origin in Florentine Mannerism; the second approaches more closely to the usual idea of the Baroque in its ingenious use of space; and the third is surprisingly calm and classical. Inside and out, SS. Martina e Luca has a tenseness in its large forms and its detail that makes it appear reactionary, coming thirty years after Sta Susanna. The same tension is noticeable in the façade of Sta Maria della Pace, but here it is part of a sweeping reorganisation of the environment and a bold disposition of several curving planes that marks this building as one of the climaxes of the High Baroque. The façade of Sta Maria in Via Lata is much more restrained in spite of some idiosyncratic details. Here, as also in Sta Maria dell'Assunzione and other buildings, we see a tendency towards extreme or comparatively extreme forms of classicism which seem to fall outside the usual notion of the Baroque. But the student of Baroque culture, and of Baroque painting particularly, is familiar with this apparent duality: the great classical tradition runs through the Baroque, and the study of the remains and writings of antiquity was considered as essential as it had ever been.

This applies even to the churches of Borromini, although in many ways the buildings of this strange man depart radically from the traditions of humanist architecture and therefore were denounced as bizarre and extravagant by contemporaries in Rome and by later generations elsewhere, until the name of Borromini stood for all that was against good judgment and taste. The little church of San Carlo alle Quattro Fontane ('San Carlino', 1638-41, façade 1665-67) was his first commission, and he lavished great care on it. It is often said that this church is so small that it would fit inside one of the piers of St Peter's; what is perhaps more significant is the way its intricate plan and internal elevation seem to spring from Michelangelo's St Peter's. The plan of the interior is so complicated that it is not easy to tell where the main divisions come, and the elevation echoes Michelangelo's giant order and massive entablature. Over it hovers an elliptical dome, coffered with unusual, deeply cut forms that look like an ingenious invention of the architect's but are borrowed from a Roman ruin. The church of Sant'Ivo della Sapienza (1642-50) is in some ways similar. Borromini had to insert it into an existing sixteenth-century courtyard; this gave him the lower part of the exterior, deceptively calm. Above this there thrusts forward a six-lobed drum which gives way to a stepped, conical roof leading up to a tall lantern with six concave sides and coupled columns (similar to the temple of Jupiter at Baalbek), crowned by a diminishing spiral that fades out in an ironwork cusp. The plan of Sant'Ivo, like that of San Carlino, is based on interlocking isosceles triangles. The complex shape that results is underlined by the severe sequence of giant pilasters carrying a deep entablature. The same shape is taken up by the dome and gradually transformed to the smooth ring which forms the base of the lantern. The church of Sta Agnese is only partially by Borromini, who worked on it between 1653 and 1657: he created the wide, concave façade, the tall drum and dome and the west towers, but these were slightly altered. The façade of San Carlino was built long after the church itself and is Borromini's last work. The three bays, concave, convex, concave, of the lower storey are turned into three concave bays in

798

799

1-803

4, 806

805

798

799

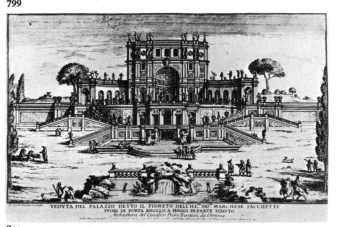

800

798 Sta Maria della Pace, Rome. Façade. 1656-57. Pietro da Cortona
Façade and piazza were designed together to give one scenic effect of contrasting curves in space. The setting has been made to show the façade to its best advantage.

799 Sta Maria in Via Lata, Rome. Façade, 1658-63. Cortona
More restrained in design. The details show an extreme form of classicism. A self-conscious study of antiquity ran parallel with the use of freer form in building.

800 Villa del Pigneto, Rome. c. 1630. Cortona
Little survives of this interesting building by Cortona. The contrast between the severely designed entrance front and the ornate garden is striking. The imposing silhouette, staircases in tiers, and the way in which the whole composition is held together with curves which advance and retreat, had great influence on subsequent architects.

801-803 San Carlo alle Quattro Fontane, Rome. 1638-41. Façade. 1665-67.
Francesco Borromini
Exterior, plan and cupola.
Instead of being based on the Renaissance circle, this plan is based on the oval and is crowned with an elliptical dome.
There is a flowing sculptural quality in the whole construction, which was the greatest contribution of the Baroque architects.
The inside area is so small it has been said that it can fit into one of the piers of St Peter's.
The façade in two tiers is rich in sculptural ornament, but it is subordinated to the passion and movement of the whole.
The ideal Renaissance church was light, with its interior harmonies plainly exposed to view.
The small Baroque San Carlo, on the other hand, is particularly dark. Light comes from a small source at the apex, the lantern illuminating the complicated sculptural decoration of the dome and leaving the rest in mystery.
The effect is dramatic and aimed at the onlooker deliberately.

801

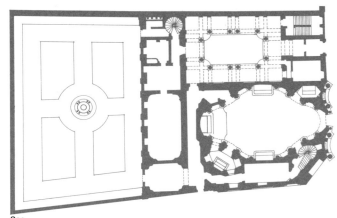

802

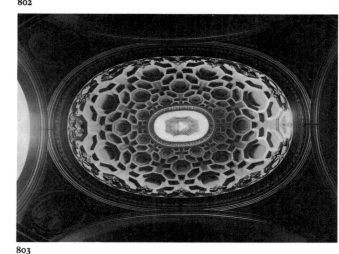

803

the upper storey. The dividing entablature forms a strong horizontal line in an otherwise dominantly vertical organisation that becomes freer and looser as it moves upwards.

Only a few of the other great works of the High Baroque can be mentioned. In St Peter's, Bernini erected the Baldacchino over the high altar (bronze, 1624-33), a semi-sculptural, semi-architectural commission that marks the beginning of his architectural career; thirty years later (1656-66) he created the Cathedra in the west apse of the church, a fusion of architecture and sculpture in many materials designed to make real to us the divine institution of the papacy. Bernini's transformation of the Cornaro Chapel in Sta Maria della Vittoria (1645-52) is a similar act of presentation and persuasion by means of paint, stucco, marble, space and light. The ecstasy of Sta Teresa, realistically 808 enacted above the altar, is observed by members of the Cornaro family on the side walls; above them, the vault of the chapel penetrates into heaven. The oval and trapezoidal piazza Bernini formed outside St Peter's out of sobre 717 architectural elements (designed 1656-57) brings to Baroque Rome the spirit of ancient Greece, triumphing over great difficulties of site and programme. His Scala Regia (1663-66), a staircase constructed in a very constricted space, receives drama and magnificence from the use of exaggerated perspective lines and controlled light. Bernini, Cortona and Borromini also produced important domestic and institutional buildings.

The later years of the seventeenth century show a decline in artistic activity in Rome; fewer great commissions were available to men of unexceptional talent. Carlo Fontana (1634-1714), trained by Bernini, is the dominant architect. Like his master he inclined to the more classical side of the Baroque and handled this kind of architecture with aplomb but little originality. His project for the completion of the piazza of St Peter's (1694) is perhaps his most impressive work. By adding a trapezoidal forecourt, he intended to present Bernini's piazza and the church as an enormous stage-set from which the spectator is separated by the projecting ends of Bernini's colonnade. A similar scenographic trend is noticeable in other works of this period and in the eighteenth century; by contrast, the High Baroque architect sought to place the spectator within the work of art, but Bernini's Cornaro Chapel, which can be fully appreciated only from the nave, i.e., from outside the chapel, heralded this trend.

Outside Rome the High Baroque period showed a variety of provincial pursuits usually of small interest. Most architects looked to Rome, without necessarily imitating the best or the most revolutionary. There were two outstanding exceptions: Longhena and Guarini. Baldassare Longhena is remembered for one brilliant building, the church of Sta Maria della Salute in Venice (built 1631-85). Take away p. 269 the splendid scrolls from its picturesque outline and you 811 are left with a remarkably austere building full of reminiscences of Palladio. The plan of the main body of the church, perhaps derived from the Byzantine church of San Vitale in Ravenna, is unique in the Renaissance. Longhena uses the form of the octagon with ambulatory and chapels to offer a set of lucid views to anyone standing at the centre of the building, and a vista of arches from the en-

804

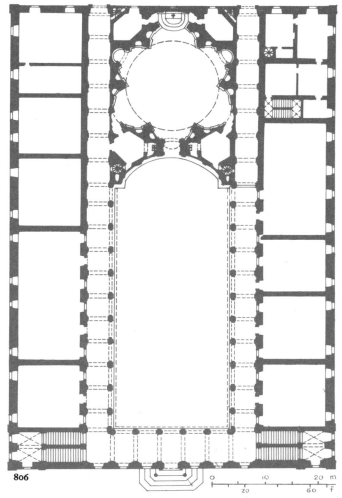

806

807

805

808

804, 806 Sant'Ivo della Sapienza. 1642-50. Borromini
Courtyard and plan.
Built inside an existing court whose loggia has been fused with the façade.
In plan it is a six-pointed star. At the six inner points pilasters rise to the cornice and carry the eye upwards, through the lines of the segmented dome, to the cupola and infinity. The lantern is treated like a piece of sculpture, spiral on the outside, twisting up into the sky. The whole building treats movement in space in an inspired architectonic way.

805 Sta Agnese, Rome. Façade. 1653-57. Borromini
The design was begun in 1652 by Carlo Rainaldi.
In effect it seems a broad oval running parallel with the façade, but it is really an octagon inside a square extended by transeptal chapels. Borromini's façade is concave with two north Italian towers.

807 Sta Maria dell'Assunzione, Ariccia, near Rome. 1662-64. Bernini
Modelled directly on the Roman Pantheon.
A far more direct imitation of antique building than anything before the days of Neo-classicism.
Pilasters and entablature are suggested in terms of decoration on the body of the church.

808 Bernini, 'Sta Teresa in Ecstasy'. 1645-52
One of the finest expressions of the High Baroque in sculpture. It was done by Bernini for the Cornaro chapel of the Sta Maria della Vittoria in Rome. Bernini placed the work so that it could only be seen from the nave, exactly on the central axis of the chapel. Golden light from a glazed opening above bathes the group and makes it seem to hover in the surrounding gloom.

809 Piazza del Popolo, Rome (from Piranesi). c. 1660
This entrance to the city is an early example of the 'rond-point', used extensively in France. The Porta del Popolo leads into the 'place' from which radiate three main streets. Their start is marked by Carlo Rainaldi's twin churches.

809

810 Palazzo Pesaro, Venice. Begun 1679. Baldassare Longhena
Rustication and small rectangular windows of the lower floors set off the upper part. This is so open that it resembles two superimposed loggias. The sharply diminishing size of the columns and the hovering putti deepen the recesses and give a theatrical effect.

810

811 Sta Maria della Salute, Venice. 1631–85. Longhena
One of the few churches not on the Gesù pattern of the High Renaissance. It is octagonal, and the ambulatory and chapels offer a set of lucid views from the centre.

811

812 Palazzo Carignano, Turin. Begun 1679. Guarino Guarini
Guarini here applies the three-dimensional form pioneered by Borromini (see 801) to a palace. Between the rectangular end-units of the building the façade swings backwards and forwards in a double S curve that is echoed by the pediment over the centre. The form and detail of this building influenced early eighteenth-century palace design in Austria.

812

trance door to the high altar. Here again is the scenographic interest. Guarino Guarini, Theatine monk, lecturer in philosophy and mathematics, dramatist, as well as architect, belongs to a younger generation than Longhena, and the great men of the Roman High Baroque (1624–83). He is, in fact, the disciple of Borromini, and took his invention further. This makes his buildings peculiarly difficult to describe briefly. Roughly speaking, his planning was Borrominesque, while his vaulting was highly personal; the effect of his interiors depends on the interaction of the two. The

814   plan of San Lorenzo, Turin (begun 1668) could be described as a square with incursions, an octagon with excursions, or a curvilinear Greek cross, but none of these formulations hints at the spatial ambiguities set, nor at the

815   strange rib-vaulting which is often compared with Moorish vaulting in Spain but is used by Guarini, quite differently, to create mysterious effects of light and space. Guarini worked mainly in Turin, but made designs for churches in Lisbon, Paris and Prague; particularly in Roman Catholic central Europe his influence was decisive. The publication of Guarini's papers, *Architettura civile* (1737; edited by Vittone), confirmed this influence.

FRANCE IN THE SEVENTEENTH CENTURY

After the turmoil of the civil wars came a period of reconstruction and rationalisation, mirrored in the architecture of the first decade of the century. While a few private buildings continued the Mannerist tendencies of the preceding decades, the scene is dominated by practical schemes for the improvement of Paris and by unpretentious buildings whose simple harmonies clear the ground for the refined classicism of the later seventeenth century. The Pont Neuf was completed, the Rue Dauphine planned, the

817   Place Dauphine and the Place des Vosges (originally Place Royale) were built. These 'squares' are enclosed residential units, but the Place de France (planned 1610; not executed) was intended to provide an imposing entrance to the city: a city gate would have led into a semi-circular space and to eight radiating streets named after the provinces of France, symbolising the hoped-for unity of the country.

The first great building of the century is the Palais du

816   Luxembourg in Paris, designed by Salomon de Brosse (begun 1615). De Brosse based himself in his planning on the château of Verneuil and on de l'Orme's intentions for the Tuileries palace, while his elevations are governed in character by his use of rustication derived from Ammanati's courtyard of the Palazzo Pitti in Florence (his patron's, Marie de Médicis's, home). The result is a building of great mass and solidity. De Brosse's debt to de l'Orme is illus-

818   trated also by his façade for the church of St Gervais (1616): in order to cover the tall late Gothic nave, he adapted the Anet frontispiece and thus established an influential type of church front. When de Brosse died in 1626, his post of *premier architecte* to the king went to Jacques Lemercier, most of whose effort was spent, however, in service of the king's chief minister, Cardinal Richelieu. For him Lemercier designed and built the château of Richelieu, a large formal lay-out between Charleval and Versailles, the little town of Richelieu on a chequerboard plan, and the church

22, 823   of the Sorbonne in Paris. With this church (begun 1635),

813

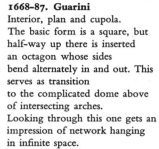

813–815 San Lorenzo, Turin. 1668–87. Guarini
Interior, plan and cupola.
The basic form is a square, but half-way up there is inserted an octagon whose sides bend alternately in and out. This serves as transition to the complicated dome above of intersecting arches.
Looking through this one gets an impression of network hanging in infinite space.
The whole thing has been achieved architecturally, not, as later, with trompe-l'oeil painting.

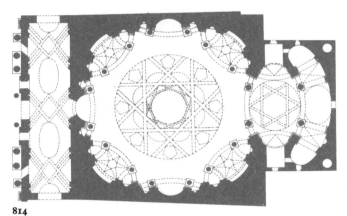

814

815

**816 Palais du Luxembourg,
Begun 1615.
Salomon de Brosse**
The planning was based on the
château of Verneuil and the
elevation echoes in its rustication
the courtyard of the Pitti palace.
The result is a building
of great mass and solidity.

**817 Houses, Place des Vosges,
Paris. 1605-12**
Housing development in Paris,
as in Amsterdam, began
to be planned. As well as the large
hôtels, the equivalent of the
Italian palazzos,
smaller houses began to be built in
squares, like the Place des
Vosges, which were enclosed
residential units.

**818 St Gervais, Paris.
Façade. 1616.
Salomon de Brosse**
This façade had to correspond
to the tall Gothic interior.
De Brosse adapted for this purpose
the French Renaissance frontispiece
as used by de l'Orme at Anet
and Lescot on the Louvre (765)
and thus established a new kind
of church front that was much
imitated in France and elsewhere.

**819 Val-de-Grâce, Paris.
Begun 1645.
François Mansart and
Jacques Lemercier**
A longitudinal church with a
centrally planned crossing.
Mansart was responsible for
the planning of the church
and its execution
up to the first cornice;
Lemercier completed the building,
the dome particularly
revealing his style
(see the dome of the Church
of the Sorbonne, 822).

**820 Church of the Invalides,
Paris, 1680-91.
Jules Hardouin Mansart**
There is a fluidity here which the
earlier Baroque of the Sorbonne
lacks, particularly apparent
in the handling of the base of the
cupola. The west front projects
in bays towards the centre,
and the columns
are very freely arranged.

**821 Hôtel Lambert, Paris. 1640.
Louis le Vau**
Increasing prosperity in France
led to the building of magnificent
town houses.
The general pattern consisted of
living quarters shielded from
the street by a forecourt
with garden, and sometimes other
courts beyond.

816

817

818

819

820

821

a great age of classical Baroque church-design opens in France. It owes much to the contemporary early Baroque of Rome and combines with this an emphatic verticality that seems reactionary, but it heralds later Baroque developments, and a remarkably cool classical interior.

The middle of the seventeenth century in France is marked by the flowering of a culture at once classical and national, that echoes the classical climax of a hundred years earlier but far exceeds it in breadth, depth and refinement. It is the age of Descartes, Corneille, Poussin and Claude, and in architecture, pre-eminently, of François Mansart (1598-1666). In his mature works Mansart succeeded in creating a style that is generally classical but embodies idiosyncratic and Baroque elements. The Hôtel de la Vrillière, Paris (1635), shows Mansart imposing clarity and dignity on a building type still troubled by planning difficulties and by Mannerist elaboration of surface. He contributed to the château of Blois a wing (1635-38) that retains the massive monumentality of a de Brosse building but replaces his weighty detailing with a surface of unprecedented finesse; in its planning he solved brilliantly problems arising from different ground levels and different centre axes on the court and garden side. The château of Maisons (begun 1642), completely his and apparently designed and redesigned with great freedom, represents Mansart's genius at its height. Two short returns at either end of the *corps de logis* are the only remnants of the traditional wings, but two modest buildings stood some distance from the house flanking the approach to it. The centre of the entrance front is marked by a frontispiece, a sophisticated descendant of that of Anet; other elements, such as the high, divided roofs, help to break the building into pavilion-like units, held together by the unifying elevational treatment. The oval rooms in the one-storey end bays of the short returns suggest kinship with the Baroque, as does the open-centred, coved ceiling over the staircase, through which one looks into a dome lit from hidden windows. The entrance hall and staircase are white throughout: columns, mouldings and occasional pieces of carefully placed sculpture are given full and individual value by the light in which they exist. In ecclesiastical architecture, too, Mansart made important contributions. The centrally planned church of Ste Marie de la Visitation, Paris (begun 1632), is a development of the chapel in Anet. In the little chapel at Fresnes (c. 1645) he uses a central plan with three apses forming chancel and transepts, and the same arrangement, derived from Palladio, is used for the eastern portion of the large longitudinal church of Val-de-Grâce in Paris (begun 1645). The upper portions of this church, above the first cornice, are not Mansart's, but his is the splendid plan, the projecting portico, the fine detailing of nave and aisles. Val-de-Grâce joins the church of the Sorbonne and the later church of the Invalides to form the great trio of Parisian seventeenth-century churches which made Paris second to Rome as a centre for monumental, modern church design.

Louis le Vau (1612-70) lacked Mansart's inventive genius and his fine handling of detail, but through his more harmonious nature and greater adaptability he was acceptable to the social world of his time. The Hôtel Lambert (1640) and the Collège des Quatre Nations, now the Institut

825

824

819

821
826

822

823

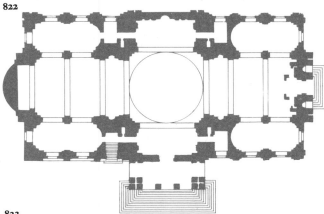

824

825

822, 823 **Church of the Sorbonne, Paris. Begun 1635. Jacques Lemercier**
Exterior and plan.
Restrained compared with the contemporary Roman churches, there is considerable freedom in the handling of the Greek cross with its two elongated arms. This church foreshadowed a great age of Baroque church building in France.
Together with the Val-de-Grâce and the Invalides, it made Paris second to Rome as leader in modern church design.

824 **Château of Maisons. Begun 1642. François Mansart**
Mansart entirely remodelled an older E-shaped house.
The entrance-front has a magnificent centrepiece, from which the wings swing out in two main and classically demarked storeys.

825 **Hôtel de la Vrillière, Paris. 1635. François Mansart**
Designed for Louis Phelypeaux de la Vrillière, this town house was to serve as the model for many others. It has a clarity and simplicity which has rarely been surpassed.

826 Collège des Quatre Nations, Paris. Begun 1661.
Le Vau
An institutional building conceived in the classical manner.
Each portion (e.g. chapel and library) is concealed
in the symmetry of the overall design.
The designer's chief concern is the façade and the scenic effect of the cour d'honneur. The building is now the Institut.

826

827 Château of Vaux-le-Vicomte. Begun 1657.
Le Vau
Here the open style of château was brought for the first time
to its logical conclusion.
The steep roof contrasts strangely with the classical cupola.
Classical portico and pediment, the giant Ionic pilasters,
and symmetrically placed windows compose a façade whose appearance has little structural relevance to the rooms behind it.
Here is embodied an experiment which was later developed
at Versailles.

827

828 Versailles
An enormous undertaking which took nearly a hundred years to build and which still remains in the imagination
the pattern for a supreme palace of an absolute monarch.
Originally a hunting lodge, it was enlarged by Louis le Vau, and later by Jules Hardouin Mansart.
The gardens were begun in 1667 by André Le Nôtre.
The roof line is severely horizontal instead of steeply pitched.
The repetition on this scale of windows and classical orders, in perfect symmetry,
is monotonous. As in Vaux-le-Vicomte the gardens and park are an integral part of the design
and are planned along a central axis springing from the centre
of the building.

828

827 (begun 1661), show his Baroque concern with the expressive shaping of space, and in the château of Vaux-le-Vicomte (begun 1657) he created one of the most magnificent monuments of this rich age in French culture. A wing-less sculptural mass, it has splendid interiors decorated by the foremost artists of the age and stands in a park designed by Le Nôtre to continue the axis of the house. All this manifested an ideal of courtly splendour which was soon to be realised on an even greater scale at Versailles.

831 Something of France's growing self-confidence in cultural matters can be gauged from the story of the completion of the Louvre. In 1665 Louis XIV's chief minister Colbert invited the renowned Bernini to make designs for the royal palace. Bernini came to Paris and made his designs; the king laid the foundation stone of the new buildings; Bernini departed. Almost at once work stopped. In 1667 a committee consisting of Le Vau, the *premier architecte*, Le Brun, the *premier peintre*, and Claude Perrault, physician and amateur architect, produced a new design which was in fact carried out, which is radically different from Bernini's or any Italian Baroque building, and which established a new type of semi-traditional, semi-Baroque but entirely French, secular architecture. The long east façade is broken by central and terminal projections, but its low roof is hidden by a balustrade (*à l'italienne*), and the horizontal division of the façade into a massive base and an upper portion recessed behind coupled columns lend to the whole a horizontality which reappears at Versailles.

828-830 There Le Vau encased and extended an early seventeenth-century hunting-lodge (from 1669) and later Jules Hardouin Mansart (1646-1708) added generously to Le Vau's already large building. With all the skill lavished on its interior, and the cyclopean gestures made over the unpromising terrain by Le Nôtre, with the several splendid buildings erected in the park, not to mention grottoes and fountains, Versailles became a paradigm of regal magnificence, which rulers all over Europe were tempted to emulate.

820 Jules Hardouin Mansart was much more than the enlarger of Versailles; he was in fact a far more impressive architect than he is often given credit for, even if he did not quite prove his artistic right to the use of his great-uncle's name. His Invalides church (1680-91) is a handsomely detailed and very dramatic example of French Baroque, and his Place Vendôme (1698) is one of the masterpieces of Baroque town architecture. Baroque in its conception of a square as setting for the statue of a king, it is classical in the design of the house façades, and adventurously practical in the arrangement that the uniform façades were built by the city authorities who could then sell the plots behind the façades to individuals to build on as they wished. To make possible his great activity, J. H. Mansart organised a large architectural office, out of which emerged several of the leading architects of the next generation.

SPAIN IN THE SEVENTEENTH CENTURY

Spain, in the century of Ribera, Zurbaran, Velasquez, Cano and Murillo, of Cervantes, Tirso de Molina and Calderón, produced surprisingly little of architectural interest. Politically she is in decline, and as the century progresses this decline turns into a collapse. On all sides she is beset,

829

830

829, 830 Royal Chapel, Versailles. 1699-1707. Robert de Cotte and Jules Hardouin Mansart Exterior and interior. Even this royal chapel is treated in the most grandiose classical manner such as was used for large churches. The exterior decoration is far more exuberant than Mansart's earlier work at Versailles.

831

831 The Louvre. East facade, 1667-70 The design of this wing of the Louvre represents a triumph of French architects over Bernini, who had been brought to France especially to make designs for this part of the Louvre; as finally built, this structure represents the total assimilation within French traditions of the classical idiom.

832, 833 Queen's House, Greenwich. 1616-35.
Inigo Jones
Exterior and first floor plan.
Inigo Jones based his classicism
on Palladio and the north Italian
architects. His lack of ornament
is in contrast with the Baroque.
This has a large central gallery
or saloon, a façade of great
symmetry and simplicity with
rusticated ground storey,
flanked by unadorned wings.
The staircase shown is the
garden entrance – the main
entrance being inside the building
which was originally built
astride the old London-Dover
road. This building is now
the National Maritime Museum.

832

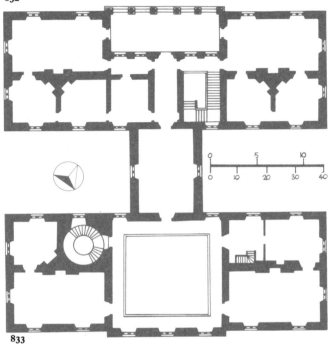

833

834 Banqueting House, Whitehall. 1619-22.
Inigo Jones
Such a building as this was
revolutionary in England.
Classicism suddenly replaced the
conglomeration of Tudor
and medieval styles which up till
then had shown classical
influences only in their decoration.

834

835 Houses on Prinzengracht, Amsterdam
The seventeenth century saw
an enormous planned development
of Amsterdam.
Built along canals in a continuous
façade, the brick houses
are tall and thin because of lack
of room.
The house façades are harmonious
but different, unlike
the uniformity of Parisian
and English 'squares'.

835

and by 1701 she is the property of the Bourbons. It would
almost be sufficient to say that architecturally Spain is a
distant province of Italy. After Herrera's classicism comes
a phase of looser Mannerism which continues through most
of the century but is occasionally injected with invigorating
shots of Baroque spirit. An unusually magnificent illustration of this is the chapel of San Isidro added to the church
of San Andrés in Madrid (1642-69, by Pedro de la Torre).
In the later part of the century links with Rome are strengthened by the increasing employment of Italians on outstanding commissions and by the closer study by Spaniards
of contemporary work in Italy. Carlo Fontana himself designed the great Jesuit Collegium Regium at Loyola (1681):
a large plain rectangular building interrupted and almost
dominated by a circular church (like Sta Maria della Salute
in Venice, but much duller). What saves this period of
Spanish architecture from utter provincialism are the occasional signs that native traditions are beginning to re-assert
themselves against stylistic domination. When Francisco
Herrera the Younger designed the church of Nuestra Se-
ñora del Pilar in Saragossa (1680) he sought to rival the
great churches of the late Middle Ages and the early Renaissance in size and splendour and planned it on essentially
traditional lines; even in its much altered execution, the
church, with its *azulejo*-covered domes, is in many ways
a non-Renaissance building. In the following century this
affirmation of Spanish taste coalesces with Rococo and other
influences to present a brief flowering of inventive design.

PALLADIANISM IN NORTHERN EUROPE

Palladian elements have been noted in the work of François Mansart and can be found elsewhere, but in northern
Europe, particularly where Protestantism produced some
aversion from Roman Baroque splendour, Palladio's example provided an alternative tradition of adaptable classicism,
acceptable to countries where hitherto the understanding
of classical design had been partial at best.

In England, Palladianism was imposed on a public accus-
tomed to a *mélange* of Tudor and northern Renaissance
elements by one man, Inigo Jones (1573-1652). It is true
that the Jacobean age brought with it a wave of humanism
associated with the names of Ben Jonson, Francis Bacon
and George Chapman, but there is nothing in English architecture to make a transition from the mixed style of
Hatfield House (1607-11) to the Mediterranean classicism
of Jones's Queen's House at Greenwich (1616-35) or his
Banqueting House (1619-22). These buildings suggest not
merely a real understanding of Palladio's work, which
Jones had studied in Italy, they also show that Jones's grasp
of classicism was sufficient to allow him to range beyond
Palladio to the High Renaissance, to enable him to distinguish between classical and Mannerist elements in Italian
design, and to permit him to handle them creatively.

778
832, 8
834, 8

The Palladian style came to the Netherlands in the 1630s,
possibly under English influence. There too it represented
a sharp departure from current style: it emerged in The
Hague as a comparatively aristocratic fashion, whereas architectural activity had until then been dominated by Amsterdam and by Hendrik de Keyser. De Keyser (1565-1621)
had transformed the medieval Dutch house into a Renais-

sance building by applying pilasters and strapwork. He had also built the first important Protestant churches by adapting medieval plans and using Renaissance detail: the Zuiderkerk and Westerkerk in Amsterdam (1603 and 1620 respectively). His third church, the Noorderkerk (1620), is planned on the Greek cross basis and is the first of a long series of Protestant centrally planned churches. The Netherlands had also experienced a short period of French-inspired architecture connected with Prince Frederick Henry of Orange and his court: Honselaarsdijk Castle (begun 1621) is clearly inspired by de Brosse.

The new classicism is announced by two town houses in The Hague, both of them begun in 1633: Constantin Huygens's house, designed by Huygens with the architect Pieter Post (1608-69), and the nearby Mauritshuis designed by Pieter Post and the gentleman-architect Jacob van Campen (1595-1657). Neither is simply imitated from Palladio: Huygens's house inclines to contemporary French planning, while the Mauritshuis suggests Palladio seen through the eyes of Inigo Jones, but both mark the arrival of self-assured classicism. Others soon followed, such as the Sebastiansdoelen in The Hague (1636) and the Leiden Cloth Hall (both by Arent van 's Gravesande). In 1648 van Campen began the great Amsterdam town hall, a monument to Dutch civic pride and thus the Netherlands' equivalent to the royal palaces of other countries: the nearest thing the Dutch produced to a real palace is the modest Huis ten Bosch, designed by Post (begun 1645)

The building of the great Augsburg town hall (1615-18) can be taken to mark a Palladian moment in Germany. Designed by Elias Holl, it makes an extreme contrast with the almost purely medieval buildings that stood around it, but its stylistic debt suggests northern Italy generally rather than Palladio in particular. Holl himself designed one or two other classical buildings, but no Palladian movement followed, and the Thirty Years War (1618-48) left the German states little scope for ambitious architecture for most of the century.

ENGLISH ARCHITECTURE
FROM THE RESTORATION TO GEORGE I

Although the cultural climate of England in the second half of the century is very different from that of the first half, the classicism of Inigo Jones continues as the basis of design. The long exile of the English court in the Netherlands and in France encouraged wide eclecticism, and the Roman High Baroque influenced England directly and through French adaptations. An extreme example of debt to the Netherlands is seen in Hugh May's Eltham Lodge, Kent (1663), but more typical is the interweaving of these influences as often seen in the work of Sir Christopher Wren (1632-1723). Wren brought to architecture the learning and practical sense of a great scientist. As a result of the Great Fire of London (1666), he found himself engaged on replanning the whole City, designing fifty-one churches as well as rebuilding the cathedral of St Paul, apart from many other commissions from kings, universities, etc. His Greek cross project for St Paul's (1673) would have given England a more exciting and more Baroque building than the clergy could accept, so Wren produced a deceptively

836

837

838

836 Mauritshuis,
The Hague. Begun 1633.
Pieter Post
and Jacob van Campen
This building suggests Palladio seen through the eyes of Inigo Jones because of its restraint and elegance.

837 Amsterdam town hall
(now the Royal Palace).
1648-65.
Jacob van Campen
Main entrance hall.
The classical style which is the chief characteristic of the plan and façade of the palace (see 774) is perpetuated in the interior.

838 New Church, The Hague.
1649-56.
Van Bassen and Noorwits
This attenuated Baroque church type is more common in Belgium than in the Netherlands.
The plan is composed of two overlapping squares with six apsidal bays.

839-841 St Paul's Cathedral, London. 1675-1710.
Sir Christopher Wren
Exteriors and interior.
Originally Wren designed
St Paul's in the form
of a Greek cross.
He was forced to adapt this to
the traditional longitudinal shape.
The aisle is proportionately small
to the original central shape
crowned by the dome.
The building is serenely classical.

839

840

841

842 Royal Exchange, London. 1671 (burnt 1838).
Edward Jerman
In spite of the classical
buildings of Jones and Wren,
classicism apart from court,
church and university architecture,
was still a strange
idiom, handled without real
understanding of its syntax
or principles.

842

traditional design (1675) which he was allowed to alter in execution. The result, the first Protestant cathedral, is a conglomeration of Renaissance styles, great in many of its parts although not satisfactory in its totality, and a remarkable victory over conservatism.

Wren dominated both church and court architecture. The needs of lesser patrons were met by, on the whole, less learned architects, such as Edward Jerman, whose Royal Exchange in London (1671) gives some idea of the limited hold that classical design still had outside court, church and university circles.   842

The end of the century saw the creation of a new style that can be called Baroque but differs considerably from the Baroque of Italy and France and has some of the anti-authoritarian characteristics of Mannerism. Individual expression, the leaning on picturesque effects and extra-architectural associations, warrant such descriptive names as 'Romantic Baroque' or even 'proto-Romanticism'. The most obvious characteristic of the style is its emphasis on physical mass and weight. This was hinted at in Wren's Cambridge library; it appears clearly in the designs he and his assistants made for a new Whitehall Palace (about 1699). Something of the kind already appears in William Talman's additions to Chatsworth, Derbyshire (1687-96). Fully   844
exploited, it marks the work of Nicholas Hawksmoor, who designed a group of London churches between 1712 and 1723, and Sir John Vanbrugh.

Vanbrugh (1664-1726) came to architecture the amateur's way. In 1699 he built a very original, keep-like little house for himself and was commissioned by a friend to build a large country house, Castle Howard in Yorkshire. In 1705 he was commissioned to design another large country house, Blenheim, near Oxford. In both cases he had the help of the experienced Hawksmoor, to whom some of the credit for these buildings must go. Blenheim is the   846
masterpiece of the style: a palace and a castle, and a vast monument to the Duke of Marlborough's victory over the French in Bavaria. At Greenwich, Vanbrugh built for him-   847
self a little brick castle, turrets and all, with an asymmetrically placed entrance and otherwise an Elizabethan plan. A similar plan is used for Seaton Delaval, Northumberland (1720), Vanbrugh's finest independent work, full of his sense of drama and the superhuman.

NETHERLANDS: LATER SEVENTEENTH CENTURY

Some later seventeenth-century buildings suggest that England's massive Baroque style may have been learnt from the Netherlands, at least in part. The Trippenhuis in Am-   852
sterdam (Justus Vingboons, 1662) suggests the direction of Talman's Chatsworth. The New Lutheran church in Amsterdam (Adrian Dortsman, 1669) has something of the English architects' aggressive monumentality. The town halls of Enkhuizen (1686, S. Vennekool) and Deventer   854
(1693, J. Roman) have some of the tough detailing of Hawksmoor.

By this time, however, the Netherlands are already falling under the spell of France. Soon it is difficult to distinguish between provincial French and Dutch architecture, and the Dutch contribute little to European architecture between 1700 and the end of the nineteenth century.

843

843 Greenwich Hospital. 1662-1814. Webb and Wren
Inigo Jones's Queen's House (see 832, 833) forms the centrepiece of this great symmetrical composition (right centre). John Webb, a pupil of Jones, added the 'King Charles Block' (1662-69) by the river (lower right).
The enormous Corinthian order was echoed by Wren in his complete plan which constitutes a large-scale, composite building in the classical manner. The buildings are now the Royal Naval College.

844

845

844 Chatsworth House, Derbyshire. 1687-96. William Talman
This is Talman's most important work, although he was not responsible for the whole. The plan, living groups arranged round a courtyard, is rather dull, but the Ionic façade and other enrichments are magnificent.

845 Clarendon Library, Oxford. 1714. Hawksmoor and Townesend
Townesend, a mason-architect who had a hand in most of the Oxford buildings at this time, built the University Printing House (now Clarendon Library) to Hawksmoor's design. Its most distinctive feature is the giant Doric portico.

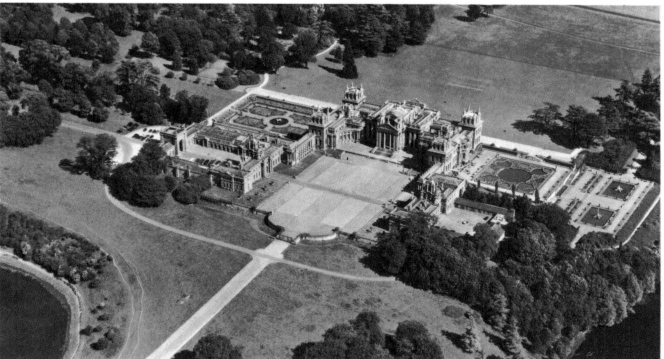

846

846 Blenheim Palace, Oxfordshire. Begun 1705. Sir John Vanbrugh
Presented by the nation to Marlborough, this was to rival the great palaces of the continent. A great cour d'honneur is flanked by two blocks, each built round a secondary court, the whole perfectly symmetrical. The curved colonnade decoration of the entrance front and its broken line are in contrast to the otherwise rectilinear form. There is a Baroque profusion of decoration, which is particularly heavy and clumsy as handled here.

847 Vanbrugh castle, Greenwich. c. 1717. Vanbrugh
Vanbrugh built this 'bastille' for himself about six years after his house at Esher.
Built of brick with pointed roofs and round towers, it has asymmetrically placed entrances and other 'medieval' features, although with an Elizabethan plan.

847

848 Augsburg town hall. 1615-18. Elias Holl
Palladian influence showed itself throughout northern Europe.
In Germany the movement was cut short by the Thirty Years War.

848

849 Heerengracht, Amsterdam
First of the three great concentric canals to be built in the seventeenth century, the others being the Keizersgracht and the Prinzengracht. The romantic combination of buildings and water, the elegance of the bridges, have made later travellers call Amsterdam the 'Venice of the North'.

849

FRANCE FROM ABOUT 1715 TO ABOUT 1760: ROCOCO AND THE CLASSICAL TRADITION

The death of Louis XIV permitted the emergence of a growing reaction against the formal magnificence of the Versailles court. The following decades see much domestic building activity in Paris and the climax of a new style, primarily one of decoration, the Rococo. In many ways the Rococo contradicts the Baroque style, out of which it was developed: it opposes lightness and fluency to the more solid and formal qualities of the Baroque. Architecturally it is marked by simplified façades, using the orders only rarely, with large windows and comfortable scale and proportions. Planning is more gracious than imposing, and great advances are made in convenience and hygiene. As a style of domestic architecture, the Rococo was widely imitated; in central Europe it was combined with Italian Baroque to create a joyous style of church architecture.

Although architects in France continued to support classical principles of design, the Rococo style did imply a weakening of the hold of these principles on their practice. Soon, however, a return to the classical tradition showed itself. The façade of St Sulpice in Paris (J. N. Servandoni, 1733) is severely classical in its lower storeys. English contemporary Palladianism may have aided the exorcism of the Rococo: certainly English influence appears in the work of the greatest French architect of the period, Ange-Jacques Gabriel (1698-1782), whose buildings give little indication that the Rococo had ever happened. The Petit Trianon, Versailles (1762), is his most perfect work: a modest building, owing its simple proportions and the external use of columns to English example, square in plan, rectilinear in its internal divisions and external forms, where the Rococo had liked to use curves. The Ecole Militaire in Paris (begun in 1751) adds a French type of dome to a Palladian porticoed block. Nevertheless, the dominant characteristic of Gabriel's work is a return to the French tradition as defined eighty or ninety years earlier. This is the quality, for example, of his Place de la Concorde (begun 1757) and its buildings, which should be compared with the contemporary, but Rococo, town-planning scheme in Nancy by Héré de Corny (begun 1752).

The 1750s and 1760s witnessed also an international debate questioning the principles and practices of Renaissance design, to which France made important contributions and which spelled the end of the Renaissance period.

BAROQUE AND ROCOCO IN CENTRAL EUROPE

Baroque architecture came to the Catholic countries of central Europe in the last decades of the seventeenth century, usually at the hands of second-rate Italian designers. In northern Germany, architectural allegiance was primarily to the Netherlands. The end of the century saw the emergence of a number of native architects, some of them outstanding by any standards, who had the good fortune to coincide with a great wave of building activity almost everywhere in this part of Europe.

The first generation of German and Austrian architects is dominated by Schlüter, Fischer von Erlach and Hildebrandt. Schlüter (c. 1674-1714) worked in Prussia, endeav-

850

852

854

851

853

855

850 Flemish Academy, Ghent. 1745.
D. 't Kint
At a time when the Low Countries were under Austrian tutelage, Flemish architecture was inclined to show characteristics of Austrian and French as well as native styles.
The Flemish Academy presents a synthesis of the various elements, yet for the period it is more Flemish than otherwise.

851 St Sulpice, Paris.
Façade, begun 1733.
J. N. Servandoni
A combination of tower and two-tiered portico.
This is an early example of the stricter classicism that succeeded the Rococo.

852 Trippenhuis, Amsterdam. 1662.
Justus Vingboons
Built for the two brothers Tripp, this is larger and more grandiose than most Dutch town houses of the time. It is similar in design to Vingboons's Stockholm Riddarhuset.

853 Ecole Militaire, Paris. 1751-53.
Ange-Jacques Gabriel
Gabriel's plan for the Ecole represents a marked development in the planning of large, complex public buildings.
The façade culminates in a huge portico surmounted by a four-sided version of the Roman dome.

854 Enkhuizen town hall. 1686.
S. Vennekool
Typical of the late seventeenth-century Dutch work, which turns more directly to the Baroque and was soon to become very close to provincial French building of the period.

855 Hôtel Soubise, Paris 1705-09. Delamair
This represents a transition between the older, grandiose hôtels of the previous century and the smaller, more intimate ones of Louis XV.
Externally the old palazzo features of pediment and portico are still there, joined here with a colonnaded formal garden-court.

856 Royal Palace, Berlin.
1698-1707
Part of south façade.
Built by Andreas Schlüter
for Frederick I of Prussia, the
Berlin Schloss is an impressive
example of Baroque classicism.
(Now destroyed.)

856

857 Schönbrunn Palace,
Vienna. Begun about 1695.
Fischer von Erlach
Fischer von Erlach had spent fifteen
years in Rome where he came
under the influence of Borromini
and Bernini.
His enormous project
for Schönbrunn seems however to
hover between the Italian
and the French.

857

858 Karlskirche, Vienna.
1716-37.
Von Erlach
Here Baroque planning is
combined with strong classicising
elements such as the
temple-front entrance and the
historiated columns flanking it.

858

859 The Upper Belvedere,
Vienna. 1721-24.
L. Hildebrandt
The ideal of a palace adjoining
a landscaped park set by Versailles
became widely sought after.
This summer residence built for
Prince Eugene of Savoy is
deliberately fantastic and Romantic.

859

ouring in his Berlin Royal Palace (1698-1707) to express
something of the rising state's power. He consciously strove
for Roman grandeur; his own villa, the Landhaus Kamecke,
near Berlin (1711-12), shows a curiously naked kind of
Borrominesque Baroque. Opportunities were greater in
Vienna, now playing the rôle of imperial capital. J. B.
Fischer von Erlach (1656-1723) had spent about fifteen years
in Rome and was particularly familiar with the High Baroque of Bernini. But his enormous project for a royal
palace at Schönbrunn (about 1695) seems intended to rival
French architecture, and in fact his architectural style hovers
between the French and the Italian, as well as demonstrates some knowledge of English architecture and considerable knowledge of the ancients'. His familiarity with
Roman Baroque appears in the four churches he designed
for Salzburg, including the large Kollegienkirche (1696).
The Batthyany-Schönborn Palace, Vienna (1700), is a subtly
shaped building, using delicate ornament and a slight projection with great effect. The suburban Palais Trautson
(1710) is more severe and suggests a tendency towards
Palladianism which may have been caused by a visit to
England. Generally, however, Fischer von Erlach's later
buildings are comparatively severe. The Karlskirche in Vienna (1716-37) is an extraordinary building, combining Baroque planning with strong classicising elements (such as
the temple-front entrance and the historiated columns flanking it) and organising these to great scenic effect. Like
Blenheim, the Karlskirche is a sculptural monument as well
as a building, full of symbolical content; it shows something of Fischer's historical scholarship, more fully represented in his *A Plan of Civil and Historical Architecture* (1721).
His last work, the Vienna Hofbibliothek (begun 1722)
shows him again at his more delicate, detailing the exterior
most elegantly in a predominantly French manner; internally he fashioned an essentially Baroque space.

Johann Lukas von Hildebrandt (1668-1745) is the more
ingratiating architect and the one most imitated by contemporaries. He had served as military engineer under
Prince Eugene in northern Italy, and it was for the prince
that he undertook to design the Lower and Upper Bel-
vederes (1714 and 1721) in the suburbs of Vienna. He was a
more painterly architect than Fischer, delighting in a
varied surface for his façades and in rich interiors. He made
important contributions to church architecture, introducing, in his church of St Lawrence at Gabel in Bohemia
(1699), Guarini's modelling of space, and, in the Benedictine abbey of Göttweig (begun 1719), setting a new
standard in magnificence for these great religious palaces.

In Bavaria there developed two distinct architectural
streams, that of the court, firmly inclined towards French
architecture, and that of the Church, inclining more towards
Italy and embodying local traditions. Court architecture
was dominated by the Flemish-born, Paris-trained François Cuvilliès (1695-1768), one of the finest Rococo designers anywhere, seen at his best in the delightful little
Amalienburg, in the grounds of the Nymphenburg Palace
near Munich (1734-39). Church architecture was dominated
first by the brothers Asam—Cosmas Damian, 1686-1739,
and Egid Quirin, 1692-1750; painter-architect and sculp-
tor-architect respectively—who had studied in Rome;

856

857

858

859

860

XLII

XLIII

and then by Johann Michael Fischer (1691-1766). The Asams made full use of Baroque forms of central planning and Baroque purposeful lighting, together with great displays of their skills as painter and sculptor. Fischer is the more inventive planner, tackling again the familiar Baroque problem of how to combine central and longitudinal elements. Thus he turned the church of Ottobeuren (1748-66), the foundations of which had already been laid, into something approaching a centrally formed space under the drumless dome, and achieved a comparable compromise in the church of Rott-am-Inn (1759-67). Decoration, by various highly skilled artists, is subjected to the clearly formed spatial units. There were other church builders active in Bavaria at this time, many of them comparatively simple men, capable of producing churches of great beauty. The most famous of them is Dominikus Zimmermann (1685-1766; the exact contemporary of Bach, Handel and Domenico Scarlatti), whose pilgrimage church at Wies (1746-54) is one of the most brilliant creations of the period.

These architects took little interest in the complex space modulation that Hildebrandt had learned from Guarini and exploited in his Gabel church. It is experimented with by the Dientzenhofers: Christoph Dientzenhofer's abbey church of St Margaret at Břevnov, near Prague (1709-15) shows it developed longitudinally, and this is done again on a larger scale in Johann Dientzenhofer's abbey church at Banz in northern Bavaria. But Balthasar Neumann (1687-1753) is the hero of this spatial polyphony, creating its greatest monument in the church of Vierzehnheiligen, near Banz (designed 1744), and exploring it in several other churches. The large abbey church of Neresheim (begun 1747) is comparatively simple and calm and suggests that Neumann was turning to a more classical phase in his last years. Neumann also built one of the greatest palaces of the period, the Würzburg Residenz (begun 1719), a fusion of French Rococo with Austrian Baroque. There, and in the palaces of Bruchsal and Brühl (1728 and 1741), Neumann created three of the most splendid staircases in an age of great splendour.

In Saxony there was a similar split between the architecture of the ruler and of the others. Augustus the Strong commissioned the Baroque extravaganza of the Dresden Zwinger from Matthäus Daniel Poppelmann (1662-1736), and sent him to Vienna and to Rome to prepare himself for the work. But when the Protestant city council wished to build a great church, they commissioned the city carpenter, Georg Bähr, who produced a magnificent centrally planned building which is at once Baroque and northern in character. Further north a fine synthesis of southern Baroque, with French and Dutch Palladianism, was achieved by Konrad Schlaun (1695-1773). In Prussia the Francophile Frederick II demanded, and in part supplied (fifty years too late, according to Voltaire), the French Rococo style for his dwellings. The middle years of the century in fact witnessed considerable stylistic confusion that will be referred to again below, but may be indicated briefly here by reference to the Gothic Neuen Gate in Potsdam (1755, designed by Frederick himself), the surprisingly classical Potsdam town hall (1753), and the New Palace, designed in 1750 in imitation of English and Dutch buildings.

ITALY: EARLY EIGHTEENTH CENTURY

After a lull in the first quarter of the eighteenth century, Rome enjoyed an architectural revival at the hands of Francesco de Sanctis (the Spanish Stairs, 1723-25), Nicola Salvi (the Fontana Trevi, 1732-62), Ferdinando Fuga (façade of Sta Maria Maggiore, 1741-43), and Alessandro Galilei (façade of San Giovanni in Laterano, 1732-35). It is significant that all these could be described as primarily scenic works whose value lies in their environmental impact. Piedmont produced two outstanding architects: Filippo Juvarra (1678-1736), who designed the vast royal palace at Stupinigi (1729-33) and the monumental church of La Superga near Turin (1717-31); and Bernardo Vittone (1704/5-70), the editor of Guarini's papers, who sought to fuse the styles of Guarini and Juvarra. Vittone's best work is the church of Sta Chiara at Brà (1742). In Naples and Sicily a light late Baroque was followed by a phase of Baroque classicism which found its climax in the great royal palace at Caserta (begun 1752, by Luigi Vanvitelli). This kind of Baroque classicism was at this time becoming an increasingly international style for palace architecture and can be found in later eighteenth-century Europe from London to St Petersburg.

SPAIN: EARLY EIGHTEENTH CENTURY

The court style of Spain's Bourbon rulers, as seen in the royal palace in Madrid (begun 1738 to the designs of Juvarra's pupil G. B. Sacchetti), represents a Franco-Italian synthesis devoid of Spanish characteristics. More interesting, therefore, are such provincial achievements as the Transparente chapel in Toledo Cathedral (1721-32, Narciso Tomé), and the sacristy of the Charterhouse in Granada (begun 1713, decorated 1742-7). Here Spanish enthusiasm expressed itself in a free richness that comes closer to the paper inventions of early Renaissance northerners than to, say, Bavarian Rococo. Other striking examples of this last great flowering of Spanish architectural genius are seen in the façade of the cathedral of Santiago de Compostela (1738-49), and, in the same town, the gatehouse of Sta Clara (c. 1750). A royal edict of 1777, designed to eradicate regionalism from Spanish architecture, ordered the submission of all designs for civil and religious buildings to the architectural academy for approval. Thus Neoclassicism was imposed on Spain.

ENGLAND: 1715-1760

The establishment of the Hanoverian dynasty on the English throne was accompanied by a considerable change of cultural atmosphere. Almost at once there is a sharp reaction against the English Baroque of Wren, Vanbrugh and Hawksmoor, and a new Palladian movement is established with the powerful backing and example of Lord Burlington (1694-1753). Through his own designs, through the designs of his associates, and through his and their books, the Palladian style is firmly established all over the country. It is a style that provincial squires and provincial designers can learn to handle almost as well as the metropolitan architects, and there results a remarkably high level of architectural production everywhere, supported by fine

XLII *Mansart: Grand Trianon, Versailles* XLIII *Burlington: Chiswick Villa, London*

**860 Amalienburg,
Nymphenburg palace,
near Munich. 1734-39.
François Cuvilliés**
Built in the grounds of the royal
palace of Nymphenburg,
this shows strong French influence.
Cuvilliés, Dutch-born, trained
in Paris before working for the
dukes of Bavaria.

**861 Würzburg Residenz.
1719-44.
Johann Balthasar Neumann**
Neumann consulted with French
and Austrian architects over
the plans for this episcopal palace.

**862, 864 Church at Wies,
Bavaria. 1746-54.
Dominikus Zimmermann**
Exterior and interior. One of the
many Bavarian churches built at
this time by German architects
showing the influence of Italy.
This pilgrimage church is one
of the most brilliant.

**863 St Margaret abbey church,
Břevnov, near Prague. 1709-15.
Christoph Dientzenhofer**
The spatial experiments which
culminated in Germany
in the church of Vierzehnheiligen
were carried out to some
extent longitudinally in this work
of Christoph Dientzenhofer.

**865 Church at Ottobeuren,
Bavaria. 1748-66.
Johann Michael Fischer**
Longitudinal foundations had
already been laid, but the architect
achieved something like a
centrally formed space under
a drumless dome.

**866 Church at
Vierzehnheiligen, near Banz.
1744. Neumann**
The interplay of spatial relations
is brought to a pitch in
this late Baroque German church.
The plan, at first sight simple,
does in fact consist of overlapping
ovals. At vault height they are
separated by three-dimensional
transverse arches.

860

861

862

863

864

865

866

867

868

869

870

871

867 Frauenkirche, Dresden. 1726-40.
Georg Bähr
A magnificent centrally planned building, the Frauenkirche, unfortunately destroyed, was one of the best examples of eighteenth-century Protestant building.
The oval dome was built of stone, and the whole was arranged somewhat like a pyramid.

868 The Zwinger, Dresden. 1711-22.
M. D. Poppelmann
This orangery and grandstand for pageants was meant to be part of an enormous electoral palace for the rulers of Saxony. It has the most exuberant decoration, swarming putti and broken and swinging pediments – Roman Baroque reduced in value.

869 Royal Palace, Caserta. Begun 1752.
Luigi Vanvitelli
In Naples and Sicily a light late Baroque was followed by a phase of Baroque classicism which found its climax in the great royal palace at Caserta.

870 San Giovanni in Laterano, Rome. Façade. 1732-35.
A. Galilei
Two superimposed porticoes are the basis for this façade.
The idea of a wall has gone; the façade is more like a screen dropped in front of the building. It is broken into balconies.

871 La Superga, Turin. 1717-31.
Filippo Juvarra
The whole church is turned round, so that the dome and apse come to the front.
An entirely different kind of façade is therefore possible. This north Italian architecture remained nearer the classical and was less Baroque than the southern.

**872 Royal palace, Madrid.
Begun 1738.
G. B. Sacchetti**
The court style of Spain's Bourbon
rulers, as seen in the royal
palace, designed by a pupil of
Juvarra, represents a Franco-Italian
synthesis devoid of Spanish
characteristics.

**873 Plan of Chiswick Villa,
near London. 1725.
Lord Burlington**
Burlington has based his building
on Palladio's Villa Capra,
with apartments ranged round the
tall, domed hall.
The dome is octagonal with
arched windows in the drum.

**874 Potsdam town hall,
Germany. 1753**
A surprisingly classical building
for the time and place.
Within five years of this building
there appeared in Potsdam
the Gothic Nauen Gate and the
New Palace,
an imitation of Castle Howard.

**875, 876 Holkham Hall,
Norfolk. Begun 1734.
William Kent**
Exterior and plan.
Palladian architecture in England
belonged par excellence
to the large country house, where,
unlike in France, the nobility
spent most of their time.
The central portico, as here, was
widely used, giving importance
to the entrance-front.
These houses were designed
to be surrounded by parkland.

**877 Transparente,
Toledo Cathedral. 1721-32.
Narciso Tomé**
The greatest excesses of illusionist
architecture were reached in
Spain. A window was
made in the existing Gothic vault,
the aperture concealed by
sculpture, to light from behind and
from the top the sculptural
scenes above the altar.
The sacrament is lit in a glass box
over the altar, hence 'transparente'.

**878 Assembly Rooms, York.
1730. Burlington**
Typical of the reaction against the
Baroque of Wren,
Vanbrugh and Hawksmoor is this
Neo-classical building based
on Vitruvius's account of the
Egyptian Hall.

872

874

877

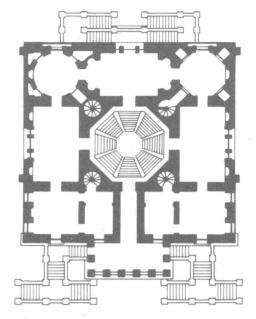

873

875

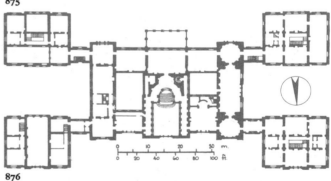

876

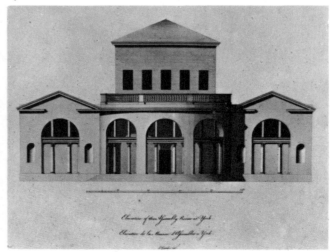

878

craftsmanship and extraordinarily reliable taste.

Burlington himself stands above his fellows by virtue of the moral intensity with which he pursues his aim of achieving, via Palladio's architecture and scholarship, a revival of truly Roman classicism such as the Renaissance had not as yet seen. His Chiswick Villa, London (1725), is Palladio's Villa Capra purified of sixteenth-century elements and classicised in terms of Palladio's reconstructions of the Roman baths. Holkham Hall, Norfolk (begun 1734), attempts something similar on a larger scale. The York Assembly Rooms (1730) were based on Vitruvius's account of the Egyptian Hall, again interpreted with the help of Palladio. From Burlington and his circle there also emerged the concept of the English landscape garden, equally a classicising invention, ideally suited to set off the formal lines of the Georgian country house, but of particular importance in that it involved the first systematic exploration of informal, 'picturesque' designing, still the basis of most town planning and much architecture.

p. 288, 873

75, 876

878

DISINTEGRATION OF THE RENAISSANCE

The middle of the eighteenth century saw the demolition of the fundamental principles and assumptions of Renaissance architecture. The primacy of Rome was questioned by archaeologists and architects who studied the ruins of the Acropolis and found there a different and, as many maintained, a superior kind of beauty. Others discovered that Imperial Roman architecture was only one phase of an architectural development, and that there were in the Near East remnants of a Roman architecture of freer and less austere design. Soon travellers brought back sketches of Egyptian, Indian and Chinese architecture, while nationalist feeling encouraged a new interest in medieval buildings, until styles came to be treated as ornamental surfaces little related to the structure beneath and therefore interchangeable according to the taste of patron or its supposed appropriateness to the building's function.

At the same time writers questioned the function of mathematical proportions, of symmetry and uniformity, of rules as such. While architects, artists and men of taste argued over the rival merits of Greek and Roman design, philosophers demolished the basic assumption that beauty was in any way related to objective criteria.

On the whole architects were not hasty to exploit the freedom these tendencies suggest: the rule of taste continued after its premises ceased to exist. In Britain, where philosophers like Hume and Burke, and artists like Hogarth, had played a leading part in this assault on the Renaissance, and where Renaissance classicism had just flowered so finely in the work of Burlington, the Palladian tradition continued without serious challenge for some decades, gradually being transformed into a more personal, more Romantic, style. By the time of Sir John Soane, what looked like cool classicism had become a means of highly Romantic subjectivism. Britain played a large part in peripatetic exploits: Robert and James Adam measured Diocletian's palace at Spalato; James Stuart and Nicholas Revett drew the ruins of Athens; Robert Wood's party did the same for Baalbek and Palmyra (all in the 1750s). And there were others. The Gothic style, always available in England for

879 Queen Square, Bath. 1728. John Wood the Elder
The greatest contribution to domestic architecture was made by the architect-speculators working in Bath and London. The Palladian façade with pediment is here stretched to cover a row of small houses.

879

880

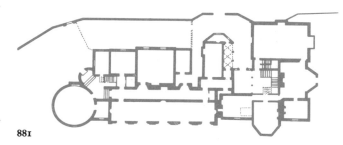

881

880–882 Strawberry Hill, Twickenham. 1748 onwards
Exterior, plan and interior. The Gothic style was adopted by Horace Walpole for the enlargement of his cottage. Until that time its rôle in the Romantic movement had been confined to follies and ruins. This 'Gothic' house departed self-consciously from the classical rectilinear plan, aiming at an asymmetry of layout, with medieval towers and long galleries, which manifest the hand of many separate designers. The ceiling in this gallery recalls the vaulting of the Henry VII chapel in Westminster Abbey. The photograph of the exterior includes nineteenth-century additions.

882

**883 Lacock Abbey,
Wiltshire. Hall, 1753-55.
Sanderson Miller**
In England the Gothic Revival
caught the imagination
more than the cult of chinoiserie
or any of the other Rococo fads.
It was an expression of Romantic
sentiment which affected
all the arts, particularly literature.

**884 Ecole de Médecine, Paris.
1769-86.
J. Gondoin**
Only a part of Gondoin's elaborate
project for this institution was
realised, but that has all the dignity
of French Neo-classicism.
The relief, by Berruer,
was substituted in 1794
for one representing Louis XV.

**885 Palladian bridge,
Stowe House,
Buckinghamshire. c. 1775**
Such pavilions and bridges
were non-functional and were
sometimes one-sided like stage
scenery and were used
solely to compose classical
landscapes like
those in the pictures of
Claude Lorraine.

**886 Pagode de Chanteloup,
Fôret d'Amboise. 1775-78.
Le Camus**
Chinoiserie often appeared
in garden ornament, sometimes as
bridges as well as pagodas.
This setting in the French forest
provided just the note of
exotic romance and unlikelihood
that made all such 'garden
furniture' one of the crazes
of the Romantic Revival.

**887 Casina at Marino, Dublin.
1769.
Sir William Chambers**
A little pleasure house for the
'pastoral life' built for the Earl
of Charlemont near Dublin.
It is based on Palladio's ideal
symmetrical villa and develops
his idea of the temple façade
to run round the building.

**888 Chinese teahouse,
Sanssouci, Potsdam. 1744.
Von Knobelsdorff**
In the gardens of Sanssouci,
designed for Frederick the Great,
this building copies the French
fashion for chinoiserie.
Tea-drinking was new and
fashionable, as tea in central
Europe was a recent commodity.

883

884

885

886

887

888

special purposes, was established as a style suitable for gentlemen's residences through the success of Horace Walpole's asymmetrical enlargement of Strawberry Hill, Twickenham (1748 onwards). Those who continued to use a classical idiom could now use a variety of classical sources, or, according to temperament, could fasten their attention on one source and exploit that with archaeological thoroughness. The former is seen at its most fruitful in the work of Robert Adam (1728-92), familiar with a variety of ancient sources as well as sixteenth-century Roman architecture and heir to English Palladianism. A domestic planner of great skill, and a decorator of genius, Adam was in great demand in the 1760s, 1770s and 1780s, and his composite style, as used by himself and many imitators, dominated domestic design for three decades and influenced France and Germany. His contemporary Sir William Chambers was of the more single-minded kind. His classicism had been tempered by close contact with French contemporaries such as Soufflot, and in the little pleasure house at Marino, near Dublin (1769), he created one of the most perfect buildings of the Renaissance.

In France, for a time, reason and objectivity seemed to have gained the day when the Jesuit Abbé Laugier, developing thoughts recently put forward by the Venetian Padre Carlo Lodoli, published a widely admired book, the *Essai sur l'Architecture* (1752). In the name of reason, Laugier demanded a return to a functionally justifiable use of the classical language: the function of columns is to support, not to decorate; the size of intercolumniations must follow from the lengths of stone in the entablature (Renaissance intercolumniations were habitually much wider); pediments represent the gable-ends of low-pitched roofs and are not to be used as ornaments over windows, and so on. Germain Soufflot's church, now the Panthéon, in Paris (begun 1752), is to a large extent a realisation of Laugier's hopes and seemed to his contemporaries to join Greek simplicity to Roman detail. Jacques-François Blondel, a powerful figure in French architecture through his teaching at the Academy, encouraged this severe classicism, and we can see his influence in such buildings as J. Gondoin's Ecole de Médecine, Paris (1769-86), and in V. Rodriguez's School of Surgery in Barcelona (1761).

Everywhere, whether classical principles were still followed or had been abandoned, architects sought a greater intensity of personal expression. For this any style would serve; the essential premise was superiority to the rules, if not independence from them. As the French author of a book on Roman architecture wrote: 'Let us learn from the ancients to submit even the rules to genius. Let us remove that mark of servitude and imitation that our buildings display' (Clérisseau, *Antiquités de la France*). So too thought Piranesi, the Italian archaeologist and architect, whose prints reassemble or distort classical buildings to make them overpowering or horrific. Whatever style they used, architects demanded the freedom presumably enjoyed by its creators. And so the study of the history of architecture became a necessary part of an architect's grounding.

889

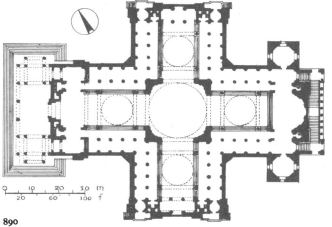

890

891

880-882

887

889-891

884

889-891 Panthéon, Paris. Begun 1752. Germain Soufflot
Exterior, plan and interior. The reaction against the free Baroque use of classical elements which was brought in by the Age of Reason is expressed in the Panthéon. Columns are no longer used as decoration (as in the Invalides); they support a giant portico. Soufflot attempted a return to the classicism of Greece and Rome, but the effect was self-conscious and cold.

Pre-Columbian (see next page)
The architecture of ancient Central and South America somewhat resembles that of the ancient civilisations of the Middle and Far East. However, its main development is parallel to the Middle Ages of western Europe, only coming to an end with the Spanish conquerors after 1492. The resemblance between ancient America and other civilisations lies in the development of the pyramid, stepped, terraced and even circular, both as cairns and sun temples, great trabeated halls and cyclopean masonry. Relief sculpture and frescoes were freely used.

892 Teotihuacán. 300–900
Teotihuacán is one of the few real
cities in ancient Mexico,
other comparable groups
of buildings being purely reserved
as religious centres.
The city covers an area of some
seven square miles.
All except the great temples and
palaces were adobe buildings
which have reverted to mud.

**893 Circular pyramid
in Calixtlahuaca, Mexico**
This pyramid in 'coiled' form is
dedicated to Quetzalcóatl,
the mythical plumed serpent,
who took the form of a
rattlesnake clad in the brilliant
green tail-feathers of the beautiful
quetzal bird.

**894 Great pyramid
of Teotihuacán, Mexico**
Built of adobe bricks faced
with volcanic stone and covered
with plaster or pre-conquest
cement, the pyramid is 700 feet
at base and 200 feet high.
There are five tiers, on top of
which was a temple to the cult
of Teotihuacán, god of the sun.

**895 Temple of Kukulkan,
Chichén Itzá, Yucatan**
Also known as El Castillo,
this temple has been carefully
reconstructed.
It is a square-based pyramid,
180 feet by 78 feet high, with
nine tiers. Large stairways on each
side are guarded by great
serpent heads.
The temple measures about
20 by 15 feet and has a door in
each side.

**896 Machu Picchu, Peru.
1000 onwards**
A mountain stronghold, Machu
Picchu was said to be reserved for
the king, priests and a nunnery of
virgins. The Incas had no
wheeled traffic, and communication
was by llama or on foot
along stepped mountain roads.

**897 Temple of Warriors,
Chichén Itzá, Yucatan**
The entrance pillars represent
serpents whose heads form the
base, the bodies the column itself,
and the tail-rattles the capital.

**898 Temple of Warriors,
Chichén Itzá, Yucatan**
Chichén was founded at the
beginning of the sixth century
by the Itzá and finally
developed in the tenth.
This temple, together with the
Group of the Thousand Columns,
bounds one side of the
main square.

**899 Fortifications
of Sacsayhuaman, Cuzco,
Peru. 1400 onwards**
The cyclopean stone walls of this
mountain stronghold contain
single polygonal blocks of
sometimes more than sixteen feet
in one dimension.

892

893

894

895

896

897

898

899

Eiffel Tower, Paris. View into tower

MODERN

INTRODUCTION

The closing years of the eighteenth century—a period of anticipation and of upheaval in political, social and economic endeavour—witnessed a series of creative events that heralded the appearance of a new art.

Paradoxically, one of the initial breaks with the senescent humanist tradition of the Renaissance took the form of a return to a remote past, as a series of revivals of earlier styles came about. Unlike the architects of the Renaissance, whose chief interest in the past concerned the forms of Roman antiquity, the architects of the late eighteenth century proceeded with encyclopedic objectivity to resuscitate Grecian as well as Roman paradigms, capped this accomplishment with a thorough revival of medieval styles, and, finally, caused the introduction of architectural styles of the Near and Far East. This plurality of mode and manner supplanted the established and relatively unitary style of the late Renaissance-Baroque period, a style which for centuries had formed a living heritage and had maintained a creative vitality until late in the eighteenth century.

These scholarly and re-creative efforts to recapture the past provided, at least until the middle of the nineteenth century, sufficient fuel with which the development of architecture could be sustained. However, it inevitably nurtured frustration and resentment among the more independent spirits of the day, and after the middle of the century, these pent-up energies were released in a series of radical movements. Indeed, the evolution of architecture, both in the nineteenth and in the more radical-seeming twentieth century, has reflected a certain Janus-faced character of modern art as a whole, in which elements of tradition and convention tend to be present, if only as foils, in the most radical of innovations. Many of the innovations that took place in architecture at this time were more related to new materials and new methods of construction than to a preconceived vision of novel forms. The introduction of iron, and later of steel and of reinforced concrete, has been somewhat over-emphasised as a *determining* factor in the creation of a new style, yet it remains commonplace that many of the forms and spaces that are uniquely characteristic of modern architecture would not have been realised had the Industrial Revolution, with its manifold technological, social and economic consequences, not taken place.

Another contributing factor in the evolution of modern art and architecture was the intellectual ferment of the late eighteenth century, with its new attachment to nature, its political idealism, its scepticism in the face of tradition, and admiration of simpler and more direct forms of expression. One of the earliest manifestations of this tendency was the *Essai sur l'Architecture* of Marc-Antoine Laugier, first published in 1752. Laugier's ideas, typical of the rational leanings of the period, appear to have influenced such diverse personalities as the startlingly original English architect Sir John Soane, on the one hand, and Goethe on the other. Without doubt, Laugier's doctrines contributed to the anti-Baroque tendencies of the Neo-classic movement at the end of the eighteenth century, and

helped in directing the new architectural movement towards formal clarification and geometrical simplicity.

Nearly a century after Laugier, another impassioned amateur, John Ruskin, produced a vast, unwieldy body of architectural commentary and criticism, which in its own way provided an index of the aspirations of mid-nineteenth-century architecture and its public. In his writings, the familiar and accepted criteria of beauty and of aesthetic value are implicitly, when not explicitly, rejected. Ruskin exhorts architects to rediscover goodness and truth in their art, as if this process were identical with the establishment of a code of ethical and spiritual behaviour. The sentimental associative values of the eighteenth century were now transformed into moralistic ones.

More than anything else, these ideas reflect his basic dissatisfaction with the characteristic appearance and condition of contemporary architecture, and especially of such new phenomena as the railroad station, or of such radical, unheralded structures as the Crystal Palace of the Great Exhibition of 1851, which Ruskin despised. However, his criteria do provide a reasonably accurate indication of the architectural values that were instinctively cherished by the bourgeois nineteenth century.

922, 923

In contrast to the irascible Ruskin, there are the equally impatient strictures of the French medievalist, Viollet-le-Duc. Of a temperament that easily gravitated to controversy, and the indirect heir of the rational architectural thought of the 'Enlightenment', as represented by Laugier, he was in a position to develop the more materialistic aspects of that attitude. It was the specific accomplishment of Viollet-le-Duc to arrive at an understanding of Gothic architecture, in which the integration of form and structure was proclaimed as the chief virtue of this style. However, Viollet-le-Duc did not rest with the assertion of a historical, archaeological interpretation of a style from the distant past, but rather applied it to a theory of contemporary architecture, and particularly to the idea of creating a new style out of an analytical study of the past, and the application of rational constructive principles to the new material, technical and industrial potential of the nineteenth century. In this way, Viollet-le-Duc developed an architectural theory that approximated to the popular, if imprecise, notion of functionalism, whereas Ruskin's endeavours were primarily concerned with the outward appearance of architectural construction, and not with the method of its inner structure.

921

Both contributed to the development of a more searching approach to the judgment of a building, in which the visual phenomena, whether they be related to the skeleton of the building or the material raiment of its exterior, are stressed almost to the exclusion of other considerations. Correctness of proportion or detail, or the inner meaning of the design, exclusive of its physical qualities, becomes a matter of secondary importance. The building's ultimate significance now comes to depend not so much upon a generative idea or concept of design, as upon its expressed technical concept, and upon its real, physical embodiment. These new doctrines, both in specific texts and in their widespread reflection in the climate of ideas current at the time, materially affected the thought and work of many diverse creative personalities at the end of the nineteenth century: Louis Sullivan, Frank Lloyd Wright, H. P. Berlage, Henry van de Velde, Victor Horta, Antoni Gaudí, and Auguste Perret. All represent various facets of progressive architecture at this juncture. In turn, this group of pioneers opened the way for the second radical generation of the twentieth century: Gropius, Mies van der Rohe, Le Corbusier, Oud, Lurçat, and others who helped shape what subsequently became known as the International Style. In effect, these two generations of architects synthesised the multitudinous elements that the modern tradition had been gradually accumulating over a period of more than a century.

ROMANTIC CLASSICISM: THE STYLE OF 1800

An interpretation of modern architecture which takes for its point of departure the historically oriented Revivalist movements, such as Neo-classicism or the Gothic Revival, is obliged to stress the original features of the styles, as well as their dependence upon specific sources, and their occasional penchant for literal imitation. Significant as such abdications of creative responsibility are in the copying of a specific building from the past, they are merely negative symptoms of the disturbances which inaugurated a new architectural tradition. There was no universal style which dominated this period, unless by style one means a related group of abstract visual characteristics which remain constant, irrespective of the decorative vocabulary and historical pedigree employed in the individual building. The admired, sought-after qualities of this period were simplicity and clarity, as well as appropriateness with respect to character and expression.

The architects of 1800 were not temperamentally equipped to absorb into their work the innate character of the historical styles they were endeavouring to revive. In Greek art (and, for that matter, in all of classic art) they perceived the order and clarity of its discipline, and the purity of its supposedly white forms set against the rich palette of nature. However, this generation of Neo-classicists overlooked the life-like vitality, and the sense of individuality contained within the universal implications of each form, which was an essential feature of Hellenic classicism. Hence the revival of antique art tends to exaggerate the purist, abstract and academic element. The forms of Neo-classicism, whether literal or general in their derivation, tend to be more rigidly geometric and over-simplified, in contrast to the more subtle, vivid effects of their prototypes. In this respect, the architecture of 1800 reflected certain ideals of the enlightenment, which concerned the admiration of primitive-seeming, as well as of simple forms. In addition, it provided a foretaste of the severe geometries characteristic of the early twentieth century, and of the overtly original International Style.

In picking and choosing other sources of inspiration from the myriad styles of the Middle Ages, the architects of the late eighteenth and early nineteenth centuries were equally arbitrary. Although their imagination was stirred by the tempestuous qualities of Gothic, and its evocation of both nordic and Christian sentiments, they tended, especially at first, to convert the wall surfaces of their Neo-Gothic buildings into papery abstract planes, which were more in keeping with a Georgian or Neo-classical attitude than with the linear screen concepts of the authentic Gothic. In effect, the medieval styles were reduced and simplified, 'classicised' in the sense of the word as understood at that time. Equally the details of Gothic architecture might be applied with gusto and abandon, but often in unseemly places, and with little sense of scale or usage. Here, indeed, one discovers that the period's concern with a building's character and appropriateness often tended to be remarkably superficial. The awkward phrase, *Romantic Classic*, is a useful label to specify these ambiguous style-tendencies of the 1800 period, and, in addition, it has gained a degree of general acceptance.

The 'Neo-classic' architecture of this period is Romantic, since it represents the projection of a modern point of view upon the aesthetic of antiquity, while the Gothic architecture of 1800, already Romantic by virtue of its associations of an irrational and mysterious sort, was subjected to a 'classicising', i.e., regularising, process in which the letter but not the spirit of the original was maintained. Consequently, the idea of Romantic Classicism manages to transcend several of the superficial stylistic contradictions of the period.

The most spectacularly inventive architects at this time were two forgotten French designers: Etienne-Louis Boullée and Claude-Nicholas Ledoux. Occasionally their buildings affected a literal Neo-classicism, but more commonly they were distorted by unfamiliar scale relationships and the use of exaggeratedly simple geometric contrasts, with results that might better be characterised as sublime, rather than beautiful. Typical of these tendencies are Ledoux's Paris Barrières, or Toll Houses, of 1785-89, a series of variations upon a set theme, which provided the architect with one of his best opportunities. His ideal city of Chaux was at least in part constructed at Arc-et-Senans, in a remote district of the Franche Comté, though certain of its more novel projects—for example, the house for the surveyor of the river Loue—were never built.

A further instance of the creative side of Romantic Classicism is to be found in the work of Boullée. His 1784 project for a spherical, planetarium-like cenotaph, dedicated to the memory of one of the heroes of the enlightenment, Sir Isaac Newton, indicates the potential of this revolutionary style. The sphere derives in all likelihood from the Roman precedent of a hemispherical dome—a form which appears in other projects of the same epoch by Boullée. However, it has been transformed into a shape that is very nearly a pure mathematical concept, and simultaneously a flaunting of architectural convention. By its literal expressiveness as a microcosmic representation of the universal world-machine, as conceived by the eighteenth-century rationalists, it necessarily becomes constructively preposterous.

The mysterious and evocative projects of the precocious German architect, Friedrich Gilly, typify the Romantic extreme, and their creator did not survive his thirtieth year, dying in 1800 without having the opportunity of executing a single significant building. On the surface, it would seem that some of his potential was realised by

902

900

903

**900 Etienne-Louis Boullée.
Newton Cenotaph. 1784**
An example of the extremes
to which Romantic Classicism
could go. Dedicated to
the memory of Sir Isaac Newton,
its spherical form, reminiscent
of a planetarium, expresses the
typically eighteenth-century
view of the world-machine.
It was never built.

900

**901 Peter Speeth.
Würzburg Women's Prison.
1809-10**
The Romantic tendencies
of Friedrich Gilly were partly
realised in the work of
Peter Speeth, with his sometimes
startling designs.
The heavy rustication of
the round-arched basement was
typical of the bolder designs
of 1800, and it foreshadows
similar effects in the work
of the American architect
H. H. Richardson, around 1880.

901

**902 Claude-Nicholas Ledoux.
Arc-et-Senans. 1775-79**
Entrance to the enormous salt
works which was planned to
include a model village
for the people working
there. The whole conception
was highly Romantic;
the stones were heavily
rusticated and carved
spouts of water, stalactites
and stalagmites and artificial
rock grottoes were used freely
as symbolic decoration.

902

**903 Friedrich Gilly.
Monument to Frederick the
Great. 1797**
Gilly's Doric temple, posed
on a mammoth overscaled
stylobate, owes its Romantic
sublimity to the example
of Boullée and Ledoux and
foreshadows Leo von Klenze's
Valhalla at Regensburg.

903

the scholarly and prolific Karl Friedrich Schinkel during
the first three decades of the nineteenth century, but in
reality, the subjective, emotional quality in Gilly's projects
is a world apart from the aloof, rational manner of his
successor. Instead, we find the Romantic tendencies of the
youthful prodigy better realised in the occasionally startling
designs of Peter Speeth (in the most unusually scaled façade of the Women's Prison, Würzburg, 1809-10), or of   901
the better known Danish Neo-classicist, C. F. Hansen.   907
Other architects achieved distinction in this *mitteleuropa*
'international style' of the early nineteenth century. Schinkel's disciple, Ludwig Persius; the Bavarian court architect,
Leo von Klenze; the French-born architect of the St
Petersburg Bourse, Thomas de Thomon; and the Danish
brothers Theophil and Hans Christian Hansen, whose most
conspicuous Neo-classic work was done in Athens and Vienna, all made individual contributions to the mode. However,
none displayed the adventurous, pioneering spirit of the
first revolutionary classicists, and a learned simplicity and
clarity is frequently all that saves their work from a descent
to the perfunctory. Of all the works of this *pléiade* of Teutonic Neo-classicists, none is more remarkable than
Klenze's Valhalla at Regensburg, a strict copy of the Parthenon set above the Danube, on a massive podium that
nearly engulfs the temple above.

By way of contrast, the employment of a Romantic Classic
style in the United States immediately after the War of
Independence, was, thanks to the activity of Thomas
Jefferson, a political as well as aesthetic decision. Jefferson
made use of the antique mode with political intent, hoping
thereby to provide an architectural backdrop for the revival
of other republican aspects of ancient life and thought.

A literal-mindedness with respect to the prototypes
employed, coupled with a hesitancy to assume creative
responsibility, inhibited many of the classic revival designers in the United States. A certain bookishness, an
outgrowth of his amateur's background, was a considerable
drawback to Jefferson's architecture, even in his inventive
lay-out for the University of Virginia, in which a kind   904
of museum of classical styles was essayed. Of all the architects of the new republic, only Benjamin H. Latrobe, with   906
his English background, keener taste, and concern with
engineering as well as architectural projects, was able to
make a distinctive contribution to the new style. More
typical of the American achievement in this vein was the
work of Thomas U. Walter, whose octastyle Corinthian
temple, serving as an academic building for Girard College,
Philadelphia (1833-47), is a 'correct' replica of a pagan
monument, yet one which is significant chiefly as a curiously inappropriate quotation out of context. Far more
striking an example of the adaptation of antique temple
forms to an academic programme is to be found in Thomas
Hamilton's picturesquely sited and complexly massed Royal
High School, Edinburgh, begun in 1825.   905

There is an improvisatory quality that distinguishes much
of the otherwise classically inspired design in British architecture in the first years of the nineteenth century. The
busiest, most ingenuous and most royally favoured architect of this period was John Nash. Much of his work is
slapdash, and drawn from a bewildering variety of sources.

904

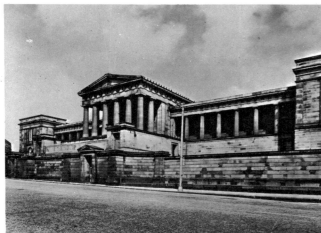

905

906

907

904 Thomas Jefferson. Library, University of Virginia, Charlottesville. 1817
Bookishness, the product of an amateur's background, was the weakness of Jefferson's architecture. It is evident even in his lay-out for the University of Virginia, in which many classical styles were reproduced.

905 Thomas Hamilton. Edinburgh Royal High School. Begun 1825
This is an examples of a strikingly successful adaptation of antique temple forms to an academic programme. The stern Doric temple form provides a fulcrum for the symmetrical façade and also evokes a determined classicism.

906 Benjamin H. Latrobe. Interior, Roman Catholic Cathedral, Maryland. Executed project, 1805-18
Among the great outcrop of formal and public building produced by the birth of the new republican state in America, Latrobe's work ranks as the most distinguished.
Here, there are obvious echoes of the Panthéon in Paris.

907 C. F. Hansen. Vor Frue Kirke, Copenhagen. 1811-29
The head of a family of architects, C. F. Hansen was the first notable exponent of the Neo-classic style in Denmark, where the Copenhagen Academy had taken it up to the end of the eighteenth century.

**908, 909 James Wyatt.
Fonthill Abbey, Wiltshire.
1796-1813**
Exterior and plan.
Built for the great eccentric and
connoisseur, William Beckford,
Fonthill Abbey realises
the Picturesque and Sublime
in the 'cardboard' Gothic style.
Just as the architects of the
revolutionary generation in France
had modified their antique
source material, so the architects
of the Gothic Revival reduced
its Gothic intricacies to mural
details and its structural flow to
four-square, typically late
Georgian compartments.

908

909

**910 Sanderson Miller.
'Castle' at Hagley Park,
Worcestershire. 1747**
Miller was an architect-squire
who started by providing
designs for his friends. This pseudo-
medieval 'ruin' at Hagley
is only one of many which he
built throughout England,
as the Gothic movement spread.
His best work is the new
Lacock Abbey (see 883).

**911 John Nash.
Diamond Cottage, Blaise,
Gloucestershire. 1803**
One of a hamlet of nine cottages
designed by Nash for
J. S. Harford, and built on his
estate. Each cottage was of a
different design, and each was given
a picturesque name such as
Sweetbriar, Jessamyn, or Diamond.

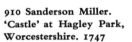

910

911

**912 John Nash.
Brighton Pavilion. 1815**
Nash rebuilt and embroidered the
Royal Pavilion into something
impossibly exotic, part Moslem
and part Indian. Cast iron was
freely used in this building.
The kitchen has cast-iron columns
which sprout palmettes at the top;
staircases everywhere are of
cast-iron sections and a great deal
of the fretted decoration found
throughout the building is cast iron.

912

In spite of this quality, it was Nash, and, to a similar degree, his contemporary, James Wyatt, who effected a blending of the stern, severe Romantic Classicism of the continental architects with the looser, Anglo-Saxon Picturesque tradition. This tendency, which developed out of the pre-Romantic, naturalistic landscaping practices of the eighteenth-century, provided the basis for a gradual revolution against the geometric regularity of the classical revivals. In its first phase, the Picturesque provided a complementary foil for the formal precision inherent in Romantic Classicism, and established a setting in which its abstract forms could acquire a sentimental or expressive significance. Nash's unique project for Regent Street and Regent's Park, London, begun in 1812, combines elements of the rigid architectural vocabulary of the day with a sequential arrangement, that is partly formal and axial, yet frequently devious and serpentine. Nash's preferences are also to be seen in his popularisation of the 'Italian villa', the Picturesque architectural mode *par excellence*. It was a type of vernacular domestic architecture which, at its source, in the timeless villas and farmhouses of central and northern Italy, already possessed a blend of irregular, accidental features in conjunction with more or less classicising details. These principles were developed in such illustrated publications of the period as J. B. Papworth's *Rural Residences* of 1818, in which a variety of stylistic tendencies, medieval, rusticised Neo-classic or simplified Regency appeared in fitting and plausible association.

The most impressive monuments dedicated to the exploitation of the Picturesque taste were, however, of a more dramatic kind. Nash rebuilt and embroidered the Royal Pavilion, Brighton, into something impossibly exotic, being part Moslem, and part Indian. The whole bizarre confection was erected with the aid of cast-iron columns on the interior, thus introducing a novel material which was ultimately destined to help revolutionise structural aesthetics later in the century, but was used here in a carnival-like atmosphere. The Picturesque, since it was not a style but an attitude, could be encouraged through the development of a taste for the Middle Ages as well. In 1747, a sham medieval castellated 'ruin' had been erected as a hermitage in Hagley Park. The taste for contrived decay was to be found in many French as well as English garden fabrics of the period. The most artful of these would appear to be the colossal 'ruined' column built as a residence by M. de Monville in the 'Desert de Retz', near Paris, in the 1780's.

However, the most breathtaking realisation of the Picturesque and the Sublime, on both a formal and ideational level, was James Wyatt's Fonthill Abbey, built for the great eccentric and connoisseur, William Beckford, in 1796-1813. Wyatt, sometimes known as the 'great destroyer', because of his drastic and over-enthusiastic restoration of certain English medieval cathedrals, created a colossal garden folly in a stylised 'cardboard' Gothic. Instead of the rich textures and linear patterns that we are in the habit of seeing as the most fundamental visual features of genuine Gothic buildings, at Fonthill, Wyatt gives us a series of four-square, typically late Georgian spaces, that are only slightly modified by the cautious, spindly efforts at Gothic detailing.

913

914

915

913 John Nash.
York Gate, Regent's Park, London. Begun 1812
The most ambitious project of John Nash's was the redesigning of frontages in London, from Regent Street to Regent's Park. His Neo-classic ideas are best expressed in these eclectic but impressive façades, which at least give unity where there was none before.

914 John Nash.
All Souls Church, Langham Place, London. 1822-25
Constructed of Bath stone, this classical temple building is one of the many churches built at this time to serve the increasing town populations. The lower portico is Ionic, and the conical spire is ringed by Corinthian columns.

915 H. L. Elmes.
St George's Hall, Liverpool. Designed 1839-40; completed after the architect's death in 1849 by C. R. Cockerell
Typical of contemporary municipal building produced in the midlands and north by the new industrial wealth. This design is based on the tepidarium of the baths of Caracalla in Rome with additionally a colonnade design. Elmes's design was also influenced by the Berlin architecture of Karl Friedrich Schinkel.

**916 Sir John Soane.
Dulwich Art Gallery, 1811-14.
Founder's mausoleum**
At times Soane's design bordered
on mannerism.
The scale and shape of familiar
objects and details have
been warped, and in a nominally
Neo-classical design one
sees heralded a modernism
where familiar elements are re-
used in abnormal or inverted ways.
The gallery was designed
to house both the collection
and the tomb of its donor.
The mausoleum,
shown in the picture,
was dramatically toplit
through amber glass windows.

916

**917 Thomas Telford.
St Katharine's docks, London.
1824-28**
This remarkably simple
utilitarian design in stock brick
is carried on stout cast-iron piers
of a very archaic Doric shape.
This derivative use of a new
industrial age material is typical
of the conflicting character of
architecture at that time.
Nonetheless, the simple elevations
in brick are worthy of
comparison with the later
American buildings of
Richardson and Sullivan.

917

**918 Peter Ellis. Oriel
Chambers, Liverpool. 1864-65**
Iron is not only used for
the framework of this office block;
there are cast-iron panels used
as cladding.
Pre-fabrication is carried further
than ever before.

918

Just as the architects of the revolutionary generation in
France had modified their antique source material through
simplification, generalisation and abstraction, the architects
who worked in the Gothic Revival reduced the intricacies
of its structural and decorative systems to flat, mural details, and its mysterious, dynamic flow of space to clear,
largely rectilinear compartments.

This process of clarification, in which the elements taken
from the most diverse periods of the past are served up
in the same *lingua franca*, can be seen to good advantage in
one of the best-known publications of the day, the so-
called *Grand Durand*, more exactly, *Recueil et parallèle des
édifices en tout genre, anciens et modernes*, Paris, 1800, of J.-
N.-L. Durand, a follower of Boullée and Ledoux. Here
the reader finds a vast melange of historic monuments,
drawn from antiquity, the Middle Ages, the Renaissance
and modern periods, in which the idiosyncrasies of scale,
style, circumstance and material are disregarded in the
fastidiously simple line drawing. These are extraordinary, if
not especially compelling, reductions from reality, and as
such are superb illustrations of the unique architectural
vision of the period.

One architect of 1800, Sir John Soane, would seem to
offer in his work a résumé and synthesis of the conflicts
of the age. His adaptations and modifications of classic
themes, as in the wantonly destroyed interiors of the Bank
of England, built over a long period, beginning in 1788,
are not grandiose in the manner of his continental contemporaries. Instead, the variations that he introduces in the
shaping of domes, arches, pendentives and lunettes, seem
to be based upon his knowledge of the Abbé Laugier's
ideas concerning the rationale of architectural systems.
Coupled with this visual evidence of Soane's intellectual
testing of classical forms and prototypes, there is a certain
crankiness, even a perversity, which borders upon mannerism, that prevails in compositions such as that of his
Dulwich Museum and Art Gallery of 1811-14. Here,   916
historical generalisation has been enriched by deliberate and
wilful disturbances, in which the scale and shape of familiar objects and details have been warped, and normal
relationships have been inverted (as in the recessed entablature above the brick piers), giving a sense of precarious imbalance. Thus, in this nominally Neo-classic
work, there is, paradoxically, a lack of familiar, even classic
resolution in the way in which the parts of the design go
together. All of these tendencies, anti-classic and anti-
academic in principle, appear at this time within the context of a nominal classic revival, and in many ways herald
the appearance of a more immediately recognisable modernism, where familiar elements are torn out of their
normal context and re-used in abnormal or inverted ways.

If one element of modernism comes about in a clandes-
tine way, in the midst of a revival of the very kind of
architecture that the new movement will ultimately and
violently reject in the twentieth century, another train
of developments leading to the familiar radicalism of our
own day emerges with the growth of a new technology
in the wake of the Industrial Revolution. The impact of
this phenomenon upon the evolution of architecture for
the next century and a half is subtle, complex, and devious

in the line of its development. The inaugural monument of this movement was the work of the Shropshire ironmaster, Abraham Darby III: the elegantly arched cast-iron bridge at Coalbrookdale, nominally the design of the architect Thomas F. Prichard, in 1777. Its span of 100 feet was soon outclassed, both in distance and in elegance of design, by the graceful arches of Thomas Telford's numerous bridges of the 1800 period, culminating in the two masterpieces of early suspension bridge art, that over the Menai Straits of 1819-26, and the more superficially castellated one at Conway. While the piers of the latter were concocted in a superficial Gothic, out of deference to the nearby castle, the Menai bridge is one of the most expressive monuments of English architecture in the whole period. Its splendid silhouette formed by the pylon-like rusticated towers, contrasted with the long, low curve of the supporting suspension chains, themselves brilliantly detailed in iron, is unequalled in the work of any other English architect of the day, with the exception of Soane. This same expressive quality—which some have deigned to interpret as an early instance of the functional tradition—is to be found in Telford's St Katharine's docks, London (1824-28), where smooth brick walls, punctuated by regularly spaced segmental-arched openings, inserted in five- and six-storey round-arched embrasures, are perched upon widely spaced, but archaic-looking, cast-iron Doric columns.

The presence of conventionally 'stylistic' features in the engineering structures of the nineteenth century should not be viewed as a matter of either surprise or alarm. Indeed, if these bridges, market halls, railroad sheds and similar structures are subjected to an art-historical analysis, as opposed to a simple technical commentary, it will be seen that their development follows an evolutionary path consonant with the more familiar architectural idioms of the day. From the classicising utilitarianism of Telford, the development leads to the more frankly non-stylistic railsheds of Robert Stephenson at Euston and at Derby Trijunct in the 1830's, or his tubular Britannia bridge over the Menai Straits (1845-50), and culminates in Sir Joseph Paxton's unique stroke of inspiration, the original Crystal Palace for the Great Exhibition of 1851. This superb, if over-familiar, monument represented a major instance of mid-nineteenth-century Victorian architecture which reflected the traditions of regularity and simplicity of the architecture of 1800. Simultaneously, it utilises to the full the principles of assemblage and re-use of elements that was made possible by early techniques of mass-production. In this respect the Crystal Palace reflects not so much the period in which it was built, but rather an aesthetic and point of view that shares elements in common with its immediate past (the first, Romantic Classic phase of modern architecture), and of the future (in the more frankly modernistic architecture of the twentieth century).

More typically and immediately Victorian in their style were such iron structures as J. B. Bunning's Coal Exchange, London (1846-49), and Paddington Station, the latter the result of a collaboration between I. K. Brunel and M. D. Wyatt (1852-54). Indeed, Brunel was the most characteristic engineer-artist of the mid-nineteenth century, in the way that Telford represents the early industrial-classic

919

920

921

919 J. B. Bunning.
Coal Exchange, London.
1846-49
This, one of the finest Victorian iron-and-glass buildings, has now been demolished. It was on a circular plan with galleries on all three levels. The interior had decorative panels of fossils found inside coal.

920 Dutert and Contamin.
Galerie des Machines,
Paris. 1889
Part of the Paris Exhibition. This was the largest free span attempted at this time. The giant metal three-hinged arches rest on points, giving the building an appearance of extreme lightness.

921 E. E. Viollet-le-Duc.
Project for concert hall
with iron-ribbed vault. 1864.
(From 'Entretiens sur
l'Architecture',
Volume 2, 1872)
Bridging the gap between traditional historicising architecture and the structural nationalism of the machine age are a series of projects by the pioneer medieval archaeologist of the nineteenth century, Viollet-le-Duc. Although he was the heir of eighteenth-century nationalist doctrines and the restorer of Notre-Dame, Paris (begun 1845), his schemes seem bizarre if only because of their uncompromisingly national tone and their blatant structural expressionism. The diversity of Viollet-le-Duc's preoccupations, ranging from the past to the future, are a vivid reminder of the various conflicting ideals of the mid-nineteenth century.

**922, 923 Sir Joseph Paxton,
designer.
Fox and Henderson, builders.
Crystal Palace, London,
1850-51; demolished and
re-erected at Sydenham, 1853;
destroyed by fire, 1936**
The first of the great glass palaces
that were a feature of
nineteenth-century international
exhibitions. Promoted with the
assistance of Prince Albert,
designed by Paxton, who had
been gardener to the Duke of
Devonshire at Chatsworth, where
he had constructed conservatories
and laid out farm villages,
it strained the resources of the
then-developing iron and glass
industries in Great Britain.
Both the interior and exterior
views show the result of industrial
methods of standardisation and
pre-assemblage. The interior
view of the transept (whose
prefabricated wooden arches
were made necessary to preserve
a tree on the site) shows the
even, regular repetition of the
same structural elements of
iron column and truss.
The exterior view shows the
Crystal Palace as re-erected
at Sydenham, its bulk and
massiveness increased by the
addition of a barrel vault
over the length of its nave.
This addition represents a
compromise between the purity
of Paxton's earliest concept
and the prevalent taste of the
day for bulkier, more
ostentatious forms.
While we rightly admire this
work for its technological
precocity as well as for its
striking anticipation of the glass
architecture of the mid-twentieth
century, we ought equally
to recognise that in the purity
of its forms and the regularity
of its detail Paxton's masterpiece
is as much a belated manifestation
of earlier Romantic Classic
taste as it is an explicit
foreshadowing of the machine age.

922

923

period. Brunel's *style*, as shown in the sheds of Paddington Station, his colossal steam-sail transatlantic ark, the Great Eastern, launched in 1858, or in the Clifton suspension bridge (designed 1829, but not begun until 1837 and completed by W. H. Barlow, the designer of the shed of St Pancras, in 1864), is richer and more recognisably Victorian in effect than that of his predecessors, without achieving the breath-taking, spidery monumentality of Gustave Eiffel.

If the Crystal Palace represents a paradox in the form of a simultaneous throwback as well as harbinger of things to come, much the same is true of the contemporary round-arched façade of Lewis Cubitt's King's Cross Station, London, and of Henri Labrouste's Bibliothèque Ste Geneviève, Paris, (1843-50). Here, a sober-elegant procession of round arches on the exterior houses a twin-naved, barrel-vaulted space fabricated in cast-iron. However, Labrouste, the most thoughtful French architect of the mid-century, is rather conventionally academic in his detailing; and in his later multiple cast-iron domes of the Bibliothèque Nationale, Paris (1861-69), there is a puzzling if effective blend of modernistic with conventional taste and technique. Labrouste was recognised by his contemporaries as the founder of a rational school in France, and some of these tendencies of a markedly materialistic sort are to be found in England in the writings of the 1830's and '40's of Augustus Welby Northmore Pugin.

Pugin, whose publications antedate those of Ruskin and of Viollet-le-Duc, represents a curious blend of ideals related to the ecclesiastical, ritualistic revival that took place both within and without the established church in England, during the nineteenth century, and of an architectural philosophy which hews a path to functionalism and the logical expression of structure. All of this is conceived within the context of a renewed and purified Gothic Revival, in which the fashion of the earlier, Romantic Classic 'Gothic', with its extravagances like Fonthill and its chic decorative paraphernalia, are castigated with a furor that matches his denunciation of the classically inspired styles. His ideals were only partly achieved in the bewildering number of churches designed in his all-too-brief active career, which was cut short by his death in 1852, at the age of forty. Only in his own house, The Grange, Ramsgate (1841-43), and the neighbouring St Augustine (1846-51), do we find a completely new, characteristically Victorian mode of Neo-Gothic: severe, harsh and aggressively pious. Here, the sentimental, romantic aesthetic of the later eighteenth century is transformed into the self-righteous 'realism' of 1850, a bud that will soon burst into the full bloom of red-brick-and-polychrome High Victorian style, in the hands of Butterfield, Street, Scott and Burges.

The new Gothic Revival of Pugin could not have come about without the Industrial Revolution, its influence upon the arts and crafts, and impact upon the patterns of urban life and society, nor without the particular religious revival of the period. Paradoxically, while his ideals indicate a profound nostalgia for the better days of a vanished medieval world, many of his characteristic buildings manifest, in their simple, direct use of brick and stone, often of an indifferent appearance, something of the sober materialism

924

925

29, 930

26-928

924 Gustave Eiffel. Tower. 1889
Erected for the Paris Exhibition of 1889, it is 984 feet high.
The arches are merely decorative links, the tower being formed of four immense pylons which flow into one.
This is of course more a feat of engineering than of architecture. Eiffel was a bridge-builder, and his genius is expressed in this edifice.
It should be noted that metal structures such as this are not very durable in comparison with conventional buildings of stone and timber, and the tower only survives as a result of constant maintenance and repainting.

925 Eiffel Tower under construction, 1888
This shows clearly the four bridge-like pylons which form the tower, before the decorative arches were added.
This form of ornamentation over a solid construction occurs later in Art Nouveau structures.

**926, 927 Henri Labrouste.
Bibliothèque Nationale,
Paris. 1861-69**
Interior and view of book stacks,
Metal and glass have been used
here to great effect.
The book stacks occupy four
storeys, all surmounted by a glass
ceiling. The gridiron floor
plates allow light to penetrate
to all floors.

926

927

**928 Henri Labrouste.
Bibliothèque Nationale,
Paris. 1861-69**
Detail of pillar and vault.
The twelve slim columns which
support the domes are
decorated very ornately in pseudo-
Corinthian, which also runs
along the arch soffits.

**929 Henri Labrouste.
Bibliothèque Ste Geneviève,
Paris. 1843-50**
A classicising building using
an interior metal frame,
although the exterior is of
conventional masonry. The style
is hybrid but has a quiet
attractiveness suitable
to the building's use.

928

929

**930 Henri Labrouste.
Bibliothèque Ste Geneviève,
Paris. 1843-50**
Thick stonework on the outside
enclosed an iron construction
which is self-supporting
The first attempt to use cast iron
and wrought iron in an
important public building,
from the foundation to the roof.

930

of the Industrial Age. This is also true of those church architects of the post-Puginesque High Victorian phase, of whom William Butterfield is both typical and unique. His first and most lasting masterpiece, All Saints, Margaret Street, London (1849-59), seizes with a vengeance upon the latent materialism of Pugin's aesthetic, and raises it to a feverish pitch, which, in the garishness of its constructive colouration and a Pre-Raphaelite-like precision of detail, was later equalled, but never surpassed. Its decorative effort would have been gratuitous had All Saints not been intended, from the start, to be the model construction of the High Church party, and the intricacy of its decoration is historically comprehensible only in this context, even though its stunning effects can, today, be appreciated, by a less ostentatiously devout generation, as a most curious anticipation of the violent colour of much modern painting. These atonal colour effects, echoing the strident, brutal massing and occasionally exaggerated structural detail, are to be found in such domestic interiors as those created by William Burges for his own residence of the 1870's, or, on a more monumental scale and in the context of a commemorative, public monument, in Sir George Gilbert Scott's Albert Memorial, London (1863-72). However, in arriving at this most personally Victorian of all mid-nineteenth-century monuments, we also come to the consideration of a series of official public buildings of great symbolic, as well as stylistic, importance.

NATIONALISM AND IMPERIALISM

In the nineteenth century, two tendencies in the realm of politics made their presence felt upon architecture in unique ways: nationalism and imperialism. With the coming of the French Revolution, and the ultimate and irresistible transformation of this movement into the empire of Bonaparte, official patronage of the arts took on a new character. It is probably no coincidence that the 'Empire Style' was oriented towards an orderly 'reform', one that was directed against the more permissive aspects of the half-bourgeoise, half-aristocratic Rococo of the eighteenth century.

In its Napoleonic formulation, this movement seems to have discouraged even the more personal of the revolutionary classic efforts. Napoleonic Neo-classicism, exception made for the best interiors of Percier and Fontaine, is pedestrian, cautious and self-important. Even more than the republican classicism of Jefferson and Latrobe in the United States or the Teutonic classicism of Klenze or Schinkel, it is bookish and overly learned. Old routiners, like Chalgrin, were called up to design the ironically triumphal Arc de l'Etoile, in a ponderous if fashionable style. It is easy to appreciate how far short the architects of Napoleon's empire fell in their efforts, when one considers the puzzlingly ineffectual Temple de la Gloire, now the church of the Madeleine, begun in 1806, but not completed under Napoleon. The Bourbon restoration that followed brought a reaction that was neither colourful nor a true reversion to the old order of things. Indeed, after a pause, this epoch went to work to complete those very Napoleonic monuments that had been left unfinished by the events of 1815.

931

932

933

931 J. F. Chalgrin.
Arc de Triomphe de l'Etoile, Paris. 1806-36
One of the first of its kind to be built, using the Roman triumphal arch, to commemorate the new imperialism.
This was one of the many monuments erected by Napoleon to the glory of the 'Grande Armée'.

932 Sir George Gilbert Scott.
Albert Memorial, London. 1863-72
Considered by many the perfect example of the High Victorian style. On the death of the Prince Consort, a competition for a memorial was won by Scott who produced this typical work which took nearly ten years to complete.

933 William Butterfield.
All Saints, Margaret Street, London. 1849-59
Butterfield's first important building in which the Gothic Revival reached fever pitch. The highly ornamented interior and structural details overpower. The colours were intense and atonal.

934 Sir Charles Barry and A. W. N. Pugin. Houses of Parliament, London. 1840-65
Barry was responsible for the layout and river façade, both clearly classical in origin. Pugin's work is the Gothic inspired decoration and detailing. The result, a satisfactory fusion of the two main styles in England in the mid-nineteenth century.

934

935 Godde and Lesueur. Hôtel de Ville, Paris. 1837-49
At a time when France was concerned with preserving and restoring its monuments, the Paris Hôtel de Ville was being rebuilt and expanded by two minor architects in an early Renaissance style. It was an attempt to create a national style for better or worse, Burnt down in 1871, the Hôtel de Ville was rebuilt 1874-82 by Ballu and Deperthes.

935

936 L. J. Duc. Palais de Justice, Paris. 1857-68
This western façade shows a certain mannerism appearing in the Second Empire style during its reign in France. Consider the archaicising of the details in conjunction with large segmental-arched window openings.

936

937 Charles Garnier. Opéra, Paris. 1861-74
The most ornate Parisian example in the Second Empire vein when the Baroque element had begun to appear. Here the exaggerated ornateness of the style suits the nature of the building which was to house entertainments of the most splendid and rich type. This is a view of the side.

937

For the rest, France, during the period prior to the Second Empire of Napoleon III, witnessed the rehabilitation of Versailles as a national shrine, as well as the beginnings of the movement directed towards the restoration and preservation of Romanesque and Gothic monuments, which were beginning to fall into decay following the neglect and depredations occasioned by the secularisation of the church during the revolution. This crusade was led by a writer, Prosper Mérimée, and two young architects, Lassus and Viollet-le-Duc. Only one other major accomplishment can be registered in favour of official architecture at this period: the expansion and rebuilding of the Paris Hôtel de Ville (1837-49), by two minor figures, Godde and 935 Lesueur. Here, the use and re-use of the local early Renaissance style of the sixteenth century must be considered of some significance.

Likewise, in England, the stipulation of a 'national' style in the competition for the Houses of Parliament, won by 934 the otherwise Renaissance-inspired Sir Charles Barry in 1836 (construction not begun until 1840), is of particular significance, given the period, although, here, 'national' referred to a late Gothic or Tudor mode. Barry established an association with the dedicated and devout Pugin in the actual execution. The latter was responsible for the small-scaled richness of the exterior detailing, and certain Picturesque touches such as the placing of the towers, while Barry himself determined the regular, indeed academic, lay-out that resulted in the symmetrical river façade, which Pugin is reputed to have castigated as 'all Greek'. Nonetheless, despite this implausible partnership, it is an eminently satisfactory design from nearly every point of view. Above all, the building is not the customary result of compromise, but would seem to contain the best of its two creative minds. Here, the Romantic Classic heritage and the more viable Picturesque tradition are fused in a single work, and provide still another landmark pointing to the stylistic equipoise of the mid-century. To a somewhat lesser degree, the Hôtel de Ville in Paris represents the same balance of forces, since here the choice of an early Renaissance style indicates a desire to find a compromise between classic regularity and Gothic irregularity.

This period of equilibrium did not long outlast the 1840's. Picturesqueness was re-vamped and popularised in a new guise by the Ecclesiologists and the High Victorians, and the Romantic Classic tradition was, at the moment of its demise, reincarnated in that official, eclectic idiom that subsequently became known as the 'Second Empire style', whether in France or abroad. To a degree, this fashion grows out of the sixteenth-century Renaissance used in the extensions of the Hôtel de Ville, and of the seventeenth-century modes that were employed for the sake of consistency in the continuation and completion of the Louvre. The final stages of this vast project were undertaken first by Visconti and subsequently, in 1853, by Hector-Martin Lefuel; the work being completed on the eve of the Franco-Prussian war. The style gained a certain spontaneity by the lavishness with which it made use of the Mansard roof silhouette and bulbous, square-based domes, and by the pneumatic, inflated scale of the masses. If the most ornate Parisian monument in this vein was Charles Garnier's be-

p. 321, 937 loved Opéra of 1861–74, an alternate, more sombre mode is struck by the façade on the Place Dauphine of the Palais de Justice by L.-J. Duc, designed in 1857. Garnier's theatre was so aptly designed to catch the spirit of its destination that the quip 'architecture as frozen Meyerbeer' was perhaps inevitable. On the other hand, there is a certain *froideur* to the various parts of Duc's Palais that can be attributed to the disturbingly manneristic handling of archaicising antique details, in conjunction with the large segmental-arched window openings, and by an aggressively constructive handling of the elements of the domical vault on the interior.

The exportation of this official style to other countries led to its frequent application in bureaucratic programmes.
940 This is the case with the State, War and Navy Building (now the Executive Offices), Washington (1871–75), by Arthur B. Mullet, or with the extraordinarily controversial
938 Foreign Office, London, a more or less imperial design by the habitually loyal Gothic practitioner, Sir George Gilbert Scott. The latter was the distant outgrowth of an 1857 competition, in which designs in the Second Empire as well as Gothic manner were received (as opposed to the 'national' style sought for the Houses of Parliament, twenty years earlier). The machinations of the wily Scott ultimately secured approval of his own Gothic-inspired design, when the results of the competition were set aside. His Gothic scheme was, in turn, disposed of by the whim of a new ministry which prevailed upon the hapless medievalist to produce something more classic. The final result is perfunctory, though its style is no less appropriately official for that reason.

The massive, super-scaled Second Empire style enjoyed noteworthy successes in other major capitals as well. In
939 Vienna, there was Gottfried Semper's Burgtheater of 1874–88; in Brussels, Joseph Poelaert's mammoth Palais de Justice. The latter combined the familiar scale-inflations with a spirit that is nearly Piranesian in dramatic power. In Budapest, Imre Steindl designed and built the massive Parliament (1883–1902), utilising a supercharged and academicised Neo-Gothic up to its pinnacles, beyond which rises a formidable Second Empire dome. By such standards, the rather jumbled sequence of constructions comprising the U.S. Capitol in Washington, with its cast-iron dome, the work of Thomas U. Walter (finished in 1863), is a model of stylistic coherence, even though it was begun in a mode partly late Georgian in derivation, and proceeded through a Classic Revival face-lifting by Latrobe, before attaining its thoroughly imperial scale through Walter's additions of the mid-nineteenth century. Indeed, the very nature of this thumping, oratorical style of European imperialism was its exportability.

Perhaps its happiest offshoot comes in the early twentieth century, with the designs of 1912 for the Viceroy's
941 House, New Delhi, India. Here, the clamorous hyperbole of the mode, in its late nineteenth-century examples, is subdued by the broad, restful horizontals and simplified detailing of Sir Edwin Lutyens's manner—qualities which hark back to the Romantic Classic era of a century before, and which also reflect two noteworthy tendencies that had crystallised in American architecture around 1900: the

938

939

940

938 Sir George Gilbert Scott. Foreign Office, London. 1860–75
Originally Neo-Gothic, Scott was persuaded by the government to substitute the classical or Second Empire style. Originating in France it had by now become the accepted style in Europe for all public and bureaucratic buildings.

939 Gottfried Semper. Burgtheater, Vienna. 1874–88
Typical of the theatres built at this time, all closely allied to Garnier's Paris Opéra. Though Semper kept to the fashionable pattern, he was far more interested in construction and engineering than most architects of the time, and adopted the Renaissance styles because of the soundness of their construction.

940 Arthur B. Mullet. Former State, War and Navy Building (now Executive Offices), Washington, D.C. 1871–75
These bulky forms derived from the new works of Second Empire Paris, but with an important difference — they were more loyal to their seventeenth-century prototypes than were such buildings in France itself. Mullet built post offices and federal office buildings in principal American cities at this time, often resembling this bureaucratic monument.

**941 Sir Edwin Lutyens.
Viceroy's House, New Delhi,
1912**
A later, Anglo-Indian version of the
Imperial style in which the
hyperbole of the nineteenth
century has been simplified.
Although the central dome is
used in the European manner,
its form is based on the Buddhist
stupa, and Lutyens tried to invent
typical 'Indian' detailing to
replace Renaissance decoration.
The horizontal accents of the
design may be compared with
the Prairie Style of Frank Lloyd
Wright, especially as manifested
in the Imperial Hotel, Tokyo.

941

**942 McKim, Mead and White.
Pennsylvania Station,
New York. 1906-10**
The familiar glass-and-metal shed
leading to the trains was fronted
by a great hall in almost literal
imitation of the tepidarium
of the Roman baths of Caracalla.
The station has
recently been demolished.

942

ground-hugging horizontal planes of Frank Lloyd Wright's prairie style and the dignified, almost puritanically sober Neo-classic version of the Imperial mode, popularised by the work of McKim, Mead and White, Carrère and Hastings, and a host of minor followers. As for the new 'official' movement in the United States, it was a branch of the academic Beaux-Arts 'export style' and had received its first stimulus from the so-called White City, the World's Columbian Exposition in Chicago (1893). From this almost carnival-like setting, whose tone was ironically pedantic, the newly purified Imperial style spread. Although applied to a number of different programmes, perhaps its most typical and effective building was Pennsylvania Station, New York, 1906-10, in which the familiar glass-and-metal shed, leading to the trains, is fronted by a great hall in almost literal imitation of the tepidarium of the Roman baths of Caracalla.

Such text-book applications of the Beaux-Arts principles of design involved very carefully studied sequences of symmetrically disposed spaces and masses, sequences in which modifications in scale and size were instituted for reasons of circulation or of change of function. Ultimately such planning techniques derive from Renaissance Italy, but the direct thread of this tradition, in which the plan itself was the generator of design, goes back to another book by J.-N.-L. Durand, the *Précis des Leçons d'Architecture* of 1802-05, the 'Petit Durand', to differentiate it from the 'Grand Durand'. These two-dimensional confections of hypothetical space have had their influence upon the more independent, creative architectural movements of the early twentieth century, as well as upon the more perfunctory Imperial modes.

In this respect, mention must be made of Frank Lloyd Wright's Imperial Hotel, Tokyo, of 1916-22, a building for which the label 'export style' is likewise fitting. This was not the only occasion on which Wright drew heavily upon the methodology of official tradition for the development of an intricate but highly ordered and symmetrical plan. To further complicate the stylistic melange here, Wright has avoided the expression of any kind of *japonisme* in the elevations, employing instead an idiom of his own, which some have seen as an outgrowth of certain indigenous Pre-Columbian American styles. In this context, 'imperialism' takes on a new meaning, one which is very nearly tangential with the idea of international, a word that will become the label for a subsequent *avant-garde* phase of twentieth-century architecture.

TOWARDS A NEW ARCHITECTURE

The creative architecture of 1800 was suspended between two opposing forces: one was Romantic Classicism; the other can be summed up under the heading of Picturesque. A dynamic balance between the two was possible, and an equilibrium between their competing forces was maintained until the 1840's. At that time the Picturesque, having worked as a kind of solvent or acid, eating away at the regular geometric surface of Romantic Classicism for a generation or so, finally transformed itself into a style. This mid-century metamorphosis of the Picturesque into a specific mode of architectural expression is represented

942

943, 944

943

944

945

943, 944 **Frank Lloyd Wright. Imperial Hotel, Tokyo. 1916-22** Exterior and interior. For this hotel in Tokyo, Frank Lloyd Wright drew on official tradition for the development of an intricate, highly ordered, symmetrical plan. Wright's knowledge of engineering was put to good use in this building, which took seven years to complete. In the earthquake of 1923 which hit Tokyo the hotel, which had been built of concrete slabs carried on concrete piles, was one of the few large buildings to survive. Wright avoided any expression of Japanese motifs, employing instead a personal idiom.

945 **Henry Bacon. Lincoln Memorial, Washington, D.C. 1917** A strange harking-back to a classic theme, a modern equivalent to the mausoleum.

946 Philip Webb.
The Red House, Bexley Heath,
Kent, 1859–60
Built for William Morris,
this continues the line of
Picturesque residence designs
but is important for its simple,
rather vernacular, exterior which
contrasts with the flamboyantly
'stylistic' designs of the more
brash Victorian architects.
Its rustic materials
and local bricks, tiles and timber
produce an effect that was
almost revolutionary in its time.

946

947 C. F. A. Voysey.
The Pastures, North Luffenham,
Rutland. 1901
While Voysey's work was
founded on local rural
building traditions, the
smooth surfaces and carefully
considered rhythmic
masses of his typical houses
make him, perhaps unwillingly,
an important precursor of
twentieth-century modernism.

947

by two major fashions. One of these was the colourful High Victorian Gothic, the other the bloated Imperial or Second Empire mode.

The High Victorian style of the 1850's and '60's is in this respect a culmination of the Picturesque tradition, and simultaneously represents a significant aspect of the architectural *avant-garde* at this time, in marked contrast to the conservative rôle played by the Imperial mode. The significance of Butterfield's All Saints, Margaret Street, London (1849-59), a cramped asymmetrical composition, shoved unceremoniously into an unattractive urban district, has already been noted. Just as the 'model' decorative scheme for this small High Church edifice was being completed, a new movement in domestic architecture and interior furnishings was set afoot with the design, by Philip Webb, of the Red House, Bexley Heath (1859-60), a simple, stylistically anonymous house for William Morris, who provided his own interior designs.

946

Here, one reform movement was superimposed directly on top of another. Morris's rôle, not in architecture but in the decorative arts, was an exemplary one for the subsequent generation. In many respects a moralist, like his immediate predecessors, Pugin and Ruskin, he nonetheless seems to have avoided the pessimistic, brooding side of the attitudes represented by these earlier figures. His work avoids the overwrought fervour, characteristic of the mid-century. While he participated in the general denunciation of the 'evils' of industrial civilization, he did not convey so pronounced a sense of bitterness or frustration as did his predecessors. His ideals concerning the return to handicrafts and to medieval patterns of work seem to be a spontaneous escape from contemporary realities. A genteel, unpretentious atmosphere pervades the design of the Red House. In contrast to the strained, over-explicit effects of a determinedly 'high' Victorian church by Butterfield or Street, Webb's design for Morris is the essence of composure, almost of self-effacement.

Morris's Red House occupies a position in the history of mid-nineteenth-century domestic architecture which is similar to that of Paxton's Crystal Palace in the development of ferro-vitreous architecture, or by the Houses of Parliament in the development of an official architecture of state. Whereas such buildings as Butterfield's All Saints or Garnier's Paris Opéra represent an extreme expression of mid-century taste, the less forceful-seeming buildings of Webb and Morris, of Barry and Pugin, and of Paxton manifest broader, less temporal implications. This latter group possesses a greater significance for the continuing evolution of modern architecture, and, consequently, they anticipate its subsequent development in a way that the overtly stylish buildings of the time cannot do.

p. 321

The history of modern architecture must, therefore, be viewed as a dual sequence of events and accomplishments. On the surface, there is the succession of styles and fashions: the various revivals—Greek, Roman, Gothic or exotic—of the early nineteenth century, or the High Victorian and Imperial styles of the mid-century, or later, *Art Nouveau* and the International Style. Each of these styles is a focal point, a recognisable pinnacle which is the result of a specific synthesis of the various elements of the modern

948

949

950

948 Sir Thomas Deane and Benjamin Woodward, with the advice of John Ruskin. University Museum, Oxford. 1855-59
This building, used to house the Natural History collections of the university, was exteriorly one of the most important early High Victorian Gothic buildings. Ruskin made an abortive effort to carve some of the detail himself, and was in any case responsible for the design of the bewildering variety of naturalistic sculpture in capitals, archivolts, etc. The iron-and-glass interior is unexpected in view of his hostility to the use of Industrial Age materials.

949 J. M. Schadde. Antwerp Bourse. 1868–72
One of the most curious buildings of its epoch, contrasting late Gothic masonry arcades with an extremely original naturalistic, virtually proto-Art Nouveau, design for the metal vault. In other works Schadde combined metal and masonry in a single structure in the manner of Viollet-le-Duc's distinctive projects.

950 H. P. Berlage. Amsterdam Bourse. 1898-1902
Brick is combined with metal and glass to give a quasi-Romanesque effect. The walls have been left unplastered; the pillars have no projecting capitals, and the decoration is structural.

tradition. Each, by virtue of being an explicit statement of form and space, tends rapidly to become a source for superficial imitation, rather than a basis for further development and evolution.

Consequently, most of the familiar phases of modernism, in architecture or in painting, have had a surprisingly brief creative existence, and the various successive developments have tended to proceed by fitful reactions and innovations, rather than by patient, consistent evolution. However, behind this sequence of surface developments, there is a variety of themes and ideals that link the various individual efforts together. One of these themes is the Picturesque itself; another is the characteristic kind of symmetrical planning of diversely shaped elements, which is initiated by Romantic Classicism only to become the perfunctory cliché of the academic tradition in the late nineteenth century. Other *leitmotifs* of the modern aesthetic have to do with the traditions of materialism and functionalism, or with the rise of structural technologies in metal and concrete. Each of these has played a specific role in most of the outwardly recognisable stylistic configurations of the last two hundred years.

It is this duality which differentiates the nature, *but not the importance*, of the several achievements of Butterfield, Garnier, Burges and Scott on the one hand, and of Morris, Webb, Telford and Paxton on the other. Both sides have made invaluable contributions to the evolution of the modern movement. However, as opposed to the stylistic fixation of the High Victorian age, which descended to the order of a cliché in slightly more than a decade, the broad movement in domestic architecture, of which the Red House is a part, tends to avoid such specific stylistic commitments and aggressive formal statements which are usually present in ecclesiastical and official architecture. Instead, Morris's Red House belongs to a continuing sequence of Picturesque residence designs, reaching back to the 'Italian villas' and related rustic structures of Nash and Papworth, as well at to Pugin's Grange. The work of Webb and Morris looks forward to the subsequent domestic works of Richard Norman Shaw, H. H. Richardson, C.

947 F. A. Voysey, Frank Lloyd Wright and Charles Rennie Mackintosh. Following the First World War, this line of development contributes to the appearance of the International Style on the continent, and is the progenitor of subsequent tendencies in mid-twentieth-century architecture.

The early domestic architecture of Richard Norman Shaw, dating from the 1860's and 1870's, is more striking in its appearance than the works of most of his contemporaries, and its style represented an additional stimulus for domestic architecture for the remainder of the century. Conventionally called 'Queen Anne', this manner, in reality, begins with the free revival of Elizabethan and Jacobean elements of the sixteenth and early seventeenth centuries, and only gradually comes to embrace certain Wrenian, or pre-Georgian features. Shaw's early Pictur-

951 esque work, like Leyswood, near Withyham, Sussex, 1868, is richer and more lavish in surface texture than the self-effacing Red House, as it has a brick, tile and half-timber exterior, in contrast to the uniform brick of Morris's residence. However, the introduction of such unifying ele-

ments as the grid pattern of half-timbering, or the mullions of the oriel windows provided a matrix in which a progressively simpler and more abstract stylistic treatment could result.

Shaw's work had a marked influence on a parallel late Victorian mode in the United States, which came about through the efforts of Henry Hobson Richardson. Richardson's domestic architecture of the early 1870's reflects not only its ostensible Norman Shaw prototypes, but is likewise an indirect outgrowth of a particularly American type of structurally expressive domestic architecture in wood, known as the Stick Style. This naturalistic, organic mode is a regional offshoot of the Picturesque cottage style of Nash, Papworth and their contemporaries, and was given its characteristic theoretical and formal orientation by Andrew Jackson Downing, a horticulturist and landscape designer, as well as architect. Downing's particular contribution to this line of development, which got under way in the 1840's, was his advocacy of the use of wood as a constructive material in a frank, expressive way. From his

953 earlier, tentative thoughts on domestic architecture, he arrived, in his *The Architecture of the Country House* (1850), at a point of view which might be characterised as Romantic Naturalism. In his statements championing the expression of the nature of materials and of appropriate structure with respect to a wooden cottage, Downing not only echoes Pugin but anticipates the broader statements by Viollet-le-Duc on this subject. Downing's ideas are reflected in the houses of his contemporaries, like John Notman, A. J. Davis and Calvert Vaux, and they also

952 influenced the mid-century work of such foreign-trained and less Picturesquely inclined American architects as Richard Morris Hunt and Leopold Eidlitz. The latter, an architect of German birth and education, provided, in the Willoughby House, Newport, R. I. (1854), an elaborate

954 example of the Downingesque mode.

From this engagingly half-sophisticated aesthetic of Downing and his followers, the line of development jumps to the work of Richardson, which grows in part out of an instinctive, perhaps even unconscious, understanding of this genre. But for the rest, Richardson, perhaps the most gifted architect of the entire century, owes his initial development to many other facets of the English and continental tradition, both Picturesque and academic, domestic and Imperial. His first masterpiece, the Watts Sherman

955 House, Newport, R. I. (1874), is heavily indebted to the early manner of Richard Norman Shaw. Here, a certain ruggedness of massing, with long sloping roof diagonals, is enriched by a small-scaled intricacy of surface texture, in which rough masonry, half-timbering and a variety of differently shaped wood shingles produce an active, faintly impressionistic effect. Richardson obtained other and more dramatic successes in his monumental public works, and in his later houses this monumentality comes through in a broad, relaxed amplitude in the masses and the more regularised surfaces of shingle, which gave rise to the term Shingle Style.

Richardson's attention to surface qualities on his exteriors is rivalled for sensitivity only in the earlier work of William Butterfield, but with an extraordinary difference

951

952

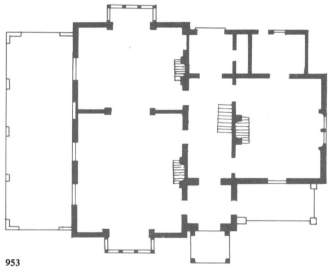

953

954

955

951 Norman Shaw. Leyswood, near Withyham, Sussex. 1868
A fine example of the 'Queen Anne' of Shaw. His work introduced a variety of new elements into domestic architecture, which were to reappear in various guises for the rest of the century, for instance here, the grid pattern of half-timbering and mullions of oriel windows.

952 Alexander Jackson Davis. Henry Delamater House, Rhinebeck, New York. 1844
An example of the American offshoot of the Picturesque cottage style of Nash and Papworth and their contemporaries. The vertical board siding of this 'board and batten' house expresses the nature of the material and the technique of construction.

953 Andrew Jackson Downing. Plan of a board and batten cottage. 1842
Downing was the chief advocate of the frank use of wood construction seen in Davis's Delamater House.

954 Leopold Eidlitz. Willoughby House, Newport, Rhode Island. 1854
The cottage style became prevalent in America. It is reflected here in the work of the foreign-trained and less Picturesquely inclined Eidlitz, who produced a melange of the Downingesque Romantic rational stick style.

955 Henry Hobson Richardson. Watts Sherman House, Newport, Rhode Island. 1874
In this building Richardson was strongly influenced by the early houses of Norman Shaw. Many other architects also built shingle-covered houses in the early Shaw manner.

**956 Stanford White.
Kingscote dining room,
Newport, Rhode Island. c. 1880**
Kingscote, in Newport, R. I.,
was built by Richard Upjohn in
the early sixties as a 'Tudor'
house at a time when
the Picturesque dominated much
of domestic architecture. Some
twenty years later, White
added the dining room with
much of the orientalising that
went into his work.

956

**957 Henry Hobson Richardson.
Ames Gate Lodge,
North Easton,
Massachusetts. 1881**
An example of Richardson's
transmutation of the styles of
Nash and Downing. An inspired
statement of the theme of
regional particularism.

957

**958 Frank Furness.
Provident Life and Trust
Building, Philadelphia. 1879**
An American architect of
a violently expressive,
exaggeratedly Victorian
sensibility, Furness may have
been influenced by
certain projects of Viollet-le-Duc.
Significantly, Louis Sullivan
was much attracted to Furness's
work and briefly held a
position in his office.
While Sullivan's own personal
style of ornament is far
removed from the strident,
overscaled shapes of Furness,
his penchant for novelty
and originality must stem
in part from this
unlikely source.
The building illustrated
here has been demolished.

958

of temperament, expression and scale. The smooth, sleek,
intricately detailed and brilliantly coloured tile-and-brick
planes of Butterfield are replaced in Richardson's characteristic idiom by sombre hues, broad, large-scaled elements, with the various naturalistic tonalities enhanced by
a rich, sculpturesque texture. In this vocabulary Richardson
drew together many of the tendencies of the High Victorian and of the Imperial styles, and with a simple, direct
power of control and organisation produced a sponta-
neously monumental architecture in such buildings as the
Allegheny Court House and Jail, Pittsburgh (1884–88), or
in the Crane Memorial Library, Quincy, Massachusetts
(1880–83). This synthesis is not achieved through the formulation of an arbitrary style, or by arriving at a compromise between opposites, but by rising above the parochial differences of the various fashions of the day and
by confronting each building as a unique design problem.

This imperturbable detachment does not really separate
Richardson's individual buildings from the everyday styles
of the 1870's and 1880's. Instead, he established his unique
superiority over his contemporaries, in much the same
way that Sir John Soane had some seventy-five years earlier: by using the common elements of the current aesthetic in a way which suggests the continued questioning and
searching for ever-different yet familiar and understandable
resolutions to the functional and style problems of a specific design. The transcendental achievements that were
possible when an architect of Richardson's powers came
on the scene can be appreciated best in the Ames Gate   957
Lodge of 1880, and the Marshall Field Warehouse, Chicago   959
(1885–87). The former is an inspired statement of the theme
of regional particularism, and of Romantic Naturalism, so
far as the relation of the form to the chosen material is
concerned; it is also an extraordinary monumentalisation
of the cottage styles of Nash and Downing. The latter is
an equally sombre, yet refined, distillation of the utilitarian tradition that has its origins in the work of Telford.
Curiously, Richardson, in his brief career (he died, aged
forty-eight, in 1886), subsumes much of the past, as well
as the present, of the latter nineteenth century, without
exhausting its possibilities and, more important, without
establishing a fixed static type that would be inimical
to further development. Paradoxically, it was out of Richardson's characteristic masonry architecture that the aesthetic of the steel-frame skyscraper emerged in the years
immediately following his death. The vitality of his contribution stems least of all from the closed, concise appearance of his individual buildings, and more from their
suggestive, provocative, indeed 'unfinished' qualities. The
breadth and largeness of scale that is characteristic of even
his domestic work makes him the heir of Romantic Classicism, as represented by Boullée and Ledoux, while at the
same time he provides a spectacular fulfilment for that
aspect of mid-nineteenth-century taste that had brought
forth the work of Garnier and Poelaert. And, finally,
Richardson's architecture fulfils the promise of the various medieval revivals, extending from Wyatt to Norman Shaw.

The lines of descent issuing from the work of Richardson
are two in number: the less fertile of the two leads into

the early work of McKim, Mead and White, and, by an evolutionary process, further and further away from the dynamic equilibrium between order and freedom that sparked the best of the master's work. The final result of this path was a return to a purely academic, Imperial point of view, albeit an academic style that, in works like Pennsylvania Station, has been purged of many of its decorative accretions, and can be re-appreciated for some of its Neo-Romantic Classic qualities. If this way leads to a sparking of what might be called the anti-modern tradition of recent architecture, then the other line of development issuing from Richardson is, during the last decade of the nineteenth century, one of the most creative of all movements. It is from here that the Chicago school of skyscraper design, from Burnham and Root to Adler and Sullivan, bursts out of mere local importance, and, equally, the domestic architecture of the prairie style, which is all but dominated by Frank Lloyd Wright, comes to life largely as a consequence of Richardson and his followers.

The European counterpart to these capital developments from the United States, which suddenly blossomed into international architectural prominence in the last third of the nineteenth century, goes under the name of *Art Nouveau*. A radical movement that was paradoxically related to the academic and medievalising architecture of the 1870's and 1880's, its chic, novel, affectedly 'modernistic' effects were made possible by a coy blending of these historicising modes with either the new expressive potentialities of metal technology, or with the more or less arbitrary forms that could be derived either literally or by principle from the revolutionary movements in painting, mostly inaugurated in the 1880's, and known collectively under the heading of Post-Impressionism. But at least a part of the ideology, if not of the outward forms, of *Art Nouveau* can be traced to the same source from which stems a part of the Anglo-American domestic tradition of Webb, Shaw, Richardson and Wright—namely to the writings of William Morris and of John Ruskin. Their outspoken appeals against the insensitivity of much of the modern visual spectacle struck a responsive chord in the European architects of the *fin de siècle*: Van de Velde, Horta, Berlage, Gaudí and probably Guimard. This is much the same group who also came under the spell of the structural aesthetic of Viollet-le-Duc, whose ideas had, perhaps, been familiar to the Paris-educated Richardson, and in any event were much admired by his successors, McKim and Wright.

Candour was, of course, the momentary virtue of Chicago commercial architecture in the late 1880's and early 1890's, although, sadly, the pattern swiftly changed around 1900, and the influence of the persistent Imperial style made itself felt in the design of skyscrapers. Before that moment, however, two buildings by Burnham and Root, the Monadnock Building, the last significant non-steel-frame skyscraper (1891), and the totally different, skeletal Reliance Building (1890), suggest the degree to which the nature of the material and constructive system could determine, and not just 'influence', the form of the building. However, it is in the best of Sullivan's office buildings, the Guaranty Building, Buffalo (1894), and the Carson, Pirie and Scott's store, Chicago (1899, with subsequent ad-

960

p. 322
62-964
961

959 Henry Hobson Richardson. Marshall Field Warehouse, Chicago. 1885-87
A utilitarian work – stark, simple, and of great dignity.
Eclectic in that its sources are both Romanesque and Renaissance, it rises far beyond the limits of ordinary revival architecture.
The building has been demolished.

959

960 Burnham and Root. Reliance Building, Chicago. 1890-95
Another famous early example of the construction determining the form of the building.
The base of this metal-framed building is stone-faced; the rest glass and white tile.
Decoration is used solely to underline the horizontality of the windows.

960

961 Louis Sullivan. Carson, Pirie and Scott's store, Chicago. 1899
Recognisably in the style of today.
The metal skeleton imposes the grid-like façades; its apertures become windows which let in the maximum light.
The tower at the corner was included at the owner's insistence.

961

**962 Louis Sullivan.
Guaranty Building, Buffalo.
1894**
Buildings like these, which were
offices, were the first
to demonstrate the potentialities of
metal-frame construction.

962

**963, 964 Guaranty Building,
Buffalo. 1894**
Details of ground storey.
Sullivan has ingeniously contrived
to give the piers of the
building an appearance of free-
standing columns by bending
back the shop windows at the top.
The piers and the rather
delicate moulding which faces
the shafts around the shop
windows are in terra cotta.
These exhibit certain
characteristics of Art Nouveau.

963

964

ditions), to name but two of his successes, that the science
of skyscraper production becomes an instinctive art.

The same spirit of invention and of sensitive accommodation to the problems of the modern house is integral to
the domestic work of Sullivan's pupil, Frank Lloyd Wright.
Wright's domestic architecture is the mid-western outgrowth of the eastern Richardsonian tradition as filtered
down in the work of the 1880's, i.e. McKim's Appleton
House, Lenox, Massachusetts (1883-84), Stanford White's
Tiffany House, New York (1882-83), or Bruce Price's Van   965
Buren House, Tuxedo, New York (1885-86). Wright's
first truly independent effort, the Winslow House, River
Forest, Illinois (1893; ironically, the year of the Columbian Exhibition), is not just an isolated juvenile effort, but
an inaugural work which, save for a certain lingering
Sullivanesque character to the general lay-out, would be
a sudden and convincing personal masterpiece. However,
a period of incubation—about five or six years—was necessary before Wright could arrive at his own unique
manner in the decade immediately following 1900, in a
series of houses that challenge and finally surpass the qual-
itative and suggestive achievement of Richardson a quar-
ter-century before.

From a stylistic point of view, the history of twentieth-
century architecture begins some years before the turn of
the century, at the moment at which the wilfully progressive
Art Nouveau consciously endeavours to establish a new
style, which, at least in outward appearance, breaks with
the historicism of the recent past. The epoch '1900' represents the beginning of a period of realisation and climax after more than a century of preparation. Significantly, the first experiments in *Art Nouveau* and related
manners come about in provincial capitals that are relatively isolated from the old centres of Paris and London.
Hence, there is Victor Horta's Tassel House (1892-93), in
the former Rue de Turin, Brussels, as well as his more
extensive Maison du Peuple (1897-99), in the same city;   967
Olbrich's Sezession gallery, Vienna (1897); Mackintosh's   969
Glasgow art school of 1897-1909; and Gaudí's numerous   970
buildings in Barcelona, culminating, for the purposes of   973-97
Art Nouveau, in the Casa Milá of 1905. In particular,   971
Horta's works, along with the smart, fashionable Parisian
works of Hector Guimard, express a deliberately ambiguous, partly rationalised, partly whimsical architectonic
poetry, in which elements of technology, naturalism, functionalism, symbolism and even of liberal social consciousness
are blended in a heady, unstable mixture. Further uniting
these varied works is a cultivated air of decadence.

In contrast to this volatile, neurotic fashion, a second,
new style—in some ways a counter *Art Nouveau* style—
comes to the fore within a decade. It preserves much of
the preciousness and even the decadent air, but it substi-
tutes a more rectilinear, relatively abstract and rational
design vocabulary for the curvilinear exuberance of the
previous decade. This comparative sobriety in the architecture of the period, which reaches its culmination around
1910, forms, thus, the transition from the naturalistic, foliate art of the '90's to the severe, almost monastic, cubic
geometry that emerges after 1918 and swiftly coalesces
into the International style. The two most representative

XLVI

XLVII

XLVIII

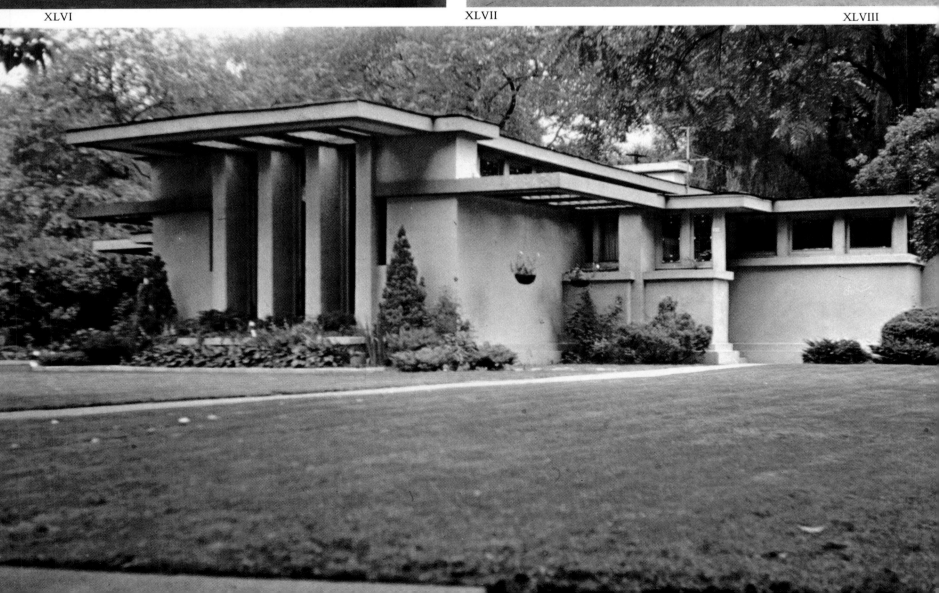

965

965 McKim, Mead and White.
Tiffany House,
New York. 1882-83
A type of luxurious American
town house that owed a debt
both to Norman Shaw and
Richardson. The simple
fenestration and blank surfaces
of brick and stone
tended to obscure
the historicising character
of the overall Picturesque design.
The building has
now been demolished.

966

966 R. M. Hunt.
'The Breakers'
Newport, Rhode Island. c. 1870
Europe's obsession with the
historical styles is paralleled here
in the American idea
of a Renaissance palazzo adapted
to a private house.

XLVI *Adler and Sullivan: Guaranty Building, Buffalo* XLVII *Wright: Walter Gale House, Oak Park, Illinois*

XLVIII *Wright: Avery Coonley Play House, Riverside, Illinois*

**967 Victor Horta.
Maison du Peuple, Brussels.
1897-99**
Built at the same time as Berlage's
Stock Exchange in Amsterdam
(see 950), this is far more advanced
in its use of glass and iron.
They fill the entire façade.

967

**968 Otto Wagner.
Karlsplatz subway station,
Vienna. 1894**
The ornamental ironwork and
hemispherical roof are a
prolongation of nineteenth-century
characteristics, but the
wall, of thin marble slabs, points
towards the new architecture.
Wagner designed the whole of the
Vienna subway.

968

**969 Joseph Olbrich.
Sezession gallery, Vienna. 1897**
Olbrich was, like Joseph Hoffmann,
a disciple of Otto Wagner's
in Vienna.
This Austrian school concerned
itself with crafts as well as
architecture, so that Art
Nouveau decoration in some of
its buildings tends to become
treated as a separate consideration.

969

**970 C. R. Mackintosh.
Glasgow Art School,
North Wing. 1907-09**
Mackintosh designed buildings
remarkably ahead of his time, but
had little influence in his own
country. In his work Art
Nouveau is the architectural form,
and is not used only as applied
decoration.

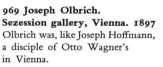

970

buildings of this counter *Art Nouveau* epoch—outside of
the buildings of Wright's early maturity—are Joseph Hoffmann's Stoclet House, Brussels (1905-11), and Olbrich's   972
Exhibition Hall and Wedding Tower at the Art Colony,   976
Darmstadt (1907).

Like so many of the important buildings of the nineteenth century, these first masterpieces of the twentieth
century exhibit an individual and particularised balance
between the demands of the academic-classic tradition and
the permissiveness of the Picturesque point of view. The
Stoclet House possesses a remarkable degree of elegant
surface finish both inside and out (there are intriguing
mosaics by Gustav Klimt, in the dining room, for example), and the compact asymmetry of the street façade is
counterbalanced by the brilliantly original, yet symmetrical, massing of the garden side. In contrast to the near-
repression of Picturesque elements in Hoffmann's design,
Olbrich's Exhibition Hall is free and syncopated in its
massing, although it undertakes a more specific, less 'decadent' utilisation of familiar historical motifs (the corner
loggia, for instance). In its loose, discursive stringing-
together of various elements, it is more frankly eclectic
and derivative than Hoffmann's more aristocratically conceived mansion.

The same air of detachment and originality, coupled
with a certain Romantic, perhaps pseudo-eclectic quality
in minor detailing, comes to the fore in the characteristic industrial buildings of this period—the monuments of the
first machine age. Peter Behrens's several shops and works
for the A. E. G. in Berlin, and his subsequent gas works
in Frankfurt-am-Main (1912), are indicative of yet an-   977
other tension latent in this early twentieth-century style:
that between a wish to reveal factory-inspired forms in
their basic and essential shape, and an irresistible desire to
touch up these forms, to give them an added accent of
rhythm or of scale that they might otherwise lack if they
had not been 'designed'. Consonant with this tendency is
a series of quasi-conventional buildings: Berlage's Bourse,   950
Amsterdam, 1898-1902; Paul Bonatz's railroad station in
Stuttgart (begun 1911); and Hans Poelzig's chemical fac-   978
tory in Luban, likewise of 1911. All these buildings would
seem to be perpetuating a part of the late nineteenth-
century tradition that was so well exemplified by Richardson's heroic accomplishment in the United States, though
there is no certain evidence to link any of these works
directly with any building by the earlier architect.

Another innovation at this time is concerned with the
development of architecture in reinforced concrete. The
crucial figure in this field is the Parisian architect-builder,
Auguste Perret, whose flats in the rue Franklin, Paris,
1903, are a major landmark in urban residential architecture, but of a type that was not followed up, except in
the architect's own work, either before or after the First
World War. More emphatic spatial effects were created
in the concrete ribs of Anatole de Baudot's St Jean-de-
Montmartre, Paris (1894-1904), whose effect is faintly, but
not specifically, Neo-Gothic, or in the spiritual, cathe-
dral-like space of Eugène Freyssinnet's Orly hangars of
1916, whose huge span is accomplished in a great parabolic arch, but without the faintest reference to any style

971

972

973

974

975

**971 Antoni Gaudí.
Casa Milá, Barcelona. 1905**
Known in Barcelona as the
'quarry', an apt description
of Gaudí's cut-stone building which
looks as though it were made
of clay.
The whole plan is executed in
curves round two kidney-shaped
courtyards.

**972 Joseph Hoffmann.
Stoclet House, Brussels. 1905–11**
The naturalistic, foliate
Art Nouveau of the nineties
emerges into more severe forms.
The flat surfaces of this
banker's house are made of white
marble slabs, treated rather
like framed pictures.

**973–975 Antoni Gaudí.
Sagrada Familia,
Barcelona. Begun 1884**
Art Nouveau has the strangest
effect of all when used in
church architecture. One
of the many buildings of this
kind built by Gaudí in Barcelona;
it was begun in 1884.
and work has been going on ever
since. It remains uncompleted.
The four striking towers
were not completed until after
Gaudí's death.
The building is perhaps the most
extraordinary church to have
been conceived
in the past hundred years.
It goes beyond any influence
which might have been
forthcoming from the international
Art Nouveau movement,
and actually foreshadows
the Expressionist movement in
twentieth-century architecture.

**976 Joseph Olbrich.
Exhibition Hall,
Darmstadt. 1907**
Olbrich, an Austrian, was invited
to Darmstadt by the Grand
Duke in 1899, and he worked
there until his death in 1908,
This exhibition hall, a rather plain
and formal building, has a
classical appearance which is
something of an exercise for the
architect in a different style.

976

**977 Peter Behrens.
Frankfurt Gas Works. 1912**
The new forms
of buildings which were emerging
as a result of industrialisation
began to be seen in terms
of architectonic shape. Behrens's
industrial and factory
buildings, like Freysinnet's Orly
hangars, gave architecture
a new dimension.

977

**978 Hans Poelzig.
Chemical Factory, Luban. 1911**
This building is simply
a functional shell to house
a chemical process.
The stepped roof follows through
the lines of filter beds
from which solutions descend.
There is a distant similarity
between this type of building
and the early English mills
and warehouses, which arose
out of closely related architectural
problems.

978

of the past. In effect these colossi represent a level of creative initiative in concrete architecture on a par with Paxton's iron Crystal Palace of 1851 or Eiffel's steel tower for the Paris Exposition of 1889.

All these buildings, which follow in the wake of *Art Nouveau* in Europe during the first decade and a half of the twentieth century, are in one way or another reflections of the modernist aesthetic, but as a group they are not homogeneous. A new art was very much in the air; in Paris, Munich, and other cities, a new painting was at that very moment in the process of becoming an historic fact with the emergence of Fauvism, Cubism, Futurism, Die Brücke, and Der Blaue Reiter. Matisse, Picasso, Klee, Kandinsky, Marcel Duchamp and Piet Mondrian were already painters to be reckoned with on the basis of their work before 1914. Yet no European architect of this period, which witnessed the initial wave of twentieth-century painting, was able to approximate in his own work the cohesive level of invention that had been attained by the painters. In contrast to this creativity, architecture was not just in flux, it was in a period of ebb and uncertainty; it lacked a sense of positive, objective purpose, to judge either by the buildings themselves, or by the theoretical utterances of the period, numerous and perceptive as they were.

The sole, heroic exception to this condition was the architecture of Frank Lloyd Wright as it evolved over the period 1900-09 in the expanding suburbs around Chicago. p. 322 Alone among architectural designers of the period, Wright's style had a degree of intellectual and perceptual cohesiveness that equalled that of the contemporary Parisian and central European painters. Despite the clarity and definitive precision of many of Wright's formulations in domestic architecture at this epoch—despite their seemingly perfect, closed finality, which gives them at once a memorable, indelible character that no work by Olbrich, Hoffmann or Behrens possesses—these buildings, published by the Wasmuth firm in Berlin, in widely circulated monographs in 1910 and 1911, sparked the next stage in the development of European architecture after the end of the First World War. Then, after a curious interlude in Wright's own development, they became both the direct and indirect source for his ultimate manner, his 'late style' of the period from the mid-1930's to his death in 1959. It is next to impossible to select from the numerous major designs by Wright, without in one way or another introducing a distortion. However, the plans and exteriors of two houses, that for Ward Willitts, Highland Park, Illinois 979, 980 (1902), and that for Robert Evans, Chicago (1908), indi- 982 cate in very different ways the polar tensions between the regular and irregular, the academic and the Picturesque, and the intricate yet precise way in which Wright has brought about their reconciliation. In the Evans House, the classic cube has been exploded by the projections of porch and *porte-cochère*; in the Willitts House, the same surging flow of interior space bursts outward from a central core of fireplaces around which the living areas have been arranged in a most original fashion. These designs are characterised by their horizontality, which gives them the appearance of hugging, as well as echoing, the flat prairie sites; but, at the same time, these houses 'float' on the surface of the ground and are not rooted below the surface with deeply excavated cellars. These tendencies are even more dramatically expressed in the outward-flung horizontals of terrace and veranda in the small yet implicitly monumental Robie House, Chicago (1909).

The particular appropriateness of Wright's prairie style in domestic architecture is indicated by the fact that when confronted with the problem of a modern office in the design of the Larkin Building in Buffalo (1904), he came up with a form that was more solid, more aggressively vertical and urban in scale. At the same time, the Larkin Building was a novelty in principle as well as in exterior appearance. In lay-out, all the offices on five floors were tied together through a central light-well, so that instead of compartmentation, there was an easy flow of space throughout. As commercial architecture, the whole interior ensemble possessed a dignity and quality that is rarely achieved even in purely official or ceremonial buildings. It marked a particular level of accomplishment in the monumental architecture of the early twentieth century, in which the synthesised tradition established by Richardson was reconstituted in the idiomatic style of his greatest successor, at a time when analogous efforts were being made in Europe by Berlage, Behrens and Poelzig.

There are many parallels between the work of Europe and America in the years around 1900. In England, the movement in domestic architecture which traced its origins back to the generation of Nash was then reaching a new degree of independence and originality in the houses of Voysey and Mackintosh, as well as an Edwardian sumptuousness in the similarly inclined work of Sir Edwin Lutyens. All these men designed works which, in a bland, less forceful way, present re-interpretations of the same Picturesque principles that were being more emphatically adapted and transformed by Wright.

Unlike the work of Wright, which enjoyed a currency among the post-1910 continental *avant-garde*, that of these English architects was rapidly forgotten. The level of creativity in their houses fell off before the first decade of the twentieth century was over, and unlike the subsequent recoveries in the checkered career of Wright, there was no significant continuation of this modern tradition in English architecture.

On the other hand, there were sporadic achievements on the part of early twentieth-century American architects, who had been touched by Wright's extraordinary achievement, or by the same grouping of influences that had initiated it in the first place. Notable in this respect are Bernard Maybeck's Christian Science Church, Berkeley, California (1910); the Bradley House, Woods Hole, Massachusetts, of Purcell and Elmslie (1911); or, somewhat later, the Lovell House, Newport Beach, California (1926), by R. M. Schindler, a Viennese-trained architect, who had been an assistant of Frank Lloyd Wright. Wright's own Ennis House, Los Angeles (1923), while striking out in a new direction from the typical prairie style dwelling of his earlier period, also represents a creative continuation of the initial achievement of the first decade of the century.

981

983

984
985

986

979

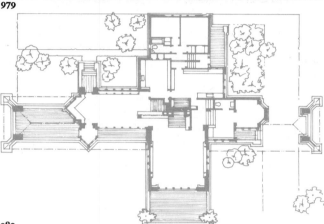

980

981

982

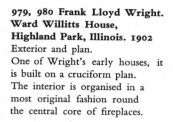

979, 980 Frank Lloyd Wright. Ward Willitts House, Highland Park, Illinois. 1902 Exterior and plan. One of Wright's early houses, it is built on a cruciform plan. The interior is organised in a most original fashion round the central core of fireplaces.

981 Frank Lloyd Wright. Robie House, Chicago. 1909 A town villa in Chicago; a more sophisticated version of Wright's ground-hugging prairie house. The outward-flung horizontals of terrace and verandah give a floating effect. The interplay of space with solid has been refined and made more complicated.

982 Frank Lloyd Wright. Evans House, Chicago. 1908 Wright was concerned with breaking down the cube conception of the house. With projecting eaves or terraces he relates his solids to the space around them. He has done this here with the porch and porte-cochère.

**983 Frank Lloyd Wright.
Larkin Building, Buffalo. 1904**
Wright's most important early
monumental or commercial
effort was an office building
with the various floors built
around a central 'nave' or
light-well, illuminated from
above by a skylight. Wright
himself designed the then novel
metal furnishings and fixtures as
an integrated part of the interior
ensemble. The building exerted
considerable influence upon
European architects, and was
visited by Berlage, architect of the
Amsterdam Bourse, in 1911.

983

**984 Bernard Maybeck.
Christian Science Church,
Berkeley, California. 1910**
This curious, still emphatically
eclectic design presents a complex
of interlocking squares that
rivals even the ingenuity of Frank
Lloyd Wright.
The timber detailing of the interior
conceals a concrete structure.

984

**985 Purcell and Elmslie.
Bradley House, Woods
Hole, Massachusetts. 1911**
Showing the influence of Frank
Lloyd Wright.
The new domestic architecture in
America was a far stronger
growth than its English
contemporary.

985

**986 R. M. Schindler,
Lovell House, Newport Beach,
California. 1926**
An example of the influence of
Frank Lloyd Wright
and of the new post World
War I architecture in
Europe. Schindler was a Viennese-
trained architect who had been
an assistant of Wright.

986

THE CLASSIC MOMENT IN MODERN ARCHITECTURE

In spite of these frequently vital American designs the
main line of architectural development re-established its
centre of gravity in Europe during the decade of 1910-20.
Activities in central Europe definitely outshone those elsewhere for a period of almost twenty years, which over-
laps the upheaval of the First World War, and this creative spurt continues in the work of Gropius, Mies van der
Rohe and others, down until the Nazi catastrophe of 1933.
Perhaps the crucial building at the beginning of this development is Gropius's Administrative Building and Hall   987
of Machinery, designed in collaboration with Adolf Meyer,
for the Deutsche Werkbund exhibition at Cologne in 1914.
Here the sensibly Romantic quality of so much of Behrens's
(Gropius's master) industrial work is given a more abstract
touch, with an unusually generous use of glass walls on
the façade. At the same time this important building
had a horizontality, as well as an emphasised symmetry
in its elevation, which is both general and specific in its
derivation from the recently published drawings of Wright.

The architectural history of the post-war period, the
1920's, has been commonly written as an account of the
International style. This familiar phrase is the one habitually used to describe the characteristically rational geometry of the early work of Gropius, Mies, J. J. P. Oud, Le
Corbusier, André Lurçat and their followers. However,
there is an alternate, relatively subjective and Romantic
trend in the 1920's, identified by the word Expressionism.
Under this banner, one finds temperaments as diverse as   988
Erich Mendelsohn, Hans Poelzig and Otto Bartning. The   989
distinction between the rational, cubic International style
and the non-geometric free forms of Expressionism is confused by the early works of architects like Mies van der
Rohe and Gropius, of the period roughly from 1918 to
1922, which pre-date the emergence of the International
style, and which show a manifestly Romantic, Expressionist character in their curving, irregular forms.

In contrast to this wave of irrational non-geometric shapes
is the appearance, in 1917, of the *De Stijl* movement in
Holland, the result of a banding together of painters (Mondrian), architects (Oud), designers (Rietveld), under the   990
driving force of an artist-writer-polemicist, Theo van
Doesburg. The early projects of Oud, notably his Purme-
rend factory project of 1919, provide an interlocking composition of horizontal and vertical slab-like elements on the
façade, which is most certainly an outgrowth of a consideration of Wright's forms, but with the more abstract pictorial compositions of Mondrian equally in mind. Along
with this synthesis of two further aspects of early twentieth-
century visual invention, there are the partly independent
achievements of Dudok in Hilversum (Holland), and in the
even more block-like cubic (not Cubist) geometricisms of
Djo Bourgeois in Brussels and of the better-known Robert
Mallet-Stevens in Paris. The latter's personal variant of the
new idiom can best be appreciated in the Noailles Villa at
Hyères (1924), a stark, Picturesque pile of forms that, by
its scale, merits comparison with the similar but more refined composition of Hoffmann's Stoclet House, begun two
decades before. In their similarities and differences, these

two luxurious houses illustrate both the continuity, as well as the stylistic evolution of European architecture. The culmination of this intricate cubic geometry comes in the architectural masterpiece of the *De Stijl* movement, Gerrit Rietveld's Schroeder House, Utrecht (1924), where the horizontal and vertically situated slab-like elements offer a precarious, tenuously balanced composition of seemingly weightless planes and surfaces.

On a monumental scale, the new spatial, constructive and functional aesthetic of the International style, bringing together innumerable strands of the modernist tradition, reaches a climax in Walter Gropius's Dessau Bauhaus (1925-26), and in Brinkman and van der Vlugt's van Nelle Factory in Rotterdam (1927-28), the latter presumably designed by Mart Stam. Once vaunted as examples of functional buildings, these works of the 1920's now appear much more significant as instances of the realisation of a new architectural style. It was not, certainly, the most pervasive of the twentieth century, but it was undoubtedly the one in which the invention of unheralded concepts that transcend the normal and customary ideas concerning the individual rôles of form and space, of 'interior' and 'exterior', are demonstrated in a concise, indeed spectacular, fashion. The ultimate, transcendental expressions of this aesthetic of weightless, hovering, screen-like forms occurs in Mies van der Rohe's Barcelona Pavilion of 1929 and in Le Corbusier's Villa Savoye, designed in the same year. Mies's lavishly executed marble-and-glass structure is a refined and distilled design which is the outgrowth of many interests and tendencies. In the first instance it culminates a spatial and planimetric type that was first broached in Wright's prairie houses, nearly thirty years before. At the same time, there is a cool, intellectually detached character to the detailing of the Barcelona Pavilion which owes something to the abstract art and architecture of *De Stijl* and, further back, to the scholarly Neo-classicism of Karl Friedrich Schinkel, more than a century before.

As for Le Corbusier's Villa Savoye, it is at once more simple and more complex as a unique statement of the new style. Full of allusions to Hellenic architecture and planning in the placing of a clean, regular form upon regularly spaced, thin steel columns, thus dramatically liberating the form from the ground, it nonetheless reveals these historical contacts through inversions, paradoxes and conceits. For instance, the Villa Savoye gains its isolated, haughty detachment through the use of an apparent void, whereas an analogous effect is produced in a Doric temple through the use of a massive stylobate. The uniform envelope of the Corbusian villa encloses a complex space which includes a generous terrace or hanging garden open to the sky, as well as conventionally roofed living areas, whereas the classical temple with its regular peripteral colonnade, encloses a simple, uniform and almost invariably roofed *cella*. In such compositional and spatial practices, the familiar architectonic conceptions of mass, load and support are either negated or perversely modified. These incisive and forthright contradictions are characteristic of the International style idiom.

This precarious, elastic balance of diverse elements in a highly charged stylistic mixture could not remain long in a stable synthesis. Only a very limited number of architects

987

988

989

990

987 **Walter Gropius. Deutsche Werkbund Exhibition, Cologne. 1914**
Gropius's Administrative Building was quite symmetrical.
The influence of Frank Lloyd Wright shows in the projecting slab roofs of the raised corners.

988 **Erich Mendelsohn. Schocken Store, Chemnitz, Germany. 1928**
Mendelsohn designed other Schocken Stores in Germany of steel and glass. Their bold sweeping curves follow the bend of the streets. There is a strong element of wilful self-expression.

989 **Hans Poelzig. Schauspielhaus, Berlin. 1919**
Poelzig was one of the leading Expressionist architects after the First World War.
His redesigning of this Berlin theatre is a perfect and extreme expression of the movement. The ceiling is a huge stalactite dome which hovers over the circular stage.

990 **J. J. P. Oud. Kiefhoek Church, Rotterdam. 1928-30**
A product of the De Stijl movement in Holland of which Oud was a member. The basis of De Stijl lay in the strictly rectilinear geometry which is seen in the paintings of Mondrian. Like the painters of the movement the architects used strong vertical and horizontal lines coupled with white, black, grey and the three primary colours. They fully exploited schemes of geometrical proportion to regulate and control all the elements in the building.

991, 992

993-995
997

999
000, 1001
1003

**991, 992 Gerrit Rietveld.
House at Utrecht. 1924**
Two views
showing similar characteristics
to Oud's work.
The De Stijl movement was
responsible for much of the
extensive town planning and
residential building in Dutch towns
during the twenties.
This important house,
though small, is the first
to condense the elements
of modern plane architecture.

991   992

**993-995 Walter Gropius.
Bauhaus, Dessau. 1926**
Plans and exterior.
The skeleton is of ferroconcrete.
The glass-curtain walling
folds itself round the building
with no outward sign of support;
the white bands are
merely decorative strips which
emphasise the horizontality
and floating air of the building.
The plan reveals a series
of interrelated cubes reaching
over the ground,
suggesting movement in space,
which has been seized and held.
The Bauhaus was
the first large building which so
completely crystallised
the new space conception.

993 Ground plan

994 First floor

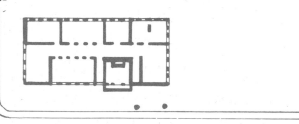 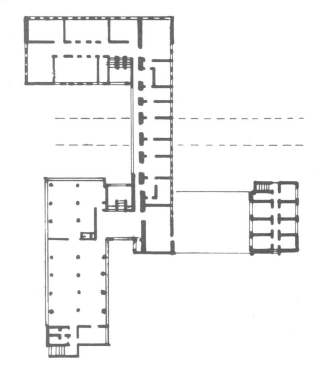

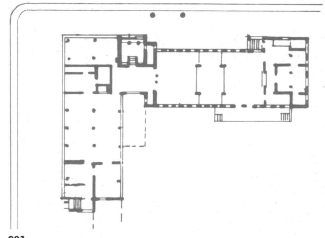

993   994

995

participated in the more rarefied achievements of the new style, with its unique manipulation of space and form, and these had indeed so far extended themselves beyond a point of familiarity through their inventive daring that a reaction became almost inevitable. After 1933, this reaction developed ugly political connotations in Nazi Germany and Communist Russia, putting an end to the vigorous and diversified modern movement in the former, and equally snuffing out the creative forces of Russian architecture, which had achieved a provocative Constructivist monument in Golossov's Worker's Clubhouse, Moscow, of 1929. The more significant tendencies that emerge as an aftermath to the uproar of the 1920's were not narrowly reactionary, but instead are better pictured as somewhat introspective consolidations of the new aesthetic, and represent a re-evaluation of the principles that motivated the onslaught against outmoded compositional techniques.

THE EXPANSION OF MODERN ARCHITECTURE

The subsequent development of modern architecture in the second third of the twentieth century took place in an atmosphere which recognised the achievements of the recent past and viewed them as a coherent, articulate, unified statement. This heroic period had created and codified an aesthetic that later modern architects could either embrace or reject: the International style was taken as the representative of a particular, specific modernist ideal; it was romanticised in history, and by mid-century was largely isolated from contemporary reality by retrospective critical evaluations, which, whether positive or negative, tended in their accounts to give their subject the status of a myth. A first consequence of this idealisation of the new past would seem to be that the most successful subsequent developments tended to be the work of those who participated in the original creative phase of the movement itself.

The transition from a creative to a retrospective and evaluative phase in twentieth-century architecture begins in the 1930's, and is manifested in a series of outstanding buildings such as Le Corbusier's Swiss Dormitory at the Cité Universitaire, Paris (1931-32), or Frank Lloyd Wright's Kaufmann House, 'Falling Water', of 1936. Each building is a re-interpretation and re-evaluation of *avant-garde* themes that were first put forward in the previous decade, but with an unmistakable tendency to re-phrase the new idiom in a somewhat more conventional way. In the case of Le Corbusier's dormitory, the clearly defined and detached cube, complete with glazed wall, is combined with an expressionistically curved mass on its reverse side, and the entire form is realised in carefully patterned masonry which conceals a steel frame, and consequently gives a degree of tactile monumentality to the building. This is at variance with the more papery and even ambiguous surface effects of Gropius's Bauhaus or Brinkman and van der Vlugt's van Nelle Factory, of the previous decades. The result is not to be interpreted as a rejection of the earlier, heroic style of modern architecture; rather, it is an effort at expansion and enrichment through the use of materials that originally seemed inimicable to the impalpable geometry of the International style. Indeed, the tendencies revealed in the Swiss Dormitory, that seem to suggest a reorientation in the

1006

1008

996

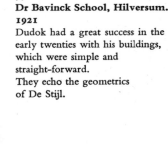
996 W. M. Dudok.
Dr Bavinck School, Hilversum.
1921
Dudok had a great success in the early twenties with his buildings, which were simple and straight-forward.
They echo the geometrics of De Stijl.

997

997 Brinkman, van der Vlugt and Stam. Van Nelle Factory, Rotterdam. 1927-28
The walls here, letting in the maximum light, are merely screens. The building is supported by reinforced concrete floors resting on mushroom-headed columns.

998

998 Fritz Höger.
Chilehaus, Hamburg. 1921
The most impressive of the large buildings erected in Germany in the twenties. The irregular site was used to produce a long double curve on one side of the building, making an acute angle at the corner, which is the building's most distinctive feature.
This is further accented by the receding upper three storeys.

999 Mies van der Rohe. German Pavilion, Barcelona. 1929
Steel skeleton and rectangular planes of marble, glass, onyx placed vertically or horizontally, freely, so that space seems to flow through them.
This use of the open plan achieves extreme lightness and movement. In the interior, materials have also been juxtaposed in such a way as to produce an effect of extreme richness and contrast.

999

1000, 1001, 1003 Le Corbusier. Villa Savoye, Poissy. 1929
Exterior and section.
A unique statement of a new style. The ferroconcrete structure means that space can penetrate the house from beneath, above, and through the middle. The walls are shells merely, or screens with no structural purpose; hence the open planning. Roof garden and terrace are included in the basic cube of the house. A gentle ramp instead of staircase, running within and without, connects the floors, as can be seen in the view of the courtyard (1003).

1000

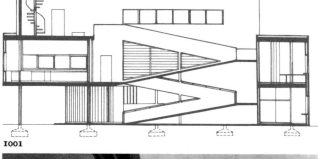

1001

1002 Le Corbusier. The Centrosoyus, Moscow. 1928-36
Le Corbusier was selected in 1928 to design this official building, now the Ministry of Light Industries, and it displays much of his inventiveness, for example the freeing of the building from the ground.

1002

1003

1004 Le Corbusier. 'Voisin' plan of Paris. 1925
One modern architectural problem is to check the spread of dense masses of houses.
In one of many such plans, Le Corbusier built upwards in zigzag blocks, leaving room for green spaces between.

1005 Le Corbusier. La Tourette, Eveux-sur-l'Arbresle, near Lyons. 1955-59
This concrete monastery comprises a U-shaped building and a rectangular chapel round a central court, built on a hillside.
The cells are cantilevered out over the storeys below.
Great attention has been given to providing shade, light and air.

1004

1005

work of Le Corbusier are only fulfilled in his subsequent masterpieces of the 1940's and '50's, the Unité d'Habitation, Marseilles, and Notre-Dame-du-Haut, Ronchamp.

Wright's most flamboyant, if not his most characteristically personal work of the 1930's, 'Falling Water', is even more of a museum-piece of contemporary architecture, insofar as it offers a résumé of the Romantic domestic tradition of the nineteenth century, in conjunction with the austere geometries of twentieth-century abstract art and the structural daring of the machine age. The triumphant *élan* with which the concrete balconies of the house both imitate and challenge the horizontal rock-beds of the water course above which 'Falling Water' is perched, is matched by the intricate meshing of horizontal and vertical elements in the composition, suggestive of the interlocking forms of *De Stijl*. The severe shapes of 'Falling Water' blend with the site, suggesting, in its integration with the natural surroundings, that it is an extension of the landscape and geological formations, rather than an intrusion. From this organic point of view it is recognisable as an ultimate consequence of Downing's century-old principles of Romantic Naturalism, applied with a totally different temperamental and creative flair.

Numerous minor tendencies in European and American architecture, appearing on the eve of the Second World War, and in the years immediately afterwards, brought the whole *avant-garde* architectural development to an inconclusive resting point. The caesura in stylistic evolution, doubtless encouraged by this catastrophe but which is already noticeable in the late 1930's, would not have been appreciably different had events exterior to architecture not brought about a halt in building activity. In the subsequent period of reconstruction, which gained momentum only in the late 1940's, and was afterwards prolonged by the commercial construction boom which began in the U.S.A. in the early 1950's, the modern movement made an effort at a new beginning. Such developments of the 1940's as New Empiricism, coming from Scandinavia, and of the western U.S. 'Bay Region style', coupled with a new popular and scholarly interest in the Picturesque tradition, all conspired to temper and soften the original geometric rigour of the International style aesthetic, as well as to replace its often spectacular feats of hovering, weightless forms with more conventional, prosaic ground-hugging shapes. These tentative developments reached their culmination in the layout for the Festival of Britain on the South Bank, London (1951), where in such permanent structures as the Royal Festival Hall, the work of Sir Robert H. Matthew and Sir Leslie Martin, the abstract architectural features of the pre-war modern style were softened by casual shaping and massing, and deliberately inconclusive detailing.

These efforts already seem ephemeral at only a decade's distance, and much of the studiously informal architecture of the post-war years now seems a bit naive and outmoded. The most durable attractions of this period—and the ones which also seemed the most spectacular at the time—were the new designs and constructions turned out by the old, familiar names long associated with the heroic struggles of modern building. Auguste Perret's last and, ultimately, posthumous work, the reconstruction of the central quarter of

1009

1015

1006

1007

1008

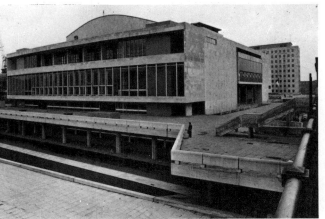

1009

**1010-12 Le Corbusier.
Unité d'Habitation,
Marseilles. 1947-52**
Exterior and roof detail.
A unique living unit housing
1,600 people. The flats are
not planned horizontally on floors,
but as interlocking rectangular
units. As a result, each 'flat' has a
two-storey living room.
Shops, day nurseries and
recreational facilities are included
in the building.
The marks of the moulds are
deliberately left in the concrete
to emphasise this bold
rough-hewn look. The roof is
deliberately designed as an
artificial landscape with its
monumental clover-leaf shaped
ventilation tower, a gymnasium
hall, a school and children's
playground and a promenade with
a view over marvellous open
country towards mountains.

1010

1011

1012

Le Havre, projected in 1945, was the first indication that the dyke of official academic hostility towards modern architecture, long a feature of French bureaucracy, had, at last, been burst. However tentative in style and in planning the new Le Havre may have been, reflecting Perret's concrete frame style of almost half a century before, it was a harbinger of something else: Le Corbusier's long-awaited opportunity to carry out his proposals for mass housing, which went back ultimately to a series of manifesto-like projects of the 1920's.

1010
1011
1012

This materialised with the official commission for the Unité d'Habitation, built over the years 1947-52. Of a remarkable conception, which provided each duplex apartment with a two-storey studio-living room, a private, isolated balcony and other commodious features, it was equally an unforgettable exterior shape, whose surface textures were enriched by both deliberate and accidental features left in the concrete by the irregularities of the form work. A seventeen-storey mass of robust scale and emphatic detailing rose clear above the ground on expressively shaped *pilotis*, and was capped by a hanging garden on the roof. This latter element was equipped with recreational facilities, housed in a concrete 'landscape' of fantastic, largely irrational forms. The residential principles realised in the late 1920's in the Villa Savoye, where the principle living spaces were elevated and visually detached from the ground, and the roof was given over to hanging gardens and terraces, were here, in the Marseilles Unité, re-phrased in a monumental, popularised and less aristocratic fashion, yet one no less effective.

In contrast to this rugged, incisively moulded late style of Le Corbusier is the simplified, polished late style of Mies van der Rohe. Having left Germany for the United States in the late 1930's, following the example of other German architects like Gropius and Mendelsohn, Mies settled in Chicago as a professor at the Illinois Institute of Technology. He was responsible for the master-plan of the campus

p. 340

(1939-40), and for a continuing series of buildings of sharply varying functions on that campus, constructed through the 1940's and '50's. The remarkable character of these structures was their uniformity, both with respect to a pre-established scale and module, and their persistent use of a highly simplified and perfected idiom of black steel, light brick and glass. All the buildings took the shape of closed, inviolable rectilinear cubes, with generally symmetrical façades, so that out of the process of reduction and rationalisation, an implicit temple-like image emerged on the exterior. The result, tacitly Neo-classic in its cool regularity, is not the consequence of arbitrarily selecting a preconceived form. Rather, the outer demeanour of Mies's campus buildings seems to be the consequence of a long, arduous analytical process, by which the extraneous is gradually and inexorably rejected. The same qualities carry over into

1013

Mies's Lake Shore Apartments in Chicago (1949-51), buildings whose scale, height, and destination allow close comparison between his personal summation of the modern architectural idiom, and that arrived at by Le Corbusier in his contemporary Unité.

In growing out and away from the main current of the International style, Mies has been drawn towards the pro-

1013

1013 Mies van der Rohe. Lake Shore Apartments, Chicago. 1949-51
A scheme of flats in Lake Shore Drive, which are masterpieces of precise engineering depending for their aesthetic effect on subtlety of proportion, fitness of material used and mechanical precision of finish.

1014

1014 London County Council Architects Department. Roehampton Estates. 1956-57
Aerial view.
Low-cost housing using pre-fabricated concrete parts, which achieves variety and atmosphere by varying the size and height of the buildings, by keeping the trees to intersperse them and retaining the natural rise and fall of the ground.

1015

1015 Auguste Perret. Reconstruction of Le Havre, projected 1948
One of the few significant ensembles to result from post-war reconstruction. Perret's designs for rebuilding the centre of the destroyed French port, together with those of his followers there, remain loyal to the stylistic and constructive principles first manifested a half-century earlier in his 1903 flats in the rue Franklin, Paris.

1016, 1017 Eero Saarinen. TWA Building, Kennedy (Idlewild) Airport, New York, 1956-61
This is an attempt to link directly the idea of an airport terminal with the adventure and aestheticism of the aeroplane and high speed flight with an unmistakable Expressionistic quality. The same plasticity is adhered to in the interior, down to the shapes of signs, telephone booths, air conditioning units, etc.

1016

1017

1018 Alvar Aalto. House of Culture, Helsinki. 1958
This modern secular temple houses a congress-concert-hall, cinema, restaurants and garage.
The concrete walls have been faced with bricks made to Aalto's special design.
The surface is curved to make the maximum play with light and shade. The roof, steeply pitched, is of copper.

1018

1019 Pier Luigi Nervi. Palazzetto dello Sport, Rome. 1958
The dome is made of pre-cast concrete coffers in nineteen different sizes.
Total roof thickness, including insulating and waterproofing, is 4.75 inches. Inside, the concrete thrusts are left visible.
Concrete Y-shaped supports take the thrust diagonally into the ground like medieval flying buttresses. The immense arena holds 5,000 people.

1019

duction of pristine, simplified forms, with a detailing which is logical, as well as Romantic, in its employment of dark hues for the exposed metal members, and the careful, craftsman-like adjustment that he imparts to the rhythms and proportions of his façades. On the other hand, the relatively spontaneous-seeming forms of Le Corbusier—which have their own particular quality of arbitrariness—have made possible a more supple, imaginative late style, one which is a contrast to the relative austerity of his early, purist manner. His richer, sculptural style of Ronchamp and Chandigarh, in the 1950's, evolved from an earlier restrictive, closed geometry, to shapes that fling themselves across the building-site in a series of dramatically effective gestures. In the work of these two consummate masters of the twentieth century the full variety and richness of formal invention characteristic of the period can easily be appreciated.

1012, p. 340
1007

No account of this middle third of the twentieth century can, however, be complete without reference to the continuing and constantly enriched work of Frank Lloyd Wright. The fact that in his last years his buildings were executed with a growing lack of concern for details, and even of gross carelessness in cases like the Guggenheim Museum, New York (1943-59), in no way lessens the extent of his significance. His contact with pre-twentieth-century lines of development, and particularly his extraordinary rôle in the re-interpretation of the Picturesque tradition of Nash, Downing, Shaw and Richardson, provides his late style with further roots buried deep in the almost hidden sources of modern architecture, and has given his ultimate works an abundant and archetypal character. They are, along with the buildings of Mies and Le Corbusier, convincing declarations that while modern architecture may have taught itself to resist the wiles of eclecticism and revivalism, the magnetic attraction of the past—of styles both historic and primitive—is perhaps even stronger today than it was a century ago.

1020

The architects of the subsequent generations, whose activity commenced after the initial effort of the International style had become a matter of history and legend, have understandably laboured under a twin shadow. They came upon the scene at an especially awkward moment, arriving in the wake of the greatest collective creative moment in architecture since the end of the Baroque. In addition, they had to establish personal identities for themselves and their work in the shadow of a group of major figures, whose instinctive personal mastery of a new idiom was equally unprecedented. Under the circumstances, it is surprising that the fundamental reaction against the new architecture —leaving aside such superficial and historically ephemeral developments of the 1930's, sponsored by Nazism and Fascism—did not take unmistakable shape until the late 1950's, and then evolved only in the most surreptitious fashion out of the ranks of the modern movement itself.

The new orientation towards an overt formalism, with an emphasis upon mannered, arbitrary shaping of spaces and exteriors, is, in part, attributable to the late styles of the older generation. Furthermore, this tendency was concealed within the ostensibly functional and abstract designs of their early careers. In general, the inclinations of the younger generation, especially since 1950, have been towards the exploitation of this quasi-subjective, quasi-academic element in twentieth-century architecture, to the point where it becomes the major rather than the minor theme. By 1960, the trend towards arbitrary formality engendered a resurgence of an ingenuous, superficial historicism. This manifests itself in a pseudo-scholarly affectation of features drawn from the great buildings of the past, a technique which has more in common with the eclecticism of the nineteenth century than with the less explicit evocations of the past that appear in the functional architecture of the first third of the twentieth century. Beneath the surface of superficial pandering to this or that momentarily fashionable 're-interpretation' of the past, the more serious architects of the mid-twentieth century seem to be carrying on a profound re-evaluation of the various achievements of the past two centuries. Part of this movement takes the form of a search for a point of departure in some incompletely explored facet of the early modern tradition lying behind the too articulate, too specifically formulated style of the 1920's. The recent disinclination to pursue the rational and functional attitudes of the International style is to be explained not so much by a wish to be rashly and irresponsibly anti-functional, as it is by a partly concealed desire to evade the stylistic formulae and the involved cubist-inspired spatial ambiguities that were fundamental to a Bauhaus or a Villa Savoye. In this respect, the current reaction that has grown up in contemporary architecture, is in part directed against the liberties of the first third of the twentieth century.

Within the pattern of this stylistic retrenchment, the houses of so diverse a group of architects and designers as Philip Johnson, Oscar Niemeyer, Paul Rudolph and Charles Eames, most of which were built about 1950, indicate the conflicting preoccupations of a transitional moment. In 1022 principle, Eames's Case Study House represents a particular refinement of the 'machine for living', the industrialised house ideal, since the detailing of its various component parts was determined by the forms and shapes of elements available from manufacturers' catalogues. In contrast, the houses of Johnson and Niemeyer, while growing out of the respective personal styles of Mies and Le Corbusier, manifest a certain detached formalism and scholarly paraphrase of the original concept. Johnson's museum design for the Munson-Williams-Proctor Institute, Utica, New York (1958-60), and Niemeyer's government buildings for the P. 339 new capital of Brasilia indicate a more individual stage of accomplishment for these architects, as well as for mid-twentieth-century architecture as a whole. Johnson's Proctor Institute has been cited as a 'Miesian' design, but, in fact, it is 'Miesian' only in the generalised severity of its exterior. As a rigid cubic form, slipped within a colossal bronze-clad concrete frame, it is a much too self-conscious, classic fixation to be truly derived from the analytic and deductive design procedures of the older modernist aesthetic. The formalising character of Johnson's architecture does not result from Mies's relentless logic (sometimes misapplied), nor is it the outgrowth of patient, personal stylistic development, but is, instead, an assumed mantle, a derived 'style'. It is important to compare the four-square arbitrariness of Johnsons's Proctor Institute with the more unex-

1020 Frank Lloyd Wright. Guggenheim Museum, New York. 1943-59
The museum is arranged round a continuous spiral ramp. The outside expresses this coil interior as clearly as a snail's shell. This is the last major work carried out during the architect's lifetime.

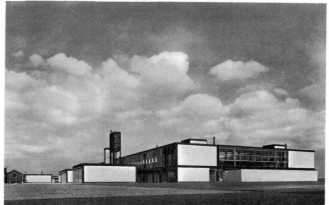

1021 Alison and Peter Smithson. Hunstanton Secondary School, Norfolk. 1954
The idea is severely rectilinear. Variety of form has been achieved by the one large block being surrounded by smaller units; variety of surface by exposed brick and steel contrasting with glass. It is influenced by the work of Mies van der Rohe.

1022 Charles Eames. Case Study House, Santa Monica, California. 1949
Towards the factory-made house. Eames's design consisted of standard parts already in production, even down to the detailing.

1023 Louis I. Kahn. Richards Medical Research Laboratories, University of Pennsylvania, Philadelphia. 1960
New methods of construction have been used to great effect and determine the design. Brick and concrete have been left bare to give surfaces colour and texture.
The towers house the services and determine the skyline. The laboratories may be seen between the towers.

1024 Philip Johnson. Glass House, New Canaan, Connecticut. 1947-49
The first element of Johnson's own suburban estate. The residential core is a brilliantly refined 'Miesian' essay, a generously scaled single room which, because of the sweep of glass, eliminates any sense of barrier between the occupants and the landscape. The ensemble now consists of a windowless guest house and an arcaded concrete 'folie', both conceived as foils to the Glass House proper. An underground, tumulus-like art gallery will ultimately complete the group.

1025 Paul Rudolph. School of Art and Architecture, Yale University, New Haven, Connecticut. Completed 1963
A startlingly bold conception, borrowing freely from many sources in the recent past, notably Wright, Le Corbusier and De Stijl. Yet in spite of this apparent eclecticism, the building possesses an individuality and forcefulness all its own, particularly in the abrupt contrasts of fragile glass and bulky concrete.

1026 James Stirling and James Gowan. Engineering laboratories, Leicester University. Completed 1963
One of the most widely admired recent buildings, this red brick, tile and glass structure is, for all its apparent novelty, the outgrowth of functional and structural theories first proclaimed more than a century ago by Viollet-le-Duc, and adopted by innumerable modern movements since. Its complex, startling shape contrasts with the predictable regularity of many of its contemporaries.

1024

1025

1026

pected yet equally 'unreasonable' concept imposed by Wright for the Guggenheim Museum. Though unmistakably different in their formal and spatial systems, the two buildings are paradoxically similar as outwardly imposed concepts which have only a partial and tenuous relevance to the practical problems of a museum programme. Both buildings suggest that while there has been a continuing effort in the period since 1940 to find means of *expressing the character* of twentieth-century technology and style in new buildings, at the same time there has been little or no interest in continuing the growth and evolution of modernism in architecture through a re-evaluation of new potentials.

With this in mind, the distinctive features of Niemeyer's Brasilia designs become more understandable. Having been originally inspired by the example of Le Corbusier in the 1930's and 1940's, the Brazilian architect has tended to develop the subjective, somewhat expressionistic side of the Corbusian style, while at the same time casting a sideward glance at the extravagant projects of Romantic Classic architects, notably Boullée and Ledoux. The *surréel* character of Niemeyer's brand-new capital must also be seen as an outgrowth of the majestical Imperial mode of the nineteenth century, with the iconography of nationalism as present under these modernistic domes, as it was behind the Gothic-detailed but academically composed façades of Pugin's and Barry's Houses of Parliament. Equally, comparison with Le Corbusier's group of official buildings for the Punjab capital of Chandigarh is important, in order to appreciate the spontaneous, personally motivated formalism of the elder master of twentieth-century design, when seen together with the more arbitrary, less conclusive, and somewhat overly generalised stylisations of the younger architect.

p. 339

In addition to the points of view represented, in different degrees and in varying modes, by Johnson and Niemeyer, there are the more determinedly independent efforts of architects such as Paul Rudolph and Louis I. Kahn. Both these men first emerged as distinct personalities in the early 1950's, inspired, but not overwhelmed, by the example of Mies. In this respect, they can be associated with the proponents of 'new brutalism' in England, Alison and Peter Smithson, whose Hunstanton School (1954) represents one of the most faithful tributes to Mies, one which stresses its industrial side rather than concentrating upon elegant refinement, as Johnson was doing at the same time. In the course of the last decade Rudolph has turned from the design of fragile, somewhat 'Miesian' houses to the creation of large, massive concrete structures, which combine influences from the entire gamut of early twentieth-century modernism into an emphatically articulated sequence of shapes.

1021

Unlike the repetitive, self-consciously retrospective work of others, is the sudden blossom of independence and high degree of personal character in the work of Kahn. Beginning with a Miesian mode in the early 1950's, he progressed by 1960, notably in the Richards Medical Research Laboratories, to a forthright, expressive constructive style, which, in its vigour and strength of mass and detail, contrasts dramatically with the more popular currents of architecture. While the experimental creativity of Kahn's work is its most immediately striking feature, his designs are laden with memories and recollections of many facets of the mod-

LII   LIII

LVI   LIV   LV

ern tradition. The massing of the research towers is suggestive of the Neo-Gothic university dormitories which surround them, and the type of planning and arrangements for circulation and service cores is indebted to the methodology, if not of the outward appearances, of academic architecture. Simultaneously, the relatively harsh surfaces of brick and concrete and the aggressive massing, bear analogies with the *brut* surfaces of Le Corbusier's characteristic late style, while, for certain critics, the same elements conjure up memories of the strong-surfaced qualities of Butterfield's High Victorian mode, of a century before. However, as with the works of Mies and Le Corbusier before him, the reminiscences to be found in Kahn's designs are in no way so specific or very exact as to obtrude themselves upon the total integrated and synthesised image of the building; nor do they dilute the personal expressiveness of his manner. Instead, they complement and reinforce the individual creative features of each of his buildings.

1023

Probably the only other designer of the 1950's to conceive works in accord with inventive structural systems is the Italian engineer, Pier Luigi Nervi. At their best, Nervi's structures, typical of which is the domical Palazzetto dello Sport, Rome (1958), have a constructive system that is expressively revealed by the overall design.

1019

The familiar commercial style of building in the 1950's, the glass-sheathed tower or slab, first popularised by the American firm, Skidmore, Owings and Merrill in Lever House, New York (1952), is a handsome offspring of glass-curtain wall masterpieces of the previous generation, such as the Swiss Dormitory, the Bauhaus or the van Nelle Factory. However, the dynamic cubistic vocabulary, with its rugged, futurist massing of parts and contrast of glass-enclosed elements with thin-seeming stucco surfaces is replaced by an elegantly monotonous regularity. In the hands of a true master, such as Mies van der Rohe, this demanding, refractory style has a creative potential. Nonetheless, the 1950's has witnessed the depressing vulgarisation of the glass-and-metal sheathed office building, to the point at which its un-thought-out clichés have become as nearly ridiculous as the spurious 'skyscraper Gothic' of the earlier twentieth century. Consequently, there were efforts towards the end of the 1950's to break with the appearance of the glass box, and to find alternate systems for containing the varied service and space requirements. Typical of this tendency are the Torre Velasca, Milan (1958), where the concrete frame dominates the exterior, and the John Hancock Building, San Francisco (1959), where Skidmore, Owings and Merrill, the original popularisers of the glass-curtain wall, have essayed a load-bearing wall-composition with conventional fenestration, creating a pattern of greater emphasis than had been possible with the undifferentiated glazed surface.

1026

An architect of distinguished standing in the modern movement who remains, none the less, difficult to categorise is the Finnish architect Alvar Aalto. His earliest works in the late twenties and early thirties were in pure International Style, though he shortly led the way to a more subtle, romantic, even organic type of design. His works since the Second World War have been characterised by random, often meandering, forms and a consequently informal style, which in the Säynätsalo Civic Centre (*c.* 1951-53) provides an effective relief from the dominant ordered formalism of our day.

However, in some ways the most characteristic architect of the 1950's was Eero Saarinen, the son of the distinguished Finnish designer, Eliel Saarinen, who, in a brief career of a dozen years, abruptly terminated by death in 1960, sampled most of the diverse tendencies of the period. While much of his work is extraordinarily interesting in shape and in structure, it is also frequently ingenuous and naive, as well as occasionally crude in execution. Having begun in a rather Miesian mould, Eero Saarinen's work terminates in the TWA Building, Kennedy Airport, where an Expressionistic quality is unmistakable in the undulating concrete shells that vault the building's interior spaces.

1018

The monumental side of the growing Neo-academicism, which is transforming and reshaping the innovations of the twentieth century, can be appreciated in the familiarly arranged cubic volumes of Lincoln Center, New York, in which a group of architects, including Wallace Harrison and Philip Johnson, has evolved a Neo-academic idiom of colonnades and arcades, in unexpected shapes and proportions, to mask the complexity of interior services and functions.

1016, 1017

This 'new formalism' in contemporary architecture may be contrasted not only with the aforementioned neo-romanticism of Aalto and the effervescent eclecticism of Rudolph, but with post-'new brutalist' developments in England, notably the red brick, tile and glass structure of the Engineering laboratories, Leicester University (1963), by James Stirling and James Gowan. In this provocatively shaped building the architects have hit upon a fresh, unexpected language of form while profoundly respecting the rational doctrines of the modern movement, demonstrating once again the resilience and potential of our new tradition.

From this evidence, it is clear that one large segment of ostensibly modernist architectural design has, by 1960, reached a stable Neo-academic level. Alternately, there are a number of visible lines of resistance and possible paths of further development. They are to be found in less spectacular, less superficially 'stylish' works of architects who have yet to score a popular success. Equally, the lessons of Kahn and Stirling and the continuing example of the surviving members of the great creative generation of the early twentieth century remain as an inspiration, even though their *forms* are often too great a temptation to be resisted, even by the most independent of designers. The history of architecture of the last two centuries reveals periods of great promise or accomplishment, followed by periods of disenchantment, in which routine often stifles creativity. However, it is these confining, enervating moments that provide the shock and challenge which is the springboard of future accomplishment. The modern period in architecture began in the eighteenth century with a thorough investigation of the past. Its most recent phase may find its subsequent path cleared and made smooth by a new investigation and re-evaluation of its own, two-hundred-year-old heritage.

(The material for this chapter was gathered with the assistance of Helen Searing).

LII *Mies van der Rohe: Illinois Institute of Technology, Chicago* LIII *Civic centre, Säynätsalo, Finland* LV *Asplund: Forest Crematorium, Stockholm* LIV, LVI *Le Corbusier: Notre-Dame-du-Haut, Ronchamp, France*

Abacus. The slab on top of a CAPITAL directly supporting the ARCHITRAVE. See ORDERS.

Abutment. Masonry placed so as to resist the THRUST of an arch or vault; part of the building acting as a BUTTRESS.

Acanthus. A plant with sharp pointed leaves, copied in the CORINTHIAN capital.

Acropolis. The citadel of a Greek city where the temple of the patron deity was usually built.

Agora. In ancient Greece, a public space for assemblies; same as a Roman FORUM.

Aisle. In BASILICAN buildings, one of the lateral divisions parallel with the NAVE but not as high. Sometimes used to include the nave as well (e.g., 3-aisled = nave and two aisles; 5-aisled = nave and double aisles). Transepts and chancel may also be aisled.

Amalaka. A type of CAPITAL in Hindu architecture.

Ambulatory. A continuous AISLE forming a processional path round an enclosed space. In Europe in the east end of a cathedral, in India in the shrine of a temple.

Amphi-prostyle. Greek: a PORTICO ('prostyle') at each end.

Amphitheatre. A round or occasionally oval arena with tiers of seats.

Antis, in. Literally, 'between the antae' or pilasters terminating the side walls of a Greek temple; a PORTICO in which columns stand between the projecting side walls.

Apse. Part of a building that is semi-circular or U-shaped in plan; usually the east end of a chapel or CHANCEL.

Arcade. A line of arches supported on piers or columns. **Blank or blind arcading.** Miniature arcade applied to a wall as decoration.

Arch. A structure of several units at the top of an opening which is supported only from the sides, the downward pressure being transformed into lateral THRUST. **Corbelled arch.** So-called 'false arch', consisting of blocks of stone each laid slightly overlapping the one beneath until the gap can be bridged by a single slab. **Diaphragm arch.** A stone arch built across the nave of a church when the roof is of wood (i.e. where there is no vault). **Half-arch.** An arch from the springing to apex only. See FLYING BUTTRESS. **Horseshoe arch.** A round or pointed arch shaped like a horseshoe, so that the diameter at its widest point is greater than the distance to be spanned. **Ogee arch.** An arch of double curvature, the bottom convex, the top concave. **Parabolic arch.** An arch whose curve is a parabola, one of the conic sections (the intersection of a cone and a plane parallel to its side). Used only recently in architecture. **Pointed arch.** An arch consisting of two curves meeting at an angle. **Relieving arch.** A concealed masonry arch built over another arch or a LINTEL to carry the weight. **Round or semi-circular arch.** The commonest and most elementary arch, consisting of a simple semi-circle of VOUSSOIRS. **Segmental arch.** An arch consisting of a segment only, not a full half-circle. In appearance flatter than a round arch. **Squinch arch.** An arch built diagonally across the corner of a rectangular space to be covered by a dome or spire, converting the rectangle into an octagon. A circle can be formed by the the use of PENDENTIVES. **Stilted arch.** An arch whose SPRINGING is higher than its IMPOST so that the sides seem vertical at the bottom. **Transverse arch.** An arch across a vaulted space at right angles to the walls. **Triangular arch.** An extreme form of the pointed arch, the sides being straight or nearly so. **Trilobe (or trefoil) arch.** With two CUSPS, dividing the arch into three lobes. A decorative, not a structural form. **Triumphal arch.** A Roman monumental arch, with inscriptions, reliefs, etc., built to celebrate a victory. Normally one large opening flanked by smaller ones on each side.

Architrave. The lowest position of a classical ENTABLATURE, the stone LINTEL above the columns. See ORDERS.

Arcuation, arcuated. Having arches and supports.

Arris. The sharp ridge formed by the meeting of two surfaces, in vaults called a GROIN.

Art Nouveau. Style of decoration popular in Europe *c.* 1890–1910, avoiding traditional motifs and basing itself on curving lines and vegetation-like forms.

Ashlar. Trimmed, regular masonry with flat surfaces and squared edges.

Atrium. (1) In classical architecture, a small courtyard in a house, covered along the sides. (2) In Early Christian, the forecourt of a large church, often cloistered.

Axial planning. The placing of several buildings along a single line.

Azulejos. Brilliantly coloured glazed tiles, used in Moslem and some Spanish and Portuguese buildings.

Balustrade. A line of balusters, or miniature pillars, supporting a handrail.

Banded. Having masonry of different colours or textures arranged in alternating COURSES.

Barbican. Fortified outwork guarding the gateway of a medieval city or castle.

Baroque. Style after MANNERISM in Italy, *c.* 1600, and later spread over Europe; characterised by dynamic lines and masses and the free use of classical motifs.

Base. (1) The lowest portion of any structure. (2) The lowest of the three principal parts of an IONIC or CORINTHIAN column (see ORDERS). (3) Masonry of any shape upon which a column or pier stands.

Basilica. (1) In Roman architecture, a large public hall where law-suits were heard. (2) In Early Christian and later architecture, a church consisting of NAVE and AISLES, with windows above the level of the aisle roofs (CLERESTORY).

Bastion. A projection from the CURTAIN WALL of a castle or defensive work, placed so that a zone of wall may be swept by fire from the bastions.

Batter. Slight inward slope given to a wall (battered = sloping).

Bay. A compartment of a large building, consisting, e. g., in churches, of the space between one column or pier and the next, including the wall and the vault or ceiling over it. By extension, any unit of a wall-surface divided by large vertical features or (on exteriors) by windows.

Bead and reel. A classical MOULDING consisting of alternate 'beads' (small eggshapes) and 'reels' (semi-circular discs, sometimes in pairs, set edgewise).

Bedding. Layer of cement or mortar on which a masonry course is laid.

Bema. (1) Platform in an AGORA or FORUM for public speeches. (2) Raised stage for the clergy at the east end of Early Christian churches.

Bent entry. A defended entrance involving a sharp change in direction.

Bombé. Convex, bulging.

Bond. The overlapping of bricks or stone slabs to increase stability. **Bonded.** Tied together by a single unit spanning two layers; usually the same material as the wall, or something serving the same purpose, e. g., chains or matting. See also THROUGH-COURSE. **English bond.** Brickwork in which each course consists of alternate 'headers' (the end of the brick) and 'stretchers' (the long side). **Flemish bond.** Brickwork in which complete courses of headers and stretchers alternate.

Boulevard. A wide, straight street. (Originally the ramparts of a walled town; when these were demolished in the nineteenth century, they were often replaced by wide streets – hence its present meaning.)

Bracket. Member projecting from a vertical surface to provide a horizontal support. CONSOLES are an ornate kind of bracket. See also CORBEL and CANTILEVER.

Brick. Regular block of hardened clay. **Glazed brick.** Brick with a polished, glassy surface, as distinct from a matt or rough surface. **Mud-brick.** A brick moulded by hand and hardened without artificial heat. Usually bound with straw or hair (cf. Exodus) but not always (e. g., ancient Mexico). Also called 'adobe'. **Vitrified brick.** Brick burnt to a hard, glossy consistency, water- and damp-proof.

Buke. Style of Japanese domestic building – simple houses enclosed by ditch and fence.

Buttress. Masonry built against a wall to give additional support, or to resist the THRUST of a vault or arch. **Flying buttress.** A HALF-ARCH leaning against that point in a wall where the LATERAL THRUST of an arch or vault is being exerted, and transmitting this thrust to a detached body of masonry at a lower level. A feature of the GOTHIC style.

Byzantine. Style evolved at Constantinople about the fifth century A. D. and still in use in some parts of the world. The round arch and the use of domes are characteristic.

Calidarium. The hot-water room in a Roman public bath.

Canopy. Decorative covering over a small open structure such as a tomb, pulpit or niche; often supported on columns.

Cantilever. A beam or girder supported in the middle or along half its length and weighted at one end to carry a proportionate load on the other.

Capital. The upper part of a column. See DORIC, IONIC, CORINTHIAN and ORDERS. In non-classical architecture, capitals may be of any design. **Cushion-capital.** The simplest possible transition from square to circle, a cube with the bottom edges and corners cut away.

Capping. Protective covering on top of wall or post. Also called 'coping'.

Carolingian. Style originating under Charlemagne *c.* 800 and leading to ROMANESQUE.

Cartouche. Tablet with ornate frame.

Caryatid. Pillar in the form of a sculptured female figure.

Causeway. A raised road or path.

Cella. The central body of a classical temple, without portico and colonnades (occasionally, to mean the NAOS alone). By extension, the sanctuary of other temples, e. g., Indian.

Cenotaph. Monument to a person buried elsewhere (Greek: 'empty tomb').

Central-plan. A plan symmetrical, or nearly so, in all four directions.

Centring. Temporary wooden support for an arch or vault, removed when the mortar has set.

Chancel. Space in a church reserved for the clergy, including the altar and the choir. **Chancel-screen.** Screen separating the chancel from the nave or crossing. Sometimes continued on the north and south sides to separate the choir from its aisles.

Chase. A vertical groove cut in a wall for pipes or wires or (in Egyptian buildings) wooden masts. Chased = grooved with chases.

Chevet. The combination of APSE, AMBULATORY and RADIATING CHAPELS at the east end of a large Gothic church.

Chevron. Zig-zag.

Choir. The part of a church where the choir sits. Normally the west part of the chancel. The term is often loosely applied to mean the same as chancel, although in large medieval churches the choir sat under the crossing or west of it.

Chryselephantine. Made of ivory and gold. Term applied by the Greeks to statues of which the draperies were made of gold and the nude parts of the figure of ivory – both over a hollow wooden framework.

Cistern. A large underground room (often vaulted) for the storage of water.

Classical. Greek or Roman and their derivatives, especially the use of the ORDERS.

Clerestory. The upper window-level of a large enclosed space, rising above adjacent roofs. In particular the upper window range of a BASILICAN building above the ARCADE and TRIFORIUM.

Cloister. A square court surrounded by an open ARCADE.

Coffering. Treatment of ceilings and domes consisting of sunk panels (coffers).

Colonnade. A row of columns.

Column. A circular pillar, a cylindrical support for part of a building. Also erected singly as a monument. See DORIC, IONIC, CORINTHIAN and ORDERS.

Columnar and trabeate. Using the column and 'beam', or lintel, only, i. e., not using the principle of the arch.

Composite. An ORDER invented by the Romans, combining the acanthus leaves of the CORINTHIAN with the volutes of the IONIC capital.

Concentric walls. Fortification introduced from the East by the Crusaders, consisting of one complete defence system inside another.

Corbel. A BRACKET, a block of stone projecting from a wall as a horizontal support or as the springing of a rib. See ARCH and VAULT. **Corbel table.** A projecting course of masonry supported on corbels round the top of a wall as a parapet or cornice.

Corinthian. The last of the three classical ORDERS. Characteristics: (1) High base, sometimes a pedestal. (2) Slender fluted shaft with fillets. (3) Ornate capital using stylised acanthus leaves.

Cornice. (1) The top, projecting section of a classical ENTABLATURE (see ORDERS). (2) In Renaissance architecture, a projecting shelf along the top of a wall supported on ornamental BRACKETS or CONSOLES.

Corps-de-logis. The main part of a large house (especially a French château), as distinct from the wings and other subordinate parts.

Course. A layer of bricks or stone slabs forming a wall. **Through-course.** A layer at right angles to the wall-surface to give greater strength, e. g., when the core of the wall is of rubble.

Cove, coving. Concave surface connecting a wall and ceiling.

Crenellation. A defensive parapet consisting of merlons (solid wall) and embrasures (gaps for shooting through).

Crossing. The central space of a cruciform church where the NAVE, TRANSEPTS and CHANCEL meet.

Cruciform. Cross-shaped.

Crypt. Underground space below the east end of a church, originally to house the remains of saints (Greek: 'hidden').

Cuboid. Cube-shaped. **Battered cuboid** = cube with sides sloping inwards.

Culvert. An arched channel for carrying water underneath a road or embankment.

Cupola. Sometimes means the same as DOME. More usually in English a miniature dome or turret with a lantern-top.

Curtain wall. (1) In castles, the wall between bastions or towers. (2) In modern architecture, an exterior wall serving as a screen only, bearing no load. In STEEL-FRAME buildings all the walls are curtain walls.

Cusp. A projecting point on the inner side of an ARCH, window or roundel.

Cyclopean. Walling in very large irregular stones without mortar.

Dado. (1) The lower part of a wall when given separate decoration from the rest. (2) The same as DIE.

Dagaba. A Singhalese form of STUPA or relic-chamber (lit: 'dhata' = relics; 'garbha' = womb).

Dais. Raised platform at the end of a hall.

Decastyle. Having ten columns; temple with a portico ten columns wide.

Decorated. Style of architecture in England following EARLY ENGLISH. Characterised by elaborate curvilinear tracery, unusual spatial effects, complicated rib-vaulting, cusping, naturalistic foliage carving.

Diaconicon. In Byzantine and Orthodox Greek churches, a room for the storage of vestments and sacred vessels; equivalent to a sacristy.

Die. Part of a pedestal between CORNICE and base.

Dipteral. Having two rows of columns along each side (Greek: 'two-winged'); a temple with double PERISTYLE and at least eight columns at the front.

Distyle. Having two columns. **Distyle in antis.** A temple whose portico consists of two columns between the projecting sidewalls. See ANTIS.

Dog-tooth. A row of miniature pyramid-shaped ornaments in EARLY ENGLISH mouldings.

Dome. A roughly hemispherical roof on a circular base. A section through a dome can be SEMI-CIRCULAR, POINTED or SEGMENTAL (see ARCH). A dome with segmental section is called a saucer-dome. Most west European domes have DRUMS. **Onion- or bulb-domes** are external features only.

Doric. First and simplest of the classical ORDERS. Characteristics: (1) No base. (2) Relatively short shafts, FLUTED, with sharp arrises. (3) Simple undecorated echinus and square abacus. See ORDERS. The Roman Doric was similar but had a base.

Dormer window. Vertical window in a sloping roof.

'Double-aspect' sculpture. Sculpture halfway between relief and sculpture-in-the-round, seeming to be complete from two separate view-points but not forming a unified whole.

Dowel. A peg which fixes blocks together by fitting into a hole in each.

Drafted margin. A narrow dressed border along the edges of a squared stone, usually the width of a chisel, either as a guide for the subsequent dressing of the whole stone, or as a border surrounding the rough central portion.
Dressed. Of stones, trimmed, made smooth and rectangular.
Drip-moulding. A projecting MOULDING over the outside of doors and windows to carry the rain away from the wall.
Dromos. (1) A race-course. (2) A passage or entrance-way between high walls, e. g., to a Mycenaean tomb.
Drum. A vertical wall, circular in plan, carrying a dome. Also a section of a column, which has the same shape.
Dry-jointed. Without mortar.
Dwarf-order. A miniature range of columns or pilasters, for instance the height of an attic-storey.

Early English. First phase of English GOTHIC, beginning *c.* 1180. Characterised by lancet windows or (later) geometrical tracery, rib-vaults, emphasis on thin linear articulation instead of mass and volume, sharp mouldings and the clear distinction of architectural members.
Eave. The lowest part of a sloping roof that projects over the wall.
Echinus. The lower element of a DORIC capital – a circular cushion-like member under the ABACUS. Also the corresponding member of an IONIC capital, partly obscured by the VOLUTES and carved with egg-and-dart moulding.
Ekklesiasterion. The public hall or council-chamber of a Greek town.
Engaged. Bonded into a wall; not free-standing.
Entablature. In classical architecture, everything above the columns – ARCHITRAVE, FRIEZE and CORNICE. See ORDERS.
Entasis. Slight bulge given to a column to correct the optical illusion that it is thinner in the middle.
Episthodomos. In Greek temples, a room behind the NAOS.
Everted. Turned outwards, trumpet-shaped.
Excursion. An addition or excrescence to an area or volume.
Exhedra. An apsidal recess or alcove with seat; in Renaissance architecture any niche or small apse.

Façade. The exterior of a building on one of its main sides, almost always containing an entrance.
Facetted. Polygonal in section, not curved.
Facing. A veneer of one material over a core of another.
Fanlight. Originally a fan-shaped window over a door or window. Now not necessarily fan-shaped.
Fascia, fascia-plane. A horizontal, slightly projecting sub-division of an IONIC or CORINTHIAN ARCHITRAVE.
Ferro-vitreous. Iron-and-glass, as e. g., the Crystal Palace.
Fillet. A narrow flat band between MOULDINGS, especially between the FLUTES of a column (if two flutes meet and form a single edge, it is called an ARRIS).
Flamboyant. Last phase of French GOTHIC (lit: 'flame-shaped'), characterised by complex curvilinear tracery and profuse ornament.
Flush. On a single plane, not projecting.
Flute, fluting. Channels or grooves, carved vertically down the shafts of classical columns. See ORDERS.
Footing. Course of brick, stone or concrete at the bottom of a wall, made wider than the wall itself in order to distribute the weight over a larger area.
Forum. Roman market-place or open space for assemblies, normally surrounded by public buildings.
Free-standing. Open on all sides, not attached to a wall.
Fresco. Strictly, painting applied to a wall while the plaster is still wet. Sometimes loosely used of any mural painting.
Fretting. Decoration produced by cutting away the backgound of a pattern in stone or wood and leaving the rest as a kind of 'grating' (French: 'frettes').
Frieze. Part of a classical ENTABLATURE, above the ARCHITRAVE and below the CORNICE. In Doric it was divided into TRIGLYPHS and METOPES. See ORDERS. Often used for a band of figure-carving; hence in Renaissance architecture it means a continuous band of RELIEF round the top of a building or room.
Frigidarium. The cold-water room in Roman public baths.
Frontispiece. Monumental entrance to a French *hôtel.*

Gable. The triangular end of a GABLE-ROOF; in classical architecture called a PEDIMENT. By extension, a triangular area over a doorway even when there is no roof behind, as e. g., over French Gothic cathedral portals. **Gable-roof.** Roof with two sloping sides and triangular gables at the ends. See ROOF.
Gadroon. A convex ridge, the opposite of FLUTE.
Gallery. (1) An upper floor open on one side to the main interior space of a building (e. g., galleries over the aisles of a church) or to the exterior. (2) In medieval and Renaissance houses, a long narrow room.
Geometrical. (1) Consisting of regular patterns, not representational. (2) An early phase of bar-tracery, characteristic of EARLY ENGLISH.
Giant order. Pilasters or half-columns used to articulate a façade and extending through two or more storeys.
Gopuram. In Indian architecture the large gate-tower of a temple-enclosure.
Gothic. Name given to medieval architecture in Europe from about mid-twelfth century to the Renaissance. Characterised by the POINTED ARCH, the FLYING BUTTRESS and the RIB-VAULT.
Greek cross. A cross with all four arms of equal length.
Groin. The ridge or ARRIS formed by the meeting of two vaulting sections.

Half-arch. See ARCH and FLYING BUTTRESS.
Half-column. A column divided vertically and attached to a wall, either as decoration (e. g., the Colosseum) or as the RESPOND of an arch.
Half-timbered. Having a timber skeleton, the spaces being filled by brick or other material.
Hemicycle. Semi-circular part of a building with semi-dome over; a large APSE.
Hexastyle. Having six columns; a temple with a PORTICO six columns wide.
Hip. The line formed by two sloping roofs meeting. **Hipped roof.** A truss roof with hips instead of GABLES: that is, the RIDGE-BEAM is shorter than the walls parallel with it, so that the roof slopes inwards on all four sides.
Hippodamian. System of town-planning using the criss-cross grid.
Hippodrome. In ancient Greece, a stadium for horse and chariot racing.
Historiated. Decorated with RELIEF figures.
Hood-moulding. A MOULDING following the outline of a door or window; originally functioned as a DRIP-MOULDING but later used ornamentally.
Horseshoe arch. See ARCH.
Hypostyle. A hall or large enclosed space in which the (usually flat) roof rests on columns throughout, not just along sides.

Icon. (Greek: 'image'). Sacred picture in an eastern Orthodox church. (Iconoclasm = the banning of images.)
Impost. The masonry or brickwork upon which an arch rests, usually a MOULDING marking the SPRINGING of the arch.
Incursion. A 'bite' out of an area or volume.
Inlay. Small pieces of some rich material set into a bed or background of another.
Intaglio. Incised carving, the forms being hollowed out of the surface like relief in reverse, often used as a mould, e. g., in signet rings.
Intercolumniation. In classical architecture, the space between the columns; the spacing of the columns according to a system of proportion.
Interface. A surface lying between two blocks and forming their boundary.
Interlace. Carved ornament imitating knots or tendrils; characteristic of Islamic and Celtic art.
International style. Name given to the style of architecture evolved in Europe and America shortly before the First World War, and still prevailing. Characterised by an emphasis on function and rejection of traditional decorative motifs.
Ionic. The second of the three classical ORDERS. Characteristics: (1) Elegantly moulded base. (2) Tall, slender shafts with flutes separated by fillets. (3) Capital using the volute, or spiral.

Jamb. Vertical side of a door or window.
Joist. Horizontal beam supporting a floor or ceiling.

K'ang. Raised DAIS in a Chinese house, heated by burning fuel underneath.
Keep. The innermost stronghold of a castle. Originally the only part built of stone, later surrounded by CONCENTRIC walling.
King-post. Upright beam of a roof supporting the RIDGE-BEAM and resting on the centre of the TIE-BEAM. See ROOF.
Kondo. The main sanctuary of a Japanese Buddhist temple.

Lamination. Covering in thin layers.
Lancet. Tall narrow window characteristic of EARLY ENGLISH before the introduction of TRACERY.
Lantern. (1) A tower open to the space underneath and with windows to admit light downwards. (2) Small turret with windows crowning a dome or cupola.
Lenticular. Double-convex, like the section of a magnifying lens.
Lintel. Horizontal beam or slab spanning an opening. In classical architecture the lintel is called an ARCHITRAVE.
Loggia. A roofed space with an open ARCADE on one or more sides.
Longitudinal plan. Church plan in which the NAVE-CHANCEL axis is longer than the TRANSEPTS (as in all English cathedrals).
Lou. In Chinese architecture, a wood-framed tower (an early forerunner of the PAGODA).
Lunette. The area of a wall enclosed by the arch of a vault or window; may be either solid or glazed.

Machicolation. The projecting parapet of a castle or town-wall, with openings in the floor through which lumps of rock, boiling oil, etc., could be dropped.
Mannerism. Style coming between High Renaissance and Baroque. Characterised by the idiosyncratic use of classical motifs, unnatural proportion and wilful stylistic contradictions.
Mastaba. In ancient Egyptian architecture, a flat-topped tomb with sloping sides, the forerunner of the pyramid.
Mausoleum. A rich and elaborate tomb, so called from the tomb of Mausolus at Halicarnassus.
Megaron. The principal hall of a Minoan or Homeric house (e. g., Tiryns, Mycenae).
Metope. Part of the FRIEZE of a DORIC ENTABLATURE, one of the spaces between the TRIGLYPHS, at first left plain, later sculptured. See ORDERS.
Mezzanine. A low storey between two higher ones, usually between the ground and first floors.
Mihrab. In Moslem architecture, a niche in the wall of a mosque, showing the direction of Mekka.
Minaret. Tower built near or as part of a mosque, from which a muezzin calls the faithful to prayer.
Minbar. The pulpit in a mosque.
Moat. A ditch round a fortified position, not necessarily flooded.
Module. A measure of proportion to which all the parts of a building are related by simple ratios. In classical architecture it is usually half the diameter of the column just above its base divided into 30 parts.
Monolithic. One large stone, or made up of large stones.
Mosaic. Small cubes of glass or stone (tesserae) set in a cement bedding as decoration for wall-surfaces or floors.
Mosque. The Moslem's place for prayer and exhortation.
Moulding. Decorative profile given to an architectural member; often a continuous band of incised or projecting patterning, e. g., BEAD-AND-REEL, DOGTOOTH, etc.
Mudejar. Late Spanish Romanesque, strongly influenced by Moslem architecture (fourteenth to fifteenth centuries).
Mullion. The vertical member dividing a window of more than one light. (The horizontal members are called transoms.)

Naos. The principal chamber or sanctuary of a Greek temple, where the statue of the deity was kept.
Narthex. Vestibule of an Early Christian church, a porch extending the whole width of the façade; occasionally used in later churches (e. g., St. Mark's, Venice).
Nave. (1) The central space of a BASILICA, flanked by the AISLES and lit by the CLERESTORY. (2) All of a church west of the crossing, or if there are no transepts, west of the chancel.
Neo-classicism. A style coming after the Baroque, characterised by a more academic use of classical features.
Niche. A recess in a wall, usually for a statue or ornament.
Norman. Name given to the ROMANESQUE style in England.

Obelisk. A tall stone, square in section, tapering upwards and ending pyramidally.
Octastyle. Having eight columns; a temple with a portico eight columns wide.
Ogee arch. See ARCH.
Ogival. Ogee-shaped. See ARCH. (Not to be confused with the French use of 'ogivale' to mean merely 'pointed' or 'Gothic'.)
Open-work. Same as FRETTED. 'Open-work spires' are spires where the stone is treated like lattice, so that they can be seen through.
Opus sectile. A type of MOSAIC in which the material used is cut into regular pieces.
Orchestra. In Greek architecture, the circular space in front of the stage in a theatre where the chorus stood.
Orders. Columns and their entablature, especially the various designs followed by Greek and Roman architects: DORIC, IONIC, CORINTHIAN, COMPOSITE, TUSCAN (q. v.). **Superimposed orders.** In Roman architecture, the orders came to be used as ornamental features, attached to walls and façades, two, three or four storeys high. The sequence from bottom to top was always Doric, Ionic, Corinthian, Composite.
Oriel window. A bay window projecting from the wall and supported on CORBELS.
Orientation. Strictly, alignment east-west, but used loosely for any deliberate placing of a building in relation to the points of the compass.
Orthostat. A large upright slab of stone.
Oversailing. A process by which an arch or course of bricks or stone is made to project over a similar arch or course beneath; a kind of repeated CORBELLING.

Pagoda. A multi-storeyed Chinese or Japanese building with wide projecting roof at each storey.
Palladian motif. An arched opening flanked by flat ones at impost level. When glazed, called a 'Venetian window'. Called after Palladio but not in fact invented by him.
Palmette. A leaf-like ornament used in classical architecture.
Party-wall. A wall dividing two properties or houses and forming a common boundary to both.
Pavilion. (1) An ornamental building such as a summer-house (French 'pavillon' = tent). (2) In French architecture, part of a château higher than the rest, e. g. the centre or corners. **Blind pavilion.** An imitation gable or pediment attached to part of a building to give distinction to the skyline.
Pediment. Originally the triangular GABLE-end of a Greek temple with pitched roof. Later used as a monumental feature independent of what is behind it.
Pendentive. The curved triangular surface that results when the top corner of a square space is vaulted so as to provide a circular base for a dome. A COVED CORNER. It fulfils the same purpose as a SQUINCH ARCH.
Perimeter wall. A wall round a complex of buildings.
Peripteral. Having a single row of columns all round; a temple surrounded by a single row of columns.

Peristyle. A row of columns (1) round the outside of a building (usually a Greek temple) or (2) round the inside of a courtyard (e. g., in a Greek or Roman house) and by extension the space so enclosed.

Perpendicular. The last phase of English GOTHIC, replacing Decorated during the second half of the fourteenth century and lasting into the seventeenth. Characterised by light airy proportions, large windows, straight lattice-like tracery over both windows and wall-surfaces, shallow mouldings, four-centred arches and fan-vaults.

Piano nobile. The first floor of an Italian palazzo, containing the principal apartments.

Pier. Free-standing masonry support for an arch, usually composite in section and thicker than a column, but performing the same function.

Pilaster. A flattened column, rectangular in section, attached to a wall as decoration, without structural function, but still obeying the laws governing the ORDERS. **Pilaster strip.** Vertical band of stone serving roughly the same purpose as a pilaster, but unconnected with the classical orders.

Pilotis. Posts or 'stilts' (French 'pilot' = piles) supporting a whole building, leaving the ground storey entirely open.

Plateresque. Early Renaissance style in Spain from about 1520.

Plinth. The base of a pillar, pedestal, statue or of a whole building.

Podium. Stone platform, on which a temple is built.

Porte-cochère. An open porch big enough for a coach to drive through, as shelter for people arriving at the entrance of a large house.

Portico. Colonnaded porch or vestibule. In Neo-classical houses the portico (columns and pediment) often merges into the façade.

Porticus. Word of uncertain meaning, used by pre-eleventh-century writers when describing churches. Seems to mean 'room', 'chapel', 'porch' or even 'aisle' – anything added to the main body of the building.

Presbytery. The part of the church containing the high altar; often used loosely for the whole east end. Architecturally the same as SANCTUARY.

Pronaos. Part of a Greek temple 'in front of the NAOS'; often same as the PORTICO.

Propylaeon. (Greek: 'in front of the gate'); a monumental entrance to a sacred enclosure.

Prothesis. In Byzantine and Greek Orthodox churches the chapel (or sometimes the table) where the preliminary oblation of the bread and wine is made.

Pseudo-dipteral. A type of temple planned as dipteral (i.e., with a double row of columns round the cella) but in which the inner row is omitted.

Purlin. The horizontal beam running midway along a sloping roof, resting on the principal rafters and supporting the subsidiary ones. See ROOF.

Pylon. Ancient Egyptian monumental gateway, usually composed of two masses of masonry with sloping sides.

Pyramid. Regular solid with a square base and sides sloping inwards to meet at a point.

Queen-posts. Two upright beams in a roof, standing on the TIE-BEAM and supporting a principal RAFTER and PURLIN.

Radiating chapels. Chapels added to an APSE and fanning out radially.

Rafter. The sloping beams of a pitched roof, carrying the battens for the tiles.

Reeding. Convex moulding, same as GADROON; often placed inside the FLUTES of the lower third of a column.

Relief. Carving on a surface so that figures and objects are raised against a background. High-relief (haut-relief) is deeply cut; low relief (bas-relief), is shallower.

Relieving arch. See ARCH.

Repoussé. Method of making RELIEF in metal by hammering from behind so that the figures stand out.

Respond. A pilaster or engaged half-column or pier taking the place of the end support of an ARCADE, when the arcade reaches a wall.

Retaining wall. A wall that holds back a mass of earth.

Reticulated. Net-like. Tracery with openings like the meshes of a net; is characteristic of the Decorated period in English Gothic.

Reveal. The inner side of a door or window; the thickness of the wall visible outside the frame.

Revetment. (1) A veneer or facing of stone over rubble or concrete. (2) A sloping wall holding back earth.

Ridge-beam. Beam running along the top of a pitched roof. See ROOF. **Ridge-end.** The end of the ridge-beam, the top of the GABLE.

Rococo. Characterised by flowing lines, arabesque ornament, ornate stucco-work and the obliteration of separate architectural members into a single moulded volume,

Romanesque. Style following CAROLINGIAN and preceding GOTHIC, characterised by massive masonry and thick proportions, the round arch, and the re-discovery of vaulting – first the barrel vault, then groined and finally the rib-vault.

Rose window. In Gothic architecture, a large round window with TRACERY.

Rosette. Ornamental motif like a stylised flower.

Rotunda. Any round building, not necessarily domed.

Rustication. Method of leaving the outside surface of stone building-blocks rough, to give an impression of strength; the edges are normally cut back, leaving deep grooves between the blocks.

Sanctuary. The part of a church or temple containing the main altar.

Sarai. In the Middle East, an inn for travellers, with a large courtyard.

Scallop. Carved ornament like a scallop-shell.

Screen. A dividing wall having no function of support, e.g., in medieval churches surrounding the CHOIR. **Screen-wall.** An exterior wall not part of the structure. Same as sense (2) of CURTAIN WALL.

Scroll. Sometimes the same as VOLUTE. More usually an S-shaped moulding, a double spiral. Used in Renaissance churches to connect the upper and lower parts of a façade, or as an ornamental BUTTRESS.

Semi-dome. Half a dome leaning against part of a building (often a complete dome) and acting as an extended FLYING BUTTRESS (e.g., in St Sophia).

Shaft. (1) In classical architecture, the middle, cylindrical part of a COLUMN (2) In medieval architecture, a thin vertical member attached to a wall or pier, often supporting an arch or vault-ing-rib.

Shikhara. In Indian architecture, a tower or spire.

Shingles. Pieces of wood used instead of tiles.

Shinden-zukuri. Style of aristocratic architecture in Japan, consisting of dispersed rectangular units set in elaborate gordens and linked by covered passages.

Shuttering. Wooden boards fixed as a mould for concrete and removed when the concrete has set.

Skene. Building (or façade) behind the stage of a Greek theatre, forming an architectural background.

Soffit. The underside of an arch or lintel.

Spandrel. The triangular space between two arches, or between an arch and a wall.

Springing. The point of an arch where the curve begins, usually marked by an IMPOST moulding.

Squinch arch. See ARCH.

Stalactite. Ceiling ornament in Islamic architecture supposed to resemble natural stalactites.

Stave church. Ancient Norwegian wooden church whose main supports are posts or 'staves'.

Steel-frame. A skeleton of steel girders providing all that is structurally necessary for the building to stand.

Stellate. Star-shaped.

Stoa. In Greek architecture, an open colonnaded space for public business; a long LOGGIA.

Strapwork. Style of ornament consisting of interlacing strap-like bands. Fashionable first in sixteenth-century Netherlands, and then in England, France and Germany.

Striation. Fine narrow ridges or grooves parallel with each other. It is an ambiguous term: both the FLUTES and the FILLETS of a column can be called striations.

Strut. A sloping beam at right angles to a pitched roof surface, supporting a PURLIN or RAFTER. See ROOF.

Stucco. Plaster applied with moulds to walls, usually to make interior decoration (e.g., Rococo), but also on exteriors and occasionally to simulate whole façades in stone (e.g., by Palladio).

Stupa. Originally a Buddhist burial mound; later a chamber for relics surrounded by an AMBULATORY.

Stylobate. The continuous base on which a COLONNADE stands.

Substructure. Foundations or base.

Suspension bridge. A bridge in which the path or road is suspended from chains between towers or pylons.

Taper, tapering. Decreasing in thickness towards one end.

Tatami. Straw mats used as floor-covering in Japanese houses. The traditional size (6 ft by 3 ft) long governed the proportions of the house.

Temenos. In Greek architecture, a sacred precinct enclosed by a wall and containing a temple or altar.

Tempera. Powder-colour bound by some substance, usually egg. Used for easel and wood paintings up to the fifteenth century when it was largely replaced by oil.

Tension. The force tending to stretch or pull apart any architectural member, e.g., the chains of a suspension bridge or the tie-beam of a roof are in tension. The opposite is compression.

Tepidarium. Part of a Roman public bath containing the warm water, intermediate in temperature between the FRIGIDARIUM and the CALIDARIUM.

Terracotta. Clay burnt or hard-baked in a mould; harder than brick; may be either natural brown, or painted or glazed.

Thermae. Roman public baths, containing large halls with water at various temperatures (FRIGIDARIUM, TEPIDARIUM AND CALIDARIUM) and many other amenities.

Tholos. (plural tholoi). In classical architecture, a round building with a dome or beehive-shaped roof.

Thrust. Pressure exerted by any body of masonry and tending, if not resisted, to compress, displace or distort part of a building. In walls and rigid sections the thrust is downwards, in arches and vaults sideways as well (lateral thrust): hence the need for BUTTRESSES, ABUTMENT, etc.

Tie-beam. A beam (or rod) across the base of a pitched roof, holding the two sides together and preventing them from spreading.

Timber-framing. Same as HALF-TIMBERING.

Tokonoma. In Japanese houses, a niche for the exhibition of paintings or flowers.

Torana. The gate of the enclosure of a Buddhist STUPA.

Tou-kung. In Chinese architecture, a cluster of brackets supporting a roof.

Trabeated. See COLUMNAR AND TRABEATE.

Tracery. The stone mullions enclosing the glazed areas of a large window – in practice the word means GOTHIC window tracery almost exclusively. Plate tracery, the earliest type, is basically solid wall in which holes have been cut for the glass. Bar tracery (tracery proper) uses stone ribs to form complicated patterns. See also RETICULATED, FLAMBOYANT.

Transept. Part of a cruciform church at right angles to the NAVE and CHANCEL (the north and south arms are always called 'north transept' and 'south transept'). Some cathedrals have an additional transept east of the crossing.

Trapezium. A quadrilateral with two sides parallel.

Tread. The horizontal part of a stair on which the foot steps (as distinct from the 'riser', or vertical part).

Trefoil. A panel or division of TRACERY which has CUSPS that divide it into three lobes.

Triforium. The middle storey of a Romanesque or Gothic church elevation, between the ARCADE and the CLERESTORY.

Trigylph. A block with three vertical strips divided by two grooves, forming (together with the METOPES) the FRIEZE of a DORIC ENTABLATURE. See ORDERS.

Truss. A rigid triangular framework designed to span an opening and to carry tile or lead. Most wooden roofs are trussed.

Turret. A small tower, often built over a circular staircase, or as ornamental feature.

Tuscan. A Roman addition to the classical ORDERS, resembling the DORIC but with a BASE and without FLUTES and TRIGLYPHS.

Tympanum. (1) The triangular area enclosed by a classical PEDIMENT. (2) Space between the LINTEL of a doorway and an arch over it.

Undressed. Of stone: not trimmed or made smooth.

Vault. A stone ceiling. **Barrel vault.** An arched vault, either semi-circular or pointed, having an identical section throughout, without intersections, and resting continuously on the supporting walls. Longitudinal barrel vault; a barrel vault running down the length of the building, like a tunnel. Transverse barrel vault: a vault consisting of a series of barrel vaults *across* the building, at right angles to the walls. **Corbel vault.** A vault built on the same principles as the CORBEL ARCH. **Fan vault.** A decorative type of rib-vault, in which the bay divisions and vaulting compartments are ignored and the ribs fan out from the wall-shafts in the shape of everted semi-cones each with the same curvature. The ribs have no structural function and are in fact often simply carved on to the slabs. Confined to English Perpendicular. **Groined vault.** A quadripartite vault in which the compartments meet at a GROIN, not a rib. **Quadripartite vault.** A vault of which each bay consists of two barrel vaults intersecting at right angles, making four triangular compartments. The lines where the planes meet may be ribbed or left as an ARRIS or GROIN. **Rib vault.** A development of the groin vault, in which the line of the groin is marked by a stone rib. The ribs can then be built separately like a skeleton and the spaces in between filled in, the weight being taken by the ribs. Can be quadripartite, sexpartite, or with any number of compartments. **Segmental vault.** A barrel vault whose section is a SEGMENTAL ARCH. **Sexpartite vault.** A quadripartite vault with the addition of an extra TRANSVERSE ARCH in the middle of the bay, passing through the intersection of the two diagonal arches. **Tunnel vault.** The same as a BARREL VAULT.

Veneer. The covering of one material by thin slices of another to give an effect of greater richness.

Verandah. A small open gallery outside a house, with a roof supported on posts or pillars and the floor raised a few feet off the ground.

Vestibule. An ante-room to a larger building or hall.

Vihara. A Buddhist monastery or hall in a monastery (originally a cave).

Volute. The spiral scroll, especially as it occurs in the IONIC capital.

Voussoirs. Wedge-shaped blocks forming an arch.

Wattle and daub. Primitive technique of wall-building. Wattles (or reeds) are plaited together and covered with daub (mud or plaster), which then dries and becomes hard. This is held up by a wooden framework.

Well. (1) A space open to the sky in the middle of a large building (light-well). (2) Central open space in circular staircase.

West front. The principal façade of a big church at the west end of the nave; conventionally used even when the church does not face east (e. g., St Peter's).

Ziggurat. Stepped pyramid supporting an altar or temple, built in ancient Mesopotamia and Mexico.